D1608243

The Arabs of the Ottoman Empire, 1516–1918

The Ottomans ruled much of the Arab world for four centuries. Bruce Masters's work surveys this period, emphasizing the cultural and social changes that occurred against the backdrop of the political realities that Arabs experienced as subjects of the Ottoman sultans. The persistence of Ottoman rule over a vast area for several centuries required that some Arabs collaborate in the imperial enterprise. Masters highlights the role of two social classes that made the empire successful: the Sunni Muslim religious scholars, the ulama, and the urban notables, the *aʿyan*. Both groups identified with the Ottoman sultanate and were its firmest backers, although for different reasons. The ulama legitimated the Ottoman state as a righteous Muslim sultanate, while the *aʿyan* emerged as the dominant political and economic class in most Arab cities through their connections to the regime. Together, the two helped to maintain the empire.

Bruce Masters is John Andrus Professor of History at Wesleyan University. He is the author of *Christians and Jews in the Ottoman Arab World: The Roots of Sectarianism* (Cambridge University Press 2001) as well as other books, articles, and scholarly contributions.

The Arabs of the Ottoman Empire, 1516–1918

A Social and Cultural History

BRUCE MASTERS

Wesleyan University

CAMBRIDGE
UNIVERSITY PRESS

CAMBRIDGE
UNIVERSITY PRESS

32 Avenue of the Americas, New York NY 10013-2473, USA

Cambridge University Press is part of the University of Cambridge.

It furthers the University's mission by disseminating knowledge in the pursuit of education, learning and research at the highest international levels of excellence.

www.cambridge.org
Information on this title: www.cambridge.org/9781107619036

First published 2013
Reprinted 2013

A catalogue record for this publication is available from the British Library

Library of Congress Cataloguing in Publication data
Masters, Bruce Alan, 1950–
The Arabs of the Ottoman Empire, 1516–1918: a social and cultural history / Bruce Masters, Wesleyan University.
    pages   cm
Includes bibliographical references and index.
ISBN 978-1-107-03363-4 (hardback) – ISBN 978-1-107-61903-6 (paperback)
1. Arabs – Turkey – History.   2. Turkey – History – Ottoman Empire, 1288–1918.   3. Turkey – Intellectual life.   4. Ulama – Turkey – History.
5. Elite (Social sciences) – Turkey – History.   6. Social change – Turkey – History.   I. Title.
DR435.A66.M37   2013
305.892'705609034–dc23   2012044077

ISBN   978-1-107-03363-4   Hardback
ISBN   978-1-107-61903-6   Paperback

For Giancarlo, Ussama, and Tim

Contents

Acknowledgments	*page* ix
Abbreviations	xi
Note on Transliteration	xiii

Introduction   1
Empire: Metropole and Periphery   3
The Arabs in the Historiography of the Ottoman Empire   10
A Question of Identity   12
Periodization   16

1. The Establishment and Survival of Ottoman Rule
   in the Arab Lands, 1516–1798   20
   Yavuz Selim and the End of Mamluk Sultanate   21
   Expansion to the East   30
   Expansion to the South   33
   Ottoman North Africa   35
   The Rise of "Self-Made" Governors   37
   Egypt: A Special Case   42
   Conclusion   45

2. Institutions of Ottoman Rule   48
   The Sultanate   49
   Provincial Administration: Governors   58
   Provincial Administration: Judges   63
   The Provincial Military   66
   Conclusion: Continuities with, and Disruptions of, the Past   69

3. Economy and Society in the Early Modern Era   73
   Commerce and the Wealth of Cities   75
   The Guilds   79

Was There an "Age of the Aʿyan"?	83
The Rural Landscape	88
The Tribal Frontier	95
Conclusion: Was There an Ottoman Economy?	100

4. A World of Scholars and Saints: Intellectual Life in the Ottoman Arab Lands — 103
- *The Scholars* — 106
- *Sufis and the Cult of Ibn al-ʿArabi* — 112
- *Anti-Sufis and Religious Reformers: The Eighteenth-Century "Renewal"* — 119
- *Nonelite Culture* — 126
- *Conclusion* — 128

5. The Empire at War: Napoleon, the Wahhabis, and Mehmed Ali — 130
- *Napoleon in Egypt* — 130
- *The Wahhabi Challenge to the "Protector of the Two Holy Places"* — 134
- *Internal Threats: Rebellions in Aleppo and the Peloponnesus* — 139
- *Ibrahim Pasha and the Egyptian Occupation* — 146
- *Conclusion* — 154

6. The Tanzimat and the Time of Re-Ottomanization — 157
- *Restoring the Sultan's Writ* — 159
- *Sectarian Dissonance on the Periphery* — 163
- *Sectarian Violence at the Core* — 168
- *Empowering the Aʿyan* — 177
- *The Constitution of 1876 and the First Ottoman Parliament* — 183
- *North Africa in the Era of the Tanzimat* — 186
- *Conclusion: The Tanzimat in Retrospect* — 189

7. The End of the Relationship — 192
- *The New Bourgeoisie* — 194
- *Competing Ideologies* — 199
- *The Caliphate Question* — 206
- *The Young Turk Revolution* — 211
- *The Arabs in the Great War* — 217
- *Postmortem* — 223
- Conclusion: For the Faith and State — 225

Bibliography — 233
Index — 251

Acknowledgments

Thirty-seven years ago, I began to study the history of the Arab lands in the Ottoman Empire in earnest as a graduate student at the University of Chicago. I had already lived and studied for several years in the Middle East and found that many of the questions I had concerning the Ottoman centuries were unanswered in the literature that was available then. I set out to find answers and have been searching for them ever since. Along the way, I had the help of Professor Halil İnalcık, who introduced me to the intricacies of the language and scripts of the Ottoman chancelleries and provided me with an appreciation of the workings of the empire from the perspective of Istanbul. I was also fortunate to have the mentorship and friendship of Abdul-Karim Rafeq, who helped me both to understand how the empire functioned in Syria and, by using the court records, to approach questions of how ordinary people lived it. Both men have had a major impact on my subsequent career and I thank them as a grateful student.

This work represents my research and thoughts on the Ottoman Empire that have evolved over many years. I have had the benefit of knowing many remarkable scholars who have contributed to my knowledge and understanding of the past. I would like to thank in particular Virginia Aksan, Palmira Brummett, David Commins, Selim Deringil, Dick Douwes, Edhem Eldem, Daniel Goffman, Tony Greenwood, Bernard Heyberger, Akram Khater, Dina Rizk Khoury, Najwa al-Qattan, and Madeline Zilfi for hours of good conversation. Much of the thought that went into this book is a product of having introduced Ottoman history and Arab culture to Wesleyan undergraduates for the past thirty years. I have learned from that truly remarkable group of young people and

I hope they have learned from me. I would like to single out from among them Giancarlo Casale, Ussama Makdisi, and Timothy Parsons, who left Wesleyan to become scholars and colleagues. I take no credit for their professional success but I do value their continuing friendship. Ussama has read drafts of this work, and his patience and insights have often helped me to clarify a muddle of language and thought of my own making. This book is dedicated to those three friends and scholars for giving me hope for the future of the historians' profession.

An earlier version of the discussions of the sultanate found in Chapter 2 and of the cult of ibn al-ᶜArabi in Chapter 4 was presented as a paper, entitled "Arab Attitudes towards the Ottoman Sultanate, 1516–1798," at the Swedish Research Institute in Istanbul and was published in *Istanbul as Seen from a Distance: Centre and Provinces in the Ottoman Empire*, edited by Elisabeth Özdalga, M. Sait Özervarlı, and Feryal Tansuğ (2010). Sections of Chapters 5 and 6 were presented as a part of a paper, entitled "The Political Economy of Aleppo in an Age of Modernity," at a conference honoring the fiftieth anniversary of the *Journal of the Economic and Social History of the Orient* and was published in volume 53 (2010) of that journal.

I would like to thank Dr. Stefan Weber of Berlin's Pergamon Museum for permission to use the photo that graces this book's cover.

Last, I would like to thank the editorial staff at Cambridge University Press, and especially Marigold Acland, who has recently retired, for their advice and assistance.

Abbreviations

AHR	*The American Historical Review*
BSOAS	*Bulletin of the School of Oriental and African Studies*
IJMES	*International Journal of Middle Eastern Studies*
JAOS	*Journal of the American Oriental Society*
JNES	*Journal of Near Eastern Studies*
MES	*Middle Eastern Studies*
MHR	*Mediterranean Historical Review*
REMMM	*Revue du Monde Musulman et de la Méditerranée*
WE	*Die Welt des Islam*

Note on Transliteration

I have employed a modified system of transliterating Arabic proper names and terms suggested by the *International Journal of Middle Eastern Studies*. I have chosen not to use diacritical marks and only retained the "raised c" (ᶜ) to represent the "ᶜayn" and the apostrophe to represent the "hamza." Ottoman Turkish proper names and terms are spelled according to the rules of Modern Turkish, with the exception that I have maintained the final voiced consonant that corresponds to the Ottoman spelling, "Mehmed" rather than "Mehmet." Place-names and terms that are more familiar to English-language speakers such as "qadi" and "pasha" are spelled according to common English usage.

Introduction

Two recent events illustrate the ambivalent space that the Ottoman Empire occupies in the historical imagination of Arabs living in the twenty-first century. In January 2002 Saudi developers razed Qasr Ajyad, an Ottoman-era fortress that had stood watch over Mecca for two centuries. They envisioned in its place a hotel with splendid views of the holy city that would provide luxurious surroundings for wealthier pilgrims and visitors. The decision to demolish the fortress was unproblematic from a Saudi perspective. Qasr Ajyad was of a recent vintage when compared to other Middle Eastern historical monuments, and there was no local outcry for its preservation. Nonetheless, İstemihan Talay, Turkey's minister of culture, compared its leveling to the Taliban's wanton destruction of the statues of the Buddha in Bamiyan in the previous year. With popular outrage growing at home over what was portrayed in the Turkish media as a slight to the honor of the nation, Minister Talay requested that UNESCO condemn the Saudi action as it had the obliteration of the "world heritage" site in Afghanistan. Arab commentators, in contrast, were dismissive of the protests, which they ascribed to a residual bitterness on the part of the Turks that their ancestors had lost control of the Arabian Peninsula in 1918. In the end, UNESCO decided that as the fortress was not on its list of places that merited preservation, its fate was a matter solely within the purview of the Saudi authorities.

Eight years later, Israeli soldiers stormed the freighter *Mavi Marmara* in international waters on 31 May 2010. In the process, they killed eleven people, all of whom were Turkish nationals. A Muslim charity in Turkey had hired the boat as a part of a flotilla manned by Turkish, European, and North American activists to transport medical supplies and building materials to the blockaded Gaza Strip. Turkey's tough verbal and political response to the killing of its citizens by the Israeli Defense Forces evoked an outpouring of pro-Turkish sentiment in the Arab media. With his public scolding of Israeli leaders on several occasions, the Turkish prime minister, Recep Tayyip Erdoğan, emerged as the hero of the day on the "Arab Street." Erdoğan, buoyed by his newly found popularity among his neighbors to the south, was in the forefront of world leaders who urged the Arab regimes to listen to their people's demand for political reform during the "Arab Spring" of 2011. Accompanying this flexing of Turkish political muscle in the region, some commentators in the Arab media remarked that the growing relationship between Arabs and Turks in the spheres of trade and international politics was positive. More than one noted that it marked a restoration of ties between the two peoples, who had drifted apart since the fall of the Ottoman Empire. The differing responses to the two incidents arose out of the complex web of relationships that linked the Ottoman dynasty with its Arab subjects and how the empire's historical legacy has been configured by successive generations of Arab intellectuals since its fall from the world stage.

Ottoman political and cultural influences were pervasive in the southern and eastern littoral regions of the Mediterranean Sea for four centuries from the start of the sixteenth century until World War I. Twentieth-century Arab historians, however, rarely presented the Ottoman period in a positive light. For most of that century, Arab nationalism was the dominant political discourse. Arab historians working within that rhetorical construct reduced the Arab peoples' past to an uncomplicated equation: the Turks were the masters; the Arabs were their subjects. The Arabs' struggle for independence from the European powers in the wake of World War I helped to conflate the defunct Ottoman regime with later European imperial interventions in the region. This created a persuasive narrative of foreign oppression that commenced with the Mongol destruction of Baghdad in 1258 and continued until the revolutionary era of Gamal Abdul-Nasser.[1]

Within that metahistory, the Ottomans were located in a continuum of conquerors, despoilers, and oppressors whom the Arab peoples had endured. As nationalist historians viewed the Ottoman Empire as an alien

---

[1] Muhammad Kurd ʿAli, *Khitat al-sham*, 6 vols. (Beirut: Dar al-Qalam, 1969–72); Satiʿ al-Husri, *al-Bilad al-ʿarabiyya wa al-dawla al-ʿuthmaniyya* (Beirut: Dar al-ʿIlm lil-Milayin, 1960).

occupier in the Arab lands, it seemed obvious to them that their ancestors would have felt the same way.[2] Countering the nationalist narratives,
Arab scholars and others began in the 1970s to reexamine the Ottoman
centuries, using archival sources largely ignored by an earlier generation
of historians. These include the records of the Islamic (sharia) courts in
the Arab cities as well as the chancellery documents relating to the Arab
provinces located in Istanbul. As a result, a more nuanced understanding of the history of Ottoman rule in the Arab lands is emerging.[3] The
findings and arguments developed by those historians over the past four
decades inform my analysis in this work.

EMPIRE: METROPOLE AND PERIPHERY

In the past decade, historians have expanded the definition of empire.
Earlier generations of historians took the Roman Empire as an historical paradigm and posited that empires required a network of control
extending from the center, or metropole, over a diverse population that
was maintained by a bureaucratic state and enforced by an army. To
qualify as an empire, the metropole had ideally to exercise power over
multiple subject peoples, who were typically, but not always, culturally
distinct from their rulers and from each other. No longer as interested in
the "great men" of history who created empires, historians have more
recently preferred to pursue the question of what mechanisms – political,
ideological, cultural, and so on – maintained empires after the initial conquests. As the historian of Rome Clifford Ando asks in a series of related
questions: "What made Roman power persuasive or even attractive to
the population of the provinces? What rendered provincial cultures permeable to Roman paradigms for the legitimate exercise of government?
In short, what induced quietude rather than rebellion?"[4] Other scholars
have focused their attention on related issues to understand the dynamics
of control employed by "empires," of varying complexities and defini-
tions, to elicit their subjects' acquiescence. It took more than power to
maintain an empire; it also required some level of collaboration on the

---

[2] ʿAbdallah Hanna, *Harakat al-ʿamma al-dimashqiyya fi al-qarnayn al-thamin ʿashar wa al-tasiʿ al-ʿashar: namudhaj li-hayat al-mudun fi dhill al-iqtaʿiyya al-sharqiyya* (Beirut: Dar ibn Khaldun, 1985).
[3] ʿAdel Mannaʿ, *Taʾrikh filastin fi awakhir al-ʿahd al-ʿuthmani: qiraʾa jadida* (Beirut: Muʾassasat al-Dirasat al-Filastiniyya, 1999).
[4] Clifford Ando, *Imperial Ideology and Provincial Loyalty in the Roman Empire* (Berkeley: University of California Press, 2000), 5.

part of its subjects.[5] This study contributes to that ongoing discussion by exploring how the Arab subjects of the Ottoman sultans viewed their relationship to the extraordinary metropole that was Istanbul.

Whatever definition one might choose for empire, there is a consensus among historians that the Ottoman state was one. Although Europeans contemporary with the Ottoman Empire labeled it as such, those at the sultan's court preferred to think of their state as "the well-protected domains" (*diyar-ı mahrusa*) or "the Ottoman kingdoms" (*memalik-i osmaniye*). Their ambition was for a political organization that transcended the petty notion of kingdom in a larger vision that they felt they shared with earlier states that had straddled the globe. The titles that some of the sultans took – *Cihangir* (World Grabber), *Alampenah* (Refuge of the Universe) – gave voice to that conceit. In their own estimation, they were world conquerors to be feared and obeyed.

In imagining their place in history, those at the sultan's court invoked historical precedents. Kritovoulos, a Greek historian of the Ottoman conquest of Constantinople, explicitly compared Sultan Mehmed to Alexander the Great.[6] Others at court expanded the comparison of the sultans to great leaders of the past, including the pre-Islamic Persian shahs, Byzantine emperors, Chingiz Khan, and the Abbasid caliphs.[7] The Ottoman elite understood all but the last exemplar to have been secular, that is, not condoned by Islamic traditions, and therefore supportive of an absolutist ideology that posited the sultan as both the source of legislation and the sole arbiter of justice. The precedent of the caliphate was more problematic as an expression of absolutism, however, as it left open the possibility that the corporate body of Muslim religious scholars, the ulama, might ultimately decide the definition of justice, even as they acknowledged that it was the sultan's prerogative to dispense it.

Such a limitation on sultanic authority was still a long way from being an early form of constitutionalism as the scholarly consensus among the

---

[5] Among others: Niall Ferguson, *Empire: The Rise and Demise of the British World Order and the Lessons for Global Power* (London: Allen Lane, 2002); Maya Jasanoff, *Edge of Empire: Lives, Culture, and Conquest in the East 1750–1850* (New York: Alfred Knopf, 2005); Timothy Parsons, *The Rules of Empires: Those Who Built Them, Those Who Endured Them, and Why They Always Fall* (Oxford: Oxford University Press, 2010); Pekka Hämäläinen, *The Comanche Empire* (New Haven, CT: Yale University Press, 2008).

[6] Kritovoulos, *History of Mehmed the Conqueror*, translated by Charles Riggs (Princeton, NJ: Princeton University Press, 1954), 3.

[7] Cornell Fleischer, *Bureaucrat and Intellectual in the Ottoman Empire: The Historian Mustafa Ali* (Princeton, NJ: Princeton University Press, 1986), 253–92.

empire's religiously trained intellectuals agreed with the formula ascribed to the Prophet Muhammad that "forty years of tyranny is preferable to one night of anarchy." Nonetheless, arguments by the leading ulama against policies that the sultan had decreed did at times create tension in the Ottoman court.[8] Present in the model of the caliphate was an acknowledgment that the political legitimacy of the ruler rested on Islamic legal precedents and traditions. While that formulation created problems for a sultan wishing to exercise his will with unfettered restraint, the argument that the legitimacy of the House of Osman was vested in Islamic notions of sovereignty and justice could produce a positive response from the majority of his Arab subjects. Going back to the questions raised by Ando for the Romans, it was the state's appeal to those traditions that helped secure Ottoman rule in the Arab lands.

Arab nationalist historians were correct to assert that their ancestors had been subjects of the Ottoman sultan, but they were less persuasive when it came to establishing the nature of that relationship. Ottoman armies conquered Greeks, Serbs, Bulgarians, Wallachians, Hungarians, Albanians, Kurds, and Anatolian Turks, as well as Arabs, reducing all to being subject peoples. Few communities voluntarily chose to submit to Ottoman rule. After the conquests, all of the sultan's subjects were ruled by an elite class of Ottoman officials who seldom had a deep concern for, or knowledge of, local conditions. The Ottoman regime equally exploited all of its subjects, the *reaya* (literally, the flock), for the revenues they might produce and considered them to be a largely undifferentiated mass of taxpayers. Exploitation and coercion went hand in hand to establish and maintain the Ottoman Empire, as was the case with other empires. At the same time, however, its survival over time required the cooptation and collaboration of at least some of the subject peoples. In that regard, the invocation of Islam as a political ideology was crucial as far as many Arabs were concerned.

The majority of the Arabs living within the boundaries of the Ottoman Empire were Sunni Muslims. That was also true for the Kurds, Albanians, Bosniaks, and Turks. In the early modern period, religious faith usually trumped an ethnic identity for most peoples' collective self-definition. As such, the relationship of any of the Sunni Muslim peoples to the Ottoman state was presumably more complex than that of the empire's Christian subjects in the Balkans. Christians could view the Ottomans

---

[8] Baki Tezcan, *The Second Ottoman Empire: Political and Social Transformation in the Early Modern World* (Cambridge: Cambridge University Press, 2010), 46–72.

as both conquerors and infidels. For many, there remained hope for a restoration of the Christian kingdoms that the Crescent had overturned. To feel a true sense of community with the Ottoman state, it has been suggested that a Christian in the Balkans had to convert to Islam.[9] Christine Philliou's recent study of the Phanariot Greeks in the service of the House of Osman in the early nineteenth century has challenged that reading as a projection backward of later nationalist sentiments for at least some Ottoman Christians.[10] Whether Balkan Christians in the sixteenth and seventeenth centuries viewed the Ottomans solely as oppressors is yet to be established, however.[11] What is certain is that their contemporaries among Sunni Muslim Arabs, or at least those who have left us with a written record, did not describe themselves as an occupied people.

The Arab chroniclers who witnessed the actual conquests depicted the Ottomans as foreigners, but there was also much about them that was familiar. The first public act that Sultan Selim (1512–20) performed after conquering Aleppo, Damascus, and Cairo was to lead the faithful in prayer in the Friday mosque of each city, and that action was noted by some of the chroniclers with approbation. It met, after all, their expectation of what a Muslim sovereign should do. The sultan whose name was mentioned in those prayers had changed, but the act of naming a ruler who pledged himself to uphold the political and religious dominance of Islam had not. The Ottoman conquest did not signal a radical overturn of the social order in the Arab lands as it simply replaced one reigning sultan with another. As such, there were few among the Arabic-speaking Sunni populations after 1516–17 who sought a restoration of the old regime or questioned the legitimacy of the Ottoman sultan to rule them.

The same claim could probably be made for the other Sunni Muslim populations that were the sultan's subjects. There was, however, an important difference between the Arabs and other Muslims. The Arabs were heirs to a highly developed literary, political, and religious culture that did not always conform to the culture present at the Ottoman court. Ottoman Turkish would serve as the written language used by the

---

[9] Maria Todorova, "The Ottoman Legacy in the Balkans." In *Imperial Legacy: The Ottoman Imprint on the Balkans and the Middle East*, edited by L. Carl Brown (New York: Columbia University Press, 1996): 45–77.

[10] Christine Philliou, *Biography of an Empire: Governing Ottomans in an Age of Revolution* (Berkeley: University of California Press, 2010).

[11] Johann Strauss makes a tentative step toward addressing that question. Johann Strauss, "Ottoman Rule Experienced and Remembered: Remarks on Some Local Greek Chronicles of the *Tourkokratia*." In *The Ottomans and the Balkans: A Discussion of Historiography*, edited by Fikret Adanır and Suraiya Faroqhi. (Leiden: Brill, 2002), 193–221.

Muslim elites throughout the Balkans and Anatolia, regardless of the language they spoke at home. In the Ottoman Arab lands, only a few apparently bothered to learn it in the first three centuries of Ottoman rule. Their cultural inheritance gave the Arabs a perspective on their rulers that was multilayered. The Ottoman sultans and their servants at court were undeniably fellow Muslims. Yet their interpretations of a shared religious heritage were not necessarily the same as those held by the Arab Sunni intellectual elite. The individuals who constituted that class had, therefore, to negotiate a place for themselves within the empire. They acknowledged the right of the Ottoman dynasty to their political allegiance, but they retained a supreme confidence in their role as guardians of a distinct cultural heritage that was, in their view, the equal of if not actually superior to that of the sultan and his court in Istanbul.

Depending on one's historical perspective, the Arabs can be configured as a subject people of the empire, which they were, or as collaborators in the imperial project. It is the latter interpretation that this study advances. The degree of that collaboration, however, could vary. Many Muslim Bosniaks and Albanians played an active role in the governance of the empire and constituted a reservoir of manpower in the early modern period that Ottoman officials could rely on to supplement the janissary units for the empire's armies both in the Balkans and in Asia. Furthermore, there were Muslim scholars who began their careers in the Balkans but who served the empire throughout its far-flung dominions, including in the Arab lands. With their service to "faith and state" (*din ve devlet*), these Balkan Muslims played an auxiliary role within the empire not unlike that of the Scots in the British Empire in the eighteenth and nineteenth centuries.[12] In contrast, Arabs did not die for the empire in large numbers before 1877, the year in which Arab conscripts were pressed into the empire's war with Russia. Yet most Arabic-speaking Sunni intellectuals acknowledged that the rule of the Ottoman sultan was legitimate in the earlier centuries, and they prayed for his victory over the empire's enemies. They were the empire's ideological cheerleaders, although admittedly their support was rarely tested. When the sultan did need their moral backing after the Wahhabi capture of the holy cities of Arabia in the early nineteenth century, however, their written responses were unanimously on the side of the House of Osman.

---

[12] Linda Colley, *Britons: Forging the Nation 1707–1837* (New Haven, CT: Yale University Press, 1992), 117–32.

There were multiple reasons why Arabs might choose to acquiesce to
Ottoman rule rather than seek to overturn it. In the Ottoman Empire as
in all other state systems in the early modern period, the ruler had the
capacity to apply coercive force to compel his subjects to accept his rule.
The application of military force was, however, not a common occurrence
in the Arab cities during the Ottoman centuries. While the Ottomans had
to mobilize their garrisons in the Arab lands to combat the raids of tribal
peoples or the insurrections of clans that enjoyed the protection of highland redoubts, there was little need to use those forces against urban
populations. Most outbreaks of urban unrest that did occur were, in fact,
mounted by the putative enforcers of the sultan's rule, the janissaries.

The virtual absence of rebellion among urban Arabs can be explained
by a number of factors. In the first century after the conquest, the merchant class prospered under the *pax ottomana*. In the nineteenth and
early twentieth, the large landowners in the Arab provinces who were
urban based had an economic interest in the continuity of the status
quo, as the empire had created the opportunities for their acquisition of
land, wealth, and status. The duration of Ottoman rule in the Arab lands
also depended, however, upon the legitimacy extended to the sultan by
the Sunni religious scholars and the willing collaboration of a relatively
small group of elite local families, the a*yan, who mediated the political
and social balance between the welfare of their fellow townsmen and the
needs of the central state. The acknowledgment and acceptance of the
House of Osman's right to rule them by both sets of actors, who were
often related by ties of blood or marriage, secured a large swath of territory for the empire in periods when the sultan did not have the resources
to wield the blunt force necessary to do the job himself.

Of all the reasons why the Arab elites might view the Ottoman state
as serving their interests, none was more compelling than that of their
shared religious identity. The perception that the fates of Islam as a community of believers and of the Ottoman Empire as a political state were
unalterably linked is a thread that runs through the various works composed by Sunni Arab authors in the early modern period. That confidence
was no longer universally shared by authors writing in Arabic in the late
nineteenth century as the empire ceased to be synonymous with security
and constructed political identities based on ethnicity rather than religious faith began to emerge in the public discourse.

Scholars have noted that those authors whose works have survived
from the early Ottoman centuries constituted only a small community
whose opinions did not necessarily reflect those of anyone outside their

close-knit circle of friends and relatives.[13] That is probably true as the elites in any society speak only for themselves. There were, of course, exceptions – chronicles written by those outside that elite circle: a barber in one case, men in the military in both Cairo and Damascus, and even a few Christians.[14] The dominant voice that has survived from the early Ottoman centuries is nonetheless that of the Sunni learned class, and its representatives spoke largely in unison. All the authors consulted for this study were city dwellers who were extremely proud of their respective cities' historical past and conscious of the place of the Ottoman sultans in a long line of Muslim rulers. If not wealthy themselves, they were in sympathy with those individuals whom they viewed as the *khassa* or the *khawass*, the social elite. They viewed their poorer neighbors as forming an indiscriminate rabble (*awbash, ghawgha', sifla*) who were perhaps a step up the social ladder above tribal pastoralists and peasants, but just barely so. The authors were all males, who rarely mentioned women. They also seldom, if ever, took note of the non-Muslims who might share their urban space. Despite those obvious drawbacks, I have turned to their works as a major source for my understanding of the era. We are left with few alternatives to answer the crucial question of what Arabs, albeit a small sample of them, thought about the Ottomans, if indeed that question can ever be satisfactorily answered. A limited sample of opinion, heavily weighted in favor of the religious establishment, is still better than no sample at all.

Largely on the basis of those sources, this study highlights the historical experience of the Sunni Muslim populations in the Ottoman Arab provinces. The non-Muslims were the subject of an earlier volume in which I discussed how their collective identities changed over time.[15] In writing that book, I was faced with the larger question of how Muslim Arabic speakers might have configured their place in the Ottoman Empire in which Islam was arguably the dominant political ideology. I could not help but notice that religion was in the forefront of the discourse that ran through the narratives composed by Arabic speakers, whether Muslim or Christian, in the Ottoman centuries.

---

[13] Nelly Hanna, *In Praise of Books: A Cultural History of Cairo's Middle Class: Sixteenth to the Eighteenth Century* (Syracuse, NY: Syracuse University Press 2003), 12–15.

[14] Bruce Masters, "The View from the Province: Syrian Chroniclers of the Eighteenth Century" *JAOS* 114 (1994): 353–62; Michael Winter, "Historiography in Arabic during the Ottoman Period." In *Arabic Literature in the Post-Classical Period*, edited by Roger Allen and D. S. Richards (Cambridge: Cambridge University Press, 2006), 194–210.

[15] Bruce Masters, *Christians and Jews in the Ottoman Arab World: The Roots of Sectarianism* (Cambridge: Cambridge University Press, 2001).

I acknowledge that there was perhaps a cynical use of religion as a political ideology by both the Ottoman officials and the Arab Sunni intellectual elite. It made governing the Arab lands easier for the sultan as it gave him legitimacy in a society that was wedded to a belief in a social hierarchy that God had ordained. For the Arabic-speaking Sunni elite, Islam provided a crucial link to the state, with the unspoken possibility of financial and political patronage. It also provided a justification for their acquiescence to Ottoman rule. Nonetheless, I believe religious faith and solidarity were also present in the works. Furthermore, the authors' commitment to Islam as their personal faith helps us to understand the political worldview that served as the bedrock of their relationship to those who ruled them.

THE ARABS IN THE HISTORIOGRAPHY OF THE OTTOMAN EMPIRE

P. M. Holt published his ground-breaking survey of Ottoman Arab history, *Egypt and the Fertile Crescent 1616–1922: A Political History*, in 1966.[16] As suggested by the subtitle, it concentrated on the region's political history and provided little discussion of economic or social developments. Holt based his narrative primarily on local chronicles in Arabic, supplemented by accounts written by European travelers and diplomats. Using many of those same sources, his student Abdul-Karim Rafeq published *al-ʿArab wa al-ʿuthmaniyyun, 1516–1916* (The Arabs and the Ottomans) in 1974, the first work in Arabic to explore comprehensively the Arab experience in the Ottoman Empire without a strong ideological bias.[17] Both authors' works have held up well over time and no subsequent study has significantly altered their complimentary narratives of the Ottoman past. I do not attempt to do so here. Since their publication, a number of scholars inspired by the pioneering work by Rafeq in the Islamic court records of Syria and by André Raymond in those of Cairo have explored the surviving sharia records of the various Arab cities to explore issues concerning the social and economic history of the region that were largely neglected in the sources used by Holt.[18] Research

---

[16] P. M. Holt, *Egypt and the Fertile Crescent 1616–1922: A Political History* (London: Longmans Green, 1966).

[17] Abdul-Karim Rafeq, *al-ʿArab wa al-ʿuthmaniyyun, 1516–1916* (Damascus: Matbaʿ Alif Ba, 1974).

[18] For a collection of Rafeq's articles based on the sijills, see, ʿAbd al-Karim Rafiq, *Dirasat iqtisadiyya wa ijtimaʿiyya fi ta'rikh bilad al-sham al-hadith* (Damascus: Maktabat Nubil, 2002); André Raymond, *Artisans et commerçants au Caire au XVIIIᵉ siècle*, 2 vols. (Damascus: Institut Français de Damas, 1973–74).

in those archives is still ongoing and there are undoubtedly numerous monographs yet to be produced from that extremely rich trove of documents. The Islamic court records can be problematic, however, and there is much they do not tell us for all the details they do offer up.[19]

Faced with the many silences in the court records, scholars have also begun to examine the literally millions of documents found in the archives of the central Ottoman state. The result has been a number of important monographs and articles on various cities of the Ottoman Arab provinces that have incorporated documentation from both local and imperial archives.[20] Despite the high quality of the work that has appeared over the past thirty years, there have been few attempts to replicate a broad, overarching survey of the region's history in the Ottoman centuries from beginning to end in the style of Holt and Rafeq.[21] Perhaps foolhardily, this volume is meant to update, but not to supplant those earlier works.

In choosing to focus on the Arab provinces, I have entered one of the potential minefields facing Ottoman historians. A central debate among them is whether the Arab provinces constitute a distinct subject of study from that of the history of the empire at large. Scholars such as Holt, Rafeq, and Raymond working with Arabic-language sources assumed that the Arab provinces had a unique trajectory in the Ottoman period that linked them both regionally and culturally, while distinguishing them from the provinces in the Balkans or Anatolia. The authors implicitly suggested an Arab "exceptionalism" from the general Ottoman narrative. In doing so, they followed the lead of the pioneering, if now somewhat discredited, *Islamic Society and the West* by Sir Hamilton Gibb and Harold

---

[19] Dror Ze'evi, "The Use of Ottoman Shariʿa Court Records as a Source for Middle Eastern Social History: A Reappraisal," *Islamic Law and Society* 5 (1998): 35–56.

[20] Among others: Charles Wilkins, *Forging Urban Solidarities: Ottoman Aleppo 1640–1700* (Leiden: Brill, 2010); Muhammad Adnan Bakhit, *The Ottoman Province of Damascus in the Sixteenth Century* (Beirut: The American University in Beirut, 1982); Karl Barbir, *Ottoman Rule in Damascus, 1708–1758* (Princeton, NJ: Princeton University Press, 1980); Collette Establet and Jean-Paul Pascual, *Families et fortunes a Damas: 450 foyers damascains en 1700* (Damascus: Institut Français de Damas, 1994); Dina Rizk Khoury, *State and Provincial Society in the Ottoman Empire: Mosul, 1540–1834* (Cambridge: Cambridge University Press, 1997); Amy Singer, *Palestinian Peasants and Ottoman Officials: Rural Administration around Sixteenth-Century Jerusalem* (Cambridge: Cambridge University Press, 1994); Jane Hathaway, *The Politics of Households in Ottoman Egypt: The Rise of the Qazdağlıs* (Cambridge: Cambridge University Press, 1997).

[21] Antoine Abdel-Nour, *Introduction à l'histoire urbaine de la Syrie ottomane (XVIᵉ–XVIIIᵉ siècle* (Beirut: Lebanese University, 1982); André Raymond, *Grandes villes arabes á l'époque ottomane* (Paris: Sindbad, 1985); Jane Hathaway, *The Arab Lands under Ottoman Rule, 1516–1800* (Harlow, UK: Pearson Longman, 2008).

Bowen.[22] The authors of that work divided almost every chapter into
sections that highlighted the distinctiveness of the Arab experience of
Ottoman rule from that of the inhabitants of Anatolia and the Balkans.
In contrast to an "Arabist" approach, historians of the empire whose
work is based primarily in the Prime Minister's Archives in Istanbul have
collapsed possible distinctive historical trajectories for different parts of
the empire into one metanarrative with Istanbul at its center.[23]

I will attempt to chart a middle course in this work. In my reading of
the documents issued by the officials at the sultan's court in Istanbul, the
Arab provinces were politically indistinguishable for them from the concerns of governing the larger empire. There was neither a distinctive Arab
policy at the Ottoman court nor a perception of an "Arab Question" that
needed addressing in the early modern period. Yet their rulers knew the
inhabitants of the Arab provinces were culturally distinct. The perception
of cultural "alterity" was mutual. Arabic-speaking Sunni scholars sought
to rationalize their place within the empire using a different political language from that employed by their non-Arab Muslim contemporaries
or, for that matter, from that used by their Arabic-speaking, non-Muslim
neighbors. If an "Arab exceptionalism" was largely absent from the political or economic experience of the inhabitants of the Arab provinces that
would serve to distinguish them from others of the sultan's subjects, it
would be difficult to argue that it was not present in their culture. It is
that difference that I seek to explore in this book.

A QUESTION OF IDENTITY

There is the obvious question of whom do I include when I make the distinction between Ottomans and Arabs. To be an Ottoman (Osmanlı) in
the early modern period was to be attached to the large extended dynasty
founded by Osman Gazi (d. 1324) or in its service. That would include
almost everyone who represented the sultan in some official capacity in
his Arab provinces, whether in the military that governed and policed
the provinces or in the judiciary that administered the religious courts.

[22] Sir Hamilton Gibb and Harold Bowen, *Islamic Society and the West: A Study of the Impact of Western Civilization on Moslem Culture in the Near East*, 2 vols. (London: Oxford University Press, 1950, 1957).
[23] Halil İnalcık and Donald Quataert, editors, *The Economic and Social History of the Ottoman Empire, 1300–1914* (Cambridge: Cambridge University Press, 1994); Caroline Finkel, *Osman's Dream: The Story of the Ottoman Empire 1300–1923* (New York: Basic Books, 2005).

The former were in the first two centuries of Ottoman rule often, but not exclusively, products of the *devşirme*, those conscripted through the "boy-tax" levied on many of the empire's Christian households. In the eighteenth century, most were Muslims from either the Anatolian or Balkan provinces, although men of slave origin from Christian Europe or the Caucasus region were also present in the imperial ranks. Whether they were actually slaves or freeborn Muslims, all the men who served in the sultan's military before the nineteenth century were technically his slaves and presumed to be personally loyal to his household.

In contrast, the chief judges who served in the Arab lands were freeborn Muslims who could be of any ethnic origin. Most were the graduates of the state-sponsored madrasa (religious school) system, which produced the empire's Turkish-speaking intellectual elite. In their training and outlook, those in the judiciary were as much the results of an imperial design to create men loyal to the state as those taken by the *devşirme*. The Ottoman elite, consisting of both its military/bureaucratic and religious wings, was not large in size, comprising no more than a few thousand individuals and their families in any year before 1800. We can assume that most of its membership knew each other at least by reputation, and there were ties of marriage between the royal house and individual members of both the military elite and the leading ulama. To be an Ottoman in those centuries was to belong to one large, and often quarrelsome, extended family.

Initially, Arab authors in Syria and Egypt used the word *Atrak* (Turks) to distinguish the Ottomans from the Mamluks who had previously ruled them and who were for them the Jarkasiyya, or alternatively Shirakasa (Circassians). But the Arab authors quickly adopted the term *Rumi* (plural *Arwam)* to mean an Ottoman and *Rum* to mean both Anatolia and the Ottoman Balkan provinces. *Rumi* was, however, a term loaded with ambiguity. Authors writing in Arabic employed it to mean Turkish-speaking Muslims in Anatolia outside the royal household, as well as those who were in the sultan's service, whether they were native Turkish speakers or non-Turkish Muslims from the Balkans or the Caucasus. To add further confusion, *Rumi* could also mean an Orthodox Christian generally, or more specifically one who spoke Greek. The less ambiguous Arabic term *ʿUthmani* for Ottoman officials came into general use only in the eighteenth century, although Arab authors employed it before that with reference to the ruling family or more abstractly the Ottoman state (*al-dawla al-ʿuthmaniyya*). The term "Turk" for members of the Ottoman officer and bureaucratic classes only began to make a return to narratives composed by

Arabic-speaking authors in the nineteenth century as ethnic identities began
to supplement religious ones, although even then ambiguities remained.
The father of the early nineteenth century Lebanese poet and chronicler
Niqula al-Turk, who presumably was the source of the author's nickname
(*laqab*), was actually a Greek Orthodox Christian from Istanbul.

If the definition of Ottoman could be linked to the ruling dynasty and
those who served it, what did it mean to be an Arab before the twentieth century? Today, most people accept at face value the assertion first
advanced by Arab nationalist writers in the 1920s that all those who
speak Arabic as their mother tongue are Arabs (*ᶜArabi*, with its plural
ᶜArab). That is how I use the term in this book. The modern usage of the
word is, however, much more inclusive than it would have been during
most of the Ottoman period. For the authors consulted in writing this
work, *ᶜArabi*, literally meant a Bedouin or an inhabitant of Arabia generally. But even that was not foolproof as an ethnic identifier. The other
possible plural of *ᶜArabi*, *ᶜUrban*, could be used by Arabic speakers to
mean pastoralists generically, regardless of the language they spoke, and
was applied by Arab authors to Turkmens, Kurds, and Bedouins.

Both Muslim and Christian chroniclers in Syria's cities used the phrase
awlad al-ᶜArab (sons of the Arabs/Bedouins) to describe themselves and
others as Arabic speakers. It is not as clear, however, what authors in
Egypt meant when they employed that phrase.[24] Its use in Syria points to
ambiguity about the authors' understanding of their collective identity;
they were the descendants of the Arabs and speakers of the Arabic language, but not "proper" Arabs, that is, Bedouins. There was nonetheless a
pride evident in that self-designation among the Arabic-speaking Muslim
elites who understood themselves to be the guardians of the language in
which the Holy Qur'an was delivered and that, they were confident, was
the language of paradise. Even so, pride and a sense of cultural identity
did not constitute the basis of resistance to the empire.

On the Ottoman side of the linguistic divide, the defining characteristics of an Arab were also not transparent. Ottoman officials were

---

[24] Jane Hathaway has questioned whether this term meant Arab in either a cultural or ethnic sense in Ottoman Cairo, see her "The *Evlad-i ᶜArab* ('Sons of the Arabs'). In Ottoman
Egypt: A Rereading" in *Frontiers of Ottoman Studies: State, Province, and the West*,
edited by Colin Imber and Keiko Kiyotaki, 2 vols. (London: I. B. Tauris, 2005), vol.
I, 203–16; for an alternative understanding, Michael Winter, "Ottoman Egypt, 1525–
1609." In *The Cambridge History of Egypt, vol. II: Modern Egypt from 1517 to the
end of the Twentieth Century*, edited by M. W. Daly (Cambridge: Cambridge University
Press, 1998), 15–17.

not exactly sure of who besides the Bedouins were Arabs. For those writing in Ottoman Turkish, *Arap* meant a Bedouin or an inhabitant of the Arabian Peninsula generally. But the word could also mean for them an African as most African slaves arrived in the empire by way of the markets of Cairo. Whatever the term *Arap* meant for the Ottomans, it was not solely vested in an individual's mother tongue. The inveterate seventeenth-century Ottoman traveler Evliya Çelebi (d. 1682?) was genuinely surprised that the Greek Orthodox (*Rum*) inhabitants of the Lebanese port of Sidon spoke Arabic (*Arapça*) rather than Greek (*Rumca*).[25] Even so, they remained for him *Rum* and not *Arap*, as it would be inconceivable to him that the identification of Arab could be applied to a non-Muslim.

Ottoman authors employed the term *Arabistan,* "the country of the Arabs," as a geographical designation, but it was not a place that was easily delineated in their mental geography. *Arabistan* was definitely to the east of Istanbul and began somewhere south of the Taurus Mountains that separate the Anatolian plateau from the steppe lands, which in turn quickly fade into the Syrian Desert. In regard to its vagueness, it was akin to *Kurdistan* (Country of the Kurds), whose exact location and ethnic makeup were also often inexact in the Ottoman imperial imagination.[26] In its most generous application, *Arabistan* encompassed the Arabic-speaking regions of Arabia and the western Fertile Crescent (Syria, Lebanon, Israel, the Palestinian territories, and Jordan) with the occasional addition of the province of Mosul, today northern Iraq. Ottoman officials never applied *Arabistan* to the rest of Iraq, which Ottoman sources sometimes labeled *İrak-ı Arap* (Iraq of the Arabs), using its medieval designation. Yemen, Egypt, and the various provinces of North Africa each had their own distinct topographical designation that did not carry any association with an ethnicity. The inhabitants of Yemen were definitely *Arap* in the Ottoman construction of their identity, but those of Egypt were more often simply labeled as *fellahin,* "peasants," using the colloquial Arabic plural for the agricultural class. The Ottomans posted in Cairo were cognizant of the fact that Egyptians spoke Arabic, but as was the case with the Arabic-speaking Christians whom Evliya encountered, that did not necessarily make them Arabs.

[25] Evliya Çelebi, *Evliya Çelebi Seyahatnamesi, cilt. 9–10* (Istanbul: Üçdal Neşriyat, 1984), vol. IX, 169.
[26] Hakan Özoğlu, *Kurdish Notables and the Ottoman State: Evolving Identities, Competing Loyalties, and Shifting Boundaries* (Albany: State University of New York Press, 2004), 21–42.

The Ottoman officials in the Arabic-speaking provinces were acutely aware that they were no longer in Istanbul. Such a reaction would undoubtedly have been similar in any provincial posting, as no place could quite equal for them the power, grandeur, and opportunity for advancement that were present in the capital. In Anatolia or the Balkans, however, Ottoman Turkish served as the language of command in the provincial *saray*s (palaces) and religious courts. In the Arab lands, commands in that language issued by the governor were necessarily mediated through an interpreter. Both Ottomans and Arabic speakers alike recognized that language separated them, even if Sunni Islam served to create a community that united the two.

The arrival of Ottoman armies in Damascus, Cairo, and Baghdad ushered in a time of potential change for the Muslim elites of those cities. Where they had once been both the guardians of the law and the producers of the literate "high" culture, they now faced competition from authorities who spoke a different language and had developed a different interpretation of that law and of Islamic "high" culture generally. The Arab ulama held an ambiguous position within the empire. The empire was "theirs" in that it was Muslim, but it was also administered and articulated in a language that most of them did not understand. As a result, the role Arabs played in supporting or administering the empire was largely confined to their own home provinces. That fact meant that the Arab intellectual elite often seemed provincial from the perspective of those going to the Arab lands from Istanbul. They were, however, not to be dismissed entirely as country bumpkins if the sultan's writ were to continue to hold sway in the provinces below the Taurus Mountains and along the littoral of the eastern and southern Mediterranean Sea. Whether or not the Ottoman governors felt there was a need for collaborators to maintain the sultan's authority is unknown as the strategies of dominance in the empire are yet to be explored by scholars. Even if that were not the case, however, the Arabic-speaking urban Sunni elite willingly served in that role.

PERIODIZATION

In plotting the outline of this book, I faced another potential pitfall for the Ottoman historian: the question of historical periodization. Most twentieth-century historians initially divided the empire's history into five broad periods: (1) origins (1300?–1453), (2) empire at its height (1453–1566), (3) empire in decline (1566–1808 or 1839), (4) empire revived

(1839–1908), (5) revolution and collapse (1908–18). The actual dates used to delineate each might differ, but earlier generations of historians agreed on the broad outline of rise, decline, and revitalization. The characterization of the empire as being in decline in the seventeenth and eighteenth centuries has been set aside of late, however. The prevalent view among scholars of the Ottoman Empire today is that although the empire was in flux in the eighteenth century, it was not necessarily in decline.

The editors of the recently published *The Cambridge History of Turkey* opted for a new periodization with the titles of their four volumes: *Byzantium to Turkey (1071–1453)*, *The Ottoman Empire as a World Power (1453–1603)*, *The Later Ottoman Empire (1603–1839)*, *Turkey in the Modern World*. Choosing those temporal divisions for categorizing the Ottoman centuries, they avoided the question of decline other than to note the loss of the empire's "world power" status by an omission in the title of volume 3. Their choice of the fourth volume's title gives a nod to an interpretation increasingly favored by historians of modern Turkey: namely, the empire did not completely disappear with Atatürk's revolution, but rather the last generation of Ottoman officers and bureaucrats transformed it into the Republic of Turkey, proceeding along a blueprint for modernization of the country that their predecessors in the Tanzimat era (1839–76) had first drawn up.

In thinking about the history of the Ottoman Arab provinces, I have opted for the temporal periodization chosen by my colleagues who teach and write about the history of Europe: early modern and modern. If we mean by the early modern period a time in which dynastic, land-based empires still dominated the political scene, then the first three centuries of Ottoman rule in the Arab lands easily fit the paradigm. Historians of Europe also see the "early modern period' as an era when the incipient capitalist world system was taking shape. In that process, I argued in an earlier work, the Ottoman Arab lands were increasingly drawn into the web of trade and economic interdependence that system created.[27] Last, the relationship between the Arab provinces and the capital did not change radically in the first three centuries of Ottoman rule. Although Ottoman political power emanating from the capital weakened in the region as local actors began to claim the right to serve the sultan in place of his own handpicked men, the provincial system established with the

---

[27] Bruce Masters, *The Origins of Western Economic Dominance in the Middle East: Mercantilism and the Islamic Economy in Aleppo, 1600–1750* (New York: New York University Press, 1988).

initial conquests endured. In that sense, there was neither a direct challenge to Ottoman rule in the Arab lands outside Egypt nor a decline in Ottoman prestige.

In a nod to the slow moving pace of political history in the first three centuries of Ottoman rule in the Arab lands, I have opted to organize my discussion of the period according to topical rather than temporal divisions. The first chapter discusses how the Ottoman sultans established their rule over most of what today we call "the Arab world." It then surveys briefly the political developments in the eighteenth century when the power of the central government devolved to local actors, setting the stage for a discussion of the political developments of the "modern age" in later chapters. The second chapter deals with the institutions of Ottoman rule in the early modern period, emphasizing how the Arabs viewed them and adapted to them over time. In that chapter I argue that the key to the empire's legitimacy for Arab scholars lay in the institution of the sultanate itself. The focus of the third chapter are the economy and social structure of the Arab provinces in the first three Ottoman centuries, with a discussion of the impact of Ottoman rule on the lives of ordinary people, both in the cities and in the countryside. A crucial element in that story was the emergence of the traditional elite families (aʿyan) in many Arab cities as power brokers mediating Ottoman rule. The fourth chapter deals with the intellectual life of the early modern period, discussing the various currents of thought that were present and how they evolved as the Arabic-speaking Muslim learned classes were influenced by ideas and events arising from outside their region.

The last three chapters of this work encompass the "modern period," roughly the last century of Ottoman rule in the Arab lands. An assessment of the relationship between the Arabs and the Ottomans who ruled them indicates that the nineteenth century witnessed the greatest strains on the relationship and the potential for rupture. Chapter 5 deals with the threats that undermined Ottoman sovereignty in the Arab lands in the first third of the century. During those troubled decades, the Ottomans lost effective political control of Egypt, Tunisia, and Algeria forever and came perilously close to losing permanently the Holy Cities of Arabia and their Syrian provinces as well. With British support, however, the empire rallied and embarked upon major reforms to secure and tighten the regime's political control over its remaining Arab provinces. Chapter 6 deals with the Tanzimat or reform period and discusses both the sectarian fissures that opened in that period and the attempts by the Ottoman sultans to reestablish their control over the Arab lands. It was a triumph of sorts in that by the century's end most of the sultan's Arab subjects could not imagine a political future other than remaining within his empire.

The final chapter deals with the end of the relationship between the sultans and their Arab subjects. With historical hindsight, it ended not because most Arabs critically questioned their four-century-old relationship to the sultanate, but rather that the sultanate itself had changed in what it expected of them. The era of Sultan Abdülhamid II (1876–1909) was remarkably peaceful for the Arab provinces, in contrast to what had occurred there in the preceding decades as well as to contemporary developments in the Balkans and southeastern Anatolia. The currents of nationalisms with competing visions and ambitions that undermined the foundations of empire, however, also had an impact in the Arab lands. Even so, most Arabs did not question the ideology of a political Ottomanism, as articulated by the Tanzimat reformers, as the bond that tied them to their sultan. Rather, the embrace of an ethnically defined ideology of Turkish nationalism, as well as a desire for a strong, centralized imperial government, by those ruling in Istanbul after 1908 began to undermine the long-established political alliance between Turks and Arabs as fellow Muslims. Increasingly, Muslim Arab intellectuals felt that they were no longer partners in an Islamic imperial enterprise, as they were being marginalized by, and subordinated to, Turkish national ambitions.

Most Arabs did not take up arms to end their relationship to the empire, but neither did they do so voluntarily to preserve it. Conscription rather than a spirit of patriotic volunteerism installed the sultan's Arab subjects in the ranks of his army during the Great War. Ambivalence and not rage was the dominant attitude among them toward the sultanate in its dying days. The empire came to an end in the Arab lands in 1918 with a long, painful sigh of a military retreat and not in an explosion of nationalist sentiment. There were clearly those among the Arabs who were not sorry to see the Ottoman army withdraw back into Anatolia from which it had originally come, but there were still others who preferred that it might stay. In the empire's absence, the sultan's former subjects in the Arab provinces were left with a political void that was not easily filled and faced a future for which few had prepared or even imagined would happen except in their worst dreams.

The Establishment and Survival of Ottoman Rule in the Arab Lands, 1516–1798

The Ottoman Empire expanded into the lands that today compose most of the member states of the Arab League during the reigns of Selim I (1512–20) and Süleyman (1520–66). The empire had already achieved major successes in the Balkans and Anatolia when its forces moved south in 1516. The conquest of the Arab lands marked, however, a significant geopolitical shift in the empire's territorial expansion from the European periphery of the Dar al-Islam ("The House of Islam," i.e., the lands under Muslim rule) into its historic heartland. The campaigns of the sixteenth century brought the fabled cities of Baghdad, Damascus, and Cairo under the dynasty's rule. The first two cities enjoyed prestige among Sunni Muslims as having once served as the seat of the caliphate, while a titular caliph still held court in Cairo when the Ottoman army arrived. The new territories also included Islam's three holiest cities: Mecca, Medina, and Jerusalem. Highlighting that responsibility and the honor it conferred upon him, Selim added the title "Servitor of the Two Holy Places" to the long list of titles he already held. His son Süleyman could boast, "I am Süleyman, in whose name the *hutbe* [Friday sermon] is read in Mecca and Medina. In Baghdad I am the shah, in Byzantine realms the Caesar, and in Egypt the sultan."[1]

With the new territorial additions, the majority of the Ottoman dynasty's subject peoples were Muslims for perhaps the first time in its history. Adding to its Muslim credentials, the Ottoman Empire stood with the conquests as the sole remaining Sunni Muslim political power

---

[1] Halil İnalcık, *The Ottoman Empire: The Classical Age 1300–1600*, translated by Norman Itzkowitz and Colin Imber (London: Weidenfeld and Nicholson, 1974), 41.

in the Middle East. That distinction helped to secure the legitimacy of the House of Osman in the Arab lands and further encouraged the religious scholars in Istanbul to envisage the empire as the new caliphate. Sultan Mehmed II had styled himself as the heir-apparent to the Byzantine/ Roman Empire with his conquest of Constantinople in 1453. His great-grandson Süleyman, as ruler of Damascus, Baghdad, and Cairo, could cast himself as the caliph of "the new age." The promotion of Islam as both the ideology of the Ottoman state and the source of its legitimacy seems to have worked. Generations of Arabic-speaking Sunni Muslim scholars born after the conquest were willing to link the fortunes of the Ottoman royal house to that of the "people of the Sunna" (*ahl al-sunna*), among whom they included themselves.[2]

The annexation of the Arab lands began a relationship between the Ottoman sultans and their Arab subjects that would last for four hundred years. That relationship consisted of a hierarchy of vassalage similar to the one that governed the other peoples of the empire. Perhaps uniquely among those subject peoples, however, the Arab elite could identify the Ottoman regime as being its own. The legitimacy that the Ottoman sultans gained from their position as the protectors of the hajj and the holy cities of Arabia, as well as defenders of Sunni Islam against its "infidels" and "heretics," served to transform the relationship between sultan and his Sunni subjects in the Arab lands over time into a collaboration of sorts. Real political power lay in Istanbul, but Sunni Arabs came to acknowledge that they had a stake in the continuation of the empire and they prayed for its success. That connection to their sultan stood in sharp contrast to the ambivalence that their ancestors had felt for the Mamluk sultanate that Sultan Selim overturned in 1517.

YAVUZ SELIM AND THE END OF MAMLUK SULTANATE

Sultan Selim won a stunning victory over the Mamluks at Marj Dabiq, north of Aleppo, on 24 August 1516. That outcome did not come easily. At the start of the battle, the Mamluk cavalry commanded by Sultan Qansuh al-Ghawri held the field successfully against the Ottoman advance. The tide of victory turned, however, with the skillful use by the Ottomans of cannon and an infantry armed with the arquebus, a type of

---

[2] Michael Winter, "Attitudes towards the Ottomans in Egyptian Historiography during Ottoman Rule" In *The Historiography of Islamic Egypt (C. 950–1800)*, edited by Hugh Kennedy (Leiden: Brill, 2001), 195–210.

primitive musket. The Mamluks had knowledge of both but chose not to invest heavily in the new technology in preference to good horsemanship and the lance that had served them in the past.[3] Selim's tactical advantage increased when Kha'ir Bek, the Mamluk governor of Aleppo, fled the field at the start of the battle, taking his men with him. Perhaps the Ottomans enjoyed another advantage as well. More than a century after the event, the Egyptian historian Muhammad ibn Abi al-Surur (d. 1677?) wrote that eyewitnesses to the battle swore that angels descended from heaven to aide Selim, announcing that they had come to sweep the Mamluk state (*al-dawla al-shirakasa*) from the face of the earth.[4] In a dramatic turn of events that presumably contributed to that myth, Qansuh al-Ghawri fell from his horse and died on the battlefield of no discernible cause. Suddenly leaderless, his troops fled the field in disarray. Selim allowed them to rush south toward the safety of the walls of Damascus as he proceeded to Aleppo. There the townspeople welcomed the installation of a new sultan with three days of feasting.[5]

The Mamluk regime that ruled Egypt, Syria, and the Hejaz between 1260 and 1517 was unusual in Islamic history as many of the sultans in its last century had started their careers as slaves. In Arabic, the word for a male slave is *mamluk* and in the medieval and early modern periods, it held the connotation of a slave purchased to serve in the military as slave soldiers became ubiquitous in Muslim regimes after the ninth century C.E. During the troubled thirteenth century when competing Muslim dynasties in Egypt and the Fertile Crescent battled each other as well as the remnants of the Crusader kingdoms, slave soldiers could at times seize the thrones of Muslim states for themselves. Further adding to the political instability in the region, the Mongols cut a swath through the eastern Islamic lands, destroying Baghdad in 1258 as well as most of the Muslim cities that had the unfortunate fate to lie in their path.

Qutuz, a mamluk of Turkic origin, was able to halt the Mongol drive toward Egypt in 1260 at the Battle of ʿAyn Jalut (today in Israel). Mamluks and Mongols took to the battlefield using similar tactics and weaponry. Qutuz could count, however, on Mongol allies from the Golden Horde

[3] Carl Petry, "The Military Institution and Innovation in the Late Mamluk Period" In *The Cambridge History of Modern Egypt*. Vol. 1. *Islamic Egypt, 640–1517*, edited by Carl Petry (Cambridge: Cambridge University Press, 1998): 462–89.

[4] Muhammad ibn Abi al-Surur, *al-Tuhfa al-bahiyya fi tamalluk al-ʿuthman al-diyar al-misriyya* (Cairo: Dar al-Kutub wa al-Watha'iq al-Qawmiyya, 2005), 57.

[5] Salahattin Tansel, "Şilahsor'un Feth-name-i Diyar-ı Arab Adlı Eseri" *Tarih Vesikaları* 4 (1955): 310–11.

in Russia who opposed Hülegü, the Mongol commander advancing on Egypt, in his ambitions for the Mongol khanate. Any further Mongol advance on Egypt stalled after the battle as Hülegü hastened back to the Mongol capital of Karakoram, where a dynastic struggle to determine who would be the next Great Khan was under way. Flushed with victory, Qutuz claimed the sultanate of Egypt. His seizure of the throne ended a decade of political turbulence in Cairo in which remnants of the Ayyubid family, established by Salah al-Din ibn Ayyub (Saladin) in 1171, served as figureheads while real power lay in the hands of their mamluk commanders. Qutuz's time on the throne was short-lived, however. Baybars, another mamluk in the royal court, engineered the assassination of his liege lord while he was on a hunting expedition. Baybars quickly claimed the sultanate for himself and ruled for almost two decades. He set his personal stamp on the institutions of the new Mamluk sultanate, and later Egyptian historians would credit him with the founding of the regime that would govern Egypt, Syria, and the Hejaz for the next two and a half centuries.

Baybars's son al-Saʿid Baraka (Berke) Khan succeeded him to the throne in 1277. A clean dynastic transfer of power was not to be, however. Al-Saʿid Baraka's mamluks dethroned him in a palace coup in 1279. One of those, Qalawun (Kalavun), beat out his rivals and seized the sultanate, ruling Egypt between 1279 and 1290. His descendants established a dynasty that held the reins of power in Cairo between 1299 and 1390, although its continuity was broken on several occasions when mamluks from the ruling sultan's household seized the throne. During the century in which Qalawun's descendants dominated the politics of Cairo, the transfer of power from one member of the family to another was seldom unchallenged, and the descendants of Qalawun failed to establish his lineage as uncontested. The Mamluk state had no single ruling dynasty after them.[6] Rather, mamluks in the ruling household continued to build their own coalitions with other commanders (emirs) of less exalted households that might move to usurp the throne when they felt the ruling sultan was vulnerable.

Throughout the centuries that the Mamluk emirs ruled Egypt and Syria, the process of recruitment into the grand mamluk households remained largely unchanged. All of the men taken into the system were supposedly non-Muslims at the time of their enslavement, although some

---

[6] P. M. Holt, *The Age of the Crusades: The Near East from the Eleventh Century to 1517* (London: Longman, 1986), 82–106.

apparently sold themselves into it voluntarily. Upon their arrival in Cairo, representatives of the emirs bought likely candidates for the prominent households where their socialization into Islam and the traditions of mamluk chivalry occurred. The mamluks' connection to the indigenous inhabitants was weak and many never learned Arabic properly. Adrift from both their homelands and the local population, the mamluks held primary loyalty to the head of the household in which they found themselves and to those with whom they served in the household, the cohort known as the *khushdashiyya*. In some cases, the emirs strengthened that relationship through the marriage of particularly trusted mamluks to their daughters or other female relatives.

In the first century of the Mamluk sultanate, most of the slaves arriving in Cairo were Turkic-speaking peoples from the Qipchak Steppe in what is today Russia, who had been captured by Tatar raiders. In 1382, al-Zahir Barkuk, a mamluk in the royal household, seized the sultanate for the first time and held it until 1389, when the last descendant of Qalawun, al-Mansur Hajji, briefly returned to the throne. Barkuk took the throne again in 1390 and held it until his death in 1399. Barkuk's origins lay in the Caucasus Mountains, and most of his successors were drawn from the ethnically diverse peoples who inhabited that region: Georgians, Adige, Ingush, Chechen, Abkhaz, and so on. Arabic-speaking authors collectively called these peoples "Circassians," although that term properly referred to the Adige people alone. In the period of the "Circassian" sultans (from Barkuk until 1517), there were occasional attempts at dynastic succession, but most of the men who seized the throne had been the mamluks of the ruling sultan rather than his sons. After Barkuk, no grandson of a sultan ever ascended the throne

A seemingly unstable formula for a regime nevertheless proved to have great resiliency in the post-Mongol Middle East. This was due to the immense wealth to which the reigning sultan and his allies had access. Western Europeans developed an insatiable appetite for the luxury goods of Asia in the aftermath of the Crusades. These were most readily available in the markets of Cairo, Damascus, and Aleppo in the era before Vasco da Gama's voyage around Africa in 1498. All three cities lay in the territories controlled by the Mamluk sultans.[7] Trade, coupled with Egypt's often bountiful and usually dependable harvests, provided the emirs with the wealth with which they acquired new slaves and financed

---

[7] Eliyahu Ashtor, *Levant Trade in the Later Middle Ages* (Princeton, NJ: Princeton University Press, 1983).

a resplendent material culture. Cairo glittered as the capital of a wealthy state, but not all was golden in the sultanate. There were periodic urban riots in Cairo, Damascus, and Aleppo, often arising out of food shortages or abuses by the emirs, but the mamluks, who probably numbered in the thousands, held a virtual monopoly over weaponry. Militarily impotent, the civilian elite was left to exact their revenge by writing for posterity the record of what they viewed as the impiety and tyranny of the Mamluk emirs.[8]

Internally secure, the Mamluk sultanate survived, as there were few external enemies to challenge it. The false sense of the regime's invincibility ended in 1401 when Timur (Tamerlane) sacked both Aleppo and Damascus. The self-proclaimed "world conqueror" paused in Damascus, however, and his army did not cross the Sinai Desert to Cairo. Timur may have perceived that the Ottomans to the north were a greater threat than the Mamluks to the south. Furthermore, an Ottoman advance to the east in the years preceding 1401 had threatened many of the independent Turkish sultans in Anatolia and they offered Timur their fealty. He withdrew from the field in Syria to march on Anatolia and the Mamluk regime survived. In Anatolia, Timur dealt a crushing blow to the Ottoman dynasty at the Battle of Ankara, on 28 July 1402, when he captured Sultan Bayezid (1389–1402). For the next two decades, the Ottoman Empire suffered civil wars as Bayezid's sons fought over which of them would gain their father's throne.

Following the conquest of Constantinople in 1453, an emboldened Ottoman Empire pushed again into the lands controlled by the Turkish sultans in Anatolia. In doing so, the Ottoman army challenged the dominance of the Mamluk sultanate over territories located today in southeastern Turkey. Relations between the two sultanates soured further when Prince Cem fled to Cairo in 1481. Cem was the losing contender for the Ottoman throne in yet another Ottoman civil war, after the death of his father, Sultan Mehmed II. Although Cem stayed only briefly in Egypt before seeking sanctuary with the Knights of Rhodes and ultimately Rome, the Mamluks drew the ire of his brother Bayezid II (1481–1512) for having sheltered him. The two states fought a series of border wars at the end of the fifteenth century that turned out badly for the Ottomans. The Ottoman push to the south had stalled for another generation to pursue.

[8] Robert Irwin, "Mamluk History and Historians" In *Arabic Literature in the Post-Classical Period*, edited by. Roger Allen and D. S. Richards (Cambridge: Cambridge University Press, 2006), 159–70.

The outbreak of the Kızıl Baş revolts in the first decade of the sixteenth century served as the catalyst that empowered the Ottomans finally to confront their Mamluk nemeses. The rebels were Turkmen tribesmen who believed that the charismatic Ismail Safavi (d. 1524), himself a Turkmen, was the twelfth imam of Shia prophecy, who had emerged from occultation to initiate an age of justice in the world. The Kızıl Baş initially pushed toward Bursa in western Turkey in 1511 with the fervor of men who believed they were on a holy mission. The Ottoman army was eventually able to push them back out of central Anatolia, but the rebellion in the east continued. Prince Selim, who sought to preempt his brothers' ambitions for the throne, initiated a military coup against his father, Bayezid II, in 1512, claiming that his actions were necessary to save the empire from the rebels. After first killing his brothers, Selim then mounted a brutal campaign against the Kızıl Baş, earning from later Ottoman court historians the sobriquet Yavuz, "stern, ruthless."

Shah Ismail, who by that time had consolidated his rule over much of Iran, responded with a counteroffensive to support his followers in Anatolia. The two armies met on 23 August 1514 at Çaldıran, northeast of Lake Van near the present-day Turkish-Iranian border. As would be the case two years later in Syria, gunpowder technology won the day as tribal warriors on horseback proved no match for a disciplined army with artillery. Shah Ismail retreated over the mountains to Iran and Selim pondered what to do next. With Shah Ismail's men occupying much of Iraq, the empire's southern frontier seemed particularly vulnerable to further Iranian attacks. In addition, the Ottomans were aware of Spanish advances along the coast of North Africa and Portuguese activity in the Indian Ocean and the Red Sea. Some advisers in Selim's entourage counseled him that the Mamluk regime in Cairo was ill prepared to counter the threat of Christian expansion into Muslim territories. They advised that he move quickly to the south.[9]

Whether Selim sought to topple his Mamluk rivals or simply to teach them a lesson in humility is unclear. We do know that he was aware of the vulnerability of the Mamluk regime through his network of spies. The information proved correct. The Mamluk defenses crumbled after the defeat at Marj Dabiq and Selim entered Damascus without a battle on 28 September 1516. The Ottoman army busied itself in the following months securing Damascus's hinterlands in what is today southern Syria,

---

[9] Palmira Brummett, *Ottoman Seapower and Levantine Diplomacy in the Age of Discovery* (Albany: State University of New York Press, 1994).

Lebanon, Israel, and the Palestinian territories. The region's terrain is rugged and it sheltered various tribal and religiously heterodox groups who had historically resisted the imposition of control from Damascus. Ottoman physical force, however, carried the day. With the pacification of the province of Damascus complete, Selim still hesitated to pursue the defeated Mamluk army to Cairo. He even offered to recognize the new sultan, Tuman Bay, as his vassal, leaving the last Mamluk sultan in control of Egypt.

Tuman Bay rejected the call for submission and attempted to retake Gaza in December 1516. With that response, Selim decided to act, arriving outside Cairo in January 1517. Tuman Bay made a stand at Raydaniyya to the east of the city on 23 January 1517, this time supported by cannon. Nonetheless, the battle proved to be another lopsided defeat for the Mamluks. The bulk of their forces retreated behind Cairo's walls badly bruised while Tuman Bay escaped to the province of Buhayra, northwest of Cairo, where he sought refuge among the Bedouins. After a short siege, the Ottomans again prevailed, easily taking Cairo despite its massive city walls. Selim granted his men the customary three days to loot and pillage the city, during which time the Ottoman army executed hundreds of mamluks. Tuman Bay's refuge in the countryside proved short-lived as news of Cairo's fall reached the Bedouin chieftains. Sensing in which direction the political winds were blowing, they betrayed him and pledged their loyalty to the new sultan. Ottoman troops returned Tuman in chains to Cairo. There they ignominiously hanged him from Bab Zuwayla, one of the monumental gates to the city. Sultan Selim stayed in Cairo until September 1517 before heading back to Syria and ultimately Istanbul in March 1518.

Later Ottoman court historians would popularize an account in which the last Abbasid caliph in Cairo, al-Mutawakkil, bestowed his cloak on Selim.[10] If that had occurred, it would have symbolized the transfer of the office of the caliphate from the family of ʿAbbas to the House of Osman. Neither Arabic chronicler of the conquest, Muhammad ibn Tulun in Damascus or Muhammad ibn Ayas in Cairo, recorded that that event occurred, however.[11] In contrast to the Ottoman version of what

---

[10] Mustafa Nuri Paşa, *Netayic ül-Vukuat*, 2 vols. (Ankara: Türk Tarih Kurumu, 1979), vol. 1, 123; Selim Deringil, *The Well-Protected Domains: Ideology and the Legitimation of Power in the Ottoman Empire 1876–1909* (London: I. B. Tauris, 1998), 46–50.

[11] al-Husri, *al-Bilad al-ʿarabiyya*, 42–6; P. M. Holt, "Some Observations on the ʿAbbasid Caliphate of Cairo" *BSOAS* 47 (1984): 501–7.

happened in Cairo in 1517, the Egyptian cleric Ahmad al-Damanhuri (d. 1778) summarized the end of the Abbasid caliphate as follows:

Prophecy ended with Muhammad, God bless him and grant him peace, and the caliphate ended with Muta^csim bi-llahi al-ʿAbbasi whom the Tatars killed in Baghdad in 656 (1258). However, the "nominal Caliphate" (*al-khilafa al-suriyya*) was transferred to Cairo and it continued until the time of Sultan al-Ashraf al-Ghawri. After him, Sultan Selim offered a profession of loyalty (*bay^ca*) to al-Mutawakkil ʿala Allah and took him to Constantinople (*al-Qustantiniyya*). When Sultan Selim died, al-Mutawakkil returned to Cairo and remained as caliph until he died in 950 (1543–44) in the time of Daud Pasha. With his death, the "nominal Caliphate" of the Abbasids passed from the world and nothing remains except the sultanate and the wazirate.[12]

For an understanding of how later generations of Egyptians understood the transfer of power, it is important to note that it was Selim who offered his fealty to al-Mutawakkil and not the other way around

Selim left former Mamluks in charge of two of his new provinces, Janbardi al-Ghazali as governor in Damascus and Kha'ir Bay, the traitor of Marj Dabiq, in Cairo. Both men had betrayed their former liege lord and Selim must have felt some unease that they might do the same to him. As a possible defensive measure, he posted Ottoman governors and military garrisons to Mosul, which Ottoman forces had bloodlessly occupied in 1517, and in the northern Syrian city of Aleppo. That proved to be a wise tactical decision as with his death in 1520, Janbardi al-Ghazali proclaimed himself to be sultan in Damascus. Kha'ir Bay in Cairo, however, quickly affirmed his loyalty to Selim's son Süleyman and left Janbardi to his own devices to face a vengeful sultan.

Janbardi's attempt to overthrow the newly established Ottoman regime in Syria stalled at the gates of Aleppo where the garrison held fast. Upon hearing the news of an impending arrival of an army sent by Süleyman to relieve that city, Janbardi raised his siege and retreated to Damascus. The Ottoman army pursued the rebels and defeated Janbardi's army on 5 February 1521 in a battle outside the city's walls. The Ottoman troops sacked Damascus in the aftermath of their victory, a fate that the city's unfortunate inhabitants had managed to avoid in 1516. Süleyman then appointed an Ottoman military commander as governor in Damascus, having learned from his father's mistake. Officers from the regular

---

[12] Ahmad ibn ʿAbd al-Mun^cim al-Damanhuri, *al-Nafa^c al-ghazir fi salah al-sultan wa al-wazir* (Alexandria: Mu'assasat Shabab al-Jam^ca, 1992), 44–6; A similar account was given by the late eighteenth-century chronicler Yasin al-ʿUmari, *Zubdat al-athar al-jaliyya fi al-hawadith al-ardiyya* (Najaf: Matba^cat al-Adab, 1974), 189.

Ottoman army would continue to serve in that capacity until the eighteenth century.

Sultan Süleyman left Kha'ir Bay in control of Cairo in gratitude for his loyalty to the House of Osman. He served in that office until his death in 1522. Taking advantage of the power vacuum his death created, supporters of the former Mamluk regime mounted a rebellion, but the Ottoman garrison in Cairo was able to suppress it. Egypt was still not secure, however, as Ahmed Bey, the Ottoman governor who had defeated the rebels, raised his own rebellion in anger in 1523 after his being passed over for the post of grand vizier. Sultan Süleyman granted that office instead to his brother-in-law Ibrahim and Ahmed must have felt that nepotism had trumped merit. Ahmed proclaimed himself "sultan of Egypt," reviving the Mamluk title and posing a direct challenge to Ottoman hegemony over the country. His rebellion was ill planned, however. The would-be sultan found little support locally from the Ottoman garrison or those mamluks who had escaped the general slaughter in 1517. Local allies of Süleyman were able to defeat Ahmed in 1524 without having to call on troops from Istanbul.

Egypt returned with that victory to direct Ottoman rule. Ottoman officers would serve as governors of Egypt for the next two and a half centuries. Their power was, by the eighteenth century, more fictive than real, however. The memory of an independent sultanate in Cairo remained to haunt the Ottoman dynasty's ambitions for an uncontested claim to Egypt. That created in Egypt a different power dynamic than existed in any other Arab province where there were no local challengers waiting in the wings to overthrow the Ottoman provincial regime.

The Ottomans had toppled the Mamluk sultanate, but the practice of creating mamluk households through the purchase of slaves or the hiring of freeborn Muslim retainers survived. Ottoman officials posted to Cairo adopted the local practice and others who claimed descent from the earlier mamluk emirs formed their own houses and began to jockey for power in the rough street politics of Ottoman Cairo. Some historians of Egypt have labeled such households as "neo-Mamluks" as they appear to be a continuation of the practice of household formation that dated to the old Mamluk regime. Jane Hathaway has argued, however, that the households were actually Ottoman in their inspiration, as they resembled more closely the household of the ruling family in Istanbul than that of their Mamluk predecessors.

A key point of divergence between the two eras for her was that many of the retainers in households formed in the Ottoman centuries had never

been slaves but were hired musketeers, recruited from the Muslim populations of Anatolia and the Balkans.[13] Egypt's wealth provided multiple
opportunities for those ostensibly in the sultan's service to skim off cash
to create their own households. Once they had established themselves,
however, the Ottoman grandees embraced the traditions and lifestyles
of the old mamluk emirs and the case for a mamluk cultural continuity
in Egypt is strong. The actual mamluk institution had changed but the
façade behind which it functioned remained largely the same, as did the
political language the emirs employed.[14]

EXPANSION TO THE EAST

Sultan Selim had taken the core Arab lands in his lightning campaign of
1516–17 but it remained to his son Süleyman to add most of the rest.
Süleyman did so to achieve tactical advantage over the empire's two arch-
foes: Safavi Iran and Hapsburg Spain. The Safavi shah's control of central
and southern Iraq remained firmly entrenched after Selim's conquest of
Syria. Mosul was the only Ottoman toehold in Iraq and it was from there
that Süleyman marched into Baghdad in 1534 virtually unopposed as the
local governor had fled. Once established in Baghdad, Süleyman demonstrated magnanimity toward the Shia population of the city. His acts of
reconciliation were in sharp contrast to Shah Ismail's brutal treatment
of Baghdad's Sunni population, as well as its Christians and Jews, three
decades earlier. In a show of respect to the Shia, Süleyman visited the
shrines of Imam Musa al-Kadhim and Imam Muhammad Taqi in what
were then the outskirts of the city. He later visited the shrine of Imam
Husayn in Karbala and that of Imam ʿAli in Najaf, where he helped to
defray the costs of needed repairs for both.[15]

With his financial largesse, Süleyman established the empire's toleration of the empire's Shi'i minority as his ancestors had granted a relatively
benign toleration to their non-Muslim subjects. There was a difference,
however. The state legitimated and supported the religious hierarchies of

[13] Thomas Philipp and Ulrich Haarmann, editors, *The Mamluks in Egyptian Politics
and Society* (Cambridge: Cambridge University Press, 1998); Hathaway, *Politics of
Households*, 17–31.
[14] Michael Winter, "The Re-emergence of the Mamluks following the Ottoman Conquest"
In *The Mamluks in Egyptian Politics and Society*, edited by Thomas Philipp and Ulrich
Haarmann (Cambridge: Cambridge University Press, 1998), 87–106.
[15] Stephen Longrigg, *Four Centuries of Modern Iraq* (Oxford: Clarendon Press, 1925),
24–5.

the non-Muslims, acting to enforce orthodoxy against dissident members of those communities.[16] For the Shia, it was a case of mutual nonrecognition by both the Ottoman state and the Shi'i *mujtahid*s (legal authorities). The Ottomans did not condemn the sect as heretical and generally allowed for the public observation in Baghdad of Shi'i holy days such as Ashura, marking the death of Imam Husayn. However, the Ottoman authorities neither sanctioned the validity of the Shi'i Ja'fari school of Islamic law nor accepted the pronouncement of its *mujtahid*s as legally binding. The empire would not endorse Shi'i practices or legal traditions as valid, but it would not seek to suppress them in regions where the majority of the population was Shia. Its desire for peace, security, and the revenues they produced trumped any tendency toward enforcing religious conformity on its Muslim subjects.[17]

Nevertheless, Sultan Süleyman relished his role as protector of the Sunni tradition, despite his gestures of toleration toward Iraq's Shia. During Shah Ismail's rule in Baghdad, the Iranian army destroyed the tomb of Abu Hanifa. Abu Hanifa was the scholar who founded the legal tradition (Hanafi) that was favored by the Ottoman dynasty. Drawing on that connection, Süleyman sought to raise Abu Hanifa's memory to cult status as the Sunni protector of Baghdad. When workers cleared the rubble covering the scholar's tomb, they reputedly found his body uncorrupted. That was a clear sign of Abu Hanifa's sanctity to those present, if there was any doubt as to that fact among them. Süleyman then commissioned a new mosque to enclose the scholar's tomb. Thereafter, Abu Hanifa's mosque-tomb complex and the shrine of ʿAbd al-Qadir al-Gaylani (in Arabic, al-Kaylani), a twelfth-century Sufi saint and nominal founder of the Qadiriyya order that the Ottoman dynasty supported, became the focal points of Sunni pilgrimage in the city. It was a calculated attempt to offset any potential claim by the Shia to a monopoly over the city's sacred geography.[18] Underscoring the role that the two saints played in affirming the legitimacy of the House of Osman to rule in the city, when the army of Shah Abbas occupied Baghdad in 1623, it destroyed both mosques.[19]

---

[16] Masters, *Christians and Jews in the Ottoman Arab World*, 98–108.

[17] Stefan Winter, *The Shiites of Lebanon under Ottoman Rule, 1516–1788* (Cambridge: Cambridge University Press, 2010), 26–7.

[18] Longrigg, *Four Centuries*, 21–5; Gülru Necipoğlu, *The Age of Sinan: Architectural Culture in the Ottoman Empire* (Princeton, NJ: Princeton University Press, 2005), 63.

[19] Longrigg, *Four Centuries*, 57.

Rashid ibn Mughamis, the Bedouin ruler of the port city of Basra, faced with the new political reality in Baghdad, acknowledged Süleyman as his sovereign by 1536. The sultan reciprocated the gesture and appointed him as governor. Located on the edge of empire, Bedouin dynasties often ruled in the sultan's name in Basra. The tradition ended in the eighteenth century when Hasan Pasha, governor of Baghdad, took control of the port city directly. The governors in Baghdad ruled all of central and southern Iraq for the next century and a half. Basra held strategic significance for the Ottomans in the sixteenth century as it served as the starting point for Ottoman naval expeditions to the Indian Ocean, mounted in attempts to counter the growth of Portuguese threats to Muslim shipping in the eastern seas.[20] Ottoman maritime ambitions subsided in the early seventeenth century, however, and those at court no longer sought to challenge European imperial expansion in Asia. Nonetheless, Basra remained a major transit node for commerce between the Ottoman Empire and India throughout the Ottoman centuries.[21]

The Iraqi provinces' unhappy fate for most of the Ottoman period was to serve as a frontier for the empire, with Iran on its eastern flank and the tribes of the Arabian Desert to the south and west. Mosul, Baghdad, and Basra were among the least secure of the sultan's territories in the Arab lands. In 1623, an Iranian army at the command of Shah Abbas I (1587–1629) captured Baghdad and moved north to occupy Mosul. The Ottomans recovered Mosul in 1625, but Baghdad remained in Iranian hands until 1638, when an Ottoman army retook the city. The Afshar tribal leader Nadir Khan, later to be shah of Iran, besieged Basra, Baghdad, and Mosul in 1733 but failed in his attempt to capture any of them. He returned to Basra and Mosul for a second attempt in 1743. Although he again failed, the threat that Nadir Shah posed to Ottoman sovereignty in the region underscored the tenuous control that Istanbul exercised over the region known locally as the "land between the two rivers."[22]

Another Iranian upstart, Karim Khan Zand, managed to take Basra in 1776 and the Iranians held the city until his death in 1779. During that occupation, the Iranian adventurer attempted to accomplish a meeting of the minds between Sunni and Shi'i legal scholars by holding a council in Najaf where they would discuss differences in dogma and traditions. He hoped that they would reach a compromise in which the Sunni scholars

[20] Salih Özbaran, "Osmanlı İmperatorluğun Hindistan Yolu" *Tarih Dergisi* 31 (1977): 65–146.
[21] Thabit A. J. Abdullah, *Merchants, Mamluks, and Murder: The Political Economy of Trade in Eighteenth-century Basra* (Albany: State University of New York Press, 2001).
[22] Khoury, *State and Provincial Society*, 44–74.

would recognize the Jaᶜfari legal tradition as coequal to theirs. The discussions went on for several days, but Karim Khan's hopes were unfulfilled. According to a Sunni scholar who participated in the discussions, there was much agreement between the two groups, but the conference ended when the Shi'i scholars refused to stop their practice of condemning the first three caliphs of the Sunni tradition as being usurpers of ᶜAli's rightful claim to the office.[23] After Karim Khan's death, civil war wracked Iran. With it, the military threat on the empire's eastern frontier subsided for a few decades. When trouble did begin in Iraq in the early nineteenth century, it would arise along its southern desert borders rather than from its eastern flank.

Arab nationalist historians of Iraq portrayed the Ottoman period as a time of economic stagnation and political indolence.[24] Whether or not that interpretation is justified, it is true that the elite in Istanbul viewed Iraq as a provincial backwater at best and at worst a contested borderland. The Ottoman ruling house and the military elite who governed in its name made few lasting contributions to Iraq's infrastructure through pious endowments (*waqf*) that might serve as monuments to their rule after the initial investment in sacred monuments made by Sultan Süleyman in the wake of his conquest of Baghdad.[25] The indifference of the Ottoman elite to Iraq stood in stark contrast to Syria, where Ottoman era mosques supported by markets that they had privately endowed help frame the skyline of all the major cities and towns.[26] Syria seemed to the Ottoman elite as a promising location to preserve their memory for posterity through the construction of public works while Iraq did not. Not entirely abandoned, Iraq remained low on the list of Ottoman priorities until the second half of the nineteenth century.

EXPANSION TO THE SOUTH

The Ottoman entry into the geopolitical struggle for the Red Sea was a preemptive strike against the Portuguese to secure vital trade routes.[27]

---

[23] al-Sayyid ᶜAbdallah ibn al-Husayn al-Suwaydi, *Mu'tammar najaf* (Cairo: al-Matbaᶜa al-Salafiyya, 1393/1973).

[24] ᶜAbbas al-ᶜAzzawi, *Ta'rikh al-ᶜiraq bayn al-ihtilalayn*, 5 vols. (Baghdad: Matbaᶜat Baghdad, 1935–56).

[25] André Raymond, *The Great Arab Cities in the 16th–18th Centuries: An Introduction* (New York: New York University Press, 1984), 104–5.

[26] Çiğdem Kafescioğlu, "'In the Image of Rum': Ottoman Architectural Patronage in Sixteenth-Century Aleppo and Damascus" *Maqarnas* 16 (1999): 70–96.

[27] Casale, Giancarlo. "The Ottoman Administration of the Spice Trade in the Sixteenth-Century Red Sea and Persian Gulf" *JESHO* 49 (2006): 170–98.

Sultan Süleyman feared that Portuguese incursions into the Red Sea might eventually threaten the holy cities of Arabia and so dispatched a fleet to secure the coast of Yemen in 1525. An Ottoman army took the inland city of Zabid, following quickly on the heels of the seizure of the port city of Mocha. Within two years, however, squabbling among the Ottoman commanders led to the withdrawal of Ottoman troops from the country. The imam of the Zaydi Shia, Sharaf al-Din, quickly moved into the vacuum created by their departure to assert his control over the coastal region.

The ruling family in the mountains of northern Yemen claimed descent from the Shi'i imams going back to Muhammad, through the line of Zayd, who was the great-grandson of ʿAli and the Prophet's daughter Fatima. The Zaydi Shia, unlike the more numerous Imami Shia, found in Iran, Iraq, and Lebanon, believed that their imams were present on earth to rule their followers politically as well as to serve as their spiritual guide. The Zaydi Shia did not deem their imams infallible but asserted that only those men who were in direct descent from the imams had the legitimacy to rule in Yemen. Not all Yemenis were Zaydi Shia, but the majority of the tribes in the northern mountains were. Furthermore, some of the tribes in the central highlands of the country were Ismaili Shia and they often allied themselves with a more powerful Zaydi confederation against the Sunni tribes in the central and southern parts of the country. The Zaydi imam's claim to a centuries-old tradition of religiously sanctioned rule, coupled with the tenacity and independence characteristic of mountain peoples throughout the Middle East, made Yemen a special, and extremely difficult, region for the Ottomans. Religious ideology added political cohesion to the natural resistance of mountaineers to lowland rule.[28]

The Ottomans launched a land assault on the mountain strongholds of Imam Sharaf al-Din in 1538; in the following year, they occupied the town of Ta'izz and captured the imam, whom the Ottoman commander sent in chains to Istanbul. Sanʿa, the regional highland capital, held out until 1547. Despite the loss of his capital, al-Mutahhar, the son of Sharaf al-Din, refused to concede defeat. The Ottomans faced a protracted guerrilla war that ebbed and flowed according to which tribes were willing to commit men to the fray at the call of the Zaydi imam. The tribes of the highlands finally rose in concerted rebellion against Ottoman rule

[28] Paul Dresch, *Tribes, Government and History in Yemen* (Oxford: Oxford University Press, 1989).

in 1566, again led by al-Mutahhar, who declared a holy war against the Ottoman sultans. That time, the Zaydi army drove the Ottomans back to the coast.

It was a bitter defeat for the Ottomans that had political repercussions far beyond the Yemeni highlands. As news of the rebellion reached Istanbul in the summer of 1567, those at court decided to cancel a naval mission to Aceh in northern Sumatra, forestalling the creation of an Ottoman military presence in the Indian Ocean. A mission to the island did sail in 1568, but with a much smaller complement of men and ships. As such, it was unable to support the establishment of a permanent Ottoman naval base in the eastern seas, as had been the original plan.[29] Yemeni warriors fighting a holy war had put an end to Ottoman ambitions to be a world power in the south Asian seas.

The Ottomans were able to reestablish their control over Sanᶜa in 1572 after al-Mutahhar's death as the various Shi'i clans plotted over who should replace him as imam. Despite the internal struggle for power, the Shi'i tribes remained restive in an ongoing campaign they viewed as a holy war. Under Imam al-Qasim, known in Yemeni chronicles as "al-Kabir" (the Great), the tribes' resistance to rule by outsiders again coalesced into a countrywide uprising in 1598. It was a protracted and bitter struggle, but finally in 1629, al-Qasim's son Muhammad al-Muᶜayyad retook Sanᶜa, which the Ottomans had established as the province's administrative capital. The Zaydi tribesmen succeeded in driving the Ottomans out of the entire country by 1635.

Having learned the lesson that Yemen was not worth the cost of keeping it, Ottoman troops would not return until 1872, when Sultan Abdülaziz (1861–76) felt that a modern army might accomplish what those of his ancestors could not. Those at the sultan's court soon relearned the lesson that occupying Yemen was not the same thing as securing it. Yemen remained a restive province until the formal end of Ottoman rule there in 1918, when Yahya Muhammad ibn Hamid al-Din, another descendant of Zayd, took the throne as imam of an independent Yemen.

OTTOMAN NORTH AFRICA

Ottoman expansion into the eastern- and southernmost regions of the Arabic-speaking lands had sought to block the Portuguese colonial threat;

---

[29] Giancarlo Casale, *The Ottoman Age of Exploration* (Oxford: Oxford University Press, 2010), 131–3.

the expansion westward to the port cities of North Africa (Maghrib in Arabic) was a strategic move to halt a resurgent Spain's expansion into Muslim territories. The fall of the Muslim sultanate of Granada in 1492 ended an Islamic political presence in Spain dating from 711 C.E. Taking the *reconquista* to the sea, Spanish fleets harried Muslim shipping while Spanish soldiers occupied ports along the North African coast. The Ottoman response was to increase pressure on the Europeans through the state sponsorship of Muslim corsairs, who raided Christian shipping in the western Mediterranean and launched slave raids on Christian coastal villages from Crete to Ireland. Corsairs, plundering in the name of the Ottoman sultan, established control over the cities of Algiers, Tunis, and Tripoli by the middle of the sixteenth century. Those three cities served to anchor the Ottoman political presence in North Africa throughout the early-modern period, and each would, in time, constitute a separate Ottoman province.

Although Spain and the Ottoman Empire each sought to check the influence of its competitor rather than actually extend its land empire, there was a major difference between the Spanish garrisons (*presidios*) along the North African coast and the fortified port cities of the Ottomans (*qasaba*). The Spanish forces faced hostile Muslim populations in the hinterlands beyond their walls and relied almost entirely on provisioning by sea, while the Ottomans could appeal to Islamic solidarity with their subjects to secure their ports' immediate hinterlands. The population of the Ottoman garrison cities was a cosmopolitan mixture of Turkish-speaking adventurers, Arabic-speaking refugees from Spain, Berber (Amazigh) tribal migrants, and European slaves and renegade converts to Islam. Although occasionally the Ottoman governors were at odds with the inland tribes, the ports' janissary garrisons did not have to exercise continued vigilance against land-based attacks. Still Ottoman control in the region relied heavily on the navy, and the sultans' writ rarely extended beyond the North African coastal plain.

Even a nominal acquiescence to Ottoman legitimacy in North Africa ended at the Moroccan frontier. The Moroccan sultans repelled Ottoman incursions into their territory as vigorously as they did attacks by the Spaniards.[30] The Ottomans faced a special problem with the Moroccan dynasties, first that of the Sa'dis (1510–1603) and later the 'Alawis, who ruled from 1668 until 1822, that they had not encountered elsewhere

---

[30] Andrew Hess, *The Forgotten Frontier: A History of the Sixteenth-Century Ibero-African Frontier* (Chicago: The University of Chicago Press, 1978).

in the Arabic-speaking Sunni Muslim territories. Both Moroccan dynasties claimed descent from the Prophet Muhammad's lineage as *sharifs* and thereby boasted a pedigree that was more exalted than that of the Ottomans. North African legal scholars considered both dynasties' rule in Morocco to be legitimate while they deemed the House of Osman to be usurpers. The practical result of that interpretation was that Moroccan sultans could rally Berber and Arab tribes into formidable military coalitions based on a mixture of religious devotion and political self-interest. With broad religious sanction from the local religious establishment, they effectively resisted Ottoman attempts to expand their political control into the country.[31] As a result of their successful resistance, Moroccans can today boast that their ancestors were never the subjects of the Ottoman Empire. It is a claim few other Arabs can legitimately make.

THE RISE OF "SELF-MADE" GOVERNORS

During the first two centuries of Ottoman rule, most of the governors in the Arab provinces were what might be termed "professional" Ottomans. Typically, these men were products of the *devşirme*, the "boy-tax" levied on Balkan and Anatolian Christians. The boys who showed exceptional promise received rigorous education in the school at Topkapı Palace in Istanbul to advance their martial and administrative skills.[32] Upon reaching manhood, they were nominally the sultan's "slaves" (*kul*) and constituted the ruling class of "Ottomans," that is, those belonging to the sultan's household. All of the "sultan's slaves," whether they were actual soldiers or not, were considered as belonging to the *askeri* (soldier) class, in contrast to the *reaya*, or those whom they ruled. Arabic-speaking Christians were exempt from the tax, and few men from Muslim families entered the palace school. Those who did were almost exclusively from the old Anatolian Turkish dynasties or later from Balkan Muslim families. As a result, the governors in the central Arab provinces were rarely native speakers of Arabic before the eighteenth century.

One of the rare exceptions to the general rule of professional Ottomans as governors in the core provinces of the Arab lands during the first two

---

[31] Stephen Cory, "Sharifian Rule in Morocco (Tenth-Twelfth/Sixteenth-Eighteenth Centuries" In *The New Cambridge History of Islam*. Vol. 2. *The Western Islamic World, Eleventh to Eighteenth Centuries*, edited by Maribel Fierro (Cambridge: Cambridge University Press, 2010), 453–79.

[32] I. Metin Kunt, *Sancaktan Eyalete: 1550–1650 arasında Osmanlı Ümerası ve İl İdaresi* (Istanbul: Boğaziçi Üniversitesi Yayınları, 1978).

Ottoman centuries occurred in Aleppo, where Sultan Ahmed I (1603–17) named Canpulatoğlu Hüseyin as governor in 1604. The Canpulatoğlu clan had provided leadership to the Kurds who lived in the Jabal Kurd (Mountain of the Kurds) region of Kilis, today in the borderlands between Syria and Turkey, for at least a century before the Ottoman conquest. There was resentment among the professional Ottoman military class at Hüseyin's rapid rise through the ranks, and the former governor of the province had reputedly stated that he would surrender his authority to a "black slave" before he would do so to a Kurd. Perhaps sharing such feelings, General Çağalzade Sinan Pasha summarily executed Hüseyin for treason in 1605, reputedly for his late arrival at the Battle of Urumia. The seventeenth-century biographer of Aleppo's notables, Abu al-Wafa al-ʿUrdi (d. 1661), hinted, however, that Hüseyin had been executed because of his Kurdish origins rather than for any misdeed he had done.[33] In revenge, Hüseyin's nephew ʿAli rallied their kinsmen in revolt. The revolt rapidly spread throughout northern Syria, and ʿAli reportedly represented himself in correspondence to the duke of Tuscany as "Prince and Protector of the Kingdom of Syria," while some Kurds hoped he would establish a Kurdish principality. Sultan Ahmed appointed ʿAli as governor of Aleppo in 1606 in an attempt to buy time and then raised an army to crush him in 1607.[34] No other local personality would serve as governor in Aleppo until 1801.

The "professional" Ottoman governors in the Arab lands sometimes married locally, often so that they might gain *sharif* status for their children as that exalted lineage could pass from the mother as well as the father of a child. A few endowed mosques that would memorialize their reigns.[35] Most, however, reportedly did not know Arabic and many received unfavorable reviews from the authors of the local chronicles and biographical dictionaries, written in Arabic during the Ottoman centuries. It is easy to understand why. The governors, knowing their term of office would be brief, extorted the funds necessary to purchase their next posting from local merchants and the minority religious communities. The pattern of short-term, rotating governors ended in most of the Arab provinces in the eighteenth century. Istanbul lost its authority to

[33] Abu al-Wafa' al-ʿUrdi al-Halabi, *Maʿadan al-dhahab fi al-aʿyan al-musharrafa bihim halab.* (Aleppo: Dar al-Mallah, 1987), 306–13.

[34] Masters, *Origins of Western Economic Dominance*, 18–22.

[35] Heghnar Zeitlian Watenpaugh, *The Image of an Ottoman City: Imperial Architecture and Urban Experience in Aleppo in the 16th and 17th Centuries* (Leiden: Brill, 2004), 60–122.

say who would represent the sultan in many of the governorships in the Arab lands as Ottoman military power weakened both on the European frontier and in provinces distant from the capital.

I will simply characterize these eighteenth-century governors as being "self-made men," for a lack of a better term, to distinguish them from the "professional" Ottomans who had gained their status through their connection to the ruling house in Istanbul. For the most part, governors in the former category pledged their loyalty to the House of Osman but did not emerge from its retinue. The term "locals" used by some historians is far from satisfactory as a designation for them, however, as most were not native to the provinces they ruled. Nonetheless, many succeeded in creating local bases of political/military power and displayed varying degrees of autonomy when dealing with orders emanating from the imperial capital. In that sense, they were localized actors. Even so, it is important to note that the authors of the urban chronicles, who for the most part did represent entrenched local connections and interests, did not view their governors as having local roots or representing the interests of the civilian populations they ruled.

Military officers in the three North African provinces – Sökeli Ali in Algiers, Alioğlu Hüseyin in Tunis, and Karamanlı Ahmed in Tripoli – seized control of the governorship of their respective cities in the early part of the eighteenth century. All three established hereditary dynasties, with their descendants succeeding them as governors into the nineteenth century. All were Muslims of Anatolian or Cretan origin and they, in turn, heavily recruited their armed retainers, who bore the title of janissaries, from Anatolia or the Ottoman Mediterranean islands. Although these governors were not technically Ottomans in that they were not graduates of the palace school in Istanbul, they were ethnically, or at least culturally, Turks, and Ottoman Turkish remained the language of the North African governors' administration. With that bond, the governors in North Africa remained culturally tied to Istanbul and the Ottoman dynasty, even if they did not always obey the orders emanating from there.

The sultan acknowledged the legitimacy of the governors in the three North African provinces through letters of appointment, and he could theoretically remove them at will. In reality, the sultan simply confirmed that the governors were his "loyal servants." The key factor in keeping these provinces nominally under Ottoman suzerainty was that the governor of each province saw the other two governors as his rivals in the pirate enterprise. The rivalry for dominance on the high seas forced each of the three governors to maintain a relationship with the sultan in

Istanbul for the sake of his own political legitimacy and to keep his closer rivals off balance. Actual control from the capital as manifested by obedience to the sultan's writ remained a constant point of negotiation for those in Istanbul, wavering between offers of reward for compliance and the threat of sanction in its absence.[36]

The political autonomy of the governing dynasties in North Africa created difficulties for Istanbul as European diplomats sought to apply pressure on the Ottoman sultan to reign in Muslim piracy in the western Mediterranean Sea in the eighteenth century. Piracy provided the main economic base of the North African provinces, however, and their governors rarely complied with the sultan's wishes to end their raiding.[37] The most flagrant example of that disregard occurred in 1718 after the signing of the Treaty of Passarowitz. Sökeli Ali in Algiers refused to honor the sultan's order to desist in attacking Austrian ships. The Şeyhülislam (chief legal scholar of the empire) declared him a rebel. In retaliation for his continued disobedience to the sultan's will, he banned Algerian pilgrims from participation in the hajj. The raiding continued nonetheless, and a new sultan, Mahmud I, who was not as concerned about placating the Austrians, lifted the ban some time after 1730. Nominally Ottoman at best, the North African dynasties did not feel secure enough to form their own sultanates and make a clean break with Istanbul. Tentatively, their provinces remained within the "Ottoman Kingdoms."

A hereditary dynasty of governors also emerged in Baghdad in the eighteenth century. An appointee from Istanbul, Hasan Pasha, governed the province from 1704 until his death in 1722. His length of tenure was uncommon for a career Ottoman officer in a provincial posting and reflected the awareness in Istanbul of Baghdad's precarious position on the Iranian frontier. Even more unusually, the governorship passed to his son Ahmed upon his death. Ahmed left no son when he died in 1747, but rather a remarkable daughter, Adile. After a two-year rule by a governor appointed from Istanbul, she succeeded in having her husband, Süleyman, who had been a Georgian mamluk in her father's household, named as governor. There was an interregnum upon Süleyman's death in 1762 in which a Persian servant of Süleyman named ʿAli ruled in Baghdad. Adile

[36] Tal Shuval, "The Ottoman Algerian Elite and Its Ideology" *IJMES* 32 (2000): 323–44; Houari Touati, "Ottoman Maghrib" In *The New Cambridge History of Islam.* Vol. 2. *The Western Islamic World Eleventh to Eighteenth Centuries*, edited by Maribel Fierro (Cambridge: Cambridge University Press, 2010), 503–45.

[37] Jamal Abun-Nasr, *A History of the Maghrib* (Cambridge: Cambridge University Press, 1975), 159–201.

resented ʿAli as an upstart and worked behind the scenes with the other mamluks of the governor's palace to undermine his position. Her plot succeeded as Istanbul named Ömer, the husband of her younger sister, Ayşe, as governor in 1764. Ömer had also begun his career as a Georgian mamluk in Ahmed Pasha's service.[38] Having once been a slave was clearly not a hindrance to social advancement in eighteenth-century Baghdad.

Almost all of the governors of Baghdad, from 1747 until 1831, were men who began their careers as mamluks in the governor's household, started by Hasan Pasha but secured by his female descendants. There were occasional attempts by the sultan to appoint men from outside the ruling mamluk clique to the governorship and thereby reestablish direct control over the province. Local resistance to any such appointment was intense, however, and the governors chosen by the sultan seldom remained for long.[39] Hasan Pasha had created his own small court in the governor's palace that imitated the imperial court in Istanbul in which he received his training. The governor's household in Baghdad, however, followed the much closer Iranian imperial model in its protocols and replenished its ranks with mamluks from Georgia, the same source for royal slaves favored by the Iranian shahs.

While successive sultans in Istanbul may have wished to unseat the dynasty founded by Hasan Pasha, they had to agree that the mamluk governors of Baghdad zealously defended Iraq's frontier against Iranian ambitions. A compromise emerged whereby the governor in Baghdad ruled in the sultan's name even if the sultan had no say in who would represent him. The façade of Ottoman rule continued in central and southern Iraq, as it did in North Africa, as a result of the governors' ability to secure the sultan's claim to his remote "protected realms" from challengers from outside the empire. The Ottoman Empire in the eighteenth century had come to resemble the late Abbasid caliphate after 1000 C.E. wherein the caliph in Baghdad routinely issued the patents appointing men, not of his choosing, to be his nominal provincial administrators. The Ottoman sultans in seeking to preserve the façade of empire settled for a regime in which they would have little say in who would represent them in their more distant provinces.

[38] Longrigg, *Four Centuries*, 123–200; Tom Nieuwenhuis, *Politics and Society in Early Modern Iraq: Mamluk Pashas, Tribal Shayks and Local Rule between 1802 and 1831* (The Hague: Martinus Nijhoff Publishers, 1981), 11–30; Thomas Lier, *Haushalte und Haushaltepolitik in Baghdad 1704–1831* (Wurzburg: Ergon Verlag, 2004).
[39] Nieuwenhuis, *Politics and Society*, 76–7.

Closer to home, there was a rise in the political influence exercised by two indigenous families in the core provinces of Damascus and Mosul in the eighteenth century. Throughout much of that century, the governors of Damascus were from the ʿAzm family, while in Mosul, the Jalili family provided many of its governors. In both cases, the sultans could, and did, remove governors arising from either extended family who earned their displeasure. Neither family produced a figure who forced the Porte to acknowledge his family's indispensability to rule, as was the case in Baghdad or the North African provinces, much less challenge the continued Ottoman claim to the city that they governed as did ʿAli Bey in Cairo, to be discussed later. Nonetheless, individuals from the two families served as governor for as long as a decade in some cases, without interference from Istanbul. Both families were able to build up a support base, if not actual military power, in their respective cities through patronage and their keen sense of how to play off the various local prominent families (aʿyan) against each other to their advantage. Although both dynasties had their critics, the local chroniclers in Mosul and Damascus generally appreciated the stability that their rule imposed. They, unlike many of their predecessors, were remembered as good governors.

The pattern of governors arising from outside the ruling circle in Istanbul although prevalent in the eighteenth century throughout the Arab lands was not universal. Jeddah, Jerusalem, and Aleppo had "professional" Ottoman governors for most of the century, and even in Damascus and Mosul there was the occasional Ottoman officer who resided in the provincial saray. In the case of Aleppo, the power struggles among the city's inhabitants ironically strengthened the Ottoman position. Much of the city's male population associated themselves with one of two political factions: the janissaries or the *ashraf* (singular, *sharif*, a descendant of the Prophet Muhammad). These two groups fought several pitched battles for control of the city's streets in the late eighteenth and early nineteenth centuries. Adding to the potential for chaos, the leading families of that city were often engaged in highly competitive power plays against one another. The result was that no local faction arose to offer an alternative to men appointed to the province's governorship from Istanbul.

EGYPT: A SPECIAL CASE

Egypt was perhaps the most difficult province for the Ottoman sultans to keep under their direct control. In part, that was due to the creation of militarized households there in the Ottoman period, but the collective memory in the province that Cairo had been the seat of a sultanate in its own right also served to undermine Ottoman claims of exclusivity to rule. The existence of militarized households was not unique to Cairo after all. The dominance of mamluks of Georgian origin in Baghdad's political life in the eighteenth century had a striking resemblance to the situation in Egypt. The loyalty of the mamluk regime in Iraq to the sultan in Istanbul, however, contrasted sharply with the slack obedience often manifested by their contemporaries in Cairo. In part, that was due to the multiplicity of such households that formed in Cairo as compared to a single governor's household in Baghdad, Tripoli, Tunis, or Algiers. Because of the existence of these competing centers of power, some historians of Egypt have distinguished the Ottoman regime there as having been highly decentralized, almost from its origins. That made the regime in Cairo distinct from other provincial governments in the empire, as well as from the regimes that historically preceded it and would replace it.[40]

The Ottoman sultans continued to appoint their men to the post of governor in Cairo throughout the seventeenth and eighteenth centuries, but they did not always exercise a monopoly of political power in the city. By the middle of the seventeenth century, independent militarized households began to compete for political dominance. Some of these had their origins with Ottoman officers appointed to Cairo; self-made men, often claiming mamluk origins themselves, formed others.[41] The self-styled emirs who headed the households held the balance of military power in Cairo, despite the presence of a janissary garrison ostensibly there to uphold the governor's writ and authority.[42]

In the seventeenth and early eighteenth centuries, most of the emirs in Cairo divided into two factions, the Faqariyya and the Qasimiyya, which routinely engaged in bloody faction fighting to achieve dominance in the city. Additionally, one or the other of these factions periodically confronted the janissary garrison in armed clashes on the streets of Cairo. There was a military standoff, however, and no party emerged in the factional fighting with sufficient strength to challenge the titular authority of the sultan to rule Egypt. In that precarious balance of power, Ottoman rule continued for more than a century in an uneasy stalemate.[43]

[40] Nelly Hanna, "Culture in Ottoman Egypt." In *The Cambridge History of Egypt*. Vol. 2. *Modern Egypt from 1517 to the End of the Twentieth Century*, edited by M. W. Daly (Cambridge: Cambridge University Press, 1998), 87–112.

[41] Jane Hathaway, *A Tale of Two Factions: Myth, Memory, and Identity in Ottoman Egypt and Yemen*. Albany: State University of New York Press, 2003.

[42] Winter, "Re-emergence of the Mamluks," 87–106.

[43] Michael Winter, *Egyptian Society under Ottoman Rule* (London: Routledge, 1992), 49–77.

The status quo changed in the eighteenth century when a new constellation of emirs, known as the Qazdughliyya, emerged. They first aligned themselves with the Faqariyya, but by 1754, they were the dominant political faction in Cairo in their own right. The most ambitious of those in the Qazdughliyya household, Bulut Kapan ʿAli (Cloud Seizer), otherwise known as ʿAli Bey al-Kabir, became the de facto head of Egypt in his role as *shaykh al-balad*, literally, "head of the town," between 1760 and 1766 and again between 1767 and 1772. The title had signified the dominant political personality in the city during the Mamluk sultanate, and its revival was redolent with nostalgia for the old regime. Its use also hinted at the aspirations of at least some emirs for the restoration of an independent sultanate based in Cairo.

Fears of that occurrence deepened the respect held by some individuals in the Muslim scholarly class in Egypt for the sultanate in Istanbul. Looking back over the troubled eighteenth century, ʿAbd al-Rahman al-Jabarti (d. 1825–6) began his chronicle of Egypt with a glowing account of the reigns of Sultans Selim and Süleyman, saying the Ottoman sultans had instituted the best government Egypt had known since the time of the "Rightly-Guided Caliphs" (632–61).[44] This was an implicit attempt to draw the reader's attention to the lack of justice in the author's present. Earlier, Ahmad ibn ʿAbd al-Munʿim al-Damanhuri (d. 1778), rector of the al-Azhar madrasa, wrote a classic treatise on the institution of the sultanate in which he emphasized the necessity for justice and the rule of law. Al-Damanhuri also made it clear to the reader that the House of Osman supplied the only virtuous candidate for the sultanate. His manuscript suggests that al-Jabarti was not alone in viewing eighteenth-century developments in Cairo with unease.

Shock at the audacity of ʿAli Bey's ambitions presumably provided the inspiration for the authors' support for the House of Osman. In 1768, he dismissed the Ottoman governor and refused entry into Cairo to the man Sultan Mustafa III (1757–74) had appointed as his successor. Then in an act of unprecedented defiance, ʿAli Bey appointed one of his own mamluks as governor in Jeddah in 1770, thereby undermining the Ottoman sultan's claim to be the protector of Arabia's two holy cities. ʿAli Bey's lieutenant Muhammad Bey Abu al-Dhahab invaded Syria in the following year. There, his forces allied with the powerful Arab tribal leader Zahir al-ʿUmar, who had dominated the Galilee region for several decades. Together, they succeeded in defeating an Ottoman army sent to stop them and marched into Damascus, although its garrison held out behind the walls of the city's citadel.

ᶜAli Bey's ambitions, which gave rise to his nickname, floundered at the citadel's walls, as Abu al-Dhahab switched sides and joined the Ottoman relief army. His aspirations still unchecked, ᶜAli Bey returned to Syria for another try in 1771, aided again by Zahir al-ᶜUmar. That attempt was supported by a Russian naval bombardment of Beirut, but it also failed because of a betrayal by ᶜAli Bey's lieutenant and brother-in-law, Muhammad Bey, who went over to the Ottoman side. The Ottoman sultan's authority technically was restored in Egypt with the death of ᶜAli Bey in 1773. Although plagued by internal competition among the various emirs, the Qazdughliyya faction retained its effective control of the province. The emirs did, however, accede to the appointment of nominal governors to Cairo from Istanbul until Napoleon's invasion in 1798. Having weathered the challenge, the façade of Ottoman rule in Egypt continued.[45]

CONCLUSION

There was a diminution of the sultan's authority in almost all of the Arab provinces during the eighteenth century. The loss of Ottoman power was most acute in Egypt during the third quarter of the eighteenth century, but the sultans also had to be content with governors in the North African cities and Baghdad who ruled with only nominal acknowledgment of Istanbul's sovereignty. Yet no matter how tenuous his actual control of affairs on the provincial level had become, the sultan remained unchallenged in his legitimacy as sovereign. Taxes continued to be paid to Istanbul, even if local players increased the percentage of the total they kept for themselves. More importantly, judges continued to arrive from Istanbul and they typically upheld the sultan's legal authority in his far-flung domains.

The reality of political life for the Sunni elite in the Arab lands was that there was simply no viable alternative to the House of Osman. Local

---

[45] Amnon Cohen, *Palestine in the 18th Century: Patterns of Government and Administration* (Jerusalem: Hebrew University Press, 1973), 83–104; Thomas Philipp, *Acre: The Rise and Fall of a Palestinian City, 1730–1831* (New York: Columbia University Press, 2001); Daniel Crecelius, "Egypt in the Eighteenth Century" In *The Mamluks in Egyptian Politics and Society*, edited by Thomas Philipp and Ulrich Haarmann (Cambridge: Cambridge University Press, 1998): 59–86.

actors perceived that working within the Ottoman system served them better than working outside it. Furthermore, the example of Egypt's moment of defiance demonstrated that although the sultan and the state apparatus he controlled were weaker in the eighteenth century than they had been previously, the sultan still possessed sufficient resources to put down a direct challenge to his authority should it arise. It was a measure of the prestige of the dynasty, if not its actual strength, that on the eve of Napoleon's arrival in Egypt, Sultan Selim III (1789–1807) still controlled, at least nominally, the patrimony left to him in the Arab lands by his illustrious ancestors Selim and Süleyman. Yemen provided the only exception.

Adding to an impression of unbroken continuity, the era of Ottoman rule between the initial conquests of 1516–17 and 1798 was relatively tranquil in most of the Arab provinces. There were the notable exceptions of Iraq, which lay on the frontier of the Ottomans' archrival Iran, and Lebanon, where political struggles over the emirate of the Cebel-i Dürüz (the Mountain of the Druzes), as the Ottomans called it, led to periodic rebellion. There were also rare occasions of popular uprisings such as the prolonged disorder known as the Naqib al-Ashraf rebellion in Jerusalem between 1702 and 1706, mounted against corrupt governors.[46]

Outbursts of urban unrest increased in the troubled decades of the early nineteenth century. Significantly, however, even when such uprisings occurred, the rebels questioned not the legitimacy of the House of Osman, but rather the quality of the men it chose as its stewards. Relatively free of peasant revolts or urban rebellions, the political history of the first three centuries of Ottoman rule in the Arab lands was marked more frequently by intrigues in the governors' palaces and struggles between the various armed groups that constituted the provincial military. These could be bloody but were generally short-lived. The disruption to civilian life was seemingly minimal even during what could have been major political upheavals. The account of the German merchant Wolffgang Aigen of the revolt in Aleppo by its governor Abaza Hasan Pasha in 1658 confirms this impression.[47] Trade quickly returned to normal after the rebels' defeat at the hands of troops loyal to Sultan Mehmed IV (1648–87) and the rhythms of daily life resumed.

[46] 'Adel Manna^c,' "Eighteenth- and Nineteenth-Century Rebellions in Palestine" *Journal of Palestine Studies* 24 (1994): 51–66.
[47] Wolffgang Aigen, *Sieben Jahre in Aleppo (1656–1663)*, edited by Andreas Tietze (Vienna: Wiener Zeitschrift für die Kunde des Morgenlandes, 1980), 99–102.

None of the rebels, outside Cairo or Aleppo during Canpulatoğlu ⁽Ali's brief moment on the political stage, challenged the authority of Ottoman rule. Rather they sought to ingratiate themselves into the Ottoman system. Given the weakness of the central government in the period, we might ask, "Why did Ottoman rule persist in the Arab lands in the eighteenth century?" The answer seems to lie in the institutions that the Ottoman regime put into place in the first century of Ottoman rule. More crucially, it rested in the legitimization that the Sunni Muslim elite was willing to extend to the Ottoman sultans. Without that collaboration, the domination by the House of Osman over the political life of the region would have become tenuous at best. The empire in the Arab lands did not survive by the threat of force. Rather it endured as the Ottoman dynasty had co-opted the region's elite as its willing collaborators, as will be shown in the following chapter.

2

Institutions of Ottoman Rule

The janissaries entered Syria in 1516 as the shock troops of an empire that had undergone two centuries of political evolution. In that regard, the Ottomans were unique among the various non-Arab dynasties that succeeded in seizing power in the Arab lands beginning in the tenth century as the Abbasid caliphate went into its long decline. The slave soldiers and tribal leaders who established the dynasties that ruled from Morocco to Iraq in the transitional centuries between the "classical age" of Islam and the early modern period were typically illiterate, with no experience in governing states with a bureaucratic tradition. Often alien to the culture of the cities they seized, the self-styled sultans were content to co-opt the Arabic-speaking religious elite to serve as the public face of their regimes. The arrival of the Ottomans challenged that monopoly of knowledge exercised by local scholars, whose position was eclipsed by bureaucrats who took their orders from Istanbul. Faced with a profound shift in the geographical locus of political power, the scholarly elite in Cairo, Damascus, and Baghdad had to be content with provincial rather than imperial horizons.

The imposition of Ottoman institutions on the Arab provinces required the local Sunni Arabic-speaking elites to mediate a place within the sultan's regime. The Ottomans made few concessions to adapt their rule to conditions preexisting in the Arab lands, other than to stress the commonality of their faith in Islam with that of most of their Arab subjects. The Ottoman officials who governed them spoke a language that was largely incomprehensible to the Arabs they ruled, but Islam provided a common political rhetoric both rulers and subjects could understand. In retrospect, an appeal to a common faith was the cornerstone of their

48

relationship. Sunni Muslims came to accept that their status within the empire was secure and they viewed its institutions as their own, with varying degrees of enthusiasm. Chief among those was the institution of the sultanate.

THE SULTANATE

The failure of the Ottoman dynasty to establish lasting control over Yemen or to achieve military success in Morocco was due, in part, to the distance separating either place from Istanbul. The simple fact was that military success in the early modern period was directly linked to the length of the supply line from the capital to the battlefield.[1] Yemen and Morocco were simply too far from the empire's center for it to mount a drawn-out military campaign in either. Further complicating Ottoman ambitions, the dynasties ruling in both Yemen and Morocco boasted a lineage that stretched back to one or the other of the Prophet's grandsons. The mantle of religious legitimacy that either opponent could claim offered a powerful political rallying point for those who would resist the expansion of Ottoman hegemony.[2] It was hard for the sultan in Istanbul to claim credibly to any Muslims, other than those at his own court, that his lineage was superior to that of his rivals when he faced dynasties that could claim descent from the Prophet's own "noble house."

Bothered by the Ottoman house's lack of a suitable pedigree, Marʿi al-Karmi (d. 1624) writing in Cairo in the early seventeenth century sought to create an Arab lineage for Osman Gazi, although he named no specific ancestor as the founder of the dynasty.[3] Marʿi's attempt seems to have found few echoes among his contemporaries, however. Muhammad ibn Abi al-Surur cited the assertion made by the sixteenth-century chronicler ibn Ayas that Osman Gazi was of the lineage of Caliph ʿUthman ibn ʿAffan (d. 656). Without commenting on that rather dubious claim, which seemingly rested solely on the fact that both men bore the name ʿUthman (Turkish form, Osman), ibn Abi al-Surur went on to delineate Osman Gazi's Central Asian ancestry, following the genealogy favored in

[1] Rhoads Murphey, *Ottoman Warfare 1500–1700* (New Brunswick, NJ, 1999), 20–5.
[2] Abderrahmane El Moudden, "The Idea of the Caliphate between Moroccans and Ottomans: Political and Symbolic Stakes in the 16th and 17th Century-Maghrib" *Studia Islamica* 82 (1995): 103–12.
[3] Michael Winter, "A Seventeenth-Century Arabic Panagyric of the Ottoman Dynasty" *Asian and African Studies* 2 (1979): 130–56.

Ottoman dynastic histories that he had apparently consulted.[4] Clearly, the author did not think Osman Gazi was of Arab origin. Nor did it matter to him that he was not. Rather the legitimacy of Ottoman rule over the Arab lands rested in the Muslim legal scholars' understanding of the institution of the sultanate. It was that office that legitimated the House of Osman for them rather than a dubious lineage that stretched back to Arabia. The sultanate as a political ideal was a product of the evolution of Muslim political theory that had occurred over the space of five centuries before the arrival of the Ottoman armies.

The origins of Muslim political theory lay in the state founded by the Prophet Muhammad in 622 C.E. in Medina. Known as the *umma*, it included all Muslims and those Jews and Christians who accepted the political supremacy of Islam. The Prophet was the head of state, but in that role he was understood to be acting as a political rather than a religious leader. His model of leadership that combined prophecy and polity was understood by Muslims to have been established by the Jewish Prophets mentioned in the Qur'an: Moses (Musa), David (Da'ud), and Solomon (Sulayman). All three had been political leaders as well as the receivers of divine revelation. When the Prophet died suddenly in 632, there was no clear successor and the community of the faithful settled on Abu Bakr, an early convert to Islam and the father of Muhammad's wife ʿA'isha. The Muslims believed that with the Prophet's death, revelation had ended, but the political state founded by him had not. Abu Bakr's role was to assume the political leadership of the *umma*, but he was not to serve as its religious guide. Not having a political vocabulary that provided an appropriate term for his role, Abu Bakr took the self-explanatory title of caliph, in Arabic *khalifat Rasul Allah*, literally the "Successor of God's Messenger."

The office of the caliph evolved over time, and the understanding of who had the right to hold the office and what his prerogatives were eventually created the split between the Sunni and Shi'i traditions of Islam. The initial rupture occurred in 656 when the third caliph, ʿUthman, was murdered by Muslim soldiers. He had not designated an heir and the majority of the community supported the elevation of ʿAli, who was the Prophet Muhammad's cousin, the husband of his daughter Fatima, and the father of Muhammad's only grandsons, to the office of caliph. The clan of ʿUthman, the Umayyads (Banu Umayya), refused to acknowledge

---

[4] Muhammad ibn Abi al-Surur, *al-Minah al-rahmaniyya fi al-dawla al-ʿuthmaniyya* (Damascus: Dar al-Basha'ir, 1995), 9–16.

ᶜAli's right to lead the community, however, and started a civil war. When ᶜAli was assassinated in 661, the Umayyads seized the caliphate. They would hold it until 750, when a revolution would replace them with a clan more closely related to the Prophet Muhammad, the Abbasids (Banu ᶜAbbas), who reigned from 750 to 1258.

Under the Umayyads the office of caliph was largely a political one, embodied in the title they most frequently used: "Commander of the Faithful" (*amir al-mu'minin*), a nod to their role as head of the Muslim armies. Those opposing them within the community believed that the office of caliph should also have a spiritual function, embodied in the title *imam*, literally "the one who stands in front," as in the person who leads the Friday prayers. Many of those seeking a larger religious role for the office supported the candidacy of one or the other of the descendants of the grandsons of the Prophet, Husayn and Hasan, as they believed that only those who were the Prophet's direct descendants were entitled to rule the community. Those partisans would, over time, come to be known as the Shia, a shortened form of the phrase *Shiᶜat ᶜAli*, the "party, or faction, of ᶜAli."

Sunni Muslim legal scholars began to wrestle with two main issues in their theorization of the caliphate, its function and who could aspire to the office, only during the later centuries of Abbasid rule. But even in such discussions, there was no deep speculative theory advanced in defense of the office; rather their articulations of its parameters were descriptive of the existing historical precedents. A good theory for them covered all known historical examples. The Sunni consensus held that the office was primarily political, but that the caliph also had a religious role, embodied in his title *imam*. In that function of his office, however, the caliph was limited largely to ceremonial occasions, such as leading the Friday prayers or taking charge, on occasion, of the annual hajj to Mecca. The caliph was to serve as a moral guide for the community of the believers and to embody the spirit of Islamic law as it was evolving, but he was not the source of that law, which remained the Qur'an and the traditions of the Prophet, or even a major interpreter of it. That role was left to the body of religious scholars, the ulama.

As to the question of who could hold the office, the Sunni ulama, looking back over the first three centuries of Muslim government, agreed that as all those who held the office were males from the Prophet Muhammad's tribe the Quraysh, henceforth that lineage would be one of the necessary criteria in determining whether a person could aspire to the office. For the largest sect of the Shia, known as the Imami Shia, the candidates for the position of imam who would exercise absolute spiritual authority over the believers could only be from the lineage established by the Prophet Muhammad's grandson, Husayn. The imam's political role was largely irrelevant to the Shi'i scholars and indeed none of their imams after ʿAli ever ruled a state. The Shia believed, however, that when their last imam, who went into occultation sometime after 873, returned, he would establish the rule of the righteous before the final Day of Judgment.

From the eleventh century onward, Sunni Muslim legal scholars had to deal with the reality that the universal caliph, which Islamic political theory had previously established as the only legitimate head of the Muslim polity (the *umma*), was a figurehead at best as the formerly unified Abbasid caliphate fractured into competing states. ʿAli al-Mawardi (d. 1058) suggested a compromise by which the community might recognize the existence of autonomous rulers, for whom he used the term *emir* or commander. The emirs were legitimate if they received a patent of office from the reigning caliph and governed according to Islamic law. Other scholars after al-Mawardi devoted considerable attention to the same question and ultimately adopted his model.[5] The scholarly consensus gave such rulers the title of *sultan*, derived from the Arabic word for "power." The scholars affirmed that as rule by these sultans was in accordance with Muslim law, their subjects should obey them secure in the knowledge that it was God's will that they do so.

The Sunni scholarly consensus had acknowledged the political fragmentation of the Muslim world, but it upheld the legitimacy of multiple sultans only as long as they recognized the caliph's theoretical right to supersede them should a strong caliph emerge. As a sign of that fealty to the higher office, coins in a sultan's realm would bear the caliph's name, and blessings invoked during the Friday prayers would mention the caliph's name before that of the ruling sultan. The principal obligations of the sultan were to protect the lives and property of Muslims and to govern them in accordance with Islamic law, "commanding right and forbidding wrong" in the classical formulation.[6] An additional prerequisite, the waging of war against infidels, began to appear in later treatises, written during and after the era of the Crusades. The scholars, faced with the reality of rule by non-Arabs, allowed that a particular sultan's right

---

[5] ʿAli al-Mawardi, *al-Ahkam al-sultaniyya wa al-wilaya al-diniyya* (Cairo: al-Matbaʿa al-Tawfiqiyya, 1978).
[6] Michael Cook, *Commanding Right and Forbidding Wrong in Islamic Thought* (Cambridge: Cambridge University Press, 2000).

to rule was not dependent on his descent from the Quraysh. Rather, a sultan's adherence to Islamic norms and values rather than his lineage legitimated the ruler in the eyes of his subjects. That formula created a path toward political legitimacy for the non-Arab rulers who would dominate the Middle East for the next seven centuries.

Commentaries on Islamic government, written by Arab scholars after the fall of Baghdad in 1258, further diminished or ignored any role for the caliphate in the political life of Muslims. An example of the evolution in the articulation of the caliphate is found in the *Muqaddima* of ᶜAbd al-Rahman Abu-Zayd ibn Khaldun (d. 1406). After establishing that the caliphate was the only just form of government in the history of the world, ibn Khaldun concluded that the office had truly existed only in the reign of the first four "Rightly Guided Caliphs" (632–61). Subsequent rulers enjoyed "royal authority," which could be claimed by any Muslim ruler who dispensed justice and ruled in accordance with the sharia. Such a ruler could claim whatever title, including that of caliph, he wished. For ibn Khaldun, however, the "true" caliphate of the "Rightly Guided Caliphs" was in the past.[7] In that assessment, ibn Khaldun followed the lead of the Muslim legal scholar Taqi al-Din ibn Taymiyya (d. 1328), who asserted that the caliphate had ended with the death of ᶜAli, citing the saying attributed to the Prophet Muhammad, "The caliphate will last thirty years, when it will turn into monarchy." In ibn Taymiyya's view, the "monarchy" (*mulk*) that followed was legitimate, only as long as the monarch (*malik*) followed the prescriptions of Muslim law and ruled with justice.[8] In short, actions legitimated the ruler and not his title or lineage.

In contrast to that rationalization of the sultanate in the absence of the caliphate offered by Arab scholars, the Ottoman sultan Mehmed I (1413–21) explicitly claimed the title "Shadow of God in the Two Worlds, Caliph of God of the Two Earths." This was in line with the understanding that had emerged in the Hanafi legal tradition outside of the Arab lands in the post-Mongol era that any Muslim ruler could legitimately lay claim to the title of caliph. That understanding was not in contradiction

---

[7] ᶜAbd al-Rahman ibn Khaldun, *The Muqaddima: An Introduction to History.* translated by Franz Rosenthal, 3 vols. (New York: Pantheon Books, 1958), vol. 1, 11–12, 285, 394–402.

[8] Taqi al-Din ibn Taymiyya, *Ibn Taymiyyah Expounds on Islam: Selected Writings of Shaykh al-Islam Taqi ad-Din Ibn Taymiyyah on Islamic Faith, Life, and Society*, translated by Muhammad ʾAbdul-Haqq Ansari (Riyadh: General Administration of Culture and Publication, 1421/2000), 495.

with the elaboration of the concept of royal authority articulated by ibn Khaldun. Ebu's-su'ud Efendi, who served as Sultan Süleyman's leading legal adviser, the Şeyhülislam/ Shaykh al-Islam, went beyond just using a historic title, however, when he claimed the House of Osman had not only the divine right to the title of caliph, but an exclusive one. As such the Ottoman sultan, as caliph, could assert universal sovereignty over Muslims everywhere.

Despite the propaganda on behalf the sultan/caliph that emanated from Istanbul, Arab writers before the nineteenth century never conceded the title of caliph to the Ottoman sultans.[9] For them, the title was simply not transferable to someone who was not of the Prophet's tribe. Rather, they typically acknowledged that the Ottoman sultans had inherited the "royalty and the glory of the caliphate" if not the actual office itself.[10] Abd al-Rahman al-Jabarti employed a slightly different strategy when he wrote that the early Ottoman sultans followed the precedent set by the "Rightly-Guided Caliphs" in their handling of the affairs of the *umma*, through their good governance and in raising up Islam over the "unbelievers."[11] In short, if not entitled to the title of caliph, the Ottoman sultans were as admirable and worthy of their subjects' allegiance as were those early paragons of Muslim political virtue.

Without a caliph, the Arabic-speaking Sunni religious establishment acquiesced to rule by sultans of non-Arab origin as long as they enhanced and protected the faith. Those living in the Ottoman centuries seemed much more willing to extend the mantle of legitimacy to their sultan than had their predecessors living under the Mamluk regime. In part, their acquiescence was a product of the Ottoman sultans' understanding of what actions would help propagate the perception of their righteousness in the Arab lands. Aware of the prescriptions for a just ruler in the Islamic literature on good government, they cultivated that image assiduously. Their efforts seemed to have worked. Ibn Abi al-Surur in his biographical compendium of the Ottoman sultans and their governors in Egypt stressed every sultan's commitment to wage the just war against "heretics" and "infidels" as well as his role as benefactor to Muslim charities. In contrast, he highlighted the lack of piety among the Mamluks, as well as their alliance with the "heretical Shia" (*rawafid*) in Iran as a justification for their eventual overthrow. In ibn Abi al-Surur's view, God

---

[9] Winter, *Egyptian Society*, 29–32.
[10] Winter. "A Seventeenth-Century Arabic Panagyric," 155–6.
[11] al-Jabarti. *ʿAjaʾib al-athar*, vol. I, 66.

had worked out his plan through the actions of his servant, Sultan Selim Khan. Defense of the faith, piety, and good deeds were all the qualities that were seemingly necessary to legitimate a ruler deserving of the loyalty of the "people of the Sunna."

It was, however, clear to the Arabic-speaking Sunni elite that the House of Osman did not have an exclusive claim to the sultanate. Shams al-Din Muhammad ibn Tulun (d. 1546) recorded his ambivalence to the new regime in his eyewitness chronicle of the Ottoman conquest of Damascus. He had not been willing even to extend to Selim the courtesy of the title of sultan in his account until Selim had actually captured Damascus, preferring to call him simply the "king of Anatolia" (*malik al-Rum*). "King" was a neutral title for ibn Tulun that implied no divine favor. When the rebel al-Ghazali seized the city in 1520, he became the rightful sultan in ibn Tulun's narrative while his adversary Süleyman was simply a "king." Only after Ottoman troops retook the city did ibn Tulun bestow upon Süleyman the title *Sultan al-Sham*. There had been four ruling sultans in as many years – Mamluk, Ottoman, Mamluk, Ottoman – and ibn Tulun had legitimated each sultan in turn, without editorial comment.[12] The routine manner with which he did so implies a resignation to political realities rather than enthusiasm over change.

Such ambivalence faded with time. A century and a half later Ibrahim al-Khiyari of Medina (d. 1672) wrote praise poems for Sultan Selim I and his conquest of Damascus, an act that the poet claimed restored justice to that fabled city where caliphs had once ruled.[13] Panegyric had replaced the ambivalence expressed by ibn Tulun to regime change. In retrospect, Ottoman rule had become for al-Khiyari divinely ordained. Society was hierarchical for the Sunni intellectual elite in urban centers such as Cairo, Damascus, Baghdad, and Medina and at the summit was the sultan. The scholars further believed that their society could not continue to function without someone serving as sultan; the alternative would be anarchy. For Sunni Muslims, the attachment to the sultan was tied to their religious belief in his ultimate role as dispenser of justice. As his place on

[12] Shams al-Din Muhammad ibn Tulun, *Mufakahat al-khillani fi al-zaman ta'rikh misr wa sham*, 2 vols. (Cairo: al-Mu'assasa al-Misriyya al-ʿAmma li-al-Taʿlif wa al-Anba wa al-Nashr, 1964), vol. II, 3, 41, 78, and his, *Iʿlam al-wara' bi-man wulliya na'iban min al-atrak bi-dimashq al-sham al-kubra'* (Damascus: al-Matbaʿa wa al-Jarida al-Rasmiyya, 1964), 236.
[13] Ibrahim al-Khiyari al-Madani, *Tuhfat al-udaba'wa salwat al-ghuraba'*, 3 vols. (Baghdad: Wizarat al-Thaqafa wa al-Iʿlam, 1979), vol. II, 140–1.

the throne had been ordained by God's grace, the sultan must, therefore, administer God's justice.

In legitimating Ottoman rule, Sunni Arab authors often invoked the sultan's role as protector of Sunni Islam against the alternative Shi'i interpretation of Islam that was prevalent in Iran. This was most apparent in the chronicles written by scholars in Mosul and Baghdad.[14] Appreciation of that role was shared even in cities farther afield, however. The two biographical dictionaries that have survived from Aleppo in the early Ottoman centuries, written by Radi al-Din Muhammad ibn Hanbali (d. 1563) and Abu al-Wafa al-ʿUrdi (d.1661), contained biographies of Ottoman grand viziers and chief judges of the empire who visited the city on their way to campaigns against the Safavi shahs. Typical of these was a biography written by al-ʿUrdi for Grand Vizier Hafız Ahmed Pasha, who lost his life trying to retake Baghdad from the army of Shah Abbas in 1625. After recounting how "our soldiers" (ʿaskarna), that is, the Ottomans, initially lost the city in 1623, al-ʿUrdi detailed the "martyrdom" of Sunni religious scholars in Baghdad, including the chief Hanafi judge and mufti, following the Iranian victory. The shah had pressed the clerics to curse the first three caliphs as usurpers (a ritual practice among the Shia), and when they refused, he ordered their decapitation. Al-ʿUrdi completed the entry with a prayer that the Ottoman sultan would preserve the "people of the Sunna" from error.[15]

The attitude held by the Sunni elite toward the Shia had hardened over the course of more than a century of wars waged to decide who would rule in Iraq. Earlier in that struggle, they had shown less zeal. Shihab al-Din Ahmad ibn al-Himsi (d. 1527?) recorded in Shaʿaban 928 (June–July 1522) that pilgrims from Iraq were arrested in Damascus, tortured, and executed on the suspicion that they were spies for the "Sultan of the East, Ismaʿil Shah al-Sufi." Ibn al-Himsi added that no one knew why this terrible act was done other than that it had been an order from Sultan Süleyman. He then added, "May God fight the order and the one who carried it out and judge them for this heinous act." Significantly, ibn al-Himsi did not condemn Süleyman as the issuer of that order, only the order itself. In the entry for the next year, he praised that same sultan for the capture of Rhodes and noted that the whole city of Damascus

---

[14] al-ʿUmari, *Zubdat al-athar*; Percy Kemp, *Territoires d'Islam: Le monde vu de Moussoul aux XVIIᵉ siècle* (Paris: Sindbad, 1982); Khoury, *State and Provincial Society*, 160–71.

[15] Abu al-Wafa' al-ʿUrdi al-Halabi, *Maʿadan al-dhahab fi al-aʿyan al-musharrafa bihim halab* (Aleppo: Dar al-Mallah, 1987), 146–9.

celebrated the victory over the "pirate infidels."[16] The sultan was held responsible for acts that ennobled the people of Islam and duly praised, but not for those that did not.

If the enemy in the east were Shi'i "heretics," then in the west that role fell to Christian "infidels." As an indication that the outcomes on distant battlefields were on the minds of the authors, many of the Muslim chroniclers in Syria's cities routinely recorded Ottoman victories and defeats in the Balkans. Muhammad ibn Kannan (d. 1740) provides an example of that concern in his entry for 1152 (1739–40). Having recounted the fall of Belgrade to the Ottomans and then separately the removal by Sultan Mahmud I of janissaries who had been terrorizing the population of Damascus, he conflated the two actions:

> An imperial decree arrived from his imperial majesty (*hadrat al-hunkar*) al-Sultan Mahmud, may God help him to victory in this world and the next. He is the most righteous of kings from among those whom God aides to victory, for he has taken Bi'r al-Aghrad (Belgrade, literally, "the well of the objectives") from the sect of the Unbelievers as well as more than a hundred castles and fortresses. He has freed Damascus from the vilest of tyrants and those who are the least in their degree of religion and faith (*din wa iman*). For he is like Antar and the equal of Nimrod deserving of praise; may God allot our lord sultan with the best portion, amen.[17]

Al-Khiyari, who was a visitor at the sultan's court in 1669, when news of the final conquest of Crete by the Ottomans arrived, lavished praise on Sultan Mehmed IV for that victory and composed a poem to honor the day.[18] Battles won or lost were matters of concern to Muslim scholars throughout the sultan's Arabic-speaking provinces, and the sultans who commanded Muslim armies against "infidels" and "heretics" deserved the authors' prayers.

The question remains whether the scholars' loyalty to the sultan was simply perfunctory, if not obligatory, rather than heartfelt. In 1578, orders were sent from Istanbul to the chief judges in Aleppo, Damascus, and Cairo, among other places, to ensure prayers were offered in each city's main mosque for the success of Lala Mustafa Pasha in his campaign against the Persian "heretics."[19] There was evidently an established

---

[16] Shihab al-Din Ahmad ibn al-Himsi, *Hawadith al-zaman wa wafiyyat al-shuyukh wa al-aqran*, 3 vols. (Sidon, Lebanon: al-Maktaba al-ʿAsriyya, 1999), vol. 3, 43, 49.

[17] Muhammad ibn Kannan al-Salihi, *Yawmiyyat shamiyya* (Damascus: Dar al-Tibaʿ, 1994), 511.

[18] al-Khiyari, *Tuhfat al-udaba'*, vol. 1, 317, 324–5.

[19] Necipoğlu, *Age of Sinan*, 66–7.

culture of public expression of solidarity with the dynasty through the invocation of prayers for the sultan's victory, and that sentiment must have seeped into the authors' consciousness as the correct response for men of their status in times of strife in order to demonstrate their solidarity with their religious community. The ideology of the Islamic sultanate helps to explain the apparent good wishes for the dynasty expressed by Muslim authors, but praise phrases after the recording of a sultan's name were also present in works written by Christian writers in the Arab lands.[20] From such examples, it would seem that identification of the House of Osman as the preserver of peace and prosperity could transcend communal identities for some.

While loyalty to the sultanate as an institution in the absence of a caliphate was unquestioned for Sunni Muslims, as we have seen with ibn Tulun's vacillation it did not necessarily extend to the descendants of Osman alone. Even ibn Kannan, who was extremely attentive to the affairs of the sultanate, could only offer the phrase "May God stop the fighting" rather than his usual "May God grant the sultan victory" when recording a battle between the Ottomans and the forces of Nadir Shah, whom the author believed to be a Sunni Afghan.[21] Loyalty to the Ottoman sultanate was not absolute; nor did it occur unconditionally. For the Sunni urban elite of Arabic-speaking lands, loyalty to the sultan was strong as long as he defended the sharia and upheld the unity of the empire against "heretics and infidels." If the House of Osman provided sultans who would watch over the lands of the Muslims and keep them from harm, Sunni Arab authors would rejoice in the sultan's victories and worry over his defeats. Alternative candidates for the sultanate besides the House of Osman were possible, but by the seventeenth century most Sunni Muslim scholars in the Arab lands would have been hard pressed to say who they were. Such seemingly unconditional loyalty was, however, rarely extended to the sultan's governors.

PROVINCIAL ADMINISTRATION: GOVERNORS

With the sultan physically distant from his Arabic-speaking subjects, the men appointed by him as governors and chief judges of the Hanafi

---

[20] Yusuf Dimitri ʿAbbud, al-Murtad fi taʾrikh halab wa baghdad, edited by Fawwaz Mahmud al-Fawwaz, M.A. Thesis, University of Damascus, 1978), 13, 169; Hilary Kilpatrick, "Journeying towards Modernity: The 'Safrat al-Batrik Makariyus' of Bulus al-Zaʿim al-Halabi" WI 37 (1997): 169.

[21] ibn Kannan, Yawmiyyat, 382.

school served as the face of Ottoman rule in the provinces. A key feature of Ottoman administration was the separation of those two officials' responsibilities and powers. The governor commanded the provincial military and saw to the maintenance of order and the collection of taxes. The chief Hanafi judge applied the law to both criminal and commercial cases, as well as in the more private realm of family law. He also served as a conduit for complaints from the sultan's subjects about the abuse of power by the governor. The men in either office had an independent chain of command in the Ottoman state bureaucracy that stretched back to the sultan. As such, the two officials were sometimes in conflict with each other over what constituted the sultan's best interests.

Both the governor and the chief judge were career men whose time of service in a particular city was often less than a year in the first two centuries of Ottoman rule. Given their brief tenure, Ottoman officials relied on local men to confer continuity in the structure of command as well as to provide knowledge of the regions that were entrusted to their care. It was in that secondary tier in both the provincial and judicial administrations that real power often rested. This became de jure as well as de facto in the eighteenth century, when non-Ottoman actors obtained the governorship in some of the Arab provinces. In contrast to that trend toward decentralization in the institution of the governorship, the chief Hanafi judges in the Arab provincial centers were drawn from the legal cadre trained at state sponsored schools from the time of the conquest through the end of the empire. In the realm of the law, there was no diminution of Ottoman authority. That pattern did not preclude an occasional Arab from serving as chief judge, but local commentators noted such an individual as a rarity.[22] It must be remembered, however, that most large Arab cities had more than one law court and in those local jurists almost always presided. With only rare exceptions, the language through which justice was dispensed in the courts was Arabic.

The sultans and their advisers settled on two different strategies in establishing provincial rule in the Arab lands. In provinces distant from the capital or with difficult terrain, the governor, who was often a local chieftain, held the province as a virtual principality of his own; there were no *timar*s (a fief granted for a set period to a cavalryman) and the governor recruited and paid the local military, who were his personal retainers. Provinces of this type in the Arab lands included Tripoli and later Sidon, both in today's Lebanon, and Shahrizor in Iraqi Kurdistan.

---

[22] al-ʿUrdi, *Maʿadan al-dhahab*, 135–7.

In those provinces, the local warlord governed in the sultan's name for extended periods as those at court in Istanbul felt that only men who had familiarity with those hostile regions were sufficiently experienced and ruthless to keep local tribes, or in the case of Lebanon, the Druzes, quiet. The drawback in that relationship was that the governors might be tempted to switch sides and back the shah in the case of Kurdistan or to align themselves with those who were rebelling against the sultan as was the case with the governors in Lebanon. To prevent that possibility from becoming a reality, direct Ottoman rule was extended to both Tripoli and Sidon by the end of the seventeenth century. Kurdistan, however, continued to enjoy its autonomous status until the nineteenth century.

In those provinces closer to the Ottoman heartland – Aleppo, Mosul, and Damascus – imperial surveyors counted adult males in the first century of Ottoman rule, assessed the province's potential revenues, and subdivided the cultivated lands into units known as *timars*, which were assigned to cavalrymen (*sipahis*) who would serve in the provincial military. The governor was the military commander of the province and many of the functions of government in the countryside fell to the *sipahis*. In theory, the land was periodically surveyed to ensure that only those still on active service held the right to the *timars*.[23] *Timars* were relatively small in physical size and often comprised simply a village. It was expected that the *sipahi* would reside on the *timar*, collect its taxes from the peasants, and be available for military service, with horse and retainers, should the governor require him. In the first decades of Ottoman rule, most of the *timar* holders in the Arab lands were Turks from Anatolia. Over time, however, the Ottoman authorities increasingly turned to local men to serve in that capacity.

Within fifty years of the institution of the *timar* system in the Arab lands, the government in Istanbul already encountered difficulty in keeping the *sipahis* on their *timars* as the siren song of urban life beckoned to them.[24] In the seventeenth century, the *timar* system began to atrophy and the government converted many of the villages that had constituted the *timars* into tax farms whose leases would be sold off to bidders for a set period.[25] The trend was not universal and the middle of the

[23] Bakhit, *Ottoman Province of Damascus*, 147–9.
[24] Uriel Heyd, *Ottoman Documents on Palestine 1552–1615: A Study of the Firmans according to the Mühimme Defteri* (Oxford: Clarendon Press, 1960), 67–8.
[25] *Tax-Farm Register of Damascus Province in the Seventeenth Century: Archival and Historical Studies*, edited by Yuzo Nagata, Toru Miura, and Yasuhisa Shimizu (Tokyo: Tokyo Bunko, 2006).

century actually witnessed an increase in the number of *timar*s in Aleppo Province.[26] It is not clear how effective a fighting force those who held the *timar*s were, however. In 1655, only 26 of the 130 *sipahi*s in Aleppo ordered to present themselves for a campaign to Crete showed up.[27] An order to the governor of the province in August 1690 called on him to mobilize his *sipahi*s against the Şeyhlü Kurds, who were raiding widely across the region from their base in Kilis to Raqqa on the Euphrates River, but there is no indication that any of the cavalrymen actually mobilized.[28]

The decline in the reliability of the *sipahi*s to mobilize was not confined to Aleppo Province. In the eighteenth century, the central government called on *sipahi*s in Damascus to protect those returning from the hajj, but its governors found it increasingly difficult to ensure that those holding the *timar*s would comply with their orders to appear ready to serve.[29] Inertia had incapacitated many of the institutions of the empire by the eighteenth century. As old institutions fell into lethargy, there was no zeal on the part of the bureaucrats in the capital to repair or replace them. Illustrating that reality, the *timar* system continued in name until the period of the Tanzimat reforms, when it was finally officially abolished, although no *sipahi* had mobilized for a campaign in more than a century.

Outside the Fertile Crescent, the Ottoman state established provincial regimes that differed from the classic model of provincial administration, embodied in the *timar* system. Mecca was such an exception. The control of the city was a sensitive issue for the Ottomans. The fact that the sultan's name was announced as sovereign in the Grand Mosque of Mecca each Friday at noon legitimated Ottoman rule for many Muslims. To highlight their role as "servitor of the Two Holy Places," the sultans lavished charitable works on the inhabitants of Mecca and Medina.[30] They also respected local traditions of rule. Although an Ottoman official resided in Mecca's port city of Jeddah, the governor of Mecca, titled the emir, was always from the Hashemite clan (Banu Hashim) of the Prophet Muhammad. The reason for that choice was twofold. The Ottomans recognized that they needed to treat Mecca as something more than an

---

[26] Wilkins, *Forging Urban Solidarities*, 148–50.
[27] Ibid., 182.
[28] Damascus, Dar al-watha'iq, Awamir al-Sultaniyya Halab (AS), 1: 22.
[29] Cohen, *Palestine in the 18th Century*, 298–303.
[30] Suraiya Faroqhi, *Pilgrims and Sultans: The Hajj under the Ottomans* (London: I. B. Tauris, 1994), 92–126.

ordinary province and that the Hashemites, as a respected local family, had a better chance of exercising restraint on the Bedouins than did an outsider with no tribal status. The strategy worked until the Wahhabi eruption shook the status quo in the early nineteenth century. Although there were occasional rebellions before that time mounted by contenders for leadership among the family, no one from the Hashemite clan questioned the sultan's ultimate protection over their city or his right to name its emir until the twentieth century.[31]

Egypt was another special case. It was the richest province in the empire and, with Wallachia (southern Romania), served as a major supplier of the capital's foodstuffs. While ships from the Danube ports carried wheat to feed the city's masses, those from Egypt held rice, sugar, and spices for the city's elite. In addition to supplying the capital, the agricultural surplus of Egypt was essential in feeding the native population of, and pilgrims in, Mecca and Medina.[32] Because it was far from any active frontier, the Ottomans did not expect Egypt to provide a large number of troops for imperial campaigns outside the province. Although imperial surveyors were careful to register agricultural lands and the canals that watered them, they did not divide the country into *timar*s.[33] The garrison in Cairo included cavalry units called *sipahi*s, but they were salaried rather than paid with the revenues of a *timar*.[34] Without the *timar* system, the Ottomans viewed Egypt as one large tax farm.

Administration in the Iraqi provinces of Baghdad and Basra, where the chief responsibilities of the governors were to secure the borders from the Iranian threat, more closely resembled the administration in Cairo than that of Damascus or the northern Iraqi city of Mosul in that the *timar-sipahi* system was only partially in place in Baghdad and completely absent in Basra. The same was true for Yemen as long as it remained under Ottoman control. In the North African port cities, which were largely pirate emporia, the governor and the captain of the fleet, both appointed by Istanbul, were often at odds over who would actually govern. Because of the differing provincial regimes, the experience of Ottoman rule for the inhabitants of that vast region differed considerably. As was the case with the Balkan provinces or those of eastern

[31] William Ochsenwald, *Religion, Society and the State in Arabia: The Hijaz under Ottoman Control, 1840–1908* (Columbus: Ohio State University Press, 1984), 3–9.
[32] Alan Mikhail, *Nature and Empire in Ottoman Egypt: An Environmental History* (Cambridge: Cambridge University Press, 2011), 103–23.
[33] Ibid., 40–6.
[34] Winter, *Egyptian Society*, 37–9.

Anatolia, the farther a province was geographically from Istanbul, the greater the probability that its administration would be "irregular." In such provinces, the control exercised by the central regime in Istanbul was more tenuous than it was in the "core" provinces, with greater power concentrated in the hands of the governor.

PROVINCIAL ADMINISTRATION: JUDGES

After the governors, the strongest connection between the sultan and his subjects in the Arab lands lay in the network of judges who traveled from Istanbul to administer both the sharia and the sultan's law (*qanun*). The sultan's law covered a wide array of issues from taxation to criminal punishment to foreign relations. The use of *qanun* was not an Ottoman innovation as the Mamluk sultans had issued their own decrees as well. What was new, however, was that the qadis in the Islamic courts in the Arab lands were empowered to administer both the *qanun* and the sharia. Although none of the sultan's prescriptions was supposed to infringe on the sovereignty of Islamic law, many in the legal establishment in the Arab lands felt that boundary was, in fact, sometimes breached. The tension between what those at the sultan's court deemed as permissible under the tradition of *qanun* and the understanding of its prerogatives among scholars in the Arab lands remained a potential source of friction throughout the Ottoman centuries.[35] It was not, however, simply an Arab issue, as some Turkish-speaking legal scholars shared some of those same qualms about the use of *kanun*.[36]

In addition to the change in the legal briefs of a judge's authority, the Ottomans introduced what seemed to the Arab religious establishment an innovation, the privileging of the Hanafi tradition of law. There are four legal traditions within Sunni Islam, each called a *madhhab* (*mezhep* in Modern Turkish), meaning "path." Each school is identified by the name of a leading jurist whose legal commentaries, written between the eighth and ninth centuries, inform the school's particular approach to jurisprudence. These are the Shafiʿi, Hanafi, Maliki, and Hanbali. The differences between the schools are generally slight and adherents of each recognize the others as valid ways to interpret the law. The Ottoman

---

[35] Martha Mundy, "Islamic Law and the Order of State: The Legal Status of the Cultivator" In *Syria and Bilad al-Sham under Ottoman Rule: Essays in Honour of Abdul-Karim Rafeq*, edited by Peter Sluglett with Stefan Weber (Leiden: Brill, 2010), 399–419.

[36] Tezcan, *Second Ottoman Empire*, 48–59.

dynasty established the Hanafi tradition as the official legal interpretation of the empire, but it did not compel scholars to abandon their own legal traditions to conform to that favored in Istanbul. Nevertheless, if a scholar wished to ingratiate himself with the new regime a switch might seem prudent.

There might, of course, have been other less material reasons for switching from one school to another. The seventeenth-century Aleppine biographer Radi al-Din Muhammad ibn Hanbali wrote that his grandfather, a noted legal scholar, switched from the Hanbali to the Hanafi *madhhab* as a way to signal his loyalty to the ruling house.[37] For whatever reason, the majority of Sunni scholars in Syria and Iraq were adherents of the Hanafi *madhhab* in the seventeenth century. In contrast, most of their contemporaries in Egypt, Arabia, and Kurdistan retained their allegiance to the previously dominant Shafiʿi tradition. Far from the influences emanating from Istanbul, the North African Muslim legal scholars remained loyal to the Maliki interpretation of the law that had prevailed in North Africa and Spain for centuries.

The shift to the Hanafi interpretation did not come easily. Ibn Tulun recorded shock among Damascus's ulama when Sultan Selim privileged the Hanafi *madhhab* over the other three schools not long after the conquest. That was a departure from Mamluk practice where the four Sunni legal traditions held equal status and privilege. Furthermore, Selim removed the man holding the qadiship of the Hanafi rite and replaced him with an Ottoman jurist on whom he bestowed the title of *Shaykh al-Islam*. Formerly, the ulama of the city had granted that title to the man they considered the preeminent legal scholar in the city, regardless of the *madhhab* he followed. Among the privileges that Selim established for the Hanafi rite were that its adherents would occupy the *minbar* (pulpit) of the city's main Umayyad Mosque at Friday prayers. That provoked a small-scale riot in the mosque between adherents of the Hanafi rite and the previously dominant Shafiʿi tradition after Selim left the city for Egypt.[38] From that time on, the chief judge in Damascus, as in every other provincial center in the Arab lands, was a state-appointed scholar, schooled in the Hanafi tradition.

The distinction between local scholars and Ottoman appointees emerged again in Damascus in 1590 when a new governor summarily

---

[37] Radi al-Din Muhammad ibn al-Hanbali al-Halabi, *Durr al-habab fi ta'rikh aʿyan halab*, 2 vols. (Damascus: Wizarat al-Thaqafa, 1972–73), vol. 1, vii.
[38] ibn Tulun, *Mufakahat*, 38.

dismissed the judges from the other three schools and ordered that all legal matters go before the Hanafi judge who had accompanied him from Istanbul. Sharaf al-Din Musa al-Ansari (d. 1594?), a local legal scholar and chronicler, wrote that the drastic change in legal administration was perceived as being directed at those he termed the *awlad al-ʿArab* ("children of the Arabs," i.e., Arabic speakers), a hint of the existence of ethnic antagonism between the Ottoman governor and the local Arabic-speaking jurists. The innovation did not go down well and a protest ensued. The clerks and translators at the central court resigned, bringing its work to a quick halt. The strike continued until the mufti of Damascus issued a fatwa to end the impasse. Its summation said succinctly, "If the Caliph dies, then the governors and judges he appointed can not be dismissed." The implication was that if the principle was valid for the office of the caliph, then it was sufficient to cover a change in governors. With that intervention, the governor reversed himself and the local judges were reinstated.[39]

The ruling of the mufti of Damascus highlights one of the distinctive features of Ottoman legal administration in the Arab lands; while the chief Hanafi judges in the major Arab cities were Ottoman jurists appointed by Istanbul, the chief legal theorist in those cities, the mufti, was always a local scholar. Although most of the ulama in the Syrian provinces who would serve as mufti followed the Hanafi interpretation of the law, they did not always agree with the interpretations of that tradition provided by scholars at the sultan's court. The fatwa collections of the muftis of Syria and Palestine display a tension between Arabic-speaking legal scholars and those writing in Ottoman Turkish.[40] From such disputes, it is clear that the legal establishment in the Arab lands did not feel compelled to accept rulings that emanated from Istanbul. Arab scholars perceived themselves as the intellectual and moral equals of the sultan's men, and they were not cowed into conformity with the imperial interpretations of the law.

Despite differences in legal opinions, the local chroniclers in the Arab cities generally gave the men who served as chief judge high marks. Unlike the governors, most judges were fluent in Arabic and some were praised for the eloquence of the verses they composed in that language. Nevertheless,

---

[39] Sharaf al-Din Musa al-Ansari, *Nuzhat al-khatir wa bahjat al-nathir*, 2 vols. (Damascus: Wizarat al-Thaqafa, 1991), vol. 1, 166–7.

[40] Abdul-Karim Rafeq, "Relations between the Syrian Ulama and the Ottoman State in the Eighteenth Century" *Oriente Moderno* 18(79) (1999): 67–95.

justice was seldom free. A Catholic chronicler in eighteenth-century Aleppo boasted that his community had effectively blocked all attempts by Istanbul to limit their religious freedom by bribing the various judges in his city to ignore imperial decrees compelling them to attend churches where the priests offered the "traditionalist" rites. He then proceeded to list the various judges by name and the amounts that they had been paid to look the other way.[41] Whether a judge was local or an appointee from Istanbul, there was no guarantee of his impartiality, especially if sufficient "gifts" (peşkeş) were proffered by the litigants.

Despite the prevalence of bribery in high places, the inhabitants of the empire held the judges to a higher standard of justice than they did their governors. They were, after all, much more intimately connected to the workings of the court than they were to the governor's palace. Most tried to avoid any dealing with the governor as it was sure to cost them dearly in fines or bribes. Whether it was a case of family law, a dispute over labor practices, or the registration of a loan or a sale of a house, most of the inhabitants of any Arab city or town had stood before a judge at some time in their lifetime. As a result of that intimate connection to the courts, the chronicles showed that while the inhabitants of an Arab city routinely endured a bad governor until matters were really desperate, an openly corrupt judge could provoke riots.[42]

THE PROVINCIAL MILITARY

If the lower classes could be provoked to riot by discontent with those sitting in judgment in the Islamic courts, the rioters were drawn from the ranks of the janissaries. That is, at least, how the urban Muslim elite whose written record has come down to us portrayed them. The common stereotype of the soldier in the chronicles was an impious drunkard swaggering down the street, abusing properly behaved Muslim women and demanding protection money from all he met. The military may have been a necessary evil for the maintenance of security, but more often than not the local narratives presented them as consummate outsiders and the source of most urban unrest rather than as guardians of the status quo.

---

[41] "The chronicle Niᶜmat-Allah ibn al-Khuri Tuma al-Halabi." In Mikha'il Burayk, Ta'rikh al-sham (Harissa, Lebanon: Matbaᶜat Qadis Bulus, 1930), 133.

[42] James Grehan, "Street Violence and Social Imagination in Late-Mamluk and Ottoman Damascus (ca. 1500–1800)" IJMES 35 (2003): 215–36; Hasan Agha al-ᶜAbid, Ta'rikh Hasan Agha al-ᶜAbid: Hawadith sanah 1186 ila sanah 1241 (Damascus: Wizarat al-Thaqafa wa al-Irshad al-Qawmi, 1979), 124–5.

The main component of the Ottoman military presence in the Arab cities was the janissary corps (Ottoman, *yeni çeri*). In addition, there were various irregular, hired soldiers who went under a variety of names such as the *maghariba* (North Africans) who were present in most Syrian cities in the eighteenth century. Nonetheless, it was the janissaries who would represent the Ottoman military in the imagination of the Arabic-speaking urban elites.

At the time of the Ottoman conquest of the Arab lands, the janissary corps was at its peak in terms of training and morale. The corps provided a permanent standing army for the sultan in an age when most European states relied on mercenaries while the armies opposing the Ottomans in the Middle East were often composed of mamluks, augmented by tribal levies. The janissaries were taken in the *devşirme*, as were the men who would make up the empire's military/bureaucratic elite. "Recruited" as adolescents, the boys were first sent to farms in Anatolia where they were instructed in Islam and trained to be soldiers, eventually forming infantry units armed with the latest military technology.

The decline of discipline in the janissary ranks that was a common theme in the Arab chronicles was undoubtedly due to the rapid expansion of the number of those who filled the corps' ranks in the seventeenth century. Expansion meant that fewer recruits went through the rigorous training conferred on those taken in the *devşirme* as serving janissaries enrolled their sons in the corps and they, in turn, enrolled their sons. Others simply bought their way into it. There were 12,789 janissaries stationed at the imperial palace in Istanbul in 1568; their number had swollen to 53,849 in 1670.[43] An equally dramatic growth in the number of janissaries occurred in the Arab provinces. There were 69 janissaries stationed in Mosul in 1520; there were at least 3,000 in 1631.[44] We cannot be certain when Aleppo first had a janissary garrison of its own, but at some time during the turbulent years at the start of the seventeenth century, Aleppo's notables petitioned the sultan for a permanent force of 500 janissaries to be stationed in the city's citadel; by the end of the century, there were more than 5,000 janissaries in the city. Herbert Bodman was convinced that these janissaries were all locally recruited.[45] His assumption as to the janissaries' origins is supported by their patronymics,

[43] Inalcik, *The Ottoman Empire*, 83.
[44] Khoury, *State and Provincial Society*, 50.
[45] Herbert Bodman, *Political Factions in Aleppo, 1760–1826* (Chapel Hill: University of North Carolina Press, 1963), 73–5.

registered when janissaries appeared at the city's courts in the eighteenth
century. Although some still were listed as being the "son of ʿAbdallah,"
the generic father for those who were produced by the *devşirme*, most
had fathers with names that indicated that they were Muslims. As freeborn Muslims, they could not have been enslaved and, therefore, could
not have entered the corps through the *devşirme*.

The evolution in the recruitment of the janissary garrison in Aleppo
corresponded to trends that occurred throughout the Arab provinces. As
early as 1577, an order sent to the governor of Damascus stated that
if the janissary ranks were to be opened up to "volunteers," then the
places should be given to "capable, strong, and brave young musketeers
from *Rum* (Anatolia)" and not to "natives, foreigners, and Bedouins."[46]
The practice that order suggested was common as well in Egypt, where
military officers recruited janissaries in the sixteenth century from the
Muslim populations in Anatolia and the Balkans. Local Arabic speakers
succeeded in enrolling themselves in the Azeban (another infantry corps)
in Cairo by the end of the sixteenth century. Their presence in the city
created occasional tensions between units composed of Turkish-speaking
soldiers and those whose native tongue was Arabic.[47] The putative janissaries in the North African cities were also recruited from the Muslim
populations of Anatolia and the Balkans. By the middle of the seventeenth century, almost all of those present in the janissary garrisons in the
Arab lands were freeborn Muslims.

With the entry of Muslims into the janissary corps, janissaries became
a part of the social fabric of most Arab cities. The corps offered an occu-
pational niche for tribal migrants to find their place in a new urban
setting, much like the role that the police force served in integrating
nineteenth-century Irish immigrants into cities in the United States. Many
of the janissaries in Damascus were Turkmens in the middle of the seventeenth century; others were Albanians or Kurds. The city's garrison supported the revolt of Abaza Hasan Paşa of Aleppo in 1657. In retaliation,
Istanbul sent a new unit of janissaries to Damascus. Thereafter, the two
competing units, one known as the *yerliyya* (locals) and the other as the
kapı kulları (literally "slave of the gate" but with the connotation of the
sultan's men), coexisted, although often violently, in the city.

Over time, the ranks of the *yerliyya* in Damascus were filled with local
Arabic-speaking recruits, while the *kapı kulları*, despite their name, were

[46] Heyd, *Ottoman Documents on Palestine*, 68–9.
[47] Winter, *Egyptian Society*, 54–8.

from non-Arab populations in Syria, Iraq, and Anatolia.[48] Certain quarters in the city were associated with the janissaries: Bab Musalla, Suq Saruja, and Maydan. These were outside the city walls and inhabited largely by poor rural migrants to the city. They were also the quarters most often associated with urban rioting. In contrast, most of the janissaries in seventeenth-century Aleppo lived in quarters within the crumbling city walls.[49] By the middle of the next century, however, that pattern had been reversed and those in the corps were almost exclusively identified with the impoverished quarters in the eastern suburbs of the city: Banqusa, Qarliq, Tatarlar, and Maydanjik. As their non-Arabic names suggest, those quarters also housed most of the tribal migrants to the city – Kurds, Bedouins, and Turkmen – suggesting the ethnic origins of the janissaries.[50]

The janissaries were theoretically the military arm of the provincial government, even if at times they performed those duties somewhat reluctantly. A chronicler reported that in Aleppo five thousand janissaries mustered for the campaign against Austria in March 1788, but by the time that the column had reached Antioch, two days march away, their numbers had dwindled by half as individual janissaries reappeared in their old haunts in the city.[51] Their defection was not surprising, as the janissaries' interest in actual soldiering had long before given way to civilian pursuits. It is apparent from guild depositions registered in the eighteenth century in the courts of Damascus and Aleppo that the janissaries controlled many of the service guilds and held a virtual monopoly over the butchers' guild in both Syrian cities. A similar pattern prevailed in Mosul. The janissaries, in addition to their legal trades, operated an extensive "protection scheme" not dissimilar to those offered by organized criminal gangs in other societies whereby wealthy individuals and businessmen paid them so things would not happen.[52]

CONCLUSION: CONTINUITIES WITH, AND DISRUPTIONS OF, THE PAST

As the core Arab Ottoman provinces had constituted the Mamluk sultanate, historians of the Arab Middle East are quick to point to continuities

---

[48] Abdul-Karim Rafeq, *The Province of Damascus, 1723–1783* (Beirut: The American University in Beirut, 1966), 26–35.

[49] Wilkins, *Forging Urban Solidarities*, 130–41.

[50] Bruce Masters, ""Patterns of Migration to Ottoman Aleppo in the 17th and 18th Centuries" *IJTS* 4 (1987): 75–89.

[51] ʿAbbud, *al-Murtadd*, 111–12.

[52] Raymond, *Grandes villes arabes*, 69–74.

between the two regimes: Mamluk and Ottoman. In both regimes, the political elite spoke a Turkic language and ruled over a subject population that was Arabic speaking. Both regimes were highly militarized with all officers of state holding military rank. The fiscal regimes of both sultanates used varying forms of tax farming and rested on the extraction of wealth through taxes that were viewed as exploitative by the subject population. Additionally, the reemergence of mamluk households, the "neo-Mamluks" in Egyptian historiography, created a façade of a social continuity in elite formation and culture between the two regimes. In making the case for an unbroken tradition, nothing seems more convincing than the fact that mamluk households dominated the rough and tumble of political life of eighteenth-century Cairo much as they had in the fourteenth and fifteenth centuries, even if the process by which their retainers were recruited had changed. Unquestionably, the memory of the Mamluk past continued to haunt the Ottoman present in Egypt.

While there were undoubtedly continuities between the Mamluk sultanate and that of the Ottomans, there were also major departures from it with the regime change wrought in 1516–17. These were more apparent outside Egypt, where all traces of the Mamluk political and social system vanished. But those who witnessed the transition in Cairo were still painfully aware that the center of political gravity had shifted from their city north to Istanbul. The Ottoman sultans would provide patronage in the construction of mosques in Damascus in the sixteenth century, and elsewhere Ottoman governors would replicate their munificence in creating smaller Ottoman-style mosques to mark an imperial presence in many Arab cities. Without an imperial court to sustain it, however, the splendid material culture that had been a hallmark of Mamluk rule in Damascus and Cairo withered. The long peace in most of the Arab lands during the early modern period had its drawbacks.

If there was a reduction of the imperial presence with the absence of a lavish imperial court culture in the Arab cities, the Ottoman sultanate exerted a much stronger ideological presence among the Arab elites than had its Mamluk predecessor. Although few, if any, Sunni Arab legal scholars accepted the claim of the descendants of Osman that they were the "caliphs of the age," most accepted the notion that the sultanate was divinely ordained. Aware of the threat to their security posed by European powers and the "heretical" regime in Iran, Sunni Muslim Arab scholars legitimated the Ottoman sultanate and came to identify their own fortunes with it. The Ottomans offered a different understanding of the place of sultanic decrees (*kanun*) in Islamic law than the one with which many Muslim Arab scholars were entirely comfortable. But at the same time, the Ottoman regime placed the Muslim law courts into a more central role in provincial administration than had previously been the case. Furthermore, with the exception of the chief judge, all of the other judges and the chief-judge's assistant (*na'ib*)were recruited from the ranks of the educated Arabic-speaking Muslim elite of the cities in which they served. It was in the administration of the law through the religious courts across the Arab lands that local collaboration with the imperial project was most evident.

Despite the continuities between Mamluk and Ottoman regimes, the Ottomans put their own stamp on the political institutions that governed the Arabs after the sixteenth century. As control over the Arab provinces began to weaken, governors, both Ottomans and local players, asserted varying degrees of independent action from the imperial court in Istanbul. Significantly even as they did so, they continued to profess their loyalty to the sultan. The sultans had succeeded in convincing most of the people living in the Arab lands that the system put into place by their ancestors Selim and Süleyman was the only legitimate political order that was possible. In the eighteenth century, Christian intellectuals in the sultan's Balkan provinces began to question why they should continue to live in his "protected domains." In place of the sultanate, they sought the revival of ancient kingdoms or alternatively the "nation-state" republic, a concept that was slowly filtering into the Balkans from Western Europe in the early nineteenth century. That question never arose among their Arab contemporaries, at least not until Muhammad ʿAbd al-Wahhab would ask it. The unquestioned loyalty of the sultan's Arab subjects to his regime helped to secure the Arab lands for the sultan during a century when real political power over the region had become tenuous.

Ottoman rule in the Arab lands did not provide a radical break with the past. There was still a sultan, the courts administered the sharia, and the military continued to hold all secular authority. But there were also two countervailing tendencies that distinguished the Ottoman era from that which preceded it. Ideologically, the Ottomans influenced the Arabic-speaking Sunni elites to a degree unprecedented by their predecessors. The sultanate no longer was an institution that had to be endured in the absence of a more righteous regime. It had become a righteous regime. In roughly the same period that the Ottoman regime had become legitimate in the imaginations of the Sunni intelligentsia, local Arabic speakers were achieving actual political power on the ground in cities such as Damascus and Mosul to a degree unprecedented in the Mamluk era.

The combination of the two developments created a political reality wherein Arabic speakers were the sultan's subjects, but they were also actively complicit in the empire's maintenance. Their participation helped to shore up the empire in the Arab provinces in the eighteenth century when the various internal contradictions of the Ottoman political and economic systems threatened to bring it down elsewhere. Those contradictions would give rise to national rebellions in the Balkans in the next century. But there would be no Arab revolt against the sultan's rule in that troubled century for the empire.

3

Economy and Society in the Early Modern Era

The Ottoman conquests of the Arab lands occurred in an age when the boundaries of what had been the known world were expanding. Historians of Asia have long been aware that transregional networks of commerce and cultural exchange were not unique to the sixteenth century, even if most western Europeans had been only dimly aware of them before. In contrast to their insularity, the peoples of the Middle East had played a vital role in those contacts for millennia.[1] But the incorporation of parts of the Americas into European empires and the intrusion of armed European ships into the trade of Asia in the sixteenth century greatly expanded the geographical horizons for many around the globe. The creation in 1513 of the Piri Reis map, which showed the partial Atlantic coastlines of both Africa and South America, was indicative of an awareness of a "new" world" (*yeni dünya*) among the sultan's advisers. Ottoman naval expeditions to the Red Sea and Indian Ocean in the sixteenth century were yet another sign of the sultan's recognition of the possibility for creating a global strategy. The expansion of contacts among peoples across oceans and continents led to the introduction of new crops, shifts in trade routes, and improvements in technology, as well as the arrival of previously unknown pandemics and military conquerors.

---

[1] Janet Abu-Lughod, *Before European Hegemony: The World System A.D. 1250–1350* (Oxford: Oxford University Press, 1989); K. N. Chaudhuri, *Asia before Europe: Economy and Civilisation of the Indian Ocean from the Rise of Islam to 1750* (Cambridge: Cambridge University Press, 1990); Andre Gunder Frank, *ReOrient: Global Economy in the Asian Age* (Berkeley: University of California Press, 1998).

The impact on the sultan's Arab subjects of their incorporation into this "world economy," to borrow Immanuel Wallerstein's formulation, was not as dire as it was for the inhabitants of sub-Saharan Africa or the Americas.[2] Nevertheless, there is little doubt that the Middle East suffered a contraction of its wealth after the sixteenth century. The shifts in global trade patterns in that century were partly to blame as the cities of the eastern Mediterranean ceased to be the key intermediaries in the east-west trade. The underlying cause of the decline for the Ottoman economy was more likely, however, the introduction of large quantities of silver from the Americas, which distorted the traditional ratio in the value of gold to silver in Middle Eastern economies. A continuing reliance on silver in the Ottoman Empire led to periodic debasements of coinage and sharp inflation in the seventeenth century.[3] Adding to the region's economic distress, there was a decline in the agricultural output in the Arab lands due in part to the abandonment of the fertile steppe lands on the edges of the Syrian Desert by their peasant proprietors in the wake of Bedouin raids as well as to an increasing desertification brought on by the drier climate associated with the "Little Ice Age" of the seventeenth century.[4]

Faced with a fiscal crisis in the seventeenth century, the bureaucrats in Istanbul had to scramble to create new sources of revenue. To make matters worse, they were crippled by political inertia. The Ottoman state bureaucracy allowed many of the institutions of control in the provinces to ossify or to contract through its own inaction. The weakening of the firm control formerly exercised by the Ottoman state had a devastating effect on conditions in the countryside of what is today Syria and Iraq that in turn affected life in the cities. The decline in economic conditions was perhaps more severe in the Arabic-speaking provinces in the Fertile Crescent than in the Balkans or Egypt, but even Egypt, whose agricultural base remained strong, experienced recurring economic downturns in the late seventeenth and eighteenth centuries.[5] Whether or not the seventeenth and eighteenth centuries witnessed a decline in Istanbul's

---

[2] Immanuel Wallerstein, *The Modern World System*, 3 vols. (New York: Academic Press, 1974, 1980,1989).

[3] Şevket Pamuk, "Money in the Ottoman Empire, 1362–1914." In *An Economic and Social History of the Ottoman Empire 1300–1914*, edited by Halil İnalcık and Donald Quataert (Cambridge: Cambridge University Press, 1994), 953–70.

[4] Sam White, *The Climate of Rebellion in the Early Modern Ottoman Empire* (Cambridge: Cambridge University, Press, 2011), 126–63.

[5] Raymond, *Artisans et commerçants au Caire*, I, 81–106.

political power may be debated, but there is little doubt that after the "golden age" of Süleyman, the Arab provinces showed signs of economic distress. An index of that economic malaise was an apparent decrease in population across the Arab provinces over the course of the seventeenth and eighteenth centuries. Such a conclusion must remain tentative, however, as the bureaucracy that had been so careful to register the sultan's subjects, or at least their lands, in the reign of Süleyman was less likely to do so in the seventeenth century.

COMMERCE AND THE WEALTH OF CITIES

The Egyptian Marxist historian Samir Amin suggested that in the precapitalist world system the cities of the Arab lands were in a unique position. At the juncture of three continents, the wealth that propelled the rise of the cities of the region in the Islamic Middle Ages and the culture it financed was drawn not from the "exploitation of its rural world," as was the case in feudal Europe or China, but "from the surplus appropriated from the peasantries of other countries by the ruling classes of those countries."[6] In other words, the profits that Arab merchants extracted from the long-distance caravan trade made their cities wealthy and allowed them to support a population much greater than would have been possible solely on the basis of the surplus of their agricultural hinterlands.

Although compelling in its simplicity, Amin's thesis requires modification if applied to the Ottoman era. The simple fact was merchants in the Arab lands during the Ottoman centuries benefited more from regional trade than they did from the transcontinental transit trade. Additionally, there is ample evidence of rural exploitation in the Ottoman centuries with local merchants and tax farmers exacting the surplus wealth of the peasants who resided in the hinterlands of the major cities of the region. Exploitation of the peasantry was not limited to Europe and China.

Trade whether local or international did, however, provide some of the excess wealth that allowed the Ottoman Arab cities to grow substantially in the first century of Ottoman rule. After reaching historic heights at the end of the sixteenth century, the populations of the Arab cities either stabilized or in some cases began to drop in the following two centuries. Even with a decline in their populations, however, cities in the Arab provinces continued to rank among the largest in the world.

---

[6] Samir Amin, *The Arab Nation: Nationalism and Class Struggle*, translated by Michael Pallis (London: Zed Press, 1976), 12–16.

In 1800, Cairo probably had in excess of 200,000 inhabitants, Aleppo 100,000, Damascus and Baghdad each 90,000, Tunis 80,000, and Mosul 55,000. In comparison with the Ottoman Balkans and Anatolia, the population of the sultan's Arab lands was disproportionately urban with an estimated 10 percent to 20 percent of his subjects living in cities with populations of more than 50,000.[7]

Historians studying the Arab provinces of the Ottoman Empire have long favored cities over the rural areas in their research. In part, that myopia was a result of the sources they used. Earlier studies of the region relied heavily on European travel accounts and consular reports, supplemented by the chronicles and biographical dictionaries written by members of the region's urban elite. Those sources dealt with rural conditions only when there were problems of supply, and the lives of the peasants were largely unrecorded. To correct for the silences in the earlier studies, historians have turned to the sharia court records of various provincial centers including Cairo, Jerusalem, Nablus, Tripoli, Damascus, and Aleppo for a perspective that now includes the rural hinterlands of each city. They have also turned to the central archives in Istanbul, which provide fiscal records for the provinces as well as the government's responses to various problems that arose in the countryside. Although these sources allow for the inclusion of rural areas in the historical narratives, cities retain the central focus of most studies of the Ottoman Arab provinces. That bias, in part, reflects the worldview of the people being studied. Ibn Khaldun wrote at the start of the fifteenth century that there could be no civilization without cities and no city without a wall.[8] If cities were privileged in the Muslim intellectuals' construction of their society, trade was understood by them to be the vital lifeblood of those cities.

The trade routes connecting Eurasia and Africa that were at the core of Amin's thesis were well established when the Ottoman army arrived. Those patterns of trade were, however, already facing challenges that were both internal and external. At the start of the Ottoman period, spices and other luxury goods from south and southeast Asia provided the major attraction for European merchants arriving in the trading emporia of the eastern Mediterranean. Their importance to them ebbed, however, as direct seaborne trade to Asia increased over the course of the sixteenth century. Competition from sailing ships reduced the flow westward of Asian trade goods carried by the caravans. As a concrete example of the

---

[7] Abdel Nour, *Introduction à l'histoire*, 84–7; Raymond, *Grandes villes arabes*, 62–6.
[8] ibn Khaldun, *Muqaddima*, vol. II, 243–9.

new conditions in global trade, pepper, which had been the mainstay of
Europe's trade in Aleppo in the middle of the sixteenth century, was virtually unobtainable in the city by the century's end, except at prices that
were higher than those that were being asked in Lisbon.[9]

The decline in the spice trade did not spell the end of the caravan trade
suggested by some.[10] Rather commodities produced in the Middle East
became the staples of trade with Europe. These were principally the silk of
Iran and raw cotton from Syria. Cairo exported Yemeni coffee and some
spices to Europe and slaves to Istanbul. Cotton, rice, wheat, and indigo
were also important Egyptian exports to Istanbul and the ports of the
eastern Mediterranean and the Red Sea. Technically, the Ottoman state
banned the export of these basic commodities to Europe, but the illicit
trade in wheat, in particular, often circumvented those restrictions and
found its way to European ports. Egyptian merchants, in turn, received
from the other Ottoman provinces timber, dried fruit, nuts, olive oil, and
soap. Trade between the Ottoman Empire and India was also substantial,
although Ottoman merchants paid for the cotton textiles and indigo they
imported from the subcontinent largely through the export of gold and
silver.[11]

The change in the availability of various commodities in the region's
markets occurred as the routes themselves were in flux. Increased Bedouin
raids led to a shift in the caravan trade from a route that traversed the
Syrian Desert directly from Basra to Damascus to one that hugged the
Euphrates River to Bira (today Birecik in Turkey), which was within a
few days of open country portage to Aleppo. Damascus had been the
major center of European trade in the fifteenth century, with Beirut its
port, but the caravan routes had definitively shifted to Aleppo by the
end of the sixteenth century. The Levant Company's initial charter, registered in London in 1581, listed Damascus as one of its potential centers
of activity, but no English merchants settled there. With the transit trade
moving away from Damascus, its port Beirut, which had bustled in the

[9] Fernand Braudel, *The Mediterranean and the Mediterranean World in the Age of Philip II*, translated by Siân Reynolds, 2 vols. (New York: Harper & Row Publisher, 1972), vol. I, 543–65.
[10] Niels Steensgaard, *The Asian Trade Revolution of the Seventeenth Century: The East India Companies and the Decline of the Caravan Trade* (Chicago: The University of Chicago Press, 1974).
[11] Halil İnalcık, "Osmanlı Pamuklu Pazarı, Hindistan ve İngiltere: Pazar Rekabitinde Emek Maliyetinin Rolü" republished in Halil İnalcık, *Osmanlı İmparatorluğu: Toplum ve Ekonomi* (Istanbul: Eren, 1993), 259–319; Abdullah, *Merchants, Mamluks, and Murder*, 57–63.

Mamluk era, declined and no single port emerged to replace it. Instead, Cairo and Aleppo emerged as the leading trade emporia in the Arab lands for Europe merchants in the early-modern period. Neither was a port city, and both relied on the continuation of the caravan trade to carry goods to their markets that European merchants sought and to transport those goods to the Mediterranean ports.

Transfixed by the centrality of those two cities in European commercial documents, historians have sometimes overlooked the reality that trade with Europe was not an essential ingredient to either city's commercial prosperity or that of the empire at large in the early-modern period. Commerce in the region was not limited to just one set of potential customers. In support of that thesis, Damascus's commercial role did not diminish with the withdrawal of European merchants from its markets. The merchants of both Cairo and Damascus were enriched by the yearly hajj, which could lead tens of thousands of customers to their markets over the space of just a few weeks. Approximately two months later, the pilgrims returned with coffee from Yemen and spices from South Asia that they had purchased in Mecca.[12] Damascus may not have hosted European merchants in the first three centuries of Ottoman rule, but there were North Africans, Indians, Iranians, and Central Asians mingling in its bazaars.

The importance of the hajj in the commercial life of Cairo and Damascus highlights a feature of trade in the Arab lands that was relatively unique in the Ottoman Empire at large: the presence of Muslim merchants. Their participation would have been an absolute necessity for the hajj, but even trade with the Europeans was still largely in the hands of Muslims in both Cairo and Aleppo throughout the seventeenth century.[13] Non-Muslims were, however, starting to make a place for themselves in the empire's trade within a century after the conquests. In the seventeenth century, Christian Arab merchants emerged in the historical record as commercial agents for Muslim investors in Aleppo. By the eighteenth century, Arabic-speaking Christians were among the leading merchants in that city and Armenian merchants from Iran, who had dominated the silk trade of their country, all but disappeared to be replaced by Armenians whose origins lay in eastern Anatolia.[14] In the same century, Christian

---

[12] Faroqhi, *Pilgrims and Sultans*, 158–70; Abdul-Karim Rafeq, "Qafilat al-hajj al-shami wa ahammiyatuha fi al-ʿahd al-ʿuthmani." In his *Dirasat iqtisadiyya wa ijtimaʿiyya fi ta'rikh bilad al-sham al-hadith* (Damascus: Maktabat Nubil, 2002), 169–92.

[13] Nelly Hanna, *Making Big Money in 1600: The Life and Times of Ismaʿil Abu Taqiyya, Egyptian Merchant* (Albany: State University of New York Press, 1998); Masters, *Origins of Western Economic Dominance*, 79–93.

[14] Masters, *Christians and Jews*, 71–80.

merchants from Syria began to establish themselves in Cairo, eventually gaining dominance in both that city's trade with Europe and that of the Red Sea.[15] In another sign of the transformation of the ethnic makeup of the merchant classes in the Arab lands, the late eighteenth century witnessed the eclipse of the fortunes of Iranian Armenian merchants in Basra and the rise of Arabic-speaking Jewish merchants, who handled much of Iraq's trade with India into the nineteenth century.[16]

The rise of the economic importance of the non-Muslim Ottoman merchants in the eighteenth century did not signal a retreat of Muslims from commerce. Muslims enjoyed an almost complete monopoly over long-distance trade in Damascus well into the nineteenth century, as indicated by the extensive report on Syria's economic conditions composed by Sir John Bowring and presented to the British Parliament in 1840.[17] Even in Aleppo, which probably had the largest non-Muslim commercial class of any Ottoman Arab city, members the Muslim al-Amiri family were among the city's leading merchants in the second half of the eighteenth century and other Muslim traders were very active in the nineteenth century.[18] Muslims were also among the leading merchants in Cairo at the end of the eighteenth century.[19] The survival of a Muslim commercial class in the Ottoman Arab cities stands in stark contrast to the rest of the Ottoman Empire, where finance and commerce became a virtual monopoly of non-Muslims. There are indications of occasional competition and friction between Muslim and non-Muslim merchants in the Arab lands, especially with those who enjoyed protégé status from a European power,[20] but there is also ample evidence of commercial cooperation among members of different religious communities.

THE GUILDS

The transit trade of the east captured the imagination of many economic historians in the first half of the twentieth century,[21] but guilds (*ta'ifa*, or

---

[15] Raymond, *Artisans et commerçants*, vol. II, 477–80.
[16] Abdullah, *Merchants, Mamluks, and Murder*, 99–115.
[17] John Bowring, *Report on the Commercial Statistics of Syria* (Reprint, New York: Arno Press, 1973), 94.
[18] Ibid, 80.
[19] Raymond, *Artisans et commerçants*, vol. I, 244–305.
[20] Bruce Masters, "The Political Economy of Aleppo in an Age of Ottoman "Reform" *JESHO* 52 (2010): 302.
[21] Alfred Wood, *A History of the Levant Company* (London: Oxford University Press, 1935); François Charles-Roux, *Les échelles de Syrie et de Palestine au XVIIIe siècle* (Paris: Paul Guenther, 1928).

in the plural *tawa'if*) were at the core of the economic life of any Arab city in the Ottoman period. The word *ta'ifa* simply means "group" and was applied by Ottoman authorities to many different types of social groupings, including religious communities. In the economic sphere, the *tawa'if* were voluntary associations similar to the guilds that emerged in medieval and early-modern Europe, both as to their organization and function. As was the case in Europe, guilds controlled almost every aspect of craft production and the service industries in the Arab cities in the early-modern period.

Although historians have long understood the importance of guilds in the Ottoman economy, the questions of their origins as well as their function in Ottoman society have undergone a major revision over the past few decades. In addition to expanding our understanding of the role of internal commerce in the Ottoman Empire, archival work in the court records of the Arab cities has overturned the established paradigm of the guilds created by an earlier generation of historians that imagined them as instruments of state control.[22] Guilds were an important link between a large segment of the urban population and the government, as suggested by earlier scholars, but it was a two-way street as the guilds looked to the state to support their rules. The guilds provided taxes and were capable of mobilizing the urban population in times of natural disasters or wars. In both those public functions, however, the leaders (*imam* or *mukhtar*) of the city quarters were more important in taking charge of the responsibilities placed by the state on the inhabitants of their quarters than were the heads of the guilds.[23]

Evidence from a number of Arab cities points to the fact that guilds were established, or dissolved, at the request of the members without state intervention.[24] The members controlled admission to the guild, and they chose who would be its head (*shaykh*). A qadi would formalize the appointment, but the occasions when a judge refused to name the man the membership had forwarded to him seem to have been rare. Membership in a guild was certified for an individual with a document known as *gedik* in Turkish and *khaluw* in Arabic, with both terms occurring in the court registers of Damascus and Aleppo. The qadi issued the document,

[22] Gibb and Bowen, *Islamic Society and the West*, vol. I, 281–94; Gabriel Baer, "The Administrative, Economic and Social Functions of the Turkish Guilds" *IJMES* 1 (1968), 49.

[23] For a listing of *mukhtar*s and their responsibilities, Damascus: Aleppo sijillat, vol. XXI, 212; Wilkins. *Forging Urban Solidarities*, 109–12.

[24] Among others: Raymond, *Artisans et commerçants*, vol. II, 503–85; Amnon Cohen, *The Guilds of Ottoman Jerusalem* (Leiden: Brill, 2001).

for which the recipient paid a fee to the court. As was often the case with union cards in the twentieth-century United States, these could be inherited from father to son. They also could be sold.

The guild members established the rules of their guild including how raw materials would be distributed and methods of quality control. The membership, after consultation with the judge over what was fair, also established the price for either finished goods or a service. The guild members registered rules, prices, and choice of guild leadership at court with the oral acknowledgment before the judge by the entire membership, or at least a substantial representation of it, that they consented to what their shaykh had attested, and their names were duly recorded by the court's scribe. The legal system could then be called upon to enforce the rules, but the judges did not make them. If a dispute arose between guilds or between a guild and merchants, however, a judge was free to exercise his interpretation of the law to settle it.[25] Researchers on guilds in Anatolia and Istanbul have shown that the guilds throughout the empire enjoyed the same autonomy as existed in the Arab lands.[26] As such, we now recognize that the guild system had more power and influence to form a civil society than was previously understood. Whatever they were, the guilds were not instruments of state control.

Membership in a guild was, at times, limited to a particular ethnic or religious group. In Aleppo, for example, the porters were generally Kurds; the members of a guild specializing in a certain type of bread were all Armenians from the Sasun region of southeastern Anatolia. Most goldsmiths throughout the region were Jews, while those in construction guilds in Syria were typically Christians. That said, the membership of many guilds, especially those involved in textile production in Aleppo, Damascus, and Cairo, crossed sectarian lines. If a guild contained members of different religious communities, the shaykh was always Muslim even if a large majority of the guild's membership was not. Similarly, when the guild presented itself before the court in depositions, the Muslim members were listed by name before any listing of the non-Muslim

[25] Masters, *Origins of Western Dominance*, 200–13; Galal el-Nahal, *The Judicial Administration of Ottoman Egypt in the Seventeenth Century* (Minneapolis: Bibliotheca Islamica, 1979), 57–64.

[26] Haim Gerber, "Guilds in Seventeenth-Century Anatolia Bursa" *Asian and African Studies* 11 (1976): 59–86; Suraiya Faroqhi, *Towns and Townsmen of Ottoman Anatolia: Trade, Crafts and Food Production in an Urban Setting, 1520–1650* (Cambridge: Cambridge University Press, 1984); Eunjeong Yi, *Guild Dynamics in Seventeenth-Century Istanbul: Fluidity and Leverage* (Leiden: Brill, 2004).

membership. There were occasional cases of struggles between guilds in the court records, and these could on occasion become violent. There is, however, no indication of sectarian dissonance within a particular guild or of guilds seeking to bar membership to persons because of their religion.

Despite the guilds' autonomy, the central state did impose its writ on the guilds when their practices interfered with the collection of revenues or caused a decline in them. An example of that interference occurred as the woolen cloth makers of Aleppo began to imitate cloth being imported from Europe in the second half of the seventeenth century. The competition in prices that this innovation created led to a drop in the customs duties reaching Istanbul as customers increasingly preferred the local product to the imported fabric. The state responded by levying additional taxes on the woolen cloth makers' guild to compensate for those losses. That action effectively put a stop to the innovation, as the local product lost its competitive edge in price for consumers and the guild stopped producing the cloth.[27]

As the central government increasingly looked for new sources of revenue, the intervention of the government in guild affairs intensified in the eighteenth century. In what was the most galling intrusion for the guilds, the state began to auction off the right to collect the guild's taxes to lifetime tax farmers (*malikaneci*). The selling of these positions gave outsiders entry into guild politics and challenged the traditional authority of the shaykh. In one such confrontation between contending voices of authority, cloth makers of Aleppo sided with their shaykh against the tax farmer and instituted a work stoppage that lasted for 129 days in 1772. The strike was finally settled when a judge intervened to settle the dispute in favor of the guild.[28] That action underlies the reality that while the guilds were an integral part of the urban economy of Arab cities for most of the Ottoman period, they also played a political role by providing a collective voice to their members in times of crisis. Enhancing their political role, many of the guilds in various Arab cities, as was the case in the empire at large, had by the eighteenth century a large janissary component, which provided armed enforcers should they be necessary. As a result of that connection, Arab chroniclers in the eighteenth century often conflated certain guilds with the janissaries as agents of social disruption.

---

[27] Masters, *Origins of Western Economic Dominance*, 198–9.
[28] Ibid., 210.

WAS THERE AN "AGE OF THE *A^cyan*"?

If the guilds gave voice to the lower socioeconomic classes of the Arab cities, the *a^cyan* were at the top of the urban social pyramid. The term, a collective plural noun, was employed by the Arab chroniclers to mean the prominent people of their town, corresponding to what eighteenth-century residents of the British Isles would have termed "the quality" or the gentry.[29] Who exactly was included in that category seemingly evolved over the Ottoman centuries. In the sixteenth century, when the Damascene chronicler ibn Tulun employed the word *a^cyan*, he usually meant the leading ulama of his city and not its secular elite.[30] Ottoman language documents sent to the Arab provinces in the eighteenth century routinely employed the phrase "*ülema ve ayanlar*" when speaking about, or addressing, the nonmilitary leadership in a city, suggesting that *a^cyan* referred only to those members of the urban elite who were not included among the scholarly class. But at least one eighteenth-century Damascene Muslim author continued to use the term primarily with its earlier meaning of the prominent ulama.[31]

Whoever was included by the authors employing the term *a^cyan*, it signified their understanding that there were families of "quality" in their cities who were their "natural" leaders. Families who produced generation after generation of religious scholars and those who had control over major religious endowments (*waqf*) predominated, but there were also merchant families and those who although they lived in the cities had large holdings of rural properties. In fact, most of the leading families engaged in a number of different economic enterprises. Albert Hourani labeled these men the "notables," and that translation of *a^cyan* has stuck with historians writing in English.[32] Every Arab town and city had its notable families, who were often signified in the written record by the use of a family name. The existence of notable families with lineages, which reputedly in some cases stretched back to the early Arab conquerors, was a distinct feature of Arab Muslim society within the empire as family names extending over several generations were elsewhere a rarity for Muslims.

[29] Toby Barnard, *A New Anatomy of Ireland: The Irish Protestants, 1649–1770* (New Haven, CT: Yale University Press, 2003), 21–40.
[30] ibn Tulun. *Mufakahat al-khillani*, 92.
[31] ibn Kannan. *Yawmiyyat shamiyya*, 87.
[32] Albert Hourani, "Ottoman Reform and the Politics of the Notables." In *Beginnings of Modernization in the Middle East*, edited by William Polk and Richard Chambers (Chicago: The University of Chicago Press, 1968), 41–68.

Pride in one's lineage was an essential element to a*yan* status, but the families themselves were not static. Studies of families in Damascus and Aleppo demonstrate that while some families showed great longevity and retained that position over centuries, others rose and fell with the passage of time.[33] A family had to work to maintain its status or risk falling into obscurity. Nonetheless, it seems that those living in an Arab city in any given year were well aware of who the current members of the a*yan* were. For Muslim writers, the a*yan* were exclusively Muslim. But it is significant that the Aleppine Christian chronicler Yusuf Dimitri ʿAbbud (d. 1803), writing in the late eighteenth century, employed the term a*yan* when speaking of the secular leadership in the Christian communities of his city, as distinct from the clergy.[34] An indication of that status among Christians in Aleppo was the appearance of family names for prominent Christians in the eighteenth century in the registers of the Muslim courts, a practice that was unknown in the preceding century. To be a member of the a*yan*, a family name was a prerequisite, and the self-made Christian merchant families were quick to adopt the social practice of their Muslim neighbors.

Whatever the exact meaning the term a*yan* may have had for eighteenth-century residents of the Fertile Crescent, historians of the Ottoman Arab lands have often termed that century as the "age of the Aʿyan." It is an all-inclusive phrase by which they seek to highlight a time when local actors, such as the ʿAzms in Damascus or the Jalilis in Mosul, came to dominate the political life of their cities at the expense of officials appointed by Istanbul. Hourani was first to draw attention to the role of these families in urban politics of the eighteenth century and to identify them as a political class. Hourani's class was, however, a virtual "grab bag" of individuals as he included within it the religious scholars who had served as the traditional spokesmen for the urban population, the "secular notables," or those who controlled some economic resources, and finally the leaders of the military garrisons. Hourani further suggested that these notables as a class provided the key to understanding the politics of the region in the eighteenth and early nineteenth centuries as they stepped into the political vacuum created with the weakening of

---

[33] Margaret Meriwether, *The Kin Who Count: Family and Society in Ottoman Aleppo, 1770–1840* (Austin: University of Texas Press, 1999); Linda Schilcher, *Families in Politics: Damascene Factions and Estates of the 18th and 19th Centuries* (Stuttgart: Franz Steiner Verlag, 1985).

[34] ʿAbbud, *al-Murtadd*, 22.

government control from the capital and gave voice to local interests over imperial ones.

Despite the wide-scale acceptance of the social/political category of the "ayanship" by historians, it is perhaps time to consider revising the paradigm. The most compelling reason for revisionism is that the term has been extended to include far too many people for it to be useful.[35] Margaret Meriwether noted that although officers from the janissary corps or chiefs of powerful guilds might have held political power in eighteenth-century Aleppo, they were not accepted into the social circles of the old, elite families.[36] ᶜAdel Mannaᶜ made a similar distinction in his characterization of the local elite in Ottoman Palestine between those involved in the "socioreligious" administration (*afandiyya, ᶜulama, ashraf*) and those who were appointed as governors or who had military skills (*bekat, aghawat*).[37] It was possible, of course, that after a generation or two, families of military origin might be counted by their contemporaries among the ranks of the *aᶜyan*, but the eponymous founder of the family would not have been included in that august company by his own contemporaries. While it is true that the *agha*s of the janissaries sat on the provincial councils in Aleppo and Damascus and that served as an indicator of their political power, the true *aᶜyan* of either city would not have permitted them to marry their daughters, an indication of their lower social status.

Some members of the *aᶜyan* may have wielded political power, but their ability to act on the political stage of their cities was not contingent upon, or even necessarily enhanced by, their *aᶜyan* status. Most people with local roots in eighteenth-century Syria or Iraq who achieved some degree of political power were not recognized by their contemporaries as *aᶜyan*, and of those who were designated as belonging to that elite few ever wielded any real political power, except in moments of extreme crisis when the power of local governors was at its lowest ebb.[38] In the nineteenth century, families such as the ᶜAzms in Damascus or the descendants of Küçük Ali Agha in Aleppo or the Jalilis in Mosul were properly members of the *aᶜyan*, but their ancestors who had founded the dynasties

[35] Hourani, "Ottoman Reform and the Politics of the Notables," 48–9; Schilcher, *Families in Politics*, 136–56;

[36] Meriwether, *The Kin Who Count*, 30–68.

[37] ᶜAdel Mannaᶜ. "Continuity and Change in the Socio-Political Elite in Palestine During the late Ottoman Period." In *The Syrian Land in the 18th and 19th Century*, edited by Thomas Philipp (Stuttgart: Franz Steiner Verlag, 1992), 69–90.

[38] Barbir, *Ottoman Rule in Damascus*, 67–89.

were not. Rather, they were viewed as outsiders by the chroniclers who might be considered as voices for the true aʿyan.

There is no family more paradigmatic of the aʿyan for historians of eighteenth-century Syria than the ʿAzms. But they are also problematic in our attempt to establish what it meant to be a local in the imagination of an eighteenth-century resident of an Ottoman Arab city. Isma'il Pasha al-ʿAzm was the first of several highly effective governors from the family whose ethnic origins are uncertain but who had served as tax farmers in the region surrounding the central Syrian towns of Hama and Maʿarrat al-Nuʿman in the seventeenth century. The ʿAzms dominated political life in the Syrian provinces for much of the following century with family members serving as governors of Damascus, Aleppo, and Tripoli on and off from 1725 through 1783. Asʿad Pasha al-ʿAzm (d. 1758), who governed Damascus from 1743 until 1757, enjoyed an unprecedented longevity in that position as most governors who preceded him held their tenure of office for a year or two at the longest.

Even in the case of such obvious candidates for local hero status as were the ʿAzms, there are questions of whether their contemporaries considered them as being properly members of the aʿyan of Damascus. Muhammad ibn Kannan noted in his entry for 1137/1724–5 that the governor of Damascus, Çerkes Osman Pasha (known locally as Abu Tawq), was removed and replaced by Isma'il Pasha ibn al-ʿAzm, whom he simply identified with the nisba (ascriptive title) of al-Nuʿmani in an acknowledgment of the town whence the family hailed.[39] Isma'il governed the city until 1730, when he was replaced with another Ottoman career officer, Aydınlı Abdullah Pasha. Ibn Kannan later included a poem of praise for Isma'il's brother Sulayman, who served as Damascus's governor (1734–8) and whom the author felt to be particularly just and sagacious.[40] The author went on to detail all that was good about Sulayman's reign and closed by saying that at the end of his governorship, "Sulayman Pasha set off for his country (biladihi) and he took with him his people, his children, his slave women and nothing remained of him in Damascus."[41] The author clearly did not consider the ʿAzms, although they were worthy of praise, to be Damascenes.

Although Hourani's use of the aʿyan has problems if it is taken to mean a political class, the category as a social unit remains valid. Its

[39] ibn Kannan, Yawmiyyat shamiyya, 364.
[40] Ibid., 484.
[41] Ibid., 500–1.

relevance lies in its utility to distinguish locally based families, who were viewed by their contemporaries as the "natural" leaders of their community, from the newly made men of non-Ottoman origin and from members of the Ottoman political establishment. It was largely irrelevant to their function in Arab urban society whether or not members of a*yan* families received political recognition from the Ottoman state, as their contemporaries knew who they were. In a crisis, they turned to them to give them advice and to represent their concerns to the central government. Furthermore, as Philip Khoury has demonstrated, these families continued to exercise authority through the end of the Ottoman Empire and into the mandate period, long past the so-called age of the a*yan*.[42] They, in effect, had become Syria's nobility.

Whatever the degree of actual political power the a*yan* exercised in cities such as Damascus, Aleppo, Mosul, and Jerusalem in the eighteenth century, their position in Ottoman Arab society stands in stark contrast to contemporary developments that were occurring elsewhere in the empire. The Ottoman Turkish form of the term, *ayan* (plural *ayanlar*), referred not to a collection of prominent persons but to a single, local strongman like those who emerged in various provincial centers throughout Anatolia and the Balkans in the eighteenth century. Such an individual was also known by the Turkish term *derebey*, meaning "lord of the valley." These men created hereditary dynasties (*hanedan*) that were able to seize local resources, which provided them with the necessary cash to raise armies and gain the governorships of large portions of the empire. They often acted independently of Istanbul's control and opened direct trade with European merchants.[43] The *ayanlar* of the Balkans and Anatolia, with their ability to initiate policies independently of Istanbul and to build private armies, more closely resembled the dynastic governors in North Africa than they did their erstwhile namesakes in the Arab provinces of the Fertile Crescent.

In the Syrian provinces, only Cezzar Ahmed Pasha, who from his fortified city of Acre gained the governorship of Sidon and occasionally Damascus between 1775 and 1803, created a power base, if not an actual dynasty, that resembled those of his contemporaries in Anatolia. Although historians of Ottoman Syria often link Cezzar Ahmed's career

[42] Philip Khoury, "Continuity and Change in Syrian Political Life: The Nineteenth and Twentieth Centuries" *AHR* 96 (1991): 1374–407.
[43] Fikret Adanır, "Semi-Autonomous Forces in the Balkans and Anatolia." In *The Cambridge History of Turkey*. Vol. 3. *The Later Ottoman Empire, 1603–1839*, edited by Suraiya Faroqhi (Cambridge: Cambridge University Press, 2006), 157–85.

to the phenomenon of *aʿyan* governors in the eighteenth-century Fertile Crescent, he was hardly a local personality. He was a Bosnian Muslim who started his career as a mercenary in Egypt before relocating to Palestine. Those who after his death succeeded him to the governorship were not his offspring or relatives, as was the case with the ʿAzms or the Jalilis, but his mamluks. In that regard, Cezzar Ahmed resembled more closely the mamluk dynasty ruling in Baghdad than he did the ʿAzms. Not a member of the *aʿyan* in the eyes of the Arab chroniclers, he was nevertheless viewed as a potentially unruly *ayan* by the Ottoman state in its understanding of that term.

THE RURAL LANDSCAPE

The economic position of the *aʿyan* families of the Fertile Crescent strengthened during the eighteenth century as new opportunities for wealth served to bolster their social prestige and political influence. The source of their enhanced economic power lay in the changing procedures under which cultivatable land outside the cities was registered and taxed. Under the Islamic legal traditions of landownership first articulated by the eighth-century Hanafi judge Abu Yusuf in his *Kitab al-kharaj* (The Book of the Land Tax), land outside Arabia was divided between that whose owners had submitted peacefully to the Muslim armies and that whose owners had not.[44] The land of the latter class of persons was forfeited to the Muslim community (*umma*) to be administered by the state. State lands were known in the Ottoman period as *miri* and could be distributed in the form of *timar*s or as tax farms (*iltizam*). In either case, the land technically continued to belong to the community of believers at large but was administered for their benefit by the state. The state then granted, or more accurately sold, to others the right to collect the taxes produced by the peasants working the land. Those monies were, in theory, then to be forwarded to the central state treasury, and the state employed those funds to "command right and forbid wrong," thereby upholding its obligation to the Muslim community at large.

In addition to the category of state lands, Islamic law recognized and protected private property (*mulk*). The owners of such property paid to the state taxes on the produce of the land, but they could sell the land itself as freehold. Private property was also subject to the complicated formula of inheritance laid out by the Qur'an. The category of *mulk* included

---

[44] Yaʿqub Abu Yusuf, *Kitab al-kharaj* (Cairo: al-Matbaʿa al-Salafiyya, 1962).

most urban properties, but also gardens and orchards in rural areas that required intensive cultivation. Typically, a village in the Ottoman Arab lands would consist of both state-held lands, the procedure for its distribution among the peasants varying from region to region and even within a region, and private property. The latter included olive trees or others producing fruit, nuts, or mulberries, even if they were growing on state land. As private property, the trees could be sold or inherited, but not the land on which they grew.

The long-established practice of transferring rural lands into the category of *waqf* (pious endowment) further complicated the question of who owned the land. While this was legal in the case of clearly defined private property or even the individual trees in an orchard that grew on state land, the practice became contentious when it alienated arable land that was originally in the category *miri* to support a pious foundation. Many legal scholars in the Arab provinces held that such a practice was permitted while those in the capital were not sure that it was, providing another example how a common tradition could be interpreted differently. The Ottoman scholars' queasiness at the practice of creating rural *waqf* endowments is understandable. It would have the net effect of reducing revenues to the central treasury, which in turn paid their salaries. Nonetheless, villages held as *waqf* properties were commonplace in Syria and Palestine in the Ottoman period, including those that constituted *waqf*s established by the House of Osman.[45]

As discussed in the previous chapter, the *timar* system began to experience stress within fifty years of its introduction in the Arab lands, and many of the villages that had been *timar*s in the Fertile Crescent were converted to tax farms (in the singular, *iltizam*). The tax farmers were either Ottoman military men stationed in the provincial centers in the seventeenth century or dominant rural clans like the Druze Maʿn family in the Shuf region of Lebanon or the Shi'i Harfush clan in the Biqʿa Valley. The most ambitious member of the Maʿn clan, Fakhr al-Din, controlled vast tracts of arable land throughout southern Syria and northern Palestine in the early seventeenth century.[46] By the end of the seventeenth century, the

---

[45] Baber Johansen, *The Islamic Law on Land Tax and Rent: The Peasants' Loss of Property Rights as Interpreted in the Hanafite Legal Literature of the Mamluk and Ottoman Periods* (London: Croom Helm, 1988), 98–121; Samir Seikaly, "Land Tenure in 17th Century Palestine: The Evidence from the *al-Fatawa al-Khairiyya*." In *Land and Social Transformation in the Middle East*, edited by Tarif Khalidi (Beirut: The American University in Beirut, 1984), 397–408.

[46] Jean-Paul Pascual, "The Janissaries and the Damascus Countryside at the Beginning of the Seventeenth Century According to the Archives of the City's Military Tribunal." In *Land*

government in Istanbul sought a quick infusion of cash with a scheme for selling off the right to collect taxes not for a set period, as was the practice with the *iltizam,* but for the life of the tax farmer. The name of the new unit was *malikane.* Although that name derived from the same Arabic root as the term for "private property," it did not imply a freehold for the owner. In practice, however, the tax farmers often acted as if the villages from which they collected taxes were their private fiefdoms.

There is an echo of that practice in the history of Aleppo written in the early twentieth century by Kamil al-Ghazzi. In his entry for 1693, he noted that the governor and chief qadi of Aleppo received an imperial order stating that henceforth tax farms were the private property of the holder; they could be sold for cash and could be inherited by the holder's children.[47] Although it is doubtful such an order was received as a *malikane* was not intended to be private property, Ariel Salzman's study of the *malikane* system in the southeastern Anatolian province of Diyarbakır shows that the practice there came to resemble the system described by al-Ghazzi.[48] This suggests that folk memory in Aleppo had provided a retrospective justification for what was the de facto reality of the *malikane* system, providing a legal pedigree for what had become a common practice.

The introduction of the *malikane* system provided the aʿyan of the Arab cities with the opportunity to enter on the ground floor of this potentially transformative development for the rural economy. Although the holders of *malikanes* in the Arab provinces included many in the military, their numbers were at times exceeded by men who came from the traditional elite families in most provinces of the Fertile Crescent by the middle of the eighteenth century. This pattern was at odds with that of the Balkans, where military officers continued to dominate the *malikanes* as they had their earlier incarnations as *iltizam.* The military's control of the tax farms in the rural Balkans and in much of Anatolia helps to explain the very different composition of the ayanship in those regions. Control of

Tenure and Social Transformation in the Middle East, edited by Tarif Khalidi (Beirut: The American University in Beirut, 1984), 357–65; Yasuhisa Shimizu, "Practices of Tax Farming under the Ottoman Empire in Damascus Province." In *Tax-Farm Register of Damascus Province in the Seventeenth Century: Archival and Historical Studies,* edited by Yuzo Nagata, Toru Miura, and Yasuhisa Shimizu (Tokyo: The Tokyo Bunko, 2006): 23–52.

[47] Kamil al-Ghazzi, *Nahr al-dhahab fi ta'rikh halab al-shahba,* 3 vol. (Aleppo; al-Matbaʿa al-Marwaniyya, 1923–26), vol. III, 292.

[48] Ariel Salzman, *Tocqueville in the Ottoman Empire: Rival Paths to the Modern State* (Leiden: Brill, 2004), 122–50.

*malikane*s by a few military officers facilitated the rise of regional dynasties of warlords that could challenge the authority of the state. Typically, no single family dominated the rural resources in the Arab provinces as most of the *aʿyan* families were in competition among themselves for that control. In that intense competition, the civilian elite's acquisition of their individual, smaller *malikane*s ironically helped to bind their loyalty to and intensify their identification with the state, as their economic position was only enhanced by collaborating with its representatives.[49]

It is not clear how the civilian elite displaced the military from many of the tax farms in the Fertile Crescent in the eighteenth century, although the court registers from Aleppo in the seventeenth century show an increasing participation by civilians in making loans to villagers over the course of that century. The majority of those involved in moneylending to the peasants were still from the military in the first quarter of the eighteenth century, however.[50] But by the late eighteenth century, anecdotal evidence points to the local *aʿyan* and even Christian merchant families as having made substantial loans to villagers. Additionally, the management of *waqf* property by the religious scholarly class gave the Muslim *aʿyan* additional sources of wealth with which they could invest in the new tax schemes, as well as access to the villages that they oversaw as administrators of rural *waqf*s.[51] However they came to control them, the *malikane*s provided the *aʿyan* throughout the Fertile Crescent with the economic resources to secure their social and political power.[52] Strengthening that assumption, both the ʿAzm family and the Jalilis had started off their careers as tax farmers. But competition from other prominent families in Damascus and Mosul checked either family from emerging as a full-fledged *hanedan* along the pattern established by their contemporaries in the Balkans or parts of Anatolia.

In Egypt, in contrast with the Fertile Crescent, the military retained its control of tax farms in the countryside. In particular, the reemergence of a mamluk class in Cairo was facilitated by their access to the revenues produced by rural tax farms.[53] Competition among the various mamluk households prevented the rise of a single powerful dynasty, however. Even with the predominance of mamluk tax farmers, wealth in Egypt did not

[49] Khoury, *State and Provincial Society*, 178–86.
[50] Masters, *Origins of Western Economic Dominance*, 164–75.
[51] James Reilly, "Rural Waqfs of Ottoman Damascus: Rights of Ownership, Possession and Tenancy" *Acta Orientalia* 51 (1990): 27–46.
[52] Meriwether, *The Kin Who Count*, 39–41.
[53] ʿAbd al-Rahim ʿAbd al-Rahman. *Al-Rif al-misri fi qarn al-thamin ʿashar* (Cairo: Maktabat Madbuli, 1974).

flow entirely from the villages to the cities as it did in the Fertile Crescent. In the late eighteenth century, wealthy peasants in the Nile Delta were able to gain control of some tax farms in their own villages and in neighboring ones, creating a class division in what had been a largely undifferentiated peasant class of farmers.[54] There is no indication that having neighbors in control of rents and taxes made life any easier for Egypt's peasants as rurally based landlords proved just as rapacious as those who lived in the cities. Without control of rural resources, the traditional *aʿyan* of Cairo, such as the family of the author al-Jabarti, continued to exercise moral authority but achieved little political or economic power in the eighteenth century.

The creation of the *malikane*s coincided with a trend toward the production of export crops in the western Fertile Crescent. There is, however, only anecdotal evidence to establish a direct correlation between the two as when an individual *malikaneci* (a holder of a *malikane*) would require his tenants to grow a particular crop. Olive trees had always formed an important part of the agricultural economy in the hill country of Palestine, Lebanon, and coastal Syria. Their oil and one of its by-products, soap, not only were consumed locally but were highly prized in both Istanbul and Egypt. In contrast to Egypt, whose peasants had produced cotton, rice, and indigo for export for centuries, the villages of the Syrian provinces produced some cotton but little else beyond olives and their by-products for export before the eighteenth century. Instead, the peasants were largely self-sufficient, with each village living off the produce of the land it controlled. The peasants sold whatever excess grain, vegetables, and fruit that they might produce to their near neighbors in the region's cities to raise the cash they needed to pay their taxes. That pattern of self-sufficiency largely came to an end in the eighteenth century.

With the collapse of the Iranian silk trade in the early eighteenth century, peasants began to produce silk more extensively in northern Syria and Lebanon for export to Europe, and the volume of the export of locally grown cotton began to rise as well.[55] By the mideighteenth

[54] Keneth Cuno, *The Pasha's Peasants: Land, Society, and Economy in Lower Egypt, 1740–1858* (Cambridge: Cambridge University Press, 1992), 64–99.
[55] Rhoads Murphey, "Syria's 'Underdevelopment' under Ottoman Rule: Revisiting an Old Theme in the Light of New Evidence from the Court Records of Aleppo in the Eighteenth Century." In *The Arab Lands in the Ottoman Era: Essays in Honor of Professor Caesar Farah*, edited by Jane Hathaway (Minneapolis: The University of Minnesota Press, 2009), 209–30.

century, peasants in the narrow coastal plain of northern Syria were also cultivating tobacco for export. The cultivation of both tobacco and cotton points to the interference of tax farmers in the peasants' choice of crop, as both were largely intended for export. Peasants had little access to the brokers handling that trade and would have had little incentive on their own to switch the crops that they grew. The *aʿyan*, however, were often connected to the export merchants by family ties and would have recognized the value of the new crops. Although the growth in the export trade provided an economic boon to the *aʿyan*, their participation in the rural economy of the Fertile Crescent occurred at a time when life in the countryside was in crisis.

By the middle of the eighteenth century, large tracts of land in what is today Syria and Iraq had been abandoned by their peasant cultivators. The description of abandoned plains with ruined villages was a common trope in the literature written by European travelers of the period. The Westerners used their characterization of rural decline to contrast the present with the civilization of the region in antiquity in order to highlight what they felt was the dismal state of affairs in the Ottoman Empire.[56] The travelers' descriptions of abandoned villages were not entirely the result of unfounded Orientalist stereotyping, however, as local sources document the precarious nature of rural life in the seventeenth and eighteenth centuries.

Ottoman archival records indicate that the central government was acutely aware that rural depopulation was an ongoing problem, but one that it seemed generally powerless to reverse. In 1693, the qadi of Maʿarrat al-Misrin, a large village to the west of Aleppo, requested from the governor of Aleppo that the number of taxable units (*avariz hane*) in his village be reduced from thirty-two to twenty as many villagers had moved away; villagers from Birqum came before the same chief judge in that year to say that so many of their fellow villagers had fled to the mountains that they could not pay any taxes at all.[57] In either case, the authorities could not offer any effective advice on how to stem the tide, other than to issue orders that the peasants must be returned to their native villages. Almost a century later, imperial orders to the governor of Aleppo in 1776 and 1780 noted the deleterious effects of peasant flight

---

[56] Constantine Volney, *Travels through Syria and Egypt in the Years 1783, 1784, and 1785.* English translation, 2 volumes (London: G.G. and J. Robinson, 1787), vol. II, 147.

[57] Damascus, Aleppo AS I: 75–6; 82.

and ordered the city's authorities to make all due effort to return the peasants who had settled in the city to their villages.[58]

The frequent issuance of such orders points to the low probability that anything was done to implement them. The judges in the Arab lands were extremely reluctant to compel peasants to return to their villages even when tax farmers went before the courts to seek redress for the flight of peasants from the land.[59] The net result was an even greater imbalance in the proportion of rural to urban populations than had existed in the seventeenth century. When peasants fled their villages for the cities, their motivation was sometimes a quest for security, a desire to escape rapacious tax collectors, or simply, as a group of seventy-seven Armenian males from the Sasun region of eastern Anatolia reported to the judge in Aleppo in 1661, that the fields in their home villages could no longer support them. Their families were hungry and the migrants sought a new life in the city to survive.[60]

Peasants continued to move from the countryside to the cities of the Fertile Crescent in the seventeenth and eighteenth centuries, but the dramatic growth both in population and in physical size of the Arab cities slowed after the boom years of the late sixteenth century. The reason for the net decline in population of the cities despite continued migration is tragically obvious. Endemic diseases of various strains remained prevalent in the cities of the Middle East throughout the early-modern period and periodically erupted to kill off thousands of their inhabitants. Although all segments of the population experienced the periodic pandemics, the poorer quarters that were packed with rural migrants suffered most. The sad reality was that peasants' hopes for a better life in the cities were often cut short by plague or the other diseases that stalked the cities.[61]

Peasant flight was common throughout the Ottoman Empire in the seventeenth and eighteenth centuries and not just in the Arab provinces. Among the causes was widespread drought that plagued Anatolia and the northern Fertile Crescent as a result of the "Little Ice Age." It began in the last decade of the sixteenth century and continued with varying degrees

---

[58] Hidemitsu, Kuroki, "Mobility of Non-Muslims in Mid-Nineteenth-Century Aleppo." In *The Influence of Human Mobility in Muslim Societies*, edited by Hidemitsu Kuroki (London: Kegan Paul, 2003), 126.

[59] Damascus, Aleppo sijillat, vol. III: 287; 21: 171; 45: 159; 51: 263; Aleppo AS vol. I: 100; vol. II, 141.

[60] Damascus, Aleppo sijillat vol. II: 240.

[61] Daniel Panzac, ıqMourir à Aleo au XVIIIᵉ s.ıq *RMMM* 62 (1991–4): 111–22.

of intensity throughout the seventeenth century. The drought in Anatolia helped, in turn, to create the Celali Revolt of the early seventeenth century, which disrupted rural conditions and created increased insecurity for peasant proprietors as roving bands of armed men plundered their villages.[62] Bandit gangs were also a constant threat. Firearms proliferated in the seventeenth century throughout the empire and desperate peasants sought relief from poverty by taking up a life of crime. Once they had joined a band of outlaws, the easiest targets were other villagers.

THE TRIBAL FRONTIER

In addition to bandits and oppressive tax collectors, peasant farmers in the Fertile Crescent faced the challenges created by the incursion of pastoralist raiders. These were predominantly Bedouins, but in the northern reaches of the Fertile Crescent, Turkmens and Kurds could also add to the rural mayhem. Muhammad al-Makki (d. 1722?), the early eighteenth-century chronicler of Homs, included accounts of raids by all three tribal peoples on the villages in the vicinity of Homs, as well as actual attacks mounted by the Bedouins on the city itself. Homs, although walled, did not have a large garrison of its own, being dependent on that commanded by the governor of Tripoli (Lebanon). As such, it was more vulnerable to Bedouin attack than Syria's larger cities. But even the inhabitants of Aleppo to the north were sometimes threatened by attack by Bedouins or Kurds, although an actual onslaught never materialized.[63]

Disorder along the desert frontier was a sign of the weakening authority of the central government. It is wrong to say, however, that there was always strife between the pastoralists and the settled farmers, as in times when the state had the resources to police the frontier it was quiet and the relationship between the "desert and the sown" was symbiotic. The pastoralists provided the expertise and the animals that were necessary for the caravan trade that linked the region's cities: Bedouins with their camels for the desert crossings, Turkmens and Kurds with their mules and donkeys for the routes heading into the Anatolian highlands. The peasant farmers provided the tribes with grain in return for meat and animal by-products such as wool, rugs, and hides. In some cases, a village in the

---

[62] Mustafa Akdağ, "Celali İsyanlarında Büyük Kaçgun" *Tarih Araştırmaları Dergisi* 2 (1964): 1–49; Polonyalı Simeon, *Polonyalı Simeon'un Seyahatnamesi*, translated by Hrand Andreasyan (Istanbul: İstanbul Edebiyat Fakültesi Yayınları, 1964), 93.

[63] al-Ghazzi, *Nahr al-dhahab*, III, 296; London, PRO, SP 105/118: 186, letter dated January 25, 1750.

steppe lands bordering the desert might have both pastoralists and farmers living within it. Even in those villages that did not house both, there was frequent intermarriage between the peasants and the pastoralists. The order produced by that balance between the two ecologies of production broke down, however, when tribal leaders felt that they could raid with impunity rather than trade. Raiding was the easier path to follow if there were few repercussions for doing so. It also invoked the warrior ethos that most of the tribes shared. A good raid was the stuff of poems and songs that could be passed down from one generation to the next.

For the Ottoman officials posted in the cities of the Fertile Crescent, Bedouins were emblematic of the strangeness of the region, and, indeed, they supplied the region with a possible name, *Arabistan*, "the country of the Bedouins." Most Ottomans, assigned to the Arab provinces only for short terms of office, never managed to understand them fully. There were a few notable exceptions, most notably the historian Naima (d. 1716). But he was born and raised in Aleppo, where his father was the janissary commander.[64] Naima's chronicle written in Ottoman Turkish displays a sophisticated understanding of tribal politics that is rare and largely absent even in the chronicles written in Arabic.[65] Control of the Bedouins required a deep knowledge of the various tribes' histories and internal clan politics in order to play off one faction against another. When political manipulation failed, it was also useful on occasion for the central treasury to provide a large infusion of cash to buy the tribes' goodwill. There were few other options. The tribes had mobility and unmatched knowledge of the terrain that they controlled, as well as the way to survive in an extremely hostile physical environment. Ottoman cavalry was no match in either speed or endurance for tribal warriors mounted on camels. For the troops faced with that tactical disadvantage, it was not until the arrival of the breech-loading rifle in the nineteenth century that the Bedouins' stranglehold over the rural areas was finally broken.

From the time of the conquest of the Arab lands, the Ottomans displayed two different options as to how to approach the Bedouin tribes. When they occupied Damascus, the Ottomans confirmed on the head of the clan of Hayar, which was a subset of the larger tribe of the Fadl, the title of *amir al-ʿArab* (commander of the Bedouins) in the form of a *timar*. The granting of that title and yearly payment to the paramount shaykh were simply following a Mamluk practice that the Ottomans continued

[64] Lewis Thomas, *A Study of Naima*, edited by Norman Itzkowitz (New York: New York University Press, 1972).
[65] Mustafa Naima, *Tarih-i Naima*, 6 vols. (Istanbul, Matbaʾa-yı Amire: 1864–66).

throughout the sixteenth and seventeenth centuries. In return, the clan was supposed to ensure the safety of communications across the Syrian Desert to Iraq and, more importantly, to provide the security for the annual hajj caravan.[66] To the north, the Mamluk regime had also granted the title of *amir al-ʿArab* to the shaykh of the Mawali tribe to buy peace in the desert between Aleppo and the Euphrates River and in the villages along the caravan route that followed the Euphrates River downstream to a point opposite Baghdad, on the nearby Tigris River. Rejecting that policy, however, the Ottoman government opted for a military solution in the northern Syrian Desert and refused payment to the Bedouins.

The result was a tactical disaster as the Mawali raided the northern desert with impunity. By 1574, the Ottomans conceded that bribery was the better part of valor. After that date, the sultan granted the head of the Mawali confederation a ceremonial plume from which he took his title, the Abu Risha (Father, or Possessor, of the Feather), and a yearly stipend of 6,000 Venetian ducats a year.[67] An agreement between the current Abu Risha and the governor of Aleppo in 1735 enumerated the duties of the office. He was to protect peasants and travelers from other Bedouins and bandits along the Euphrates from Bira to Ridwaniyya (today in Iraq), from which a short overland portage could reach Baghdad, and to follow all orders sent to him by the sultan.[68] Although there was an occasional lapse in the peace, as in 1644, when the garrison of Aleppo was nearly annihilated by Assaf Abu Risha after a misunderstanding, the Mawali were able to secure the desert route between Iraq and Syria for most of the seventeenth century.[69]

The fragile peace in the desert began to collapse toward the end of the seventeenth century as the ʿAnaza confederation of tribes moved out of the Najd in the central Arabian Peninsula into the Syrian Desert. It is not clear what set off the migration. Periodic mass migrations of tribes out of Arabia had occurred across millennia, but this wave may have been tied to the drought of the "Little Ice Age" that contributed to the desiccation of the steppe lands bordering the Syrian Desert. With control of the Syrian Desert in flux, the Mawali continued to protect the trade routes in northern Syria, but increasingly they left the peasant cultivators in the Euphrates Valley to their own devices.[70]

[66] Bakhit, *Ottoman Province of Damascus*, 200–4.
[67] Longrigg, *Four Centuries of Modern Iraq*, 39.
[68] Damascus, Aleppo sijillat, vol. XLV, 71.
[69] Naima, *Tarih*, vol. IV, 104–10.
[70] Damascus, Aleppo sijillat, vol. LXXVIII, 19.

Farther south, however, the Ottomans' Bedouin allies proved ineffective in their role as protectors of the hajj caravans, and at times, they even
joined in the plunder. Without effective protection, the ⁽Anaza were able
to mount a number of devastating raids, most notably in 1691, 1711, and
1757, in which thousands of pilgrims lost their property and their lives.[71]
Ibrahim al-Khiyari, traveling by caravan from Medina to Damascus in
1669, noted that scouts reported Bedouins were tracking the column.
The travelers spent a fearful night huddled in an abandoned caravansary
expecting an assault at any time. Luckily for the travelers, janissaries,
mounted on horseback, arrived at dawn from Damascus and escorted
them to safety.[72] The unsettled conditions along the desert frontier in
the eighteenth century seem to have been one of the key reasons that the
sultans consented to the long reign of the ⁽Azm family in Damascus as it
was hoped that with their local knowledge they might secure the province from Bedouin raiders.

A separate migration sent the Shammar and the Banu Tamim tribes
from the Najd into southern and central Iraq in the late seventeenth century. There, they competed with the already established tribes: the Bani
Lam, Fatlah, Muntafiq, and Khaza'il, among others. The impact and the
influence of the Bedouin in the rural areas were extreme. Faced with the
option of flight or seeking to become the clients of a dominant tribe,
the peasants chose the latter course of action. The result was a widespread tribalization of the peasant population. By the nineteenth century,
most peasants in central and southern Iraq identified with one or another
Bedouin tribe and boasted lineages that traced back to Arabia, even if such
claims were historically suspect.[73] In what would become Syria, by contrast, tribal affiliation was common only among the cultivators along the
Euphrates River, the region most exposed to Bedouin raids.[74] Elsewhere,
peasants simply abandoned their fields and moved to the hills where they
could find some level of natural defense against Bedouin predators.

The Ottoman response to the growing depopulation of the Euphrates
River valley was to settle Turkmen pastoralists along its banks. Sultan
Ahmed II (1691–5) ordered that the İlbeklü and the Bekirli Turkmens
be given lands that had been abandoned by their peasant proprietors.

[71] Barbir, *Ottoman Rule in Damascus*, 200–1.
[72] al-Khiyari, *Tuhfat al-udaba*, vol. I, 50–1.
[73] Hanna Batatu, *The Old Social Classes and the Revolutionary Movements of Iraq*
    (Princeton, NJ: Princeton University Press, 1978), 63–86.
[74] Hanna Batatu, *Syria's Peasantry, the Descendants of Its Lesser Rural Notables, and Their
    Politics* (Princeton, NJ: Princeton University Press, 1999), 22.

These would be exempt from taxes for thirty-two years in return for the Turkmens' providing security for caravans passing through that territory.[75] The plan proved ineffective, however. The İlbeklü, who had been banished from their original home near Maraş in southern Anatolia as a result of banditry, reverted to their old ways. Other tribes, adapting poorly to the desert climate, sought to return to the mountains of Anatolia. Further attempts to settle Turkmens in the abandoned lands around Homs and Hama also failed.[76] In the eyes of Muhammad al-Makki of Homs, the Turkmens were as much of a problem, and every bit as destructive, as the Bedouins whom they were meant to control.[77]

When looking across the landscape of the Fertile Crescent in the early-modern period, European travelers were struck by empty spaces. Those who ventured into the hills and mountains surrounding the lowlands were equally impressed by the industriousness and ingenuity of the peasantry there.[78] In the hills, local feudal lords could be as rapacious as any on the plains, but when faced with the choice of abusive landlords or Bedouins, the peasants in Syria and northern Iraq chose the security of the uplands. Although there were multiple causes for the depopulation of the countryside, the Ottomans' inability to control the Bedouins and protect the peasants was clearly one of them. A comparison with Egypt provides a telling counterexample.

Bedouins were a problem in Egypt as well, but the mamluks who commanded the provincial military forces often established economic ties to the tribes and, should those fail, were not above using brutal tactics against them. A combination of the threat of military retaliation and the incentive of bribes generally kept the peace. The knowledge of political rivalries in the desert that the mamluk emirs possessed proved invaluable, but the density of population in the Nile Valley and Delta also helped. Peasants who were living in close proximity to their neighbors could band together and more effectively resist the tribes than could those in the widely scattered villages in the steppe lands of the Fertile Crescent.[79] While most of the villages registered in Egypt in the sixteenth century

---

[75] Damascus, Aleppo sijillat vol. LIV, 101; Aleppo AS vol. I, 623.

[76] Yusuf Halaçoğlu, *XVIII. Yüzyılda Osmanlı İmparatorluğu'nun İskân Siyaseti ve Aşiretlerin Yerleştirilmesi* (Istanbul: Türk Tarih Kurumu, 1988), 136–40.

[77] Muhammad al-Makki, *Ta'rikh hims* (Damascus: Institut Français de Damas, 1987), 39, 43–56, 175–8.

[78] John Burckhardt, *Travels in Syria and the Holy Land* (London: John Murray, 1822), 178; Bowring, *Report of the Commercial Statistics*, 8.

[79] Mikhail, *Nature and Empire*, 79–81.

were still there at the end of the eighteenth century, large tracts of Syria and Iraq were abandoned. As a result, agriculture production in the Fertile Crescent in the eighteenth century was increasingly confined to the rich farmlands surrounding the region's major cities that could be protected by their garrisons or in the mountains and hills along the Mediterranean coast and in northern Iraq.

CONCLUSION: WAS THERE AN OTTOMAN ECONOMY?

The conquest of the Arab lands by the Ottomans coincided with the apogee of the empire's military power and economic prosperity. There is little question that the region prospered under the sultans' stewardship in the first century of Ottoman rule. Corruption had been endemic with the Mamluk emirs, and the Arab chroniclers seem to agree that the Ottomans provided a modicum of good government that encouraged trade and protected the peasantry from abuse. But the "golden age" was perhaps as much a product of good fortune as good governance. The growth of new villages in formerly abandoned lands in the Fertile Crescent that has been documented by archaeology and research in the Ottoman archives may have been a product of climate change as the arrival of the Ottomans coincided with a period of wetter winters that would have created the possibility of more irrigation projects.[80] The fact that under the *pax ottomana* the Euphrates Valley was no longer a borderland between warring Muslim states, however, also contributed to the general prosperity the region experienced in the sixteenth century.

   In crediting the Ottoman regime for the improvements, the Arab chroniclers noted that the state placed a high priority on establishing order both in the cities and along the caravan routes. The territory of most of the Arab provinces was carefully surveyed. Every province received a code of laws that asserted what the level of taxation on various commodities was to be and what kinds of punishments would be inflicted on wrongdoers. Justice was understood by the Ottomans to be the wellspring of taxes, which in turn allowed the state to function. If the system were to continue, then all aspects of administration had to be in balance. A good indication of that desire for justice is the empowerment by the Ottoman state of the Muslim courts beyond issues of family law to include all

---

[80] Wolf-Dieter Hütteroth, "Ecology of the Ottoman lands." In *The Cambridge History of Turkey*. Vol. 3. *The Later Ottoman Empire, 1603–1839*, edited by Suraiya Faroqhi (Cambridge: Cambridge University Press 2006), 18–43.

economic transactions and the enforcement of guild regulations. The qadis served as the crucial intermediaries between the sultan's subjects living in the Arab cities and their ruler in Istanbul. Lacking a notary system, which was common in the contemporary Christian Mediterranean lands, the Ottoman government further empowered the scribes at the Muslim courts with many of those same functions. This led merchants to register contracts and to bring charges against those who did not fulfill them in the Muslim courts. Without banks, lenders registered their loans at court and the courts adjudicated their repayment.

Although there now seems little reason to suspect that the Ottoman state imposed the guild system on the craft and service workers in the Arab cities, workers perceived an advantage in organizing themselves into guilds for their own protection and as a means to present a common front to the authorities. The guilds may or may not have predated the arrival of the Ottomans in the Mamluk territories, but they clearly proliferated after 1516–17 with workers in various trades deciding that they too would benefit from forming a guild. The court records of Aleppo, Damascus, Cairo, and Jerusalem establish that there was an ongoing process of new guild formation over the early Ottoman centuries as workers saw collective bargaining as in their best interests. The state system of taxation encouraged the process, but the state clearly did not impose guilds on unwilling workers. Rather, guilds became an integral part of the economy in every city, and by 1800, most male craftsmen and laborers seem to have belonged to a guild.

There were two ideological underpinnings of the Ottoman state's policies toward the economy. First, there was the Muslim principle of "commanding right and forbidding wrong" upon which Muslim scholars had devoted ink and paper for centuries. Balanced against those principles was the overriding desire to increase revenues or at least not to allow a reduction in them. In the first century of Ottoman rule in the Arab lands, the level of security and the accompanying prosperity meant that the two potentially competing aims were in balance and the sultan could enjoy both increased revenues and the approbation of his subjects that he was dispensing justice. As the economic position of the empire began to change for the worse in the seventeenth century, however, the state's bureaucrats were pushed to seek alternative sources of revenue to meet the immediate demands for cash. In that context, tax farming, which was an established fiscal tradition in the Muslim states that had predated the Ottomans, became more widespread. The handing over of tax collection to local personalities allowed for the emergence of powerful *aʿyan* families throughout the empire but also imposed greater burdens on both peasants and urban guildsmen. Caught between justice and the need for revenue, the state imposed laws such as those that required peasants to return to villages from which they had fled or created extra taxes on guilds that were seeking to meet the competition created by imports.

The disjuncture between the ideal of Islamic governance and economic realities on the ground created dilemmas for the judges in the provincial centers. Should they continue to "forbid wrong" even if it meant opposing their sultan? The tension in the sultan's court between the two conflicting desires was replicated in the provinces, where judges were sometimes required to choose between their sense of what actions were just and the necessity to obey their sultan. The tension was never completely resolved in either venue, but its existence helps us to understand the sometimes very contradictory rulings emanating from the capital and local responses to them in the sharia courts. Of course, bribes offered by one of the parties involved in a case at court could also account for a contradictory ruling from a judge.

Although the economy was firmly based in Islamic precedents, as well as in the secular models expropriated from the Byzantine and Sasanian Empires, the mania for regulation and control seems to be distinctly Ottoman in its inspiration. Thanks in large part to that desire for local knowledge, the Ottoman sultans maintained a bureaucracy that produced the records that have made possible our understanding of how that economy functioned. The bureaucrats in the capital were innately conservative in their approach toward economic developments, however. That meant that they usually missed opportunities for capitalizing on change in their desire to preserve already existing revenues. Their conservatism helped to preserve the outward appearance that the sultan was in control of his territories even as global market forces were undermining his autonomy. Throughout the eighteenth century that façade of empire stood even as many of its supports were weakening. The nineteenth century would witness its virtual collapse.

4

A World of Scholars and Saints

Intellectual Life in the Ottoman Arab Lands

Ibrahim al-Khiyari, a scholar from Medina, set out for Istanbul in 1669 following the Sultan's Road, as the pilgrimage route from Üsküdar to Mecca was called. He left for posterity a journal of his year-long adventure that led him to Bulgaria and an audience with Sultan Mehmed IV (1648–87) and then back again to Arabia by way of Cairo.[1] Although his account lacks the wealth of local color found in the more widely known travelogue of his contemporary Evliya Çelebi, he meticulously recorded those who hosted them along the way. They included Ottoman officials who had served in the Hejaz and religious scholars whom the author had met in his native city. Choosing not to travel, Muhammad ibn Kannan began a chronicle in Damascus at the end of the seventeenth century in which he noted, among other things, the Muslim scholars who stopped in his city while on the hajj. The correspondence of ibn Kannan's contemporary, ʿAbd al-Ghani al-Nabulusi (d. 1731), with scholars in Cairo, Medina, Van, Istanbul, Edirne, Tekirdağ in Thrace, and Sombor in Serbia points to a network of correspondence across the empire.[2] Such informal and often personal contacts created a network for the exchange of ideas on a variety of topics. As most of the scholarship produced by the empire's ulama was in Arabic, regardless of the language they spoke at home, Arabic-speaking scholars, most of whom

---

[1] al-Khiyari, *Tuhfat al-udaba*.
[2] ʿAbd al-Ghani al-Nabulusi, *Wasa'il al-tahqiq wa rasa'il al-tawfiq*, edited by Samer Akkach and published under the title *Letters of a Sufi Scholar: The Correspondence of ʿAbd al-Ghani al-Nabulusi (1641–1731)* (Leiden: Brill, 2010).

knew no Turkish, were active participants in an ongoing dialogue across the empire.[3]

Far-flung connections were not confined to the sultan's Sunni Muslim subjects alone. Pilgrimage to, or alternatively prolonged residence in, the holy cities of Karbala and Najaf in Iraq linked Shi'i Muslim scholars in the Ottoman Empire with their coreligionists in Iran and the Indian subcontinent. Moving in the opposite direction, Shi'i students from Lebanon and Iraq studied in the seminaries in Qom in Iran. Orthodox Christian priests and monks kept in contact with the wider world of their coreligionists through pilgrimage to Jerusalem, missions to the patriarchal see in Istanbul, or residence in monasteries on the holy mountains of Sinai and Athos.[4] Catholics of various rites could envision even wider geographical horizons, as the travel narrative of the Chaldean priest Elias al-Musili to Spanish America in the seventeenth century attests.[5] Among the Jews of the Arab provinces, Jerusalem, Safed, and Baghdad were renowned centers of learning, and they provided a haven for scholars from beyond the borders of the empire.

The scholarly elites in the Arab lands, whatever their religious community, did not live in isolation. Intellectual contact among scholars across communal lines existed, but most networks of communication lay largely within a scholar's own religious community. An illustration of this is provided in the chronicle of Dimitri ʿAbbud, a Melkite Catholic merchant in Aleppo. Embedded in the events he recorded as occurring in 1789 is a lengthy promonarchist account of the French Revolution that ʿAbbud informs his readers had come to him from Roman Catholic priests visiting his native city.[6] The communal nature of the lines for the transmission of knowledge is not surprising as the majority of those who made up the relatively small literate class that was present in the early-modern period were members of the Muslim scholarly class, Christian clergy, or Jewish rabbis.

Literacy and a love of books were not confined to the religious classes alone, however, as the research of Nelly Hanna has demonstrated.[7] In

---

[3] Khaled El-Rouayheb, "Opening the Gate of Verification: The Forgotten Arab-Islamic Florescence of the 17th Century" *IJMES* 38 (2006): 263–81.

[4] Mikha'il Burayk al-Dimashqi, *Ta'rikh al-sham, 1720–1782,* edited by Qustantin al-Basha (Harissa, Lebanon: Matbaʿat Qadis Bulus, 1930), 29.

[5] Elias al-Musili, *An Arab's Journey to Colonial Spanish America: The Travels of Elias al-Musili in the Seventeenth Century,* translated and edited by Caesar Farah (Syracuse: State University of New York Press, 2003).

[6] ʿAbbud, *al-Murtadd,* 176–81.

[7] Hanna, *In Praise of Books,* 50–103.

support of her characterization, there is the anecdotal example found in the registration of the estate of an Ottoman soldier (*jundi sultani*) named Salim Bek ibn Hajj Yusuf who died in Aleppo in 1679. Among his possessions were books – the actual number was not provided – including works of jurisprudence, grammar, and *hadith* (the sayings and traditions of the Prophet Muhammad) worth 130 *ghurush*, a valuation that was more than that of his female slave, horse, and mule combined.[8] All of the other men whose estates were listed in that same register and who owned books were, however, members of the ulama. As such, it is hard to know how representative Salim Bek was. Clearly, not all of those who were literate and valued books belonged in the ranks of the religious scholarly classes, but they were the authors of the majority of the works that survived and have shaped how we view the early Ottoman centuries in the Arab lands.

The preeminent role that the ulama had in creating the historical record has perhaps influenced historians of the period to overemphasize the role that religion played in the Ottoman past at the expense of other social markers such as class or ethnicity. There can be little question, however, that religion gave structure and meaning to those who inhabited the Arab provinces in the Ottoman centuries and informed their culture. Religious law mandated their customary behavior, and a religious worldview rendered the vicissitudes of life comprehensible and perhaps even meaningful. The inhabitants of the Ottoman Empire were not unique in that regard, as a similar claim could be made about most societies around the globe in the early modern period.[9] Beyond institutionalized religion, for which the scholars served as its guardians, most of the inhabitants of the region believed in a host of saints (*wali*, plural *awliya*), living and dead, who inhabited or could communicate with an unseen world that coexisted with the physical world of everyday concerns and tribulations.

The boundaries between the two sources of religious authority, scholars and saints, were permeable. Until the eighteenth century, most religious scholars in both the Sunni and Shi'i Muslim traditions believed that the study of law and mysticism were valid scholarly endeavors, and each had to be understood in its own terms. Religious law constituted the "outer" (*zahir*) truth that governed the smooth functioning of family, society, and the state. But the "inner" (*batin*) truth of mystic knowledge was the key

---

[8] Damascus, Aleppo sijillat XXXIII: 147–9.
[9] Raymond Gillespie, *Devoted People: Belief and Religion in Early Modern Ireland* (Manchester, UK: Manchester University Press, 1997).

to each individual's personal relationship to God. For Jewish scholars, a parallel understanding allowed students of the Halakha (religious law) and Zohar (mysticism) to coexist easily in a spectrum of knowledge that ran from a system of laws minutely governing the mundane to works that invoked the divinely transcendent. In all the religious traditions practiced in the empire, the inner and outer truths were not mutually exclusive, and one individual could have expertise in both. For the believer, it was possible to appeal to whichever tradition and way of knowing offered a solution to the particular problem at hand, without any apparent contradiction. Furthermore, in the realm of the unseen, the boundaries between religious communities, maintained by the guardians of the "outer" truth, collapsed as Muslims, Christians, and Jews sought the intercession of each other's saints and celebrated their feast days ecumenically.

THE SCHOLARS

The intellectuals of Muslim Arab society in the early modern period were its religious scholars. They were its guardians against the abuse of political authority, the preservers of religious tradition, and both the repository and producers of its "high" culture. It was not an exclusively male club. Women were included in the ranks of the learned, and some were respected sufficiently for their legal knowledge or poetry by their male contemporaries to be included in the compendia of notable persons that were popular in the Ottoman Arab lands.[10] Segregated gender roles, however, prevented women from assuming positions of responsibility in the public sphere. Without exception, male scholars interpreted and administered the law. Some women who appeared at court may have been versed in the law, but custom compelled them to let male relatives or agents speak in their place.

In theory, the ranks of the learned formed an egalitarian club as entrance was based on formal education in a madrasa, or religious school, and these were heavily subsidized by *waqf*s, pious endowments. As a result, the schools were open even to those without financial means. In reality, a small number of scholarly families dominated the ranks of the leading ulama in every Ottoman Arab city. There was room for an occasional prodigy from modest or rural origins to break their monopoly

[10] ibn al-Hanbali included the biographies of several women scholars,. *Durr al-habab*, vol. I, 39, 403–6, vol. II: 21–2.

of knowledge and become a member of the intellectual elite, thereby founding his own august lineage. These were the exceptions to the general rule of social stratification among the ranks of the learned, however. Discrimination on the basis of social class was not condoned by Islam's legal traditions, except in the case of eligibility for marriage partners, but it is evident in the literary sources that such social distinctions existed and mattered. It was easier for a merchant or a soldier with ambition and good fortune to rise to Arab society's elite than for a scholar without connections.

The ulama constituted a religious class, but their education included exposure to the classics of Arabic secular literature, which they called the "Arab sciences" (history, grammar, and rhetoric), as opposed to "religious sciences" (Qur'an, the traditions of the Prophet, and jurisprudence). They also read, recited, and composed poetry. The continuation of a literary culture in Arabic stretching back to a perceived golden age in the Abbasid period (750–1258) was a source of pride for the Arabic-speaking ulama. This contrasted to cultural developments that were occurring elsewhere in the Middle East as vernacular languages adapted to the Arabic script and reemerged as the literary language of the non-Arab Muslim elites. Acknowledging that reality, it is possible to suggest a bifurcation of the Middle East into an Arabic-speaking zone and one where Persian was the predominant language of secular literature, that is, poetry, history, and political commentary, following the composition of the Persian-language epic, the *Shahnamah*, around 1000 C.E. The two zones could be demarcated geographically by mountain ranges, with the Taurus Mountains forming the northern limit of the Arabic zone and the Zagros Mountains its eastern boundary.

With the rise of the Ottoman state, Persian gave way to Ottoman Turkish as the primary language of the literate classes in Anatolia, and it spread with the conquests into the Balkans. Nonetheless, Persian remained in vogue in the Ottoman court well into the sixteenth century. The use of Persian as the language of high culture linked the various imperial courts of the Muslim lands, Ottoman, Safavi, Mughal, and Uzbek, and provided the linguistic medium through which ideas and artists could circulate easily from one court to another. In most of the Fertile Crescent, Arabia, Egypt, North Africa, and al-Andalus (Muslim Spain), however, Arabic continued to serve as both the vernacular and the language of culture for the majority of the inhabitants. That reality did not constitute a barrier to the circulation of ideas, but it meant that works composed in Persian were often slow to find reception among the Arabic-speaking intellectual class.[11] That was perhaps not entirely a good thing.

While cultural production in Persian demonstrated great creativity between 1258 and 1500, authors writing in Arabic tended to mimic, usually poorly, the earlier classics. There were a few exceptions, most notably the historian ibn Khaldun, but generally the production of both literary and scientific works in Arabic was in decline after 1258. That trend toward mediocrity only accelerated in the subsequent Ottoman centuries. As a result, most modern scholars of Arabic literature dismiss the literary works produced in the Ottoman Arab lands as a pale reflection of what had preceded them in a "golden age" of Islamic culture.[12] On a purely abstract level of literary aesthetics, such criticism is valid. But the social context of that production should also be understood to be fair to the authors who produced works that are easily critiqued as pedantic and lacking in creative verve.

The authors who produced the Arabic-language "classics" of the Abbasid age were typically the recipients of lavish court patronage and sponsorship. The same held true for those who chose to compose their works in the neo-Persian that emerged in the eleventh century. Patronage of literature composed in Arabic continued sporadically with the establishment of the Mamluk court in Cairo, but as most sultans' command of Arabic was limited, there were few who could recognize and reward true literary brilliance. With the arrival of the Ottomans in Damascus and Cairo, even a limited court patronage withdrew from those cities. This was symbolically represented by the actual deportation of artisans from Cairo to Istanbul, ordered by Sultan Selim in 1517.[13] As they no longer housed the courts of sultans or caliphs, Cairo, Damascus, and Baghdad were reduced by the shift of political power northward to being mere provincial capitals. There were few opportunities after 1517 for patronage of the arts in the governors' sarays.

Rather than writing under the sponsorship of the politically powerful, poets and scholars in the Ottoman Arab lands composed verse, chronicles, and religious commentaries for their friends and family, as well as for the small circle of scholars in their community. In the absence

[11] For examples of works in Persian translated into Arabic, see El-Rouayheb, "Opening the Gate of Verification," cited above in note 3.
[12] See the various contributions in *The Cambridge History of Arabic Literature: Arabic Literature in the Post-Classical Period*, edited by Roger Allen and D. S. Richards (Cambridge: Cambridge University Press, 2006).
[13] ibn Abi Surur, *al-Tuhfa al-bahiyya*, 93.

of consistent patronage that might have encouraged creativity, literary production, especially of poetry, was left largely to the amateurs. Poetry was an avocation, which, judging by the poems ascribed to all manner of elite persons contained in the biographical dictionaries, almost everyone tried his or her hand at composing at some point. The recitation of spontaneously composed poetry was viewed as a social skill that demonstrated the composer's erudition. Nearly half of the three-volume travel account of Ibrahim al-Khiyari, for example, is taken up by praise poems he composed for his hosts or those that they, in turn, offered to him. With everybody a poet, truly original poetry seems to have been lost in the din of competing couplets.

Perhaps the literary value of those poems should be irrelevant to the historian, as their cultural significance should not be dismissed solely on aesthetic grounds. The survival of Classical Arabic as a literary language through the Ottoman period, represented by such poems, the chronicles, and biographical dictionaries, formed the basis of the language's literary revival in the nineteenth century. It also reminds us that the main reason that the Ottoman Arab provinces were distinct from the rest of the empire was that the dominant political and cultural language in them was, in fact, Arabic and not Ottoman Turkish. Imperial decrees were composed in the latter language, but the region's religious courts functioned in Arabic. We must assume that much of the business in the governors' palaces was carried out in that language as well, through the service of the interpreters who were omnipresent in all contemporary accounts of the provincial *divan*s.

Despite the ulama's pride in their cultural patrimony, Arab culture did not survive in a linguistic bubble as Sunni Arab religious scholars were open to intellectual influences emanating from Istanbul. The father of ᶜAbd al-Ghani al-Nabulusi studied in Istanbul before beginning a career as teacher in the school established by Sultan Selim in the Salihiyya Quarter of Damascus.[14] He was not alone in the route he chose to pursue knowledge. Approximately half of the 187 men who have been identified as being the leading Hanafi scholars in eighteenth-century Syria studied in Istanbul at some point in their careers. Those following in the Shafiᶜi School (60) generally preferred Cairo as the center of their intellectual world.[15]

---

[14] ᶜAbd al-Ghani al-Nabulusi, *al-Haqiqa wa al-majaz fi rihlat bilad al-sham wa misr wa al-hijaz* (Damascus: Dar al-Maᶜarifa, 1989), 49–50.

[15] Rafeq, "Relations between the Syrian ᶜulama and the Ottoman State," 76.

Intellectual differences among the ulama more often arose not from where they had studied but from the understanding of the nature of Islam they favored. Although there was a shared literary canon in the Arab lands, Muslim intellectuals could hold a diversity of opinions concerning it. In the region stretching from Algiers to Baghdad and south to Mecca, exponents of many differing Muslim intellectual currents, ranging from the theosophy of Muhiy al-Din ibn al-ʿArabi (d. 1240) to the text-based Qur'anic literalism of Taqi al-Din ibn Taymiyya (d. 1328), corresponded with and disputed one another. As those two influential scholars had lived and were buried in Damascus, their legacies were particularly well represented in that city, with often heated debates between the adherents of the two very different schools of thought. When there were disagreements among the scholars, however, the same shared texts were invoked and similar styles of rhetoric for disputation and proof were employed. The first three centuries of Ottoman rule produced neither a disruption in the ways by which knowledge was acquired or disseminated, nor any radical change in the cannon of received wisdom. That continuity was created, in part, by the relatively small size of the educated class and the similarity of its education.

The training of the Arabic-speaking Sunni elite was the responsibility of the network of schools, madrasas, that could be found in every major city in the region. The schools' origins lay in the eleventh century, when the proponents of the Sunni and Shi'i traditions competed with each other to establish their hegemony over both Muslim dogma and education. The Shi'i Fatimid dynasty established a school attached to the newly constructed al-Azhar mosque in Cairo in 969 to refine and propagate the Ismaili Shia doctrine. To counter the growing popularity of various Shi'i doctrines in the eleventh century, the Seljuk minister Nizam al-Mulk (d. 1092) endowed a college, the Nizamiyya, in Baghdad in 1067 to produce Sunni scholars to preserve and spread his view of orthodoxy. Other Sunni political leaders followed his lead. By 1500, every Muslim city had at least one, if not several, religious schools. Cairo was said to have had more than twenty major madrasas, each with more than a hundred students, in the eighteenth century. Damascus in that same century had at least ten such institutions with as many as sixty-five schools offering varying levels of instruction.[16]

---

[16] Steve Tamari, "Ottoman *Madrasa*s: The Multiple Lives of Educational Institutions in Eighteenth-Century Syria" *Journal of Early Modern History* 5 (2001): 99–127.

The Ottoman sultans and governors continued the practice of building and endowing religious schools in the principal cities of the Arab provinces. Sultan Süleyman founded a madrasa attached to the mosque that he commissioned the architect Sinan to design in Damascus in 1554; a grand vizier and former governor of Aleppo, Hüsrev Pasha, founded a major mosque and madrasa complex (known locally as the Khusrawiyya) in Aleppo, which was completed in 1546. There was a significant change in the Ottoman period from the practices of the earlier Muslim rulers, however. Beyond building the schools, the Ottoman state oversaw an imperial madrasa system that sought to standardize the curriculum taught in the schools, to appoint those who would teach in them, and to provide their salaries. These schools created a cadre of religious scholars who, once certified with an *ecazet* (diploma), filled the ranks of the state's religious bureaucracy as judges and clerks. At the top of this educational system was the Süleymaniye Madrasa in Istanbul, attached to the mosque commissioned by Sultan Süleyman and on whose grounds were his tomb (*türbe*) and that of his wife, Hürrem Sultan. For reasons that are not clear, the system of government-controlled madrasas was not extended to the Arab provinces. The Khusrawiyya Madrasa in Aleppo and the Sulaymaniyya in Damascus followed a curriculum closely influenced by the Ottoman madrasa system, but neither was officially designated as belonging to the imperial network of religious schools. Other schools in the region followed their own traditions and were seemingly little influenced by what was happening in the state-run madrasa system to the north.

The paramount institution of Muslim learning in the Arab lands in the Ottoman centuries was al-Azhar in Cairo. Although founded as a center of Shi'i learning, by the thirteenth century it was a major center of Sunni scholarship. During the Ottoman period, al-Azhar continued to grow and attract students from across the Arabic-speaking lands, as well as from Muslim communities in Africa and Anatolia. It distinguished itself from the schools within the official network of state-sponsored madrasas by continuing to give equal space in its classrooms and faculty to those who taught according to the Shafiʿi tradition. The Maliki and Hanbali schools were also represented in the curriculum. Ibrahim al-Khiyari visited both Cairo and Istanbul and praised the level of erudition he found in each, which he extolled in lengthy poems. Nonetheless, he wrote that the scholars of al-Azhar were the equal of, if not superior to, those of the Süleymaniye in Istanbul. For him the wisdom of the Ottomans, although profound, could not compete with the eloquence of those scholars who spoke in the Prophet's own tongue, which was the language of paradise.[17]

SUFIS AND THE CULT OF IBN AL-ᶜARABI

At the time of the Ottoman conquest, mystical, or Sufi, doctrines and practices were ubiquitous in the lives of Sunni Muslims living in the Mamluk-controlled territories. When Sultan al-Ghawri marched north toward his fateful confrontation with Sultan Selim on the plain of Marj Dabiq, he was accompanied by al-Mutawakkil, the last in the line of Abbasid caliphs as well as the chief judge of each of the four Sunni *madhhabs*. But he was also accompanied by the heads of the Sufi order of Ahmad al-Badawi and that of the Rifaᶜiyya, and the Qadiriyya, which were at the time the most popular Sufi orders in Egypt.[18] Undoubtedly, Sultan Selim had representatives of the Bektaşi order, popular with his janissary forces, and of the Mevlevi order, which served as the "official" court order of the dynasty at his side. Both regimes sought to bolster their legitimacy through state sponsorship of certain orders. They were also keenly aware that Sufi orders outside the system of state patronage had to be monitored for potentially subversive activity.

The Sufi orders (singular, *tariqa*) were both religious and social phenomena. If the biographical dictionaries, produced in the Ottoman centuries, are a reflection of reality, most prominent Muslim males before 1800 seem to have belonged to one or another of the Sufi orders and sometimes more than one. Sufi hostels (*zawiyya* in Arabic, *tekke* in Ottoman Turkish) were found in every Arab city and provided space for both ritual and social gatherings. The *zawiyyas* also accommodated visiting scholars, as well as mendicants. That function helped to strengthen the bonds between members of a particular order across the Muslim lands by creating personal connections and providing nodes for the dissemination of information. In some rural areas, the *zawiyyas* provided the only religious institution available to the peasants. As a result, Islam as practiced in the countryside in the Ottoman centuries was heavily influenced by Sufi beliefs and practices, a reality that was painfully obvious to the religious reformers of the late nineteenth century.

The variety and number of Sufi orders proliferated in the Ottoman period as those whose origins lay outside the old Mamluk territories,

[17] al-Khiyari, *Tuhfat al-udaba'*, vol. III, 67–74.
[18] ibn Abi Surur, *al-Tuhfa al-bahiyya*, 56.

such as the Mevlevis (in Arabic, Mawlawiyya) and Naqshbandis, took root and flourished in the Arab lands. The intellectual and emotional range of the various orders' activities was substantial. The outward sign of an order's emotional content was its practice of *dhikr*, literally "remembrance," through which the participants sought to connect with God on an intimate and highly personal level. At the conservative end of the spectrum of the orders were the Naqshbandis, who held that one could only join the order if God had ordained it to be so, a Muslim equivalent of Calvinism's "electorate of God." With such an elite pretense, most in the order disdained the public excesses of many of the other orders such as chanting, singing, and dancing, which they considered vulgar and unspiritual. There were exceptions, however, as ʿAbd al-Ghani al-Nabulusi (to be discussed later), who was a member of the order, wrote a treatise on the use of musical instruments in the *dhikr*.[19] Al-Nabulusi notwithstanding, the majority within the order held to the silent *dhikr*, wherein one should only commune with God internally without public spectacles. The *dhikr* of another elite order, the Mevlevis, which they called the *sema* in Turkish, was, by contrast, highly choreographed and accompanied by music. That practice earned them the sobriquet of the "dancing (alternatively "whirling") dervishes" in Western travel literature. The Mevlevi order, although of Anatolian origin, became popular with the Sunni elite in the Arab lands within a century of the Ottoman conquest. Aleppo, Damascus, and Cairo all hosted Mevlevi *tekke*s where the *sema* was performed. As it was open to the viewing public, including women and non-Muslims, their specialized form of ritual was frequently described by Europeans travelers in the Ottoman period.[20]

If there was a Sufi order for every taste and social class, there were also mendicant Sufis (*qalandar*s) who pushed the limit of what was acceptable, behaving in provocative ways that sometimes openly flouted religious taboos. Most of the population excused such excesses as the mendicant was said to be *majdhub*, or so overcome with the passion of having encountered God that he was no longer accountable for his actions.[21] Although those who would transgress the boundaries of societal norms were not as prevalent in the Arab lands as they were in the areas influenced by Persian literary culture, they did turn up in Arab cities

[19] Elizabeth Sirriyeh, *Sufi Visionary of Ottoman Damascus: ʿAbd al-Ghani al-Nabulusi, 1641–1731* (London: Routledge Curzon, 2005), 45.
[20] Alexander Russell, *The Natural History of Aleppo*, 2 vols. (London: 1794), vol. I, 207.
[21] Ahmed Karamustafa, *God's Unruly Friends: Dervish Groups in the Islamic Middle Period 1200–1550* (Oxford: Oneworld, 2006).

at times. One of the more notorious of these was Shaykh Abu Bakr ibn Abi al-Wafa (d. 1583) of Aleppo, who lived outside the city's walls and engaged in all sorts of unconventional and, by Muslim legal standards, illicit and immoral behavior including drunken debauches that included homosexual sex. After his death, however, Shaykh Abu Bakr's life was converted into a more traditional and conventional hagiography, and his followers founded their own *zawiyya* and a less socially deviant Sufi order to memorialize him.[22]

The behavior of such reputed saints was not the only aspect of Sufism that troubled some in the Sunni Muslim community in the seventeenth and eighteenth centuries. One of the most distinctive features of the intellectual life in the Arabic-speaking provinces of the Ottoman Empire in the centuries following the conquest was the centrality of the writings of the mystic ibn al-ʿArabi in many of the religious debates in which the ulama engaged. That assertion is supported by the many commentaries on his works that were produced between 1516 and 1900. Muhiy al-Din ibn al-ʿArabi was born in Spain but settled in Damascus in his later life. He died there in 1240 and was buried in the quarter of Salihiyya, which was outside the city's walls on the slopes of Jabal Qasyun, which rises to the northeast of the city. Ibn al-ʿArabi's reputation faded over time as far as most of the city's inhabitants were concerned, and his grave was in derelict condition at the time of the Ottoman conquest. In the Ottoman period, that all changed, however, as al-ʿArabi became the city's local saint and protector.

Many scholars of Islamic mysticism consider ibn al-ʿArabi to have been the most original of the Sufi theosophists. His writings are extremely dense, however, as a result of the subtlety of his arguments and the obscurity of his language. That obscurity was probably intentional as he was controversial even in his lifetime. Both ibn al-ʿArabi's detractors and his followers said his writings advanced the concept of *wahdat al-wujud*, or the unity of existence or being, although he never used that particular phrase in his voluminous writings. The phrase is, however, an attempt to capture succinctly a very complex theosophy that proposes that the only existence in the cosmos is God's. All other consciousness is a reflection of his essence without an independent existence of its own. Overly simplified, ibn al-ʿArabi proposed the existence of one transcendent reality or

[22] al-ʿUrdi, *Maʿadan al-dhahab*, 43–54; Heghnar Zeitlian Watenpaugh, "Deviant Dervishes: Space, Gender and the Construction of Antinomian Piety in Ottoman Aleppo" *IJMES* 37 (2005): 535–65.

Being (*wujud*, literally "presence"), God, from which emanates the consciousness that all sentient beings share.

In ibn al-ᶜArabi's cosmos, each individual is both separate from and a part of that larger consciousness even if most are unaware of that reality. Mindful of that ultimate reality, the distinctions among religions become trivial and wither away as one seeks the transcendent Truth, God. God's consciousness in the view of the shaykh, as he was called by those who embraced his cosmology, cannot be circumscribed by one religion's rituals. Rather the rituals of all provide the seeker of truth with a path on which to begin to approach her. Further adding to the potential for controversy, if God had a gendered nature for ibn al-ᶜArabi, it was surely as Creator feminine. God's ultimate reality was, however, for him beyond any artificial constructions, such as gender, that are imposed on God's "Presence" by humankind's limited intellect.

While ibn al-ᶜArabi's writings carefully skirted the issue of whether the sharia was ultimately irrelevant, some of his followers were less circumspect in their language. Ibn al-ᶜArabi's Muslim critics argued that his vision of the universe promoted monism, or the belief that God alone exists, and thereby collapsed the distinction between God and his creations. Furthermore, many Muslim scholars felt that what could be interpreted as religious relativism in his writings diminished the importance of following the sharia in everyday practice and denied Islam's unique truth. It is doubtful that ibn al-ᶜArabi would have conceded that point, however, as is evidenced by his advice to Sultan Kai Kaus of Konya, who questioned him how to treat his non-Muslim subjects. The shaykh responded that all of the requirements of the sharia in restricting their public worship should be applied without exception.[23] Whatever their personal relationship with God might be in the spiritual world of the *batin*, non-Muslims must conform to the rule of law in the physical world of the *zahir*.

Given the controversy surrounding him and the complexity of his vision, it is somewhat surprising that ibn al-ᶜArabi would become a figure with cult status in the Ottoman period. Nonetheless, the Ottoman sultans served as the patrons and promoters of the cult of the shaykh from their first entry into the Arab lands. Ibn Tulun recorded that one of the first acts Sultan Selim performed after his entry into Damascus was to attend Friday prayers in the Umayyad Mosque, the reputed burial place of John the Baptist's head and the most important mosque in the city. That was

[23] Muhiyy al-Din ibn al-ᶜArabi, *Ibn al-'Arabi: The Bezels of Wisdom*, translated by R. W. J. Austin (Mahwah, NJ: Paulist Press, 1980), 10.

to be expected of a Muslim sovereign. Soon afterward, he surprised the ulama by visiting the tomb of ibn al-ᶜArabi, where he offered prayers over the derelict grave site. According to Evliya Çelebi, writing more than a century and a half after the event, Selim was troubled over whether to pursue his Mamluk enemies to Cairo and hesitated to set out with his army from Damascus. In this period of personal trial, ibn al-ᶜArabi appeared to Selim in a dream and promised him Cairo if Selim would restore his grave.[24] Although it makes a good story, there was also an important political reason why Selim might have wanted to honor the saint. Accompanying Sultan Selim to Damascus was the Ottoman legal scholar and chief legal scholar of the empire (Shayhk al-Islam, or in the Turkish version of the title, Şeyhülislam) Kemalpaşazade Ahmed (d. 1534).

Kemalpaşazade followed in the tradition of Ottoman scholarship that saw in ibn al-ᶜArabi's writings a bridge between the Ottoman dynasty's role as upholders of Sunni Islam and the various popular movements present in Anatolia, such as the Kızıl Baş, that were tinged with Shi'i millenarianism. The court scholars sought to effect a union between the two disparate traditions by promoting the sultan as the "perfect man" (*al-insan al-kamil*) of the Sufi tradition. In that formulation of the cosmos, there has to be one individual who acts as the fulcrum between the perceived physical mundane world and the transcendent reality of God. This was the role filled by the Prophet Muhammad in his lifetime, but some Muslims held the belief that there must be one such individual in every subsequent generation. Ibn al-ᶜArabi had written that with the Prophet's death and the end of Prophecy, the mantle of "Perfect Man" had rested on the shoulders of God's saints (*awliya*), of whom ibn al-ᶜArabi claimed to be the last.

Without saints, there were those in the community of the faithful who fervently believed that there had to be some line of descent, either spiritual or physical, that would provide the individuals who would fulfill the necessary function as the "Perfect Man" in subsequent generations in order that the connection between God and his creation would remain unbroken. This was an echo of the belief of the Imami Shia in the absent imam as the two performed the same function in the cosmos. Promoting the sultan as the "Perfect Man," Ottoman scholars based their claim on the works of ibn al-ᶜArabi.[25] The link between the Ottoman sultans and

---

[24] Evliya, *Seyahatname*, vol. IX, 206.
[25] Tim Winter, "Ibn Kemal (d.940/1534) on Ibn 'Arabi's Hagiography." In *Sufism and Theology*, edited by Ayman Shihadeh (Edinburgh: Edinburgh University Press, 2007), 137–57.

the scholar was supported by a text, entitled *al-Shajara al-nuᶜmaniyya fi al-dawla al-ᶜuthmaniyya* (The Genealogical Tree in the Ottoman State), that reputedly was written by ibn al-ᶜArabi. It, however, only made its first recorded appearance in the sixteenth century. With apparently tremendous foresight, ibn al-ᶜArabi predicted in that work the conquest of Egypt by the Ottomans and stated that theirs would be the last, universal Muslim state, which would reign until the arrival of the Mahdi at the end of historical time and immediately preceding the Final Judgment.[26]

Yasin al-ᶜUmari, writing in Mosul at the end of the eighteenth century, cited that apocryphal text as saying that ibn al-ᶜArabi had himself predicted that Sultan Selim would restore his grave: "When the letter Sin enters the letter Shin ibn al-ᶜArabi's grave will appear."[27] It was implicit to the reader that the Sin stood for Sultan Selim and the Shin for *Sham* (Damascus). A century earlier, Evliya's story had cited that same prophecy. Ibn Tulun did not provide the reason for Selim's actions in regard to the saint's tomb, but he noted that the sultan established a *waqf* for its maintenance and for the construction of a mosque over it. That mosque was completed while Selim was in Cairo, and he prayed there as his last public act in Damascus before setting out on his return to the capital.[28] As evidence of the association between the House of Osman and ibn al-ᶜArabi, Janbirdi al-Ghazali destroyed the dome of the newly constructed mosque as one of the first acts of his rebellion against Süleyman in 1520. When Farhad Pasha restored Ottoman control over the city, he quickly moved to repair the dome. Farhad died in 1522 while still serving as governor of Damascus and was buried on the grounds of the mosque, establishing a precedent for it to serve as the resting place for some of the Ottomans who would die while governing the city.[29]

From its founding, the mosque that had been built to honor ibn al-ᶜArabi was known as the Salimiyya, not to be confused with the Sufi *zawiyya*, whose construction was financed by Sultan Selim's grandson Selim II (1566–74) and that bears that name today in Damascus.[30] The original Salimiyya, known today as simply the Mosque of ibn al-ᶜArabi, became a sacred space for Ottoman officials to perform public rituals.

---

[26] Cornell Fleischer, "Shadows of Shadows: Prophecy in Politics in 1530s Istanbul." In *Identity and Identity Formation in the Ottoman World: A Volume of Essays in Honor of Norman Itzkowitz*, edited by Baki Tezcan and Karl Barbir (Madison: The University of Wisconsin Press, 2007), 51–62.

[27] al-ᶜUmari. *Zubdat al-athar*, 185.

[28] Necipoğlu, *Age of Sinan*, 222–4.

[29] ibn al-Himsi, *Hawadith al-zaman* 3, 49.

[30] Necipoğlu, *Age of Sinan*, 224–30.

The chroniclers of Damascus noted that following Selim's example, it was often the last spot governors visited when leaving the city on their return to Istanbul for reposting. Although Süleyman would build a much grander mosque on the banks of the Barada River to serve as the starting point for the hajj out of the city, the smaller mosque built by his father seems to have continued to hold a special place in the spiritual imagination of Ottoman officials and Muslim pilgrims alike.[31]

The Arab intellectual who was most closely associated with ibn al-ʿArabi in the Ottoman period was ʿAbd al-Ghani al-Nabulusi, whose family name was pronounced locally as al-Nabulsi. Al-Nabulusi was born in Damascus in 1641 in the quarter of al-Salihiyya in a house not far from the Salimiyya Mosque. He was a prolific scholar whose extant works number more than two hundred. Most of these have not been studied by scholars and exist only in manuscript form, but their titles range from love poetry dedicated to beardless youths to a treatise on the proper care and propagation of olive trees. They also include a history of the Ottoman dynasty. But al-Nabulusi's most famous works among his contemporaries were his treatises on the works of Muhiyy al-Din ibn al-ʿArabi.

When Ibrahim al-Khiyari visited Damascus in 1669, al-Nabulusi was already an established scholar, and as such, he was one of the Muslim scholars that al-Khiyari sought out to visit. Like al-Nabulusi, al-Khiyari held ibn al-ʿArabi in reverence and recorded a poem in his honor upon visiting his shrine and another praising the wisdom of the saint's student, al-Nabulusi. The Damascene chronicler ibn Kannan referred to al-Nabulusi as *mawlana* (our master). Furthermore, he repeatedly identified al-Nabulusi as the most learned of his city's many learned men. ʿAbd al-al-Rahman ibn ʿAbd al-Razzaq (d. 1725), who wrote a compendium of the places in Damascus that were associated with various saints, also honored al-Nabulusi by citing him frequently as an authoritative source on such matters.[32] Their respect was echoed by Muhammad al-Makki, who recorded al-Nabulusi's visit to Homs and the warm reception he received from the city's leading ulama.[33] Al-Nabulusi responded by composing a poem to extol Homs's charms and another in honor of its governor, Ibrahim Agha.[34] Ibn Kannan noted in his chronicle when al-Nabulusi

[31] ʿAbd al-Rahman ibn ʿAbd al-Razzaq al-Dimashqi, *Hada'iq al-inʿam fi fada'il al-sham* (Beirut: Dar al-Diya', 1989), 170–1.
[32] Ibid., 71, 105, 121, 156, 171, 183, 187.
[33] al-Makki, *Ta'rikh Hims*, 123–5.
[34] al-Nabulusi. *al-Haqiqa wa al-majaz*, 107–10.

gave public lectures in the Salimiyya Mosque, and who from among the city's prominent men attended. These frequently included the Ottoman governor and chief judge in the city. Upon al-Nabulusi's death in 1731, there was a large public funeral, which the Ottoman governor and chief judge attended. Two years later his body was entombed in the Salimiyya Mosque near the mausoleum of ibn al-ᶜArabi.[35]

Whether or not Selim had consciously sought to do so when he refurbished the saint's tomb, the cult of ibn al-ᶜArabi helped to promote the dynasty's legitimacy in the Arab lands and establish a bond between the sultan and his subjects. The Arab authors who expressed the strongest support for the House of Osman – ibn Kanan and al-Nabulusi in Damascus, ibn Abi Surur in Cairo, Yasin al-ᶜUmari in Mosul, al-Makki in Homs, and al-Khiyari in Medina – also professed reverence for the shaykh. The legitimacy of the House of Osman rested not only on its defense of the "outward" truth of the sharia, but also on the support it received from the invisible world of the saints. Ibn Abi Surur acknowledged that link in his biography of Sultan Selim I in which he highlighted Selim's construction of the mosque over the tomb of ibn al-ᶜArabi and the reverence the sultan paid to the saint as proof of Selim's religiosity. He added that the impious Mamluk sultan whom the Ottomans had overthrown paid, in contrast, no homage to the saint. For ibn Abi Surur, faith in saints such as the shaykh of Damascus and the political legitimacy of the Ottoman dynasty were intertwined.[36]

ANTI-SUFIS AND RELIGIOUS REFORMERS: THE EIGHTEENTH-CENTURY "RENEWAL"

The cult of ibn al-ᶜArabi was not universally embraced by the Ottoman ulama, in either Syria or Anatolia. Nor did all approve of what they perceived as public antics performed as ritual by many of the Sufis. One of the earliest critics of the Sufis was Mehmed of Birgi (d. 1573), an Anatolian scholar who was educated outside the state-sponsored madrasa system. Birgili Mehmed, as he was known in Ottoman Turkish, denounced many Sufi practices as both innovations and impious acts. He also asserted that popular vices such as the consumption of coffee and tobacco, as well as practices such as shaking hands that were unknown in the time of the Prophet Muhammad were illicit. Those Muslims who said they were not,

[35] ibn Kannan, *Yawmiyyat*, 415–16, 438.
[36] ibn Abi Surur, *al-Tuhfa al-bahiyya*, 57.

he added for good measure, were themselves guilty of heresy. In the rigidity of his interpretations of Islam, Birgili Mehmed prefigured the more extreme Islamist positions current in the twenty-first century, although none of those today espousing such strident versions of Islam cite him as an inspiration. He did not, however, condemn all forms of mysticism outright, only its more unrestrained practices and claims. In particular, Birgili Mehmed found fault with the writings of ibn al-ʿArabi, which he said promoted the heretical idea of the "unity of being."

One of those influenced by Birgili Mehmed was Kadızade Mehmed (d. 1635),who created a stir in Istanbul by demanding that the Ottoman sultan Murad IV ban coffee and tobacco, prohibit music and dance, and remove the study of mathematics and the natural sciences from the state-sponsored madrasas. He soon had a movement of dissatisfied madrasa students behind him.[37] In the reign of Sultan Mehmed IV (1648–87), the Kadızadelis, as those who followed Kadızade Mehmed came to be known, were in the ascendancy. One of the movement's most prominent preachers, Vani Mehmed Efendi, served as the spiritual adviser to Sultan Mehmed. Among the other abuses of what he considered to be "true" Islam, Vani Mehmed condemned the popularity among the learned of the writings of ibn al-ʿArabi.

In 1692, al-Nabulusi wrote a stinging treatise against an unnamed Turkish (*min al-Arwam*) scholar who had written a critique of ibn al-ʿArabi for having said that Christians and Jews might enter paradise. Al-Nabulusi's essay is loaded with vitriol and makes much of the Turkish origins of the scholar with the implication that he had an imperfect knowledge of Arabic and was, therefore, unqualified to speak authoritatively about ibn al-ʿArabi's complex arguments. The essay has been interpreted by some as an indication of al-Nabulusi's ethnic pride.[38] It should be remembered, however, that he also wrote a history of the Ottoman ruling house that bordered on a panegyric. Additionally, as noted before, al-Nabulusi carried on extensive correspondence with Turkish scholars. In one such exchange in 1698, Şeyhülislam Feyzullah Efendi asked al-Nabulusi for his prayers for the Ottoman army in its

---

[37] Madeline Zilfi, "The Kadizadelils: Discordant Revivalism in Seventeenth-Century Istanbul" *JNES* 45 (1986): 251–69.

[38] Michael Winter, "A Polemical Treatise by ʿAbd al-Ġani al-Nabulusi against a Turkish Scholar on the Religious Status of the *Dhimmi*s" *Arabica* 35 (1988): 92–103; Steve Tamari, "Arab National Consciousness in Seventeenth- and Eighteenth-Century Syria" In *Syria and Bilad al-Sham under Ottoman Rule: Essays in Honour of Abdul-Karim Rafeq* edited by Peter Sluglett with Stefan Weber (Leiden: Brill, 2010), 309–22.

war with the "infidels," to which al-Nabulusi promptly responded in the affirmative.[39]

It is widely presumed that the target of al-Nabulusi's wrath was Vani Mehmed, or one of his students. Ibrahim al-Khiyari also recorded a disagreement with Vani Mehmed. Al-Khiyari had an audience with the Ottoman scholar in Istanbul during which he praised him for influencing the sultan to close down the taverns of Istanbul. After composing a praise poem in Vani Mehmed's honor, al-Khiyari added that he had taken issue, however, with the Ottoman scholar's intolerance toward coffeehouses.[40] Al-Khiyari had written an ode in praise of the Nawfura coffeehouse in Damascus earlier in his travelogue and was clearly not opposed to drinking coffee on religious grounds. Unlike taverns, which with their drawn shudders were dins of iniquity and sexual licentiousness, he reportedly told Vani Mehmed Efendi, coffeehouses provided open, airy spaces where a cultivated man could rest, talk with friends in leisure, or contemplate the world as it passed him by. Al-Khiyari did not record Vani Mehmed's response to his defense of the coffeehouse. He also did not mention whether he had broached the subject of ibn al-ʿArabi's writings in his discussions, but al-Khiyari had visited the mosque of ibn al-ʿArabi on his way to Istanbul and would return there again on his way home. Both times, he reported praying over the saint's grave, an act that Vani Mehmed would have condemned as heresy.[41] The ideological difference between the two men was obviously greater than the question of whether the drinking of coffee was licit.

Despite al-Nabulusi's essay against the unnamed Turk, the side of the divide over ibn al-ʿArabi's writings on which scholars would align themselves seems to have had very little to do with their ethnic origins. The prominent Ottoman scholar Katib Çelebi also disagreed with the followers of Kadızade Mehmed and defended ibn al-ʿArabi in his writings, as did Fezyzullah Efendi.[42] Furthermore, not all Arab ulama had problems with the stricter interpretation of Islam advocated by the Kadızadeli movement. Muhammad al-Ustawani, a scion of a family well known in Damascus for its piety and scholarship, was a leading advocate of their extreme positions in Istanbul until his death in 1661. He even had the righteous temerity to denounce Şeyhülislam Yahya Efendi for having

---

[39] al-Nabulusi, *Wasa'il al-tahqiqa*, 337–42.
[40] al-Khiyari, *Tuhfat al-udaba'*, vol. I, 164; vol. II, 74–6.
[41] Ibid., vol. I, 2, 135.
[42] Inalcık, *The Ottoman Empire*, 183–5.

written poetry.[43] Clearly, many of al-Nabulusi's contemporaries even in Damascus were wary of his admiration of ibn al-ʿArabi. He was removed from his post as mufti of Damascus in 1723 after only a few months because of the opposition of some of the city's Sunni elite, who found his rulings to be unorthodox.[44] Within both the Arabic-speaking and Ottoman intellectual elites, there were profound differences of opinion on the question of religious truths that found echoes on both sides of the linguistic divide.

The fiercest denunciation of the Sufis to arise in the Arab lands was found in the writings of Muhammad ibn ʿAbd al-Wahhab (d. 1792). His followers called themselves Muwahhidun (Unitarians), or those who proclaim the unimpeachable unity of God. But they were called by their detractors Wahhabis after the shortened family name of the founder of the movement. All Muslims, after all, would say that they accepted the indivisibility of God even while they might not agree with some of the interpretations of the faith advanced by ibn ʿAbd al-Wahhab. Muhammad ibn ʿAbd al-Wahhab was born in the Najd in the first decade of the eighteenth century. He studied in both Baghdad and Mecca before settling in the 1730s in the oasis village of ʿUyayna in the Najd, where he began to preach an uncompromising interpretation of Sunni Islam. There is no indication in his writings that ibn ʿAbd al-Wahhab was aware of the Kadızadeli movement in Anatolia, although his major work, *Kitab al-tawhid* (The Book of the Unity of God), acknowledges a debt to the writings of Taqi al-Din ibn Taymiyya, who served as the primary intellectual inspiration to the Kadızadelis as well.[45]

Muhammad ibn ʿAbd al-Wahhab shared with ibn Taymiyya and Birgili Mehmed a deep anguish that Islam as practiced by most of their contemporaries was corrupt. All three yearned for Muslim society as it existed in the age of the Prophet and his companions when they felt it had been clear to everyone in the community what it meant to be a Muslim. Unlike the case in their own times, there had been no hint then of any heresy in the Community of the Faithful. For all three, a return to that idealized past would secure the Muslims' future. The word in Arabic for ancestors was *salaf* and so the movement to return to the practices of the original Muslim community would come to be called the *salafiyya* in the

---

[43] Marc Baer, *Honored by the Glory of Islam: Conversion and Conquest in Ottoman Empire* (Oxford: Oxford University Press, 2008), 70–1.

[44] Rafeq, *Province of Damascus*, 83.

[45] Muhammad ibn ʿAbd al-Wahhab, *Kitab al-tawhid alladhi huwwa haqq Allah ʿala al-ʿabid*. Cairo: Dar al-Maʿarif, 1974.

nineteenth century, although what exactly those practices were and what a return to them might mean were not always the same for those who expressed a desire for a return to the idealized past.

The vision of what a return to origins meant for ibn ʿAbd al-Wahhab was a straightforward, if puritanical, one. Muslims could condone no practice that interfered with a believer's unwavering acceptance of the uncompromised unity of God, hence the movement's name for itself. This meant there could be no substitution for the divine presence or any diminishing of it by the invocation of intercessors or mediators. As such, the Sufi belief in saints or the belief of the Shia in the imams was heresy that must be unconditionally condemned and extirpated from Muslim practice. Any Muslim who did not see the error of his/her ways and did not repudiate such practices had veered so far from the "true path" of Islam as to become an unbeliever, *kafir*. All judged to be in such error could be forced to return to the true path or forfeit their lives. The claim of the righteous within the movement of their ability to pronounce another Muslim to be an infidel (*takfir*) promised schism in the community. Adding to the potential for disruption among the Sunnis, ibn ʿAbd al-Wahhab viewed the institution of the sultanate in its absolutist ambitions as amounting to heresy (*bidʿa*). It was for him an innovation in the Muslim body politic as there had been no sultans in the early Muslim community. Although he did not mention the Ottoman dynasty by name, ibn ʿAbd al-Wahhab's invocation of the saying attributed to the Prophet that there was no title more hateful to God than that of Shahanshah, "king of kings," was a not-so veiled reference to the Ottoman sultans' use of the title Padişah, a variant of that Persian title.

In the interpretation of Islam advanced by Muhammad ibn ʿAbd al-Wahhab, the building of a mosque over a saint's grave as Sultan Selim had done for ibn al-ʿArabi was a sin, as was the asking of a saint's intercession in a personal matter, as al-Khiyari had done in Damascus. Similarly, any sign of reverence extended to a shaykh of a Sufi order by a believer infringed upon God's unity by introducing the notion that a mortal might contain the divine. Ibn ʿAbd al-Wahhab had an uncompromising view toward most Sufi practices, as had ibn Taymiyya before him. Neither man, however, condemned the Sufi notion of an "inner truth" that could only be gained by an individual's seeking of God through the *dhikr*. Ibn ʿAbd al-Wahhab's construction of Islam did not rule out all forms of mysticism categorically, but he strongly suggested that as a belief system it was too easily corruptible by the unscrupulous and should be avoided by most.

The followers of Muhammad ibn ᶜAbd al-Wahhab, like their counter-parts among the seventeenth-century Puritans in England, were text-driven literalists. There could be no compromise with the written text of the Qur'an, which they believed was the unadulterated text given by God directly to his Prophet, Muhammad. Ibn ᶜAbd al-Wahhab acknowledged, however, that the sacred text did not provide clear answers to all human questions. In such cases, the believer had to seek to understand what the text established as the underlying principles of faith and apply them to the issue at hand. In Islamic jurisprudence, the use of such individual reasoning was known as *ijtihad*. In Sunni Islam, the legal scholars had deemed by the thirteenth century that the practice was too dangerous for the established social and political order and had reached a consensus that it should be abandoned. Among the Shia, its use was restricted to only a few of the most learned among their ulama, the *mujtahids*, as everyone else ran the risk of falling into dangerous heresy by its misuse. In contrast, Muhammad ibn ᶜAbd al-Wahhab wrote that the limited use of *ijtihad* by the learned was preferable to all the accretions that Islamic practice had acquired over the centuries and that could not be justified, in his interpretation, by the Qur'an or the traditions of the Prophet. Ibn ᶜAbd al-Wahhab's works struck a cord of approval among Muslim scholars in his denunciations of the excesses of Sufi practices and in his cautious appeal to the reintroduction of the principle of *ijtihad* in Muslim jurisprudence.[46] The same could not be said about some of the violent actions taken by his followers after their teacher's death in 1792, to be discussed in the next chapter.

A more influential intellectual challenge to extreme Sufi practices in the Arab lands arose from the Naqshbandi Sufi order, which in the eighteenth century sought to renew Islam by reforming it. The adherents of the Naqshbandi order claim a line of descent that stretches back to the first caliph in the Sunni tradition, Abu Bakr (d. 634). By creating a lineage going back to a man who the Shia believed to have been a usurper, the Naqshbandi announced that they were firmly in the Sunni camp while many other Sufi orders trace their foundation myths more ambiguously to ᶜAli. Despite that genealogy, the order's more recent history had its roots in Central Asia. From there, its preachers transported the order to India, where one of its greatest saints, Shaykh Ahmad Sirhindi (d. 1624), helped to give the Naqshbandis an international reputation. Sirhindi

---

[46] Butrus Abu-Manneh, "Salafiyya and the Rise of the Khalidiyya in Baghdad in the Early Nineteenth Century" *WI* 43 (2003): 349–72.

created problems for the Mughal emperors as he rejected the *Din illahi* proposed by Emperor Akbar (d. 1605) as heretical syncretism and urged the dynasty to return to a more orthodox version of Sunni Islam. A swing back to orthodoxy occurred in the reign of Awrangzeb (1658–1707). Nonetheless, many of Sirhindi's followers were compelled to flee India for Mecca because of their uncompromising critique of Mughal absolutism, which they viewed as substituting the emperor's decrees for Islamic law. It was an interesting parallel to many Muslim scholars' rejection of the Ottoman sultan's use of *kanun*, and that bond would guarantee the refugees of "religious conscience" a welcome by some of the sultan's Muslim subjects.

In Mecca, the order emphasized that Sufism was only acceptable if it were in compliance with the outer truth of Islam, the sharia. In this, they were following in the tradition of "sober" Sufism advocated by the prominent scholar Muhammad al-Ghazali (d. 1111). Al-Ghazali had written that all the strictures of the law must be followed without exception, but that true understanding of why those regulations were, in fact, divine could only be gained through the certainty of God's existence achieved by the mystics.[47] That duality of knowledge, inner and outer, was embraced by the Naqshbandis. By appealing to al-Ghazali, however, the Naqshbandis in Mecca had implicitly condemned many of the Sufi practices that were prevalent in the Arab lands in the Ottoman centuries, as al-Ghazali had shown little tolerance for anything in the Sufi tradition other than the highly internalized quest for God's truth. Saint worship, singing, and dancing were for him definitely outside the boundaries of proper Muslim behavior.

In regard to the question of ibn al-ʿArabi's orthodoxy, Naqshbandi commentators shifted the emphasis from the idea of God's transcendence and his connection to all consciousness that was controversial for many Muslim scholars to one of ibn al-ʿArabi's characterization of Prophet Muhammad as embodying the "Perfect Man." That change of emphasis inserted the Prophet as the idealized model that an individual believer should emulate.[48] Earlier generations of readers of ibn al-ʿArabi might have concluded that his writings advanced a relativist approach to other established religions. The Naqshbandis disagreed with that interpretation,

---

[47] Muhammad al-Ghazali, *Al-Ghazali's Path to Sufism; His Deliverance from Error (al-Munqidh min al-Dalal*, translated by R. J. McCarthy, S.J. (Louisville, KY: Fons Vitae, 2006).

[48] Itzchak Weismann, *Taste of Modernity: Sufism, Salafiyya, and Arabism in Late Ottoman Damascus* (Leiden: Brill, 2001),143–8.

saying that that when properly read, ibn al-ʿArabi's writings conformed to Holy Law.[49]

No longer a saint, ibn al-ʿArabi had become simply a profound teacher. That compromise seems to have worked. In Damascus, ʿAbd al-Ghani al-Nabulusi joined the Naqshbandi order without any apparent sense of contradiction between his championing of ibn al-ʿArabi and his embrace of the Naqshbandi path.[50] The Naqshbandi revival of the eighteenth century would lay the groundwork in the Ottoman Arab land for ongoing intellectual discussions of Islam and its place in a rapidly changing world in the nineteenth century.[51]

NONELITE CULTURE

Popular culture in the Arab lands for most of the Ottoman centuries was dominated by the coffeehouse. Coffee arrived in the core Arab lands from Yemen roughly at the same time as the Ottoman armies. In 1511, a controversy arose in Mecca over the question whether the consumption of coffee was licit for Muslims, and in 1532–3, one of Cairo's leading scholars issued a fatwa against it.[52] Other scholars disagreed with the prohibition, and by the middle of the sixteenth century, coffee shops had become ubiquitous in all Arab cities. Although Ottoman legal scholars would attempt to ban coffee and coffeehouses in the seventeenth century, Arab scholars such as al-Khiyari were known to write poems in praise of both coffee and the establishments that dispensed it.[53]

Taverns could legally be operated only by non-Muslims and were theoretically restricted to their custom; as such, they were extremely rare in the Arab cities, in contrast to Istanbul, where they flourished.[54] In their absence, coffee shops, along with the already existing bathhouses, served as the social meeting places for friends, business associates, and idle male

---

[49] Atallah Copty, "The Naqshbandiyya and Its Offshoot, the Naqshbandiyya-Mujaddiyya in the Haramayn in the 11th/17th Century" *WI* 43 (2003): 321–48.

[50] Sirriyeh, *Sufi Visionary*, 44–7.

[51] R. S. O'Fahey and Bernard Radtke, "Neo-Sufism Reconsidered" *Islam* 70 (1993), 52–87; Butrus Abu-Manneh, "The Naqshbandiyya-Mujaddidiyya in the Ottoman Lands in the Early Nineteenth Century" *WI* 22 (1982): 131–53.

[52] Ralph Hattox, *Coffee and Coffeehouses: The Origins of a Social Beverage in the Medieval Near East* (Seattle: University of Washington Press, 1985), 29–40.

[53] James Grehan, *Everyday Life and Consumer Culture in 18h-Century Damascus* (Seattle, 2007), 140–6.

[54] Ebru Boyar and Kate Fleet, *A Social History of Ottoman Istanbul* (Cambridge: Cambridge University Press, 2010), 194–201.

gossipers. Once tobacco was introduced in the region, the combination of coffee and a smoke added to the coffeehouses' popularity. As such establishments were strictly off limits to women, they enjoyed both vices in the bathhouses which were specifically designated for their use or in places that could not support multiple bathhouses, on the special days set aside for their use. Women were also entertained in the baths by female singers and storytellers. For men, the coffeehouses provided the stage for public performances.

In popular culture, as in the realm of more sophisticated intellectual pursuits, there was an ongoing exchange between the Arab lands and Turkish-speaking Anatolia. As coffeehouses spread north from the Arab lands across the empire, the Anatolian Karagöz, or shadow puppet theater, which was popular in both Anatolia and the Balkan territories, spread south.[55] The English physician Alexander Russell, a longtime resident of the city of Aleppo in the eighteenth century, described the puppet performances as usually obscene, but he added that they at times could contain political satire, as in 1768, when the character Karagöz mocked the janissaries returning from the Russian campaign for their dismal performance, causing the authorities to close the coffee shops temporarily.[56] They were much too popular to be banned for long, however, and within a week their doors were open again for business.

Despite their popularity, the often obscene antics of Karagöz and Hacıvat, the two most popular characters in the Anatolian repertoire, did not replace the serial stories of Bedouin heroes such as ᶜAntar and the Banu Hilal that were already popular entertainments for Arabic-speaking audiences in the Mamluk era. Also popular as coffeehouse entertainers were those who retold the urban stories that have come to be known in the West as *The Arabian Nights*. Already available in European language editions in his day, Russell noted that although he found only two manuscript copies of the series, known in Arabic as *Hikayat alf layla wa layla* (The Stories of a Thousand and One Nights*)* in Aleppo, some of the tales were told and retold orally in the city's coffee shops.[57] In their various incarnations with differing casts of heroes, heroines, and villains, an individual tale would be embedded in another, not unlike a serialized novel

[55] Philip Sadgrove, "Pre-Modern Drama" In *The Cambridge History of Arabic Literature: Arabic Literature in the Post-Classical Age,* edited by Roger Allen and D. S. Richards (Cambridge: Cambridge University Press, 2006), 369–83; and in the same volume, Rosella Dorigo Ceccato, "Drama in the Post-Classical Period: A Survey," 347–68.

[56] Russell, *Natural History of Aleppo,* vol. I, 148.

[57] Ibid., vol. I, 149, 385–6.

or soap opera, so that the listener would be encouraged to return on the following evening to pick up the story line and consume more coffee and tobacco.

The recital of folk poetry was also an important entertainment in coffeehouses and in public celebrations such as weddings and feasts honoring a circumcision of a son. The multiverse poems known as *mawal*, which were often sung or recited with musical accompaniment, had two genres: religious poems in praise of the Prophet Muhammad or some Sufi saint and poems of unrequited love. As these were deemed suitable for women's sensibilities by their male relatives, they were often performed at women's gatherings by female performers. In some cases, women composed them, and they are one of the few surviving literary genres in Arabic from the Ottoman era that preserve a woman's perspective. In addition to poetry, the coffeehouses also served as a venue for the performance of music, and Jewish musicians seemed to have been especially in demand in eighteenth-century Syria.

CONCLUSION

The literary production of Arabic-speaking scholars between 1516 and 1800 was considerable, and it included representatives of many of the theological and literary genres that had been established as canonical in the Abbasid period. These included Qur'anic commentary, poetry in its myriad forms, and history. Original work in the sciences, mathematics, and philosophy ceased almost completely in the Arabic-speaking lands, however. Twentieth-century scholars, both Arab and non-Arab alike, largely dismissed the Ottoman centuries as the historic nadir of Arabic literature, because of that narrowing of intellectual interests and a lack of originality in the composition of poetry in the period. As one author summed up his views on the era, "the Ottoman period is marked by a sharp decline in Arabic culture in general and literature in particular."[58]

Historians and scholars of Islamic thought have, however, been more generous to the ulama of the period, recognizing that they made significant contributions to the revival of Islamic intellectual life in the form of a critical response to the traditional canon they had inherited.[59] A full verdict on the state of the intellectual life of the Arab lands in the

[58] Husain Haddawy, translator, *The Arabian Nights* (New York, 1990), xvi.
[59] Khaled El-Rouayheb, "The Myth of the 'Triumph of Fanaticism' in the Seventeenth-Century Ottoman Empire" *WI* 48 (2008): 196–221.

Ottoman centuries awaits further scholarship. There was clearly more going on than the composition of mediocre poetry. That realization is hoped to highlight the critical need for the editing and publishing of the hundreds of volumes that were produced in the Ottoman centuries but still exist only in manuscript copies.

From this brief survey of cultural production in the Arab lands in the Ottoman period, it should be apparent that intellectuals in the Arab provinces did not live in a cultural vacuum. They were aware of intellectual developments occurring outside the region and responded to them. This was especially true in the eighteenth century with the emergence and proliferation of various movements to reform Islam, whether inspired by Wahhabi or Naqshbandi teachings. But there had been an ongoing dialogue between those scholars who represented the Ottoman state and its traditions and those who were educated in the Arab lands from the time of the initial conquest. This was the most apparent in legal discussions where Sunni Arab scholars accepted or rejected arguments advanced from the capital on the basis of their own understanding of Muslim traditions. It was also apparent in those who were attracted to mysticism as the cult of ibn al-ʿArabi and the writings of Jalal al-Din Rumi became widely disseminated among the Sunni elite in the Arab cities. While it is fair to say that few of the Arab ulama learned Ottoman Turkish, that did not mean that there was an absence of dialogue between those scholars who were the products of the official Ottoman madrasa system and those who had studied in the independent madrasas in the Arab lands. From their debates and correspondence it becomes clear that Arabic-speaking Muslim scholars did not view Ottoman culture as an alien culture, but rather as a strand of a common one that Ottomans and Arabs shared.

5

The Empire at War

Napoleon, the Wahhabis, and Mehmed Ali

In the roughly three centuries between Sultan Selim's victorious entry into Cairo and that of Napoleon Bonaparte in 1798, the regime that the Ottoman sultans imposed on the Arab lands had evolved and adapted to changes brought about by global forces. Istanbul had lost its ability over the course of the eighteenth century to influence who would represent it in much of the empire, but the Ottoman sultans had maintained their legitimacy to rule in the vast lands that stretched from Algiers to Basra. The survival of the empire in the Arab provinces was in part fortuitous as neither a military power nor a compelling political ideology had emerged to break the bond that linked the House of Osman to its Arabic-speaking subjects. Nonetheless, Bulut Kapan Ali Bey's two invasions of Syria had demonstrated that the empire was vulnerable on its southern flank. The dynasty had dodged a potential disaster in Egypt, but its ability to with-stand more formidable challengers was yet to be tested.

NAPOLEON IN EGYPT

A European army arrived on the shores of Egypt on 1 July 1798, commanded by the self-styled champion of the Enlightenment's view of "progress," Napoleon Bonaparte. The French found little opposition from the mamluk emirs and quickly advanced on Cairo. There on 21 July in the suburb of Imbaba on the western side of the Nile River, the French dealt the "neo-Mamluk" regime in Cairo a blow almost as stunning as the one their erstwhile nominal predecessors had suffered at the hands of Sultan Selim. Despite their victory at the "Battle of the Pyramids," as French spin masters labeled the clash, the French had not delivered a coup de grace and the surviving mamluk emirs continued a campaign of guerrilla-style warfare from Upper Egypt. Napoleon Bonaparte, never one to revel in understatement, proclaimed to the people of Egypt in a document marred by errors in Arabic grammar that he was merely ridding the country of the treasonous mamluks and restoring Egypt to its rightful liege lord, Sultan Selim III. No one in Egypt, or in the wider Ottoman Empire, was fooled by the charade. Sultan Selim declared war on France on 11 September and ordered the mobilization of forces in the provinces of Damascus and Aleppo. In the meanwhile, a British fleet commanded by Lord Nelson caught the French expeditionary fleet at Abu Qir, near Alexandria, on 1 August 1798 and demolished it. Napoleon was trapped in Egypt and faced an increasingly restive population that was not at all impressed by his proclamation that he was Islam's true friend, having conquered Rome and destroyed the Knights of Malta.[1]

News of the French invasion shocked the Muslim elites in the Arab provinces. Their counterparts in Istanbul had become inured to a string of defeats in the Balkans and were already beginning to explore contacts with Europeans in the capital. In some cases, they had actually traveled to Europe. The Arabic-speaking Muslim elite had, however, been largely insulated from contact with the West. A few, such as the mufti of Aleppo, who befriended the English doctor Alexander Russell, had initiated contacts with the resident Europeans in their cities, but almost no one other than a handful of merchants had actually traveled to Europe. The Arab Muslim elite were aware that the Ottoman armies had suffered defeats in the Balkans, but those lands seemed far removed from their realities. Egypt was clearly another matter. Not all seemed equally perturbed or anxious. Hasan Agha al-ʿAbid (d. 1826?) laconically recorded, "The news came to us in Damascus that the French Christians came on the ocean and seized Alexandria. Their aim is to take Cairo and then Jerusalem and the coast."[2] Clearly more alarmed, Yasin al-ʿUmari in Mosul took the news of Napoleon's conquest of Egypt as a sign that the end of Ottoman Empire was near, but he found solace in the fact that the sad turn of events had been predicted centuries before by ibn al-ʿArabi and would lead to the coming of the *mahdi* and the end of historical time.[3]

Yusuf Dimitri ʿAbbud provided a detailed account of how the news of the French occupation of Egypt was received in his native Aleppo

[1] Holt, *Egypt and the Fertile Crescent*, 155–63.
[2] al-ʿAbid, *Taʾrikh*, 36.
[3] Khoury, *State and Provincial Society*, 164–6.

and the preparations that were undertaken to mount a counterattack. ᶜAbbud was a Melkite Catholic merchant and ideologically unsympathetic to Napoleon, whom he had earlier described as a "heretical regicide" and enemy of the "Mother Church." Members of his community were, however, in the employ of the French in Aleppo and they were imprisoned or had their wealth confiscated when the news of the invasion reached the city. Those in the employ of the Austrians and the Dutch suffered similar fates after the Ottomans learned of the French occupation of the Netherlands and Austria's alliance with France. Locally, the armed factions of the janissaries and the *ashraf* who had just two years before been locked in internecine conflict mobilized and marched off to confront the French. Before departing, the janissaries swaggered through the streets of the wealthier Christians quarters, insulting those they met and demanding payment for the campaign.[4]

The situation in Damascus, as described by Hasan Agha, who had served in the local military but not as a janissary, was equally chaotic as various armies commanded by contending pashas descended on the city. Prices for food doubled and the soldiers looted both townspeople and the surrounding villages. Anxiety in both cities grew as news arrived that the French army had taken Gaza and Jaffa in late winter 1799 and both authors feared Damascus might fall next. The empire was spared further military embarrassment, however, by Cezzar Ahmed Pasha, who held fast in his citadel at Acre. With his army harassed by the British navy and decimated by disease, Napoleon abandoned his siege on 20 May 1799 after sixty-two days. There were extended celebrations in both Aleppo and Damascus as the population believed that the worst had been weathered. Troops continued to arrive in Damascus, including units of the new improved Ottoman army, the Nizam-ı Cedid, wearing the fez (*tarbush fasi*). According to Hasan Agha, the behavior of the "new order" was no less riotous than had been that of their less nattily dressed predecessors.[5] The Christian chronicler Mikha'il al-Dimashqi (d. 1843) was even more critical of the behavior of the Ottoman troops, whom he described as wearing "a strange conical hat to which bells were attached" and who extorted money from the Christians of Damascus.[6]

After his failure at the gates of Acre, Napoleon returned to Cairo, where he enjoyed at least some consolation in that his forces easily

---

[4] ᶜAbbud, *Murtadd*, 195–205.
[5] al-ᶜAbid, *Ta'rikh*, 50–60.
[6] Mikha'il al-Dimashqi, *Ta'rikh hawadith jarrat bi-al-sham wa sawahil barr al-sham wa al-jabal, 1782–1841* (Amman: Dar Ward al-Urduniyya, 2004), 85–7.

defeated an Ottoman expeditionary force that the British landed on Egypt's Mediterranean coast near Alexandria on 11 July 1799. Not willing to be bottled up in Egypt while events were quickly unfolding in France, Napoleon left the country on 22 August. A second Ottoman invasion of Egypt in 1800 also failed. Sultan Selim III acknowledged that his military was not up to the task of defeating the French and offered them safe conduct out of the country. The British, sensing a complete humiliation of their French adversaries was in the works, refused to cooperate with the plan and the French troops remained. In 1801, a combined force of Ottoman and British troops arrived in Egypt, including a force commanded by Grand Vizier Yusuf Ziya Pasha, who had marched overland through Syria, gathering troops in both Aleppo and Damascus along the way. The Ottoman troops saw no combat in Egypt as the French garrison in Cairo surrendered on 18 June while that in Alexandria did so on 3 September 1801. Ottoman rule had technically returned to Egypt.[7]

There is a discrepancy in the causes for the French withdrawal from Egypt that were given by ʿAbbud and Hasan Agha that reflects their differing worldviews. For the cosmopolitan ʿAbbud, the return of Egypt to the sultan's sovereignty depended on the might of the British fleet. He described the disorganized and chaotic mobilization of forces in his native Aleppo as they set out on campaign and their riotous return after their "victory" over the French during which they terrorized the local Christians. He had no illusions that the Ottomans had routed the French on their own.

Hasan Agha hardly mentioned the British at all. In his view, the victory over the French lay squarely in the hands of the Ottoman grand vizier, Yusuf Pasha. Furthermore, his closing passage introduces us to the sectarian prism through which he viewed the developments:

The French Christians departed, returning to their country. After that with the entrance of the Grand Vizier into Cairo, some of the Christians who had cooperated with the French were executed, others were exiled, and still others were sent over the sea to Islambul. A large amount of wealth was confiscated from them. The vizier stayed in Cairo and sent the hajj from Cairo to Mecca. After putting the affairs of Egypt in order, he returned to Syria.[8]

[7] Holt, *Egypt and the Fertile Crescent*, 155–63; Juan Cole, *Napoleon's Egypt" Invading the Middle East* (New York: Palgrave Macmillan, 2997); Darrell Dykstra, "The French Occupation of Egypt, 1798–1801." In *The Cambridge History of Egypt*. Vol. 2. *Modern Egypt, from 1517 to the End of the Twentieth Century*, edited by M. W. Daly (Cambridge: Cambridge University Press, 1998), 113–38.

[8] al-ʿAbid, *Ta'rikh*, 66.

Hasan Agha often identified both the French and the English as Christians, as in the opening line in the previous quote. It is not obvious from his narrative whether there was a clear distinction in his mind between French Christians who were the enemy and the English Christians who were the sultan's onetime ally, or the Christians of Cairo who suffered punishment for their supposed collaboration with the French. Underscoring his sectarian bias, Hasan Agha chose not to mention that Muslims had been subject to reprisals for their supposed collaboration with the French as well as Christians.[9]

Hasan Agha's association of the Egyptian Christians with the French enemy was a manifestation of the growing fear among some Muslims in the empire that their Christian neighbors were a potential fifth column for the Western powers. Several hundred Coptic Christians had enlisted with the French occupation forces in Egypt and rumors of that collaboration undoubtedly contributed to Muslim mistrust of their Christian neighbors.[10] Nonetheless, the departure of the hajj caravan signaled for Hasan Agha the return of order to Egypt. The storm had been weathered. The House of Osman was seemingly once again in control and life had returned to what the author viewed as its normal rhythms. The hajj as symbol of normalcy would also inform his subsequent description of the next crisis that would arise to upset the political order for which Hasan Agha clearly yearned.

THE WAHHABI CHALLENGE TO THE "PROTECTOR OF THE TWO HOLY PLACES"

A new crisis threatened the Ottoman regime in the Arab provinces within two years of the French departure from Egypt. It arose not from Europe, as might have been anticipated at the sultan's court, but from the remote desert tracts of Arabistan. Its source was the unique alliance that the House of ibn Saʿud had forged with the radical religious reformer Muhammad ibn ʿAbd al-Wahhab in the middle of the eighteenth century to create an ideologically driven tribal confederation. At the end of that century, ʿAbd al-ʿAziz ibn Saʿud defeated the Bedouin Shammar confederation that had previously dominated the desert to the west and south of the Euphrates River in Iraq. He then moved against the Shi'i holy city of Karbala in 1801. Shia Muslims, with their belief in the infallible imams,

---

[9] Niqula al-Turk, *Hamalat Bunabart ila al-sharq* (Tripoli, Lebanon: Jirus Burs, 1993), 223–4.

[10] Ibid., 231–2; Ian Coller, *Arab France: Islam and the Making of Modern Europe, 1798–1831* (Berkeley: University of California Press, 2011), 39–46.

represented nothing short of heresy to the Wahhabis. As such, they felt it was their religious obligation to restore the Shia to the fold of Sunni orthodoxy, by force if necessary. Complementing their self-righteousness, the booty that could be gained in looting the defenseless shrine city made it a tempting target for the Bedouin warriors.

The result was a nightmare for the Shia inhabitants, who possessed few resources to protect themselves. The tribesmen easily sacked Karbala, and hundreds, if not thousands, of civilians, including women and children, perished at their hands. The massacre was viewed as an atrocity by the outraged Sunni scholars in Baghdad, who had their disagreements with the Shia but did not consider them as being either apostates or heretics. They condemned the slaying of innocent Muslims, almost to a man.[11] A Shi'i Muslim assassinated ʿAbd al-ʿAziz in 1803 in retaliation for the destruction of Karbala and the enmity between the two sects intensified. The Wahhabi forces attacked the other major Shi'i shrine city in Iraq, Najaf, in 1806. But Najaf was prepared for the onslaught and its defenses held.

The Shia in Iraq clearly needed a better defense as future attacks seemed inevitable. The Hawza (the council of the leading Shi'i clergy) opted for a strategy of creating allies among the Bedouin tribes of Iraq, reasoning that the best defense against Bedouins was other Bedouins. It dispatched missionaries to instruct the tribal elders in the tenets and practices of Shia Islam. There had been some missionary activity among the tribes in the eighteenth century, but after the Wahhabi eruption that process accelerated. By the end of the nineteenth century, the majority of the country's Arabic-speaking population would at least nominally embrace Shia Islam.[12] Their strategy seemingly worked, as there were no further major Wahhabi attacks on the Shi'i holy cities in the nineteenth century.

It was the turn of the Sunni establishment in the empire to be shaken when the news arrived in 1803 that Mecca had fallen to ʿAbd al-ʿAziz's son, Saʿud ibn Saʿud. Although the Wahhabis later abandoned the city, they returned in 1805, advancing that time north to Medina, where they pulled down the dome over the Prophet's grave, which they claimed reeked of idolatry. The two Syrians who had reported Napoleon's adventures in Egypt also chronicled the advent of the Wahhabis. Yusuf Dimitri

[11] ʿUthman ibn Sanad al-Basri, *Mataliʿ al-suʿud* (Mosul: Wizarat al-Thaqafa wa al-Iʿlam, 1992), 241–2.

[12] Yitzhak Nakash, *The Shi'is of Iraq* (Princeton, NJ: Princeton University Press, 1994), 27–35.

ᶜAbbud had fled his native Aleppo in 1801 for Baghdad, because of the oppression of that city's governor, Katırağası Ibrahim Pasha, and was one of the first chroniclers to take notice of the Wahhabi threat. He reported that Wahhabi raiders had cut off trade between Damascus and Baghdad in 1801 and had attacked the hajj caravan from Baghdad, executing at least four hundred Persian pilgrims. In that unsettled time, plague hit Baghdad, and its governor, Büyük Süleyman Pasha, and most of his garrison withdrew from the city for the presumably healthier climate of northern Iraq. Taking advantage of their absence, the Wahhabis struck Karbala and were only deterred from entering Baghdad by the quick action of the governor's deputy, who took the troops back to the city.[13]

Hasan Agha in Damascus first mentioned the Wahhabis on 12 Safar 1218/3 June 1803, when he noted that the returning hajjis had reported that the Wahhabis seized Mecca, destroyed a number of graves there, and "killed some people." He ascribed the trouble to personal strife between ᶜAbdallah al-ᶜAzm, the governor of Damascus and leader of the hajj caravan, and the unnamed leader of Wahhabis, adding that the two "had squabbled like children." But ᶜAbdallah Pasha prevailed in the initial Wahhabi challenge to an Ottoman-sanctioned hajj and the hajjis returned to Damascus safely with most of their property intact.[14] Hasan Agha later reported the arrival of troops in Damascus from Istanbul to engage the Wahhabis on 13 October 1804. Instead of pursuing the tribesmen, however, the troops bivouacked in the Takiyya (the local name for the *tekke* built by Sultan Selim II), "drank night and day," and undertook no military activities.

Many in the city were already starving and clashes erupted between the city's local garrison and angry civilians, into which the Ottoman expeditionary force finally had to rouse itself to intervene.[15] It was difficult to sustain any initiative to pursue the Wahhabi raiders when there was anarchy in the streets of Damascus. The lack of a strong response, however, may also have been simply the product of sustained inertia that had characterized the local governor's saray for almost a half a century. There was no reward for taking decisive action and little retribution for not doing so. ᶜAbbud reported that when the governor of Damascus, ᶜAbdallah al-ᶜAzm, was ordered to move against the Wahhabis in 1803, he simply refused.[16]

[13] ᶜAbbud, *al-Murtadd*, 221–2; Longrigg, *Four Centuries of Modern Iraq*, 216–17.
[14] al-ᶜAbid, *Ta'rikh*, 86.
[15] Ibid., 122–3.
[16] ᶜAbbud, *al-Murtadd*, 226.

The Wahhabis continued to harass the pilgrims and in 1805 turned the Syrian hajj caravan back at Medina. Hasan Agha reported that coffee prices doubled with the news as pilgrims returning from the hajj traditionally enjoyed a near-monopoly over the import of coffee grown in Yemen to the city. Panic in the markets spread as people started to hoard other basic commodities and the guilds ordered work stoppages to protest the rising cost of almost everything. In the following year, the Wahhabis repeated their blockade and refused to allow Ottoman pilgrims to visit the Prophet Muhammad's grave in Medina. According to reports reaching Damascus, they stated that the pilgrims could only visit the Holy Cities if they offered fealty to the Wahhabi leader "ibn Mas'ud" (the author had not quite gotten the name right).[17] Abdallah's inaction now had consequences. Sultan Selim III replaced him as governor of Damascus with a properly Ottoman official, Genç Yusuf Pasha, in 1807 in what was one of that sultan's last acts before his overthrow in a palace coup. Yusuf Pasha started his term with a show of religious orthodoxy by imposing new regulations on the city's inhabitants, including placing a ban on the consumption of wine and 'araq by the city's Christians.[18]

A new governor in Damascus, however outwardly righteous, did not necessarily mean a firmer determination to carry out the sultan's orders. Later that year, Wahhabi raiders burned and looted villages in the Hawran, Damascus's major source of grain, which lay to the south of the city. Belatedly, Genç Yusuf went out to look for them but returned to the city without engaging the tribesmen.[19] Genç Yusuf had proven no more capable of turning back the Wahhabi threat than had his predecessor, and the new sultan, Mahmud II (1808–39), replaced him in 1809 with Süleyman Pasha. Süleyman began his career as a mamluk in the entourage of Cezzar Ahmed Pasha and succeeded him as governor in Acre upon his master's death in 1803. It is presumed that the sultan felt with his local experience and military background he might finally secure the empire's southern flank. But Süleyman also failed to act decisively against the Wahhabis and was replaced in 1811.

Sultan Mahmud II turned in desperation to Mehmed Ali, who had been formally recognized as the Ottoman governor in Egypt in 1805, to deal with the Wahhabi problem. Mehmed Ali, or Muhammad 'Ali in the Arabic pronunciation of his name, had arrived in Egypt in command of

[17] al-'Abid, *Ta'rikh*, 131–2; al-Dimashqi, *Ta'rikh*, 105–6.
[18] al-Dimashqi, *Ta'rikh*, 110–11.
[19] al-'Abid, *Ta'rikh*; 143–4.

a unit of Albanian irregulars in 1803, ostensibly to secure the province for the sultan. Gradually, however, he had managed to eliminate all local opposition and was in firm control of the province by 1811. In that year, Mehmed Ali appointed his son Tosun to the governorship of Jeddah who began preparations for campaign to take back the Holy Cities. Tosun succeeded in his initial mission, and Mecca and Medina were technically restored to Ottoman suzerainty in 1812. Hasan Agha marked the event by going on the hajj in the following year.[20]

The Wahhabi threat had not subsided entirely, as the governor of Aleppo, Ragib Pasha, received an order in March 1813 warning him to be alert for Wahhabi raiders, who were reported as being active in his province.[21] He was busy at that time, having to deal both with the continuing internal feuding in the city between the janissaries and the *ashraf* and with Kurds in the northern reaches of his province. Consequently, he paid little attention to the Wahhabis on his southern flank. He was replaced by the Anatolian *ayan* Çapanoğlu Celalettin Mehmed Pasha.[22] It was an indication of the deep concern on the part of Sultan Mahmud II to restore order in his Arab provinces that he would appoint to the important Aleppo governorship one of the very *ayan*s of Anatolia whose power he sought to destroy. But rather than moving against the Wahhabis, Çapanoğlu Mehmed simply arrested the janissary leadership in the city and sent them off to exile in Anatolia.

There was good reason for continuing concern in Istanbul. Despite his initial success in retaking the Holy Cities, Tosun was unable to defeat the Wahhabis decisively, and they continued to raid the caravan routes and vulnerable villages along the desert frontiers of the empire. Frustrated with his son's lack of success, Mehmed Ali took charge of the expeditionary force in 1813. The offensive halted, however, as he had to return to Egypt as news reached him that one of his mamluks was attempting a palace coup, with the reputed help of Sultan Mahmud II. If the second part of the rumor were true, the incident highlights the complex political machinations that Mahmud was willing to undertake to secure his throne. What seems to us as contradictory actions, Mahmud's appointment of a onetime rebel against his authority in Anatolia as governor of Aleppo due to the Wahhabi threat while seeking to unseat his governor in Cairo, who was the only man capable of ending that threat, was probably an

[20] Ibid., 156.
[21] Damascus, Aleppo AS, vol. XXXV, 90–1.
[22] Bodman, *Political Factions in Aleppo*, 129–30.

exercise of realpolitik. It was necessary to undermine the person whom Mahmud perceived as his most immediate threat. With that perspective, the Wahhabis, now confined to the Najd, did not pose a direct challenge to the dynasty's continued rule, but Mehmed Ali might pose one in the future. His elimination would also mean the return of Egypt, with all its revenues, to direct Ottoman rule.

Upon leaving Arabia, Mehmed Ali appointed his oldest son, Ibrahim, to lead the Egyptian army against the Wahhabis. It was a good choice, as Ibrahim proved to be an extremely skilled tactician, although the campaign initially stalled as the desert terrain proved an effective ally for the Wahhabis. Ibrahim was a quick learner, however, and he moved deeper into the deserts of the Arabian Peninsula, relying on those Bedouin tribes who had their own grudges against the Wahhabis. He was able in 1818 to capture Dar'iyya, the stronghold of the Wahhabi movement in the Najd, and with it ʿAbdallah, the leader of the clan of ibn Saʿud. Ibrahim dispatched ʿAbdallah to Istanbul, where he was beheaded for treason. Although the Wahhabis would not pose another serious military threat to the Ottoman Empire after 1818, the less militant aspects of the ideology of the movement's founder that called for a reform of Islam through the limited use of *ijtihad* was already disseminating among the Sunni scholars in the Arab lands.

INTERNAL THREATS: REBELLIONS IN ALEPPO AND THE PELOPONNESUS

The failure of successive governors of Damascus to counter the Wahhabi challenge pointed to a systemic decline of Ottoman authority throughout the Arab provinces in the early nineteenth century. Although the sultan could name and replace governors, the political order was rapidly deteriorating. With it came the threat of a collapse of civil order in the region's cities as armed challenges to the political establishment were no longer confined to the countryside. In the Balkans and Anatolia, Sultan Mahmud II faced the possibility of armed resistance from the private armies of the *ayan*s and that threat demanded his immediate attention. In Egypt, Mehmed Ali was increasingly expanding the parameters of his province's virtual independence. Farther afield, the Mamluk governors of Baghdad continued to hold sway over most of Iraq. In the Syrian provinces the squabbling among the rival governors of Sidon, Damascus, Tripoli, and Aleppo that had paralyzed the region during the Wahhabi crisis persisted. The people of Damascus had risen in rebellion in 1804. In a clear indication of their desperation, they drove the chief judge from the city. The extra troops sent to the city to fight the Wahhabis had suppressed that rebellion, but the underlying causes remained. The unstable political situation in the cities of the Fertile Crescent contrasted sharply to conditions in Egypt, where by 1811 Mehmed Ali had silenced all opposition to his rule. Without an equivalent military force at its disposal, however, urban anarchy threatened the continuation of the Ottoman regime in the Fertile Crescent as much as had the Wahhabi warriors.

In a demonstration of that fragility, Aleppo's inhabitants rose in rebellion on 23 October 1819 against the entourage of the city's governor, Hürşid Pasha, while he was away dealing with a revolt in Diyarbakır province. The city of Aleppo provides an illustrative example of the decline in the fortunes of the cities of the Fertile Crescent over the course of the eighteenth century. In the seventeenth century, it had been home to more than 100,000 inhabitants, making it the third largest city in the empire after Istanbul and Cairo in terms of population. By 1819, that number had shrunk to less than 80,000. Once it had served as an international commercial hub, hosting dozens of foreign merchants, but by the time of the revolt, there were only an Englishman and two Frenchmen resident in the city. During the second half of the eighteenth century, many of the city's males divided into two armed factions: the *ashraf*, who claimed descent from the Prophet Muhammad, and the janissaries. The clashes between them were often violent and one particularly severe period of unrest closed the city down for seven months in 1797–8, with barricades preventing the easy movement from one quarter to another.[23]

Given the internal factionalism in the city, no strongman emerged to take control. In 1818, Istanbul dispatched Hürşid Pasha, a professional Ottoman military officer, to be governor, and many of Aleppo's people hoped for a firm hand that could impose order. Although the later chroniclers of the city gave the new governor high marks personally, they excoriated his men as having been frequently drunk and disruptive.[24] All in all, the *aʿyan* were disappointed. Taking the opportunity of the governor's absence, some of them decided to send a message to their sultan.

There is an eyewitness account of what happened next in the chronicle of the city's Maronite Catholic bishop, Bulus Arutin (d. 1851). On the night of 22 October 1819, twelve leaders of the *ashraf* went to the eastern, extramural quarter of Qarliq, heavily populated by the janissaries

[23] ʿAbbud, *al-Murtadd*, 185–8.
[24] al-Ghazzi, *Nahr al-dhahab*, vol. III, 324; Muhammad Raghib Tabbakh, *Iʿlam al-nubala bi-taʾrikh halab al-shaba*, 3 vols. (Aleppo: Dar al-Qalam al-ʿArabi, 1977), vol. III, 312.

and their families, and raised the inhabitants in revolt. This "rabble" then went to the houses in their quarter where the governor's troops were quartered and killed them.[25] Faced with a sizable insurrection, Sultan Mahmud II dispatched orders to the governors of Adana and Kayseri to lead troops to Aleppo to join the siege of the city that Hürşid Pasha initiated upon his return. A period of prolonged negotiations followed, during which there was intermittent fighting.[26]

During the siege, the city's inhabitants split over whether or not to accept the terms of surrender offered by Hürşid Pasha. The *ashraf* agreed, but the janissaries held out for a promise that their leaders did not have to go again into exile as had occurred five years earlier during the governorship of Çapanoğlu Celalettin Mehmed Pasha. After prolonged fighting, the janissaries accepted a truce brokered by the leading merchants in the city that would permit their leaders to remain in the city if they put down their arms. But when the troops entered the eastern suburbs, they arrested the leading janissary *agha*s (officers), in violation of the truce agreement. In Bishop Arutin's explanation of the events the "people of Aleppo" in the eastern suburbs rose up to free them. Their resistance led to the sacking of those quarters by the Ottoman troops and the execution of the janissary leaders. Executions of janissaries by beheading and of their reputed Christian allies by hanging continued for several weeks afterward. Among those condemned to death was the wife of one of the janissary leaders who was hanged from one of the city's gates for having created a public ruckus by screaming for justice outside the central courthouse and throwing rocks that broke its windows. Order was restored but social tensions persisted in the city.[27]

The rebellion in Aleppo had been suppressed, but that did not mean a restoration of either order or good government. Troubles in the Arab provinces, whether from tribal incursions or urban unrest, were not at the forefront of Sultan Mahmud's concerns, and few resources from the central treasury were available to support a forceful reassertion of Ottoman authority in Asia generally. The situation in Europe continued to unravel, even as the sultan was able to crush the *ayan* families in the Balkans.

[25] Yusuf Qara'li, editor, *Ahamm hawadith halab fi nifs al-awwal min al-qarn al tasiʿ ʿashar* (Cairo: Imprimerie Syrienne, 1933), 36–7.

[26] al-Tabbakh, *Iʿlam al-nubala'*, vol. III, 320.

[27] Bruce Masters, "Aleppo's Janissaries: Crime Syndicate or *Vox Populi*?" In *Popular Protest and Political Participation in the Ottoman Empire: Studies in Honor of Suraiya Faroqhi*, edited by Eleni Gara, M. Erdem Kabadayı, and Christoph Neumann (Istanbul: İstanbul Bilgi Üniversitesi Yayınları, 2011), 165–7.

Popular rebellions in Wallachia and the Peloponnesus at the start of what would become the Greek War for Independence in 1821 took precedence in the capital over events occurring in the distant east. Adding to the political instability, some Muslims in the capital and in parts of Anatolia responded to the risings in the Balkans, as had Hasan Agha to Napoleon's occupation of Egypt, by casting the strife in sectarian terms. As news of the outbreak of rebellion in the Greek city of Patras on 25 March 1821 reached Istanbul, a mob led by janissaries hanged the Orthodox ecumenical patriarch Grigorios V from the gates of his Patriarchate on Easter 1821. Soon afterward, Muslim irregulars massacred much of the Greek population on the island of Chios in response to rumors of massacres of Muslims by Greek rebels in the Peloponnesus. The sectarian/ethnic conflicts that would plague the Ottoman Empire until its demise had begun.

There was also concern, if not rioting, among some Muslims in the Arab provinces, although fear of an actual Christian insurrection seemed to have been stronger in the governors' *saray*s than among the Muslim Arab population at large. In part, it arose out of confusion over labels. In Ottoman Turkish and Arabic, the word *Rum* meant both the community of Greek Orthodox faithful and ethnic Greeks. So exactly who was in revolt was not clear to the Muslims in the Arab lands. Simply put, the Rum for them were generically the source of the rebellion with no differentiation as to other aspects of their identity. Ethnicity as opposed to religious community still remained a largely unrecognized social construct for most. Members of the Melkite Catholic community in Aleppo, who had broken away from the larger Orthodox community in 1725, were quick to make that distinction clear, however, with the unfolding of events in Greece. They had managed to avoid prolonged government interference in their religious life throughout most of the eighteenth century. That benign toleration ended in 1818 as Sultan Mahmud II, at the urging of the same ecumenical patriarch in Istanbul who would be lynched a mere three years later, imposed a return of the Catholics to the Orthodox Church and a suppression of Catholic rites.

Taking note of the Greek insurrection, a delegation from the Melkite Catholic community went before Aleppo's chief judge on 16 April 1821 and swore that they were the sultan's loyal subjects. To clarify matters before a skeptical judge, they affirmed that while they were Rum (Greek Orthodox), they were not Yunan, a word revived from medieval Arabic to denote ethnic Greeks. Their deposition was sent on to Istanbul, supported by separate depositions from local Muslim notables affirming the Catholics' good behavior and loyalty. Sultan Mahmud II responded with an order in October that declared that the Catholics in the city were a sect (*taife*) that was indeed separate from the Orthodox. As loyal subjects, unlike the perfidious Orthodox, they were free to worship in the manner to which they were accustomed.[28]

Public anger at the Greek insurrection was not so easily dodged in Damascus, where the overwhelming majority of the Christian population of the city remained loyal to Orthodoxy. The governor of Damascus read aloud the order from Istanbul that rebellious Orthodox leaders were to be executed and all the community humbled. Muslim notables responded that there were no rebels in the city and that the Christians in the city had always behaved as they should. As such, they should not be harassed further. The governor ordered that the Christians return to wearing the black outer clothing that was required by Muslim legal tradition but was frequently ignored. The Christians responded by offering a bribe of 50,000 piasters to the governor to allow them to wear what they wished.[29] It was accepted and no other action was taken, but in Beirut, some of the Orthodox clergy were imprisoned, as were those of the laity who spoke Greek.[30]

In Jerusalem, which had a large resident community of ethnically Greek clergy and pilgrims, there was a mixture of elation and fear at the news of the rising. Neophytos, a Cypriot monk of the Order of the Holy Sepulcher, wrote: "That was a great and holy day, the sixth of April, when news arrived of the rebellion of the Greeks from the yoke of slavery!" But there was also unease over possible Muslim retribution. That fear proved justified as Muslims looted Christian homes, under the pretense of looking for arms, and there were frequent rumors of more drastic action to come. On 8 July 1821, the chief Muslim judge of Jerusalem announced at Friday prayers at the Haram al-Sharif that the few arms that the Christians held had been collected; they were loyal and none should be killed without explicit orders to do so from the governor in Damascus. With that, the Muslim *aʿyan* worked to break up any groups of Muslim commoners that seemed to be forming to attack the Christians. Subsequently, the situation in Jerusalem calmed down.[31]

[28] Masters, *Christians and Jews*, 98–108.
[29] Mikhayil Mishaqa, *Murder, Mayhem, Pillage, and Plunder: The History of Lebanon in the 18th and 19th Centuries*, translated by Wheeler Thackston, Jr. (Albany: State University of New York Press, 1988), 121–2.
[30] Assaad Kayat, *A Voice from Lebanon* (London: Madden, 1847), 26.
[31] Neophitos of Cyprus, "Extracts from the Annals of Palestine, 1821–1841," translated by S. N. Spyridon. *The Journal of the Palestine Oriental Society* 18 (1938). Reprinted under

Sultan Mahmud II's forces proved unable to dislodge the Greek rebels from their stronghold in the Peloponnesus, and he was finally forced to turn once more to his "loyal governor" of Egypt, Mehmed Ali, for military assistance. In the years following the Arabian expedition, Mehmed Ali and his son Ibrahim had built a conscript army, trained by Europeans and Americans, to fight a conventional European-style war. The Egyptian troops arrived in 1825 and the tide of victory quickly turned against the Greeks. Hasan Agha in Damascus concluded his entry for 1241 (1825–6) after having briefly recounted the uprising, "Then God gave victory to Islam and the Muslims were able after much violence and suffering to take back most of what was lost."[32]

Sultan Mahmud used the success of the Egyptian army to move in 1826 against the janissaries, who were seen not only as incompetent but also as an impediment to his building a modern army. Hasan Agha reported that news reached Damascus that twenty thousand janissaries had been killed in a massacre in Istanbul as "they had rebelled against kings, ministers, and the masters of the state to the point that they had frightened both big and small."[33] He did not record whether any action was taken against the janissary garrison in his own city, although an order abolishing their rank and privileges was received in Damascus in July of that year.[34] The governor of Aleppo received a similar order on 14 July 1826 and was told to be on the lookout for janissaries who had escaped the slaughter in Istanbul and taken refuge in Anatolia.[35] In December 1827, however, the janissaries were involved in a dispute with the coffee sellers guild in Aleppo, and it is apparent that they continued to function as a corporate group in the city after the corps' official dissolution.[36] Elsewhere in the Arabic-speaking provinces when the mamluk governor Davud Pasha received the order for the decommissioning of the corps in Baghdad, he did so and then promptly recruited those same men into a new unit commanded by a French officer.[37]

The success of Mehmed Ali's army in Greece prompted Russia, France, and Britain to intervene in the Greek struggle for independence from

the title, Farqim be-Toldot Eretz Yisrael [1821–41] (Jerusalem: Ariel Publishing House, 1979), 11–16.

[32] al-ʿAbid, *Taʾrikh*, 166–7.
[33] Ibid., 182.
[34] Damascus, Damascus Awamir al-Sultaniyya (Damascus AS), vol. III, 29.
[35] Damascus, Aleppo AS, vol. XLIII, 55–9.
[36] Damascus, Aleppo AS vol. XLIV, 128–9.
[37] Holt, *Egypt and the Fertile Crescent*, 248.

the Ottoman Empire in 1827. Within the space of a few months in the following year, Istanbul ordered the collection of large sums of money from Aleppo for the war effort, 502,500 piasters in February and another 650,000 in April, stating that such extraordinary measures were necessary, as there were "rebellion and lawlessness in Rumeli (the Balkans) and Russia, France, and England had attacked the `kingdoms of Islam' (*memalik-i islamiyye*, i.e. the Ottoman Empire)."[38] In addition, the province was required to provide 350 cavalrymen for the war effort and the governor was ordered to confiscate all weapons held by Christians.[39] Such desperate measures did not turn the tide of battle, however, and Sultan Mahmud was forced to recognize Greek independence in 1829.

The two revolts, in Aleppo and the Peloponnesus, only two years apart had much in common on the surface. Both occurred as local governors sensing that the sultan was distracted by larger matters had imposed what was viewed by their subjects as despotic and capricious rule. Although the nationalists would lay claim to the uprisings in Wallachia and Greece, it is not clear that those who had risen did so solely for the cause of the Greek nation.[40] The difference between the trajectories of the two uprisings is, however, telling. Once a revolt had occurred in the Peloponnesus, whether it was mounted in the name of Greece or Christendom, or a combination of the two as the new national flag prominently displayed a cross, Greek-speaking Christians could imagine the revolt as the opportunity to overthrow a hated regime that extended beyond the provincial *saray* to the capital itself.

The rebels in Aleppo could not envision a regime change beyond the removal of a hated governor. Their appeals to the sultan for justice, as would be the case of rebels in the same city in 1850, cast themselves as the sultan's loyal subjects, who only sought his justice. In Greece, those rebelling proudly proclaimed themselves to be rebels. In their view, they were fighting for the cause of liberty against a tyrannical sultan, if not quite yet for national liberation. Despite its limited objectives, the rebellion in Aleppo had signaled that there was a looming crisis for the continuity of Ottoman rule in the Arab lands. The Ottomans were holding on to power in the region largely as no one, other than the Wahhabis, had been bold enough to challenge the tradition that their rule was ordained by God. That would soon change.

[38] Damascus, Aleppo AS, vol. XLV, 4–5, 134–7.
[39] Ibid., vol. XLV, 26–7, 32.
[40] Roger Just, "Triumph of the Ethnos." In *History and Ethnicity*, edited by Elizabeth Tonkin, Maryon McDonald, and Malcolm Chapman (London: Routledge, 1989), 71–88.

IBRAHIM PASHA AND THE EGYPTIAN OCCUPATION

The military resources that Sultan Mahmud could muster to exercise direct control over his Arab territories were by 1830 severely limited. Orders appointing governors and chief judges still arrived in the provincial capitals, but those appointees often failed to appear. When they did do so, there is little indication that they had the resources or the inclination to rule effectively in the sultan's name. In 1830, an unnamed *mütesellim* (provisional tax collector) sent a memorandum to Istanbul outlining the political and economic conditions in Aleppo province. It was brutally frank for an Ottoman document. The author began by invoking the memory of the Umayyad "Princes" (*Ümerâ-yı Ümeviye*) and the Abbasid Caliphs (*Hülefâ-yı Abbasiye*) when the regions known as *Irak-ı Arab* (central Iraq) and *Cezire* (northern Iraq and eastern Syria) were flourishing and villages lined the Euphrates River. But afterward, he wrote, infidels from the nations of Europe had conquered the kingdoms of Anatolia. They were followed by the "enemy of the faith" (*düşman-ı din*) Timur-i lenk Han (Tamerlane), who devastated the villages and dispersed their inhabitants. In recent years, he continued, the tribes of the ʿAnaza and others from Darʿiyya in the Najd (an implicit reference to the Wahhabi confederation) had brought their herds to the Euphrates and no villages remained. Furthermore, these tribesmen were now at the very outskirts of the towns of Hama, Homs, Maʿarat al-Nuʿman, Aleppo, and Ayntab (Gaziantep), threatening trade and villagers. They were joined by formerly obedient Kurdish and Turkmen tribesmen. In the districts of Jisr al-Shughur, Jabal Samʿan, and Harim (to the west, north, and east of the city of Aleppo), the tribes had forced the abandonment of numerous villages that only a few decades before had been flourishing. Agricultural lands lay deserted everywhere, he wrote; there was no revenue and the caravan trade suffered.[41]

It was not only in northern Syria that security was unraveling in the absence of a strong Ottoman military presence in the Arab lands. The often-violent competition between the governors of Sidon and those of Damascus continued. The men holding the governorship of Sidon were connected to the "household" begun by Cezzar Ahmed and continued to rule from the heavily fortified city of Acre. In that unstable political climate, Bashir II al-Shihabi, the local strongman in southern Lebanon, played an increasingly prominent role. In 1821, Bashir joined in the

---

[41] Istanbul, BOA, Hatt-ı Hümayûn 4806.İ.

conflict between the two provincial governors by siding with ʿAbdallah Pasha of Sidon against Derviş Pasha, the governor of Damascus. The two men, who had become temporary allies, provide an illustration of the often convoluted road to power that marked early nineteenth-century Syria. ʿAbdallah was the son of the steward (*kahya*) in the household of Süleyman Pasha, governor of Sidon. Süleyman had succeeded his former master, Cezzar Ahmed, to the governor's *saray* and had also served as governor of Damascus, 1809–11. At Süleyman's death, ʿAbdallah gained the governorship of Sidon in 1820 at age eighteen through the intervention of the Jewish banker Haim Farhi, who had served both Süleyman and ʿAbdallah's father. Farhi most probably came to regret his intervention in gaining his protégé the governorship as within a year, ʿAbdallah had his old mentor strangled.[42]

Bashir's rise to power as "emir of the Mountain," as the paramount Druze chieftain in Lebanon was known, had been marked by treachery that was almost the equal of that of his new ally in Acre. Bashir waged a drawn-out campaign against the other prominent Druze clans for the title and bruised some egos along his way to the top. His family, the clan of al-Shihab, had held the position as emir from 1697, when the last male heir of the then-reigning family, al-Maʿn, died. In that political vacuum, the Druze elders chose Haydar al-Shihab as emir. Haydar was nominally a Sunni Muslim, but his mother was a Druze from the al-Maʿn clan and that seemed a sufficient lineage for the elders. Among the extended Shihab family, formal religion did not seem to be of great importance. Some were openly Christians, others Sunni Muslims, and still others Druzes. Members of the Shihab clan held the title of emir throughout the eighteenth century, deftly playing off the contending Druze clans who sought it for one of their own and cagily visiting and supporting Sunni, Druze, and Maronite Christian shrines. That was a useful strategy in the Lebanese mountains, where all three religious communities were heavily armed.

Bashir and ʿAbdallah distrusted each other and rightly so as each man in his own way had proven himself untrustworthy. United momentarily, they were able to defeat Derviş Pasha in May 1822. Their victory was short-lived, however, as it provoked Sultan Mahmud II to dispatch troops from Aleppo to aid his governor in Damascus. The Ottoman forces besieged Acre in July 1822 and Bashir fled to Egypt, where he cultivated the friendship of Mehmed Ali. Sultan Mahmud's need for Mehmed Ali's

---

[42] Philipp, *Acre*, 85–9.

support in Greece ultimately outweighed his desire to punish the two rebels. Mehmed Ali was able not only to have the onetime rebel ᶜAbdallah reinstated as governor of Sidon, but also to ease Bashir's way back to Lebanon through his influence in Istanbul. British diplomats were convinced that while he was in Egypt, Bashir had made an agreement to aid Mehmed Ali should he decide to move into Syria and they predicted that Egypt's strongman would soon attack the Ottoman Empire.[43]

It did not require much of an intelligence network to reach that conclusion. Mehmed Ali had demanded the governorship of Syria in payment for his participation in the war in Greece in 1827. Sultan Mahmud II demurred from making that grand gesture, offering him the island of Crete instead. Whatever machinations had occurred in private between the governor of Egypt and the various parties contending for power in southern Syria and Lebanon, the official reason for the Egyptian army's advance on Acre in October 1831 was that ᶜAbdallah had given shelter to several thousand Egyptian draft dodgers.

Acre resisted the Egyptian advance as it had the earlier invasion by Napoleon Bonaparte. Sultan Mahmud declared Mehmed Ali, formerly his "loyal governor," a traitor while the onetime traitor ᶜAbdallah had once again become a loyal governor. Bashir al-Shihabi, in contrast, committed his forces on the side of his old protector in an open revolt against his sultan. In early December 1831, the chief judge and *aᶜyan* of Aleppo were informed that the "rebel" Mehmed Ali had taken al-Arish and Sidon and was besieging Acre. Soon afterward, a new governor, Mehmed Pasha, arrived in Aleppo and he was instructed to raise troops and advance to aid the defenders of Acre.[44] It is not clear whether the troops from Aleppo ever materialized to help the besieged city. If they did so, they do not seem to have made a difference. With its once-formidable walls breached by the Egyptian artillery, Acre fell to Ibrahim Pasha in May 1832. Neophytos recorded the reaction to the news of the fall of Acre in Jerusalem:

For five days the people of Jerusalem, Moslems, Greeks, Franks, Armenians, and even Jews made merry. All were happy and delighted at the thought that Egyptian entry meant freedom (as it really did.) The Moslems alone could not hide their sorrow and sullenness (although they danced with the rest), because they had a presentiment that Egypt would use its power against them.... They heard and saw things which they hated to hear and see, namely regular soldiers wearing

---

[43] William Polk, *The Opening of Southern Lebanon, 1788–1840: A Study of the Impact of the West on the Middle East* (Cambridge, MA: Harvard University Press, 1963), 87–9.

[44] Damascus, Aleppo AS, vol. XLVII, 67–8.

tight trousers and carrying terrible fire-arms and musical instruments, and marching in formation after the European fashion.[45]

Ibrahim's forces then moved on Damascus. The inhabitants of the city had rebelled against their governor in 1831 and petitioned Istanbul for his replacement. At the start of June 1832, the acting governor attempted to rally them to mount a defense of their city against the advancing Egyptian army but was unsuccessful. Clearly, many in the city felt that a regime change might indeed be a good thing, and without the moral support of the city's *aʿyan*, the governor fled. Egyptian troops supported by Druze and Maronite militias from Lebanon entered Damascus unopposed. Shortly thereafter, Ibrahim defeated an Ottoman army near Homs and his forces occupied Aleppo in July. He then went on to defeat an Ottoman army sent to stop him near Iskanderun (Alexandrette) and continued his march into Anatolia. Ibrahim overcame yet another Ottoman army, led by Grand Vizier Hüsrev Pasha, at Konya in December 1832 and the road to Istanbul was open.

Konya was a crushing defeat for the Ottomans. Sultan Mahmud had prepared his new army, modeled after that of Mehmed Ali, with conscripts and Western training but it was clearly no match for that of his erstwhile governor. Desperate, Mahmud turned to Russia for support, an act that in turn frightened Britain and France into action. That may have been his intention. The Western powers brokered the Convention of Kütahya in May 1833 by which Ibrahim withdrew his troops from the Ottoman Empire's Anatolian heartland. In return, Syria was granted to his father as a lifetime governorship. For that concession, Mehmed Ali had to pay a yearly tribute to the sultan and returned to his status as "loyal governor." The façade of empire had been maintained but at a terrific cost.

Amidst all the bad news, Sultan Mahmud could be gratified by one small victory. Before the Egyptian invasion of Syria, he had granted Ali Rıza Pasha the title of governor of Aleppo and of Iraq. The latter province included the cities of Baghdad and Basra but not Mosul, where a scion of the Jalili dynasty continued to rule. An advanced party of his forces reached Baghdad in the summer of 1831 and deposed the Mamluk regime that had governed the city for almost a century. A popular uprising in the city derailed the restoration of direct Ottoman control, however, and it was not until September that Ali Rıza entered the city to establish order. The last of the mamluk governors, Davud Pasha, was

[45] Neophitos, *Extracts*, 29–30.

taken to Istanbul, from which he was allowed to go into exile in Medina. With the death of Mosul's governor, Yahya al-Jalili, in 1834, Ottoman governors were appointed there as well.[46] Ottoman control remained tenuous in the Iraqi provinces for the next decade. As an indication of that reality, Iran's Mohammad Qajar Shah offered military assistance to Istanbul against Ibrahim Pasha in Syria in return for its ceding Baghdad to Iran.[47] The Ottomans declined the offer and those at the sultan's court could perhaps take solace in the fact that although they had lost Syria, they had regained Iraq.

The Egyptian administration organized Syria, which it labeled Arabistan, into a single province with Damascus as its capital and Ibrahim as its governor. It looked briefly as if the ulama might be ready to shift their loyalty to a new dynasty as the Muslim population initially received the Egyptian occupation without outward sign of alarm. That all changed as the centralized regime that had been in force in Egypt for a decade was imposed on Syria. In particular, Ibrahim implemented two initiatives that met with almost immediate resistance: conscription and the collection of an individual poll tax from all adult Muslim males (*ferde* in Ottoman Turkish), with a sliding scale based on their wealth. Previously, only non-Muslims had to pay such a tax. Both measures were essential in order to implement the level of centralized control over the province that he envisioned.[48] A disciplined army was necessary to extend the state's control and taxes would finance it. The immediate cause of the revolt in Damascus in 1831, however, had been a similar scheme for taxing individual Muslim males directly and resistance to both the new tax and the draft was not long in coming.

Ibrahim Pasha informed the Janissary *agha*s in Aleppo in 1833, clear proof if any was necessary that the institution had not died in 1826, that their sons would have to accompany him to Gaza, where they would be a part of his new, European-trained conscript army. In response, one of the janissary leaders, Ahmad Agha ibn Hashim, organized a plot to assassinate Ibrahim and raise the city in rebellion against the Egyptian army as had occurred against an Ottoman governor fourteen years earlier. Word

---

[46] Rizk Khoury, *State and Provincial Society*, 205–12; Longrigg, *Four Centuries*, 250–76; Ebubekir Ceylan, *The Ottoman Origins of Modern Iraq: Political Reform, Modernization and Development in the Nineteenth-Century Middle East* (London: I. B. Tauris, 2011), 42–7.

[47] Ibid., 43.

[48] Khaled Fahmy, *All the Pasha's Men: Mehmed Ali, His Army and the Making of Modern Egypt* (Cambridge: Cambridge University Press, 1997), 112–59.

of the plot leaked out, however, and Ahmad was executed along with a number of other leaders of the janissary faction.[49] With that decisive, if brutal action, the janissaries were temporarily silenced and general conscription for Muslims was introduced in 1834. The result was the flight of hundreds of young men to Mosul and Diyarbakır, cities that were still under Ottoman control.[50]

The reaction to conscription was more sustained in the southern regions of the new province and armed revolts temporarily drove the Egyptians from Jerusalem in May 1834. The Egyptian forces were able to recapture the city, but scattered rebellions continued throughout Palestine and in the Hawran region of Syria during the summer. Blaming the ulama and the *aʿyan* for fomenting the resistance, Mehmed Ali arrested some of the most prominent men in Jerusalem and exiled them to Egypt.[51] The honeymoon with the Egyptian occupation had proved short-lived. Sultan Mahmud was aware of the rift and began to cultivate the Syrian Muslim establishment through letters of support and financial gifts. Mehmed Ali had shown little respect for the ulama in Egypt in his quest for power. His son followed his example by seeking to replace their central role in the governance of Arabistan's cities through the reduction of the authority and the legal brief of the Muslim courts.

To further that aim, Ibrahim created in every major Syrian city a body known as the *majlis* (alternately, *diwan*) *al-shura*, the "consultative assembly," consisting of the governor of the town, a financial officer, and representatives of the *aʿyan*. He gave these assemblies supervision over many of the economic transactions that had previously been regulated by Islamic law as well as responsibility for criminal prosecutions. The authority of the Islamic courts was to be henceforth limited only to matters of personal law: marriage, divorce, and inheritance. It was not just a question of secular versus religious jurisdiction for the provincial assemblies that elicited discontent among the ranks of the religious establishment. As their role as judges and arbiters in the Muslim courts had provided them with substantial fees, the legal innovations deprived them of income as well as influence. In addition, the Egyptian regime centralized the administration of the *waqf* properties under its control, thereby alienating the ulama from another of their customary sources

[49] al-Tabbakh, *Iʿlam al-nubala*, vol. III, 340–1.
[50] Istanbul, BOA Hatt-ı Hümayûn, 3190.
[51] Judith Rood, *Sacred Law in the Holy City: The Khedival Challenge to the Ottomans as Seen from Jerusalem, 1829–1841* (Leiden: Brill, 2004), 122–37.

of personal enrichment.[52] The Egyptian occupation was proving itself to be both a political and an economic threat to the ulama's established place in Syrian urban life. Whatever possibility there had been that Syria's ulama might accede to Mehmed Ali's rule vanished.

Further driving a wedge between the ulama and the Egyptian occupation was Mehmed Ali's treatment of the region's Christians. Maronite Christian militiamen serving under Emir Bashir played a role in policing the province and that could hardly go unnoticed by Muslims. But not all of Syria's Christians were happy with the new regime. In a stunning defeat for the Orthodox establishment in Syria, Ibrahim favored the Melkite Catholics in all their disputes they had with their former "Mother Church," forcing the Orthodox to hand over some of their churches to the rival sect and recognizing the Melkite Catholic patriarch of Antioch, Maksimus Mazlum, as legitimate and the coequal to the Orthodox patriarch of that same see.[53] Adding insult to both Muslims and Orthodox Christians, the chief financial officer of Syria was Hanna Bahri, a Melkite Catholic. Replicating his position of influence at the provincial level, the chief financial officer in each of the councils in the other cities of the province was also a Christian and usually a Catholic. Christians were also represented in the *majlis al-shura* of most towns, providing them with a political voice for the first time since the Muslim conquest of Syria in the seventh century.

As a result, many of Syria's Catholics of the various Uniate sects became enthusiastic supporters of the Egyptian occupation. In 1835, a Syrian Catholic schoolteacher in Aleppo, Naʿum Bakhkhash, began to keep a diary in which he would continue to write until his death in 1875.[54] His entries for the years of the Egyptian occupation show his appreciation for the fairness with which his community was treated. Bakhkhash took particular satisfaction in the fact that the administration's chief financial officer in Aleppo was a Melkite Catholic, who frequently entertained prominent Uniate Catholic merchants in his home.[55] Not all innovations of the Egyptian occupation were so well received by the Christians. In 1837, a number of Christians were rounded up along with their Muslim

[52] Moshe Ma'oz, "Changes in the Position and Role of the Syrian 'Ulama in the 18th and 19th Centuries." In *The Syrian Land in the 18th and 19th Century*, edited by Thomas Philipp (Stuttgart: Franz Steiner Verlag, 1992), 109–19.

[53] Masters, "The Establishment of the Melkite Catholic *Millet* in 1848."

[54] Naʿum Bakhkhash, *Akhbar halab*, edited by Fr. Yusuf Qushaqji, 3 vols. (Aleppo: Matbaʿat Ihsan, 1985, 1987, 1992).

[55] Ibid., vol. I, 46.

compatriots in a general sweep of the city by Egyptian press gangs. The Christians were eventually able to buy their way out of military service by hiring substitutes from the more bellicose Armenians of Zeytun, in the northern reaches of the province.[56]

Despite their alarm at the prospect of conscription, Aleppo's Catholic population, if the diarist Naʿum Bakhkhash was representative, viewed the Egyptian occupation favorably as Ibrahim relaxed many of the traditional restraints that Islamic law imposed on them. As an indicator of their loyalties, the Catholics in Aleppo celebrated the defeat of the Ottoman army at Nezip in 1839 and worried at the news in 1840 that the British had forced the Egyptian army to withdraw from Syria.[57] The British consul in Aleppo, Edward Barker, also commented positively on the Egyptian occupation.

> The Egyptian being a just and strong Government, it guaranteed the lives and property of all its subjects. A woman could go alone with the greatest security, carrying any amount of money from one end of Syria and Palestine to the other (in the plains, not in the mountains). Venality, corruption, was almost unknown, being very severely punished.[58]

Although Barker's characterization of Ibrahim Pasha's rule was generally positive, he acknowledged that both conscription and taxation had soured much of Syria's population toward the regime.

Muhammad Raghib al-Tabbakh reproduced in his history of Aleppo a contemporary account of the Egyptian occupation, written by a Muslim religious scholar, Shaykh Salih ibn al-Shaykh Ahmad al-Martini al-Idlibi. Shaykh Salih excoriated the Egyptians. In contrast to Barker's metaphor of a woman traveling safely in Syria under the occupation, he wrote that women were so afraid of rape by the Egyptian soldiers that they dared not venture from their homes during the occupation. Furthermore, Shaykh Salih complained that the Egyptians had imposed the *jizya* on Muslims, a reference to the *ferde*, and allowed the Christians to act insolently toward them and, on occasion, physically abuse them. Last, he added that the impious Egyptians had torn down mosques to procure the stones with which to build stables for their horses. In his own summary of the Egyptian regime, al-Tabbakh editorialized that

---

[56] Ibid., vol. I, 70–2.

[57] Ibid., vol. I, 104, 150–1; Mikhayil Mishaqa, a Christian chronicler in Damascus, also expressed a positive impression of Ibrahim's rule, *Murder, Mayhem, Pillage, and Plunder*, 204–5.

[58] Edward Barker, *Syria and Egypt under the Last Five Sultans of Turkey*, 1876, 2 vols. (Reprint, New York: Arno Press, 1973), vol. II, 204.

Ibrahim Pasha had brought no improvements or "civilization" to the country but only wars.[59]

Shaykh Salih was not alone among the Syrian ulama in his view of the Egyptian occupation. It created a dilemma for Muslim scholars in Syria. Should they accept the new regime of Ibrahim Pasha as legitimate, following the age-old formula that whoever is in charge is legitimate as long as he is nominally a Muslim, or should they seek a legal justification that would validate insurrection? One of the first of the Arab scholars to recognize the Ottoman sultan as caliph was the Damascene scholar Muhammad Amin ibn ᶜAbidin (d. 1836), who did so as a means of justifying resistance. Living under Ibrahim Pasha's occupation, he like others of his class felt the need to declare himself on the side of the righteous. Ibn ᶜAbidin found the legitimization for his position in reviving the theory of the universal caliphate.

By establishing that Sultan Mahmud II was the rightful, universal caliph, ibn ᶜAbidin cast Mehmed Ali as a rebel against God's order. He argued that Ibrahim Pasha had lost any legitimate authority he might claim over the Muslims as he had removed all distinctions between Muslims and Christians in violation of the holy law. Ibn ᶜAbidin was thus willing to accede to the claim of the Ottoman sultan to the caliphate out of necessity. In his view, Muslims were obliged to render their fealty to the Ottoman sultan as caliph as long as he maintained the rule of religiously sanctioned law and fought the jihad against infidels and heretics.[60] Implicit in that call was a characterization of Ibrahim Pasha as a heretic, if not an actual infidel. Clearly, not everyone viewed the initial attempts at the centralization of political power imposed by Ibrahim Pasha on Syria through the same lens. What the European observers viewed favorably as progress toward their vision of "modernity" and some local Christians, most notably the Catholics, saw as their emancipation, many of the Muslim residents of the newly organized Arabistan experienced as despotic oppression (*taghut*).

CONCLUSION

If there is a consensus that the early nineteenth century witnessed the potential for major change in the Middle East that would usher in

---

[59] Tabbakh, *Iᶜlam*, vol. III, 345–8; Fahmy, *All the Pasha's Men*, 231–5.
[60] Fritz Steppat, "Khalifat, Dar al-Islam und die Loyalität der Araber zum osmanischen Reich bei hanafitischen Juristen des 19. Jahrhunderts" *Correspondence d'Orient No 11: VᵉCongrès International d'Arabisants et Islamisants* (Louvain: Centre pour l'Étude des Problèmes du Monde Mussulman Contemporain, 1970): 443–62.

the "modern age," the question of when exactly that age began in the Ottoman Arab provinces remains.[61] The answer, in large part, depends on your geographical perspective. For generations of Egyptian schoolchildren, the answer was unambiguously 1798 with the French occupation of Cairo. In the Egyptian nationalist narrative, Napoleon, although the first in a long line of Western imperialists who would plague the Egyptians for the next century and a half, ended the centuries-old despotic rule of the country by the Turks, whether in the guise of Mamluks or Ottomans.[62] In the anarchy that followed the French withdrawal from the country, Mehmed Ali would impose various schemes that would give rise to a highly centralized Egyptian nation-state. Although the historical verdict on the man himself is mixed, tyrant or enlightened despot, most in Egypt would concur that Mehmed Ali was the "founder of modern Egypt."[63]

Outside Egypt, there are other dates that loom as significant. Desert warriors sacked the shrine city of Karbala in 1801 in the name of the "purified" Islam taught by Muhammad ibn ʿAbd al-Wahhab. In 1803, they occupied briefly the holy city of Mecca. They returned again in 1805 when they also occupied Medina. Those events sent shock waves throughout the Muslim world. The impact on the Shia in Iraq was obvious, and their response was the cultivation of Bedouin tribes who might protect them from further attacks. Besides shock at the violence perpetrated on fellow Muslims, the political alliance of the House of ibn ʿAbd al-Wahhab with that of ibn Saʿud signaled for Sunni religious scholars an end to the monopoly over claims of political legitimacy that the House of Osman had enjoyed through the consensus of most of the Sunni scholarly community in the Ottoman Arab lands since the conquests in the sixteenth century. The question must have arisen for some, If the House of Osman can no longer provide security for the "people of the Sunna," what was its source of legitimacy?

Mehmed Ali, although designated as the Ottoman sultan's loyal governor of Egypt, would turn on his liege lord in 1831 and order his son Ibrahim to lead a Western-trained conscript army into Syria. Some historians of the region use that year to mark the commencement of the "modern age."[64] The Palestinian historian ʿAdel Mannaʿ considers the

---

[61] Dror Ze'evi, "Back to Napoleon? Thoughts on the Beginning of the Modern Era in the Middle East" *Mediterranean Historical Review* 19 (2004): 73–94.

[62] Ulrich Haarmann. "Ideology and History, Identity and Alterity: The Arab Image of the Turks from the 'Abbasids to Modern Egypt" *IJMES* 20 (1988): 175–96.

[63] Afaf Lutfi al-Sayyid Marsot, *Egypt in the Reign of Muhammad Ali* (Cambridge: Cambridge University Press, 1984); Fahmy, *All the Pasha's Men.*

[64] Moshe Ma'oz, *Ottoman Reform in Syria and Palestine 1840–1861: The Impact of the Tanzimat on politics and Society* (Oxford, 1968), 12–20.

Egyptian occupation to be a false start toward modernization, however, as Palestinian society remained fundamentally unchanged until the period of the Tanzimat reforms (1839–76).[65] The year 1831 also witnessed the Ottoman overthrow of the Mamluk regime in Baghdad. Ironically, given its distance from the capital, Baghdad was the first of the Arab provinces to experience attempts at a centralizing regime imposed from Istanbul. That begs the question whether more control from the center, accompanied by increasingly efficient means of taxation and greater effectiveness in imposing order through the military, equals political modernization.

For the North African provinces, their experience with "modernity" was tied more closely to events in Europe after 1831 with the French invasion of Algeria rather than to Istanbul. The year 1831 clearly marked a rupture with the past for the people of Algeria, where a French-imagined "modernity" was imposed by armed force at the cost of tens of thousands of lives. A pretense of Ottoman rule would continue in Tunisia until 1881 and in Egypt until 1914. In reality, however, most of North Africa was definitively "lost" to the Ottoman Empire in the nineteenth century. For the majority of North Africans, "modernization" meant imperialism with the modernity they experienced imposed upon them by Europeans.

The three occupations – Napoleon of Egypt, the Wahhabis of Mecca, and Ibrahim Pasha of Syria – signaled that there were alternatives to Ottoman rule in the Arab lands. These included European occupation, rule by ideologically driven tribal warriors, or that by another despot who had a stronger military, none of which was particularly appealing to the traditional Sunni Muslim elites. That these challenges occurred within roughly three decades enabled members of a single generation to experience, at least vicariously, all three. The trauma that those events produced clearly shook those who witnessed the occupations even from a distance. Nothing would ever be exactly the same again for them, and many must have wondered what momentous changes lay in the future. Where once there had been a sense of security vested in the House of Osman, there was now uncertainty as to whether the old order had the resources to survive any future onslaughts. If the arrival of the violent agents of change had any message for the peoples of the Ottoman Arab lands, it was that the coming years augured future pain.

---

[65] Manna‘, *Ta'rikh filistin*, 161–4.

6

The Tanzimat and the Time of Re-Ottomanization

When Sultan Abdülmecid I (1839–61) issued his "noble decree" (Hatt-ı Şerif) at Gülhane Park in Istanbul on 3 November 1839, its preamble made it clear that reform was necessary to restore the empire to the halcyon days of its past. The surface message was that that he did not seek to impose on his subjects anything that was new.[1] Imbedded in the call to a restoration of what had been, however, were hints of a future that would see radical breaks with that past. These included the end of tax farming, a call for universal male conscription, and the rather vague sentence "the Muslim and non-Muslim subjects of our lofty Sultanate shall, without exception, enjoy our imperial concessions." Historians of the Ottoman Empire have debated how to characterize the series of initiatives that were undertaken between 1839 and 1876, which were known in Ottoman Turkish as the Tanzimat (Reordering). Because the terms "Westernization" and "modernization" have fallen out of favor for some, a consensus has lately emerged that "the age of reform" is the appropriate, nonjudgmental designation for the period.[2]

The questions of the reform of what exactly and to what ends have not produced any agreement among historians, however. Şükrü Hanioğlu has argued that the framers only inserted the language of the preamble in a final draft of the proclamation to appease potential critics of

---

[1] Butrus Abu-Manneh, "The Islamic Roots of the Gülhane Receipt" *WI* 34 (1994): 173–203.
[2] A good review of this question is provided by Christoph Neumann, "Ottoman Provincial Towns from the Eighteenth to the Nineteenth Century: A Re-assessment of their Place in the Transformation of the Empire." In *The Empire in the City: Arab Provincial Capitals in the Late Ottoman Empire*, edited by Jens Hanssen, Thomas Philipp, Stefan Weber (Beirut: Orient-Institut der deutschen morgenländischen Gesellschaft, 2002): 133–44.

the initiative among the ulama. In his interpretation, the reformers did indeed seek to "modernize" the empire, following Western models.[3] Hanioğlu thus situates himself within the Turkish republican historiographical tradition, which interprets the Tanzimat as having been both self-consciously "modernizing" and "Westernizing," initiating a process that would ultimately result in the proclamation of the Turkish Republic in 1923.[4] Despite the much needed revisiting of the period, the interpretations currently in vogue among scholars still reflect a perspective that is both Istanbul-centric and implicitly sympathetic with the ambitions of the bureaucrats who initiated the "age of reform."

What the Tanzimat bureaucrats understood as "reform" was relative to their location at the empire's center. Programs that they conceived as transforming the empire to save it seemed to those living in the provinces as attempts by Istanbul to reimpose its control over their lives. For provincial elites, the era of the Tanzimat meant a renewal of direct Ottoman rule. Not since the first century following the Ottoman conquest of the Arab lands had the central state bureaucracy inserted itself so directly into the everyday lives of the sultan's Arab subjects. That was not necessarily, from their perspective, either reform or good. Faced with that skepticism, the reformers in the capital had to convince the sultan's myriad subjects that the preservation of the empire was in their best economic and political interests. While the Tanzimat failed ultimately in its objectives to secure the European provinces for the sultan, it succeeded in the Arabic-speaking regions in reestablishing direct Ottoman control after an absence of almost a century and a half. It also prepared the groundwork of reaching that more elusive goal, winning over the hearts and minds of the provincial elites to the sultan's cause.

The empire and the sultanate had largely been abstract ideals for earlier generations of the Arabic-speaking Muslim elite of the Ottoman Empire. Most wished it well although few participated in the governance of the empire. They had witnessed locally only sporadic periods of justice from the sultan's representatives. More typically, as indicated in their chronicles, they faced a succession of government officials who claimed to be acting in the sultan's name, but whom the chroniclers often characterized as being both corrupt and oppressive (*fasid wa zalim*). That bleak assessment of local government did not, however, diminish the

[3] M. Şükrü Hanioğlu, *A Brief History of the Late Ottoman Empire* (Princeton, NJ: Princeton University Press, 2008), 72–3.
[4] Halil İnalcık, "Sened-i İttikak ve Gülhane Hatt-ı Hümayûn" *Beletin* 28 (1964): 603–2.

chroniclers' faith in the sultanate itself. The Muslim scholarly class must, therefore, have welcomed the language of the proclamation of 1839, as it promised a return to their idealized version of the past. On the other side of the emerging sectarian divide, the Arabic-speaking Christian bourgeoisie undoubtedly took heart from the ambiguous language about equality and some became supporters of the reform efforts.

The daunting task before the Ottoman reformers was to reconcile the expectations of the two groups so that neither saw the material and political improvements that the reforms created for those not of their community as their loss, in a "zero-sum game" of winners and losers. To complicate both the pace and the scope of reform, the Ottoman bureaucrats were not working in a political vacuum. There were justified fears of ongoing rebellions in the Balkans and reform had by necessity to be accompanied by increased security. There was also unrelenting pressure on the part of European diplomats at the court in Istanbul to make the empire conform to their sometimes competing visions of what a modern state should be. At the same time, those diplomats sought to impose upon the Ottoman Empire unequal treaties for the benefit of Europe's merchants and bankers. Despite their protestations to the contrary, the Europeans rarely had the best interests of the empire at heart.

RESTORING THE SULTAN'S WRIT

Given the mixed verdict on the Egyptian occupation by the residents of Aleppo, their response to the arrival of the Ottoman army on the city's streets on 29 October 1840 was equally divided in a reflection of the sectarian tensions that had emerged with the Egyptian occupation. The Muslim population, already observing Ramadan, rejoiced. The Christians stayed off the streets or took shelter in the city's easily defensible stone caravansaries (*khans*), expecting the worst.[5] But on 15 January 1841, the newly installed Ottoman governor, Esad Muhlis Pasha, called the a*ʿyan* of Aleppo together and informed them of the Gülhane Decree guaranteeing the well-being of all the sultan's subjects. He added that the sultan viewed the Christians as his loyal subjects and that if anyone insulted them, the a*ʿyan* of the city would be held collectively responsible for those actions.[6] From that date, the diarist Bakhkhash reported a growing sympathy for the new regime among the Christians. This was highlighted in 1847 when

---

[5] Bakhkhash, *Akhbar halab*, vol. I, 151–4.
[6] Ibid., vol. I, 157.

a group of young Christian men decided to don that sartorial symbol of the Tanzimat era, the fez.[7]

The Egyptian troops pulled out of Damascus on 31 December 1840. That event inspired Muhammad Saʿid al-Ustuwani (d. 1888), a young scion of a notable family long famous for producing scholars, to begin a chronicle that he would maintain through 1861 when the events that had recently transpired in his city silenced his pen.[8] He recorded that Necib Pasha arrived as the newly appointed governor of Damascus on 21 April 1841 and promptly ordered that town be decorated with lanterns for five nights. The new governor held a reception in a large tent for the leading ulama and *aʿyan*, "the like of which had not been seen before."[9] The Muslim elite of Damascus may have been ambivalent about the arrival of the Egyptian army in 1832, but they were clearly happy to see their backs in 1840.

The Egyptian occupation in Syria provided a template for the Ottomans to follow in their attempts to reform the region and reestablish direct control from the capital. But the Ottomans did not retain all of the changes that had been imposed by their predecessors. They dismantled the centralized province of Arabistan with its capital of Damascus, returning interior Syria to its historic division between the province of Aleppo in the north and that of Damascus in the south. The coastal areas were united into one province, still named Sidon (Sayda), but with its new capital situated in Beirut, rather than in the fortress city of Acre. The move acknowledged that Beirut had emerged from among the competing port cities along Syria's coast to be the major commercial gateway to the region, regaining the status it had enjoyed in the late Mamluk period. The shift in provincial capitals from Sidon to Beirut was not the first time someone had recognized the latter city's renewed importance to the commerce of the eastern Mediterranean. The United States established a consulate in Beirut in 1836 during the Egyptian occupation and the American Board of Commissioners for Foreign Missions (ABCFM) established its regional headquarters in the city in 1823, to be followed in 1866 with the establishment of the Syrian Protestant College, the predecessor of the American University in Beirut. By the end of the nineteenth

---

[7] Ibid., vol. II, 47.
[8] Schilcher, *Families in Politics*, 181–4.
[9] Muhammad Saʿid al-Ustuwani, *Mashahid wa ahdath dimashqiyya fi muntasaf al-qarn al-tasiʿ al-ʿashar 1256 h.–1277 h. 1840 m.–1861 m.* (Damascus: Wizarat al-Iʿlam, 1994), 131–2.

century, Beirut, which had been a large village at the start of the century, was one of the Ottoman Empire's premier port cities.[10]

The provincial boundaries in Syria had returned to roughly what they had been before the Egyptian occupation, but the Ottoman reorganization contained two major departures from the earlier provincial system: advisory councils to the governors and a unified military command. Both were features of the government of occupation imposed on Syria by Ibrahim Pasha, and both served to undercut the power formerly held by the provincial governors. The Ottoman administration had apparently learned its lesson from the examples of the largely autonomous governors and *derebey*s in the eighteenth century and wanted to create a new balance of power to prevent the rise of local challengers in the governors' palaces. One regional rival in Egypt was clearly enough and Istanbul did not wish to see competing centers of power emerge in either Syria or Iraq to challenge its hegemony in the Arab lands.

Governors in the Arab provinces had convened in the earlier Ottoman centuries an informal *diwan*, or council, to advise them. These councils consisted of representatives of the leading Muslim religious authorities such as the chief qadi and the *naqib al-ashraf*, some of the *a'yan*, and the head of the janissaries. Replacing that arrangement, a new provincial governing body, known in Ottoman Turkish as the *meclis*, was mandated by the state after 1840. It was established in the Syrian provinces first and was later implemented in provincial centers across the empire including Iraq. Each *meclis* was granted authority over the management of the pious foundations (*awqaf*), poor relief, supervision of the guilds, and the appointment of village headmen in the province. The *meclis* also served as an appeals court to decisions made in the local sharia courts and later, once they were established in the 1860s, the commercial courts.

The provincial governing bodies quickly appropriated many of the functions that the qadi had traditionally performed. Despite that outcome, their establishment seemingly elicited little or no opposition from the religious authorities, unlike the situation during the Egyptian occupation. The lack of a reaction may have stemmed, in part, from the fact that the ulama were heavily represented in the *meclis* of every Syrian province. In addition, other members of the body were drawn from the same elite families from which they came. The Egyptian regime had sought

---

[10] Leila Tarazi Fawaz, *Merchants and Migrants in Nineteenth-Century Beirut* (Cambridge, MA: Harvard University Press, 1983); Jens Hanssen, *Fin de Siècle Beirut: The Making of an Ottoman Provincial Capital* (Oxford: Oxford University Press, 2005).

to undercut the traditional authority that the ulama held in Syria's cities. The Ottomans were empowering them with increased responsibilities in local governance, even as they reduced the authority of the religious courts, which had long been the source of the ulama's power.

We have some insight into how an early Tanzimat era provincial *meclis* functioned, as the records of the proceedings of the *meclis* of Damascus from October 1844 to October 1845 have survived. The council consisted of twelve members and a clerk. They were all Muslims and constituted a virtual "Who's Who" from the prominent families of the city. Of the twelve, seven can be identified as belonging to the ulama. In another contrast with the civic bodies that had been established during the Egyptian occupation, there was no permanent representation of the city's Christians. In contrast, the provincial council that met in Baghdad in 1846 had twenty-three members, of whom five were non-Muslims. As was the case in Damascus, however, the Muslims on the council were drawn from the ranks of the ulama and the *aʿyan*.[11]

In both Damascus and Baghdad, the council was largely a rich man's club. It is estimated that seven members of the Damascus council and its clerk held 46.4 percent of the tax farms in the Ghuta, the fertile oasis to the south of the city. Nonetheless, the register from Damascus demonstrates that in their first attempt at a truly local, if not representative, government the members tried to work out both a just way of dealing with the 506 cases that came before them and to figure out for themselves exactly what the rather vague language in the 1839 Hatt-ı Şerif meant. In regard to issues arising from the non-Muslim communities, the council generally acted in a nonpartisan way.[12]

The cleavages that did appear among the membership in Damascus represented the fault lines and historic grievances that existed among members of the city's *aʿyan*. That suggests the old patterns of urban politics in the city had not changed. They had simply found a new venue.[13] The provincial *meclis* ruled on issues that had formerly gone directly to the governor, for example, petitions from villagers for redress of abuses perpetrated by the tax farmers in charge of their villages. That reduced the direct control the governor had over local political and economic issues. In addition, the Tanzimat reformers in Istanbul sought to limit the governors' military power by creating a central military command.

---

[11] Ceylan, *Ottoman Origins*, 113–17.
[12] Elizabeth Thompson, "Ottoman Political Reform in the Provinces: The Damascus Advisory Council in 1844–45" *IJMES* 25 (1993): 457–75.
[13] Schilcher, *Families in Politics*, 53–6.

Sultan Abdülmecid established a new Fifth Army to be known as the Arabistan Ordusu (the Army of the Land of the Arabs) with its headquarters in Aleppo in 1844. It later moved to Damascus.[14] A Sixth Army was created in 1848 to police the provinces of Basra, Baghdad, and Mosul and later the Hejaz. It was known as the İrak Ordusu (Army of Iraq) or, alternatively, the Bağdat Ordusu. Although both armies were created largely to control the Bedouins and protect the hajj, the Fifth Army was deployed against the rebels in Aleppo in 1850 and for restoration of order in Damascus after the riots there in July 1860.[15] Turkish officers commanded both armies, but local Arabic-speaking conscripts filled their ranks. They provided a level of security that been previously unknown in the region for at least two centuries and by 1880, the desert frontiers in Syria and Iraq were quiet. Conscription, however, created resentment in the Muslim population that would threaten the stability of the provincial regime that the Tanzimat reforms had put into place.

SECTARIAN DISSONANCE ON THE PERIPHERY

Muslim-Christian relations in the Arab provinces reached the point of rupture during the Tanzimat era. Stopping the deterioration in communal relations was, with historical hindsight, probably beyond the Ottomans' control. Nevertheless, those outside the empire at the time and the Christians within it would blame the Ottoman authorities for the breakdown. Some among the Muslim population of the empire would cast the blame on outsiders for the troubles as the European powers pressured the Ottoman state to push the amelioration of the conditions under which the Christians lived to the forefront of its reform agenda. Religious identity was increasingly politicized as many Muslims saw the gains made by the Christians in the Tanzimat era as undermining the Muslims' traditionally dominant role in Ottoman society. The populations of most of the Arab provinces would experience some level of intercommunal tensions during the decades following the Egyptian withdrawal from Syria, but they exploded first in the mountains along the periphery of the core Arab provinces.

The Ottoman government perennially faced difficulty in governing two regions within, or partially within, the boundaries of the Arab

---

[14] Norman Lewis, *Nomads and Settlers in Syria and Jordan, 1800–1980* (Cambridge: Cambridge University Press, 1987), 25–6.

[15] Lewis, *Nomads and Settlers,* 28–30; Virginia Aksan, *Ottoman Wars 1700–1870: An Empire Besieged* (Harlow, UK: Pearson Longman, 2007), 408–14.

provinces: Lebanon and Kurdistan. Both contained very rugged terrain and as Fernand Braudel famously noted the inhabitants of the mountains of the Mediterranean basin were difficult to rule.[16] In both regions, the Ottoman state had adopted a policy of indirect rule, granting autonomy to local lords, Druze in the case of Lebanon and Kurdish clan chieftains in the mountains along the frontier between the empire and Iran. As Istanbul sought to convert indirect rule to direct control in the period of the Tanzimat, local political interests in those two regions collided with the ambitions of the centralizing state. The existence of a modernized army allowed those at the sultan's court to imagine that they could impose the imperial will by force on those two historically rebellious regions, rather than through the mixture of coercion and co-optation that had worked in the past. Such actions would, however, have consequences that those ruling in Istanbul could not have foreseen.

In addition to the tension between the push toward centralization and the traditions of autonomy, political and economic conditions on the ground had changed in both regions. These upset the political arrangements that had governed relations among the various religious communities in the past. Struggles that might have been simply military confrontations between the countervailing forces of centralization and local autonomy took on a sectarian dimension as minor subplots in a larger narrative. It was the sectarian undertones of the rebellions that the outside observers, both European and North American, eagerly seized upon as their root cause, however. Local developments ignited the initial outbreak of violence in Lebanon and Kurdistan, but as the crises unfolded, external pressures exacerbated them and deepened the fissure between the religious communities. Because of the interconnection between the two, Ussama Makdisi has suggested that sectarianism itself was a by-product of "modernity" as the inhabitants of Lebanon attempted to work out their place in a rapidly changing world order by adopting categories of identity that had been privileged by the Western diplomats and missionaries.[17]

Today the Republic of Lebanon is smaller than the state of Connecticut in the United States, but the historic Lebanon known to the Ottomans as Cebel-i Dürüz (the Mountain of the Druzes) was smaller still, consisting of the mountains to the east and south of Beirut. With mountain ranges

---

[16] Braudel, *The Mediterranean*, vol. I, 34–41.
[17] Ussama Makdisi, *The Culture of Sectarianism: Community, History, and Violence in Nineteenth-Century Lebanon* (Berkeley: University of California Press, 2000).

rising sharply from a narrow coastal plain and running perpendicularly to the coast, it was difficult terrain for outsiders to subdue and hold. The Ottomans mounted successful campaigns against its ruling lord (*amir al-jabal*, "Commander, or Prince, of the Mountain") in 1585 and again in 1634, but rather than confront the lords of the mountain with a continued show of force, the policy from Istanbul was to co-opt the head of the dominant family in the region to serve as emir and to legitimize him with an imperial patent of office. Although the various mountain clans were often at war with one another, the fiction of the sultan's peace prevailed. Following in that tradition of indirect rule, the Ottomans simply sought to replace Bashir II, who had gone into exile with his Egyptian overlords in 1840, with another member of the same clan rather than to rethink their policy toward Lebanon.

Sultan Abdülmecid chose Bashir Qasim, whom historians have dubbed Bashir III, from the clan of Shihab for the position of emir. His immediate predecessor may or may not have been a secret Christian; Bashir III was, however, openly a communicant in the Maronite Church. That might not have mattered in the eighteenth century, but the leaders of the Druze clans refused to recognize his authority and demanded that the sultan appoint someone who was a Druze and from a different clan; that of the Jumblats was the most frequently mentioned. There was reason for the Druze elders to fear a Christian in the region's dominant political role. The fortunes of the Maronite Christian community were improving in the nineteenth century, and the equilibrium among the various religious communities was unstable. The Maronite population was increasing at a rate faster than that of the Druzes, creating competition for land. Maronite peasants began pushing southward from the Kisrawan region, which they had historically shared with Shi'i clans, but where they had in recent decades become numerically dominant, into the Matn district, in which Maronites and Druzes had coexisted for centuries, and even farther into the Shuf to the south where the Druzes had been historically the dominant group. In addition, Lebanon had become a major exporter of silk, and that trade disproportionately enriched the Maronite community, whose members produced and marketed it. As some in the Maronite community were getting rich, they sought political power commensurate with their economic power.

The Ottoman government, insisting on a return to the status quo before the Egyptian occupation, refused to back down on its choice of Bashir Qasim despite the opposition from the Druze lords. Many of the Maronite commoners supported that decision while their notables and clergy were not so sanguine about the Ottomans' choice as they feared he might upset the traditional balance of power in the mountains. A stalemate ensued with neither side willing to concede. What had been a political dispute quickly turned sectarian with Druzes fighting Maronites in an escalating cycle of "tit for tat" revenge killings. Contributing to the growing animosity between the two religious communities, the European powers pressured the Ottomans to intervene to impose order.

In the negotiation over what to do next, the British claimed to represent the Druzes while the Austrians, as a Catholic power, spoke for the Maronites. Together, they forced the Ottomans to accede to a solution whereby the Lebanese mountains were split into two political units, using the road connecting Beirut to Damascus as the north-south divide between the two. In the north the local governor, termed the Kaimmakam, would be a Maronite, while in the south he would be a Druze. Both men would be appointed by the sultan from a list of names submitted to him by their respective religious communities. Each, in turn, would be responsible to the governor in Beirut. In addition, as the southern district had a large Maronite Christian minority, the position of deputy (vekil) was created with the stipulation that the person holding that position would be a Maronite. The dual Kaimmakamlık received new regulations in 1845, but the broad outline remained the same.[18] Political confessionalism had made its appearance in Lebanon for the first time.

As in Lebanon, the Ottomans had an established policy in Kurdistan of granting the local chieftains, known as mirs, almost complete autonomy. It was politically expedient as Kurdish tribal levies, the majority of whom were nominally Sunni, usually helped to support the regular Ottoman army in its campaigns along the Iranian frontier. Even more compelling in Ottoman strategic planning was the realization that the costs of subduing the region, much less ruling it, would have been high. With the Egyptian army in Syria in 1832, however, the Ottomans made the political calculation that the portion of Kurdistan that bordered Syria had to be secured lest it slip into the orbit of Egyptian influence. The shift in policy proved to be costly for the long-term security of the region.

The Ottomans chose to move first against the Kurdish emirate of Botan, which stretched to the north and west of the city of Mosul in territory that today lies at the juncture of Turkey, Iraq, and Syria. It was one of

---

[18] For Lebanon's troubled nineteenth century, see: Leila Tarazi Fawaz, *An Occasion for War: Civil Conflict in Lebanon and Damascus in 1860* (Berkeley: University of California Press, 1994); Makdisi, *Culture of Sectarianism*.

the more accessible of the Kurdish emirates as it was wedged between the garrison towns of Diyarbakır and Mosul. After a prolonged campaign, the Ottomans seized Cizre, the capital of Botan in 1838, forcing its emir, Bedir Xan, to seek refuge in the nearby mountains. But with the defeat of the Ottoman army at Nezip in the following year, the Ottoman military presence in Kurdistan receded. With the immediate threat of Ottoman retaliation removed, Bedir Xan came down out of the mountains and reentered his capital, with a clear grudge against his former masters in Istanbul.[19]

The situation in Kurdistan was further unsettled in the 1840s when American Congregationalist missionaries entered the region and began proselytizing among the Nestorian Christians (later to be known as Assyrians). Although they spoke a dialect of Aramaic rather than Kurdish, the Nestorians were culturally and socially similar to their Kurdish neighbors. Armed and fiercely independent, their clans had traditionally been in client relationships with one or the other of the Kurdish *mir*s. As was the case with the Druze and Maronite clans in Lebanon, Muslim Kurds and Christian tribesmen were often allies in the decades before the Tanzimat; Nestorian warriors had aided Bedir Xan in the siege of Cizre. But as in Lebanon, global developments destabilized local conditions. The spiritual head of the Nestorian Church, titled the Mar Shimꜥun, sensed that the influence of Russia was on the rise while that of the Ottomans was in decline in the mountainous borderlands that linked the three empires: Ottoman, Russian, and Iranian. He, therefore, welcomed the arrival of Protestant missionaries in Kurdistan as potential allies and a possible link to the European powers. Emboldened by their presence, the Mar Shimꜥun made a grab for political power away from the traditional Nestorian clan chieftains. In the eyes of the Kurds, that upset the traditional equilibrium and threatened their political dominance in the region.

The two developments came to a head in the Tiyari district of the emirate of Hakkari, today in southeastern Turkey, in 1843, when the Nestorian clans stopped paying tribute to their Kurdish *mir*, at the urging of the Mar Shimꜥun. Independent of that action, the American missionaries built a school on a high hill commanding the valley below. To the Kurds, the structure appeared to be a fortress, seemingly indicating that the Nestorians were preparing for war. The *mir* of Hakkari appealed to Bedir Xan for support and his tribesmen moved into the region. A general

[19] Martin van Bruinessen, *Agha, Shaikh and State: The Social and Political Structures of Kurdistan* (London: Zed Press, 1992), 177–80.

massacre of Nestorian villagers ensued in which several thousand report-edly perished. The ongoing political unrest in Kurdistan was reported by the American missionaries to the British ambassador in Istanbul as being yet another example of Muslim fanaticism and resistance to reform. There was intense pressure from both the United Kingdom and France on the Ottoman state to move against Bedir Xan; it did in 1847, eventually defeating him. Bedir Xan was sent into exile and the power of the emirate of Botan was broken.[20] The tensions between the Kurdish tribes and their Christian neighbors, both Assyrians and Armenians, in the mountains of southeastern Turkey did not subside, however, and they would flare again in the last decade of the century with tragic consequences for the Christian communities.

SECTARIAN VIOLENCE AT THE CORE

In the decades between Napoleon's invasion of Egypt in 1798 and the Egyptian occupation of Syria 1832, the established social order in the cities of the Arab world was shifting, if not crumbling. The first evidence of this was the increasing class antagonism in Syria's cities as witnessed by the uprising in Aleppo in 1819 and in Damascus in 1831. Sectarian fault lines began to form as well. Rumors of events occurring in Lebanon or Kurdistan reached the populations of Damascus, Aleppo, Mosul, and Baghdad, with Christians and Muslims hearing different versions of what had transpired. A changing economic environment also contributed to a perceived religious divide.

As the Fertile Crescent was drawn more tightly into a world economy that the Europeans dominated, Christian merchants were much more willing to take advantage of the new opportunities. As a result, there was a perception in the Muslim community that the Christians were getting rich at the Muslims' expense. Furthermore, as conscription was imposed on the Muslim community but not on the non-Muslims, much of the Muslim community felt that the new order was not fair. Adding to that sense of personal injury among the Muslims, many in the Christian com-munity reveled in the liberal atmosphere of the Tanzimat and used the lessening of restrictions that had formerly been imposed upon them by the state to construct new churches and hold public celebrations, drawing attention to their wealth and status. The result was a social powder keg with Muslims nurturing their resentments while the Christians and the

[20] Ibid., 177–82; Özoğlu. *Kurdish Notables*, 70–2.

government officials were largely oblivious to their discontent. It would only take a rumor to set off the explosion.

The first of the urban riots that would shake the Arab provinces in the Tanzimat era occurred in Aleppo, which was not surprising given the city's recent past. The uprising began as protest against conscription on 17 October 1850, during the Muslim feast ʿId al-Adha, as a rumor circulated that the Ottoman authorities would begin conscription after the holiday. The city's fear of the draft was fueled by the first Ottoman census of the city's males, which had just been completed. During the Egyptian occupation, Ibrahim Pasha had first counted the city's males and then drafted them. Although the Ottoman authorities claimed the census was simply to establish who should pay a new tax, the *ferde vergüsü*, locally known as the *wirki*, most in Aleppo suspected that the Ottomans were about to follow the Egyptians' lead and do the same.

The actual number of protesters given by the contemporary accounts varies. One overly excited deposition, filed by the city's notables while under siege by the insurgents, reported thirty thousand people took part.[21] More cautious accounts say simply several hundred men participated. All accounts agree, however, that the initial crowd gathered in the eastern quarters of Banqusa, Qarliq, and Bab al-Nayrab, the neighborhoods long associated with the janissaries and from which the rioters of 1819 had come. Once formed as a group, the protesters marched to the residence of the city's governor, Mustafa Zarif Pasha. He would later claim that he had too few troops to disperse the crowd.[22] Christian versions of the events, however, said that he had cowered behind closed doors and refused to disperse the protesters while they had still not quite yet become a mob.[23] The crowd moved on to the house of ʿAbdallah al-Babnisi, who had acted as unofficial head of the former janissaries since the Egyptian occupation of the city. There, they chanted their demands "No draft, no taxes." ʿAbdallah Bey refused to lead the protesters. But his elliptical statement to them, "You know your own work," reported by several contemporary sources, was interpreted by the city's early twentieth-century historian al-Tabbakh as giving the protesters the green light for what happened next.[24]

The mob then started to loot the shops in the city's central market. Thus far, the riot had proceeded in the well-worn pattern established by

[21] Istanbul, Başbakanlık Osmanlı Arşivi (BOA) İrade Dahiliye 13185/5.
[22] Aksan, *Ottoman Wars 1700–1878*, 418–22.
[23] Istanbul, BOA, İrade Dahiliye 13185/10.
[24] Tabbakh, *Iʿlam*, vol. III, 439.

earlier risings, but in a turn from tradition, the rioters focused their rage on the predominantly Christian quarters of Judayda and Saliba, which they began to loot and pillage. There is no agreement in the sources as to the number of fatalities. An Ottoman account drawn up in 1851 gave the total as twenty dead.[25] The British consul in Aleppo, Augustus William Werry, reported eighteen Christians had died, while the Maronite bishop Bulus Arutin stated that only seven men were killed as the riots proceeded, but three hundred others, including many women, were wounded. Of these, he wrote, an additional seventy later died of their wounds.[26] A final register of the destruction compiled a year later by the Ottoman authorities gave the figure of six churches, 688 homes, and thirty-six shops as having been looted and partially destroyed.[27] The rioters had been discriminate in their targets, however. Not only had they left the older, poorer churches untouched, they had not attacked poorer Christians living in religiously mixed neighborhoods. As with the uprising of 1819, a class-based reading of the riot was possible. But as all of the targets of the mob's anger had been Christian, sectarianism was the dominant causal explanation chosen by those who had witnessed the violence.

The next day the riots continued as the local rioters were reportedly joined by ʿAnaza Bedouins. By that time, most of the city's Christians had already fled to the safety of the city's commercial *khan*s. Muslim friends or neighbors sheltered others, as was the case of the schoolteacher and diarist Naʿum Bakhkhash.[28] On Friday, the beginning of a second full day of rioting, a group of Muslim notables, supported by guards supplied by ʿAbdallah Bey, visited the afflicted quarters and urged the plunderers to go home. Having partially reclaimed their city, they agreed to present the rioters' demands to Mustafa Zarif Pasha. Their original letter, with an attached Turkish translation, was then dispatched to the Porte while the governor, with many of the city's elite, waited in the barracks. Most Christians remained in the city's *khan*s, behind their locked gates and formidable walls.[29]

For the next fortnight an uneasy calm prevailed in the city. The Christians remained off the streets. The governor and most of the notables huddled in the barracks with the town's garrison as ʿAbdallah's men

---

[25] Istanbul, BOA, İrade Meclis-i Vâlâ 6121.
[26] London, Foreign Office (FO), Letter Werry to Rose (Beirut), dated November 2, 1850, London, FO 226/107; Qara'ali *Ahamm hawadith*, 85.
[27] Istanbul (BOA), İrade Dahiliye 13493/7.
[28] Bakhkhash, *Akhbar halab*, vol. II, 208.
[29] Istanbul, BOA, İrade Dahiliye 13185/5.

patrolled the streets to prevent further looting. The long-awaited reinforcements arrived 2 November 1850, having marched overland from
Iskenderun. With them were several new artillery pieces recently acquired
from Britain. Some reports have the hostilities beginning on 5 November,
others on 7 November. But the general outline of the events is the same:
the government asked for the rebels to surrender and when they did not,
an artillery barrage opened up on the eastern quarters of the city.[30] They
were the same neighborhoods that had been sacked thirty-one years
before during the suppression of the uprising of 1819.

Following the bombardment, a house-to-house battle ensued. By 8
November 1850, the Ottomans had prevailed. Consul Werry reported,
"the insurgents, who have been entirely subjugated, and the Quarters
they inhabited have been destroyed and burnt, perfect tranquility exists
in every part of the city."[31] Werry wrote that it was reported that a thousand people had been killed and five hundred wounded by the Ottoman
onslaught, although he cautioned those figures were probably exaggerated. He added, "this lesson will serve to make the Islams [*sic!*] generally
in the north of Syria obedient to that rather too mild a government for
such barbarians."[32] Reports from the Ottoman army to Istanbul gave 9
November 1850 as the date when peace was restored to the city. They also
provided their estimates for rebel casualties: 3,400 killed, 1,500 having
fled the city, and 230 arrested.[33] The casualties suffered by the Ottomans
were extremely light in comparison, but then the Ottomans had the artillery: twenty-seven dead and ninety-two wounded.[34]

The riot in Aleppo should have been a wake-up call that the situation
in Syria was deteriorating. Instead those who had seen the mob's fury
opted for conventional explanations. If the dispatches of Mustafa Zarif
can be taken as representative, the rising was simply a reminder for the
Ottomans of the "rebellious nature of the inhabitants of Arabistan." The
people of Aleppo had risen in 1819, after all, and driven the governor's
entourage out of the city. As in 1850, order had only been restored by
force. Of course, in 1819 poor Christians and Muslims had allied themselves against the governor's forces and there had been no attacks by
the rebels on the Christian quarters. The British observers were probably
unaware of what had happened in the city in 1819, and they blamed the

[30] Istanbul, BOA, İrade Hariciye 3526.
[31] London, FO 861/2 Werry to Canning, November 8, 1850.
[32] London, FO 226/107.
[33] Istanbul, BOA, İrade Dahiliye 13495/3.
[34] Istanbul, BOA, İrade Dahiliye 13304.

riot of 1850 on the innate religious bigotry of Muslims. The Christian petitions to Istanbul favored the explanation that the Muslims were jealous of the Christians' newfound freedoms and wanted to restore the social order to what it had been before the Tanzimat, at the their expense.

In 1853, the Ottoman Empire went to war with Russia, and although France and the United Kingdom were its allies, Muslim authors viewed the war as yet another example of Christian encroachment on Muslim lands. British consular officials in the Syrian cities suspected that the Christians secretly sympathized with Russia.[35] The Christian diarist in Aleppo, Naʿum Bakhkhash, however, recorded his wishes for the sultan's victory in his "jihad" against "the enemy of peace, the emperor of Russia."[36] As a partial payment for Britain's help in the Crimean War, Sultan Abdülmecid issued his Islahat fermanı (Reform Decree) on 18 February 1856. Unlike the Hatt-ı Şerif of 1839, the new document was quite explicit in setting out the rights of the non-Muslim populations of the empire. These included the abolition of any special taxes, the right to take any disputes with Muslims to mixed tribunals rather than the sharia courts, the establishment of formal internal governance for the non-Muslim religious communities (*millets*), guaranteed participation in provincial and municipal councils, and the provision that all distinctions between the sultan's subjects "on account of their religion, language, or race, shall be forever effaced from administrative protocol."[37] It also guaranteed eligibility for conscription for young men of all the religious communities, a new freedom that the non-Muslims were undoubtedly less enthusiastic about receiving. Actual conscription of non-Muslims was, however, not imposed until 1909 as they were given the option to buy their way out of the military through a new tax, the *bedel-i askeri*.[38] It was perhaps not coincidentally set at the same rate as the cizye/jizya that had just been formally abolished.

The difference in the reception of the new decree in the various religious communities was stark. Muhammad Saʿid al-Ustawani recorded that the decree was read to him and other members of the *meclis* of Damascus on 12 March 1856 and that in response "all the Muslims were ashen-faced and we asked Him Most High to exalt the faith

[35] London, Public Record Office (PRO) Foreign Office (FO 861/4, Werry to Rose, November 26, 1853.
[36] Bakhkhash, *Akhbar halab*, vol. II, 385.
[37] Akram Khater, *Sources in the History of the Modern Middle East*, (Boston: Houghton Miflin, 2004), 14–18.
[38] Ufuk Gülsoy, *Osmanlı Gayrimüslimlerinin Askerlik Serüveni* (Istanbul: Simurg, 2000).

and give victory to the Muslims. There is no power or force except in God Most High."[39] He later praised the city's governor, Said Pasha, for standing up to the consuls, their protégés, and the Orthodox patriarch in refusing to grant Christians what they wanted, even when these demands were in accordance with the new sultanic order.[40] In contrast, Bakhkhash recorded in his entry for 2–8 March 1856 that the French consul in Aleppo held a grand reception to mark the occasion and the prominent Christians were invited to attend. All present celebrated the decree with a formal ball, replete with a Western-style orchestra.[41] For both al-Ustawani and Bakhkhash, the decree marked the dawn of a new era, but whether that meant a bright future or a dark one was a matter of perspective

Under pressure from the Europeans to grant equality to the Christians, Sultan Abdül-Mecid was losing the loyalty of the Muslim elites who had helped to keep the Arab lands Ottoman for his ancestors. In an atmosphere of increasing sectarian tension and mistrust, rumors threatening impending doom swept the Muslim and Christian communities. Those that circulated in the Christian community usually involved tales of a conspiracy among the Muslims to rise up and kill them. For Muslims, there were reports of intrigues by local Christians to act as a fifth column for an impending invasion by one European power or another. Into that very volatile mix of rumors, news arrived of actual events occurring in Lebanon, which when filtered through the rumor mills in each community only worked to confirm its darkest fears. The rising demand for land among Maronite peasants in the district of Kisrawan, coupled with their understanding of what the Reform Edict of 1856 had promised, led them to agitate against their feudal lords, the Maronite Khazin shaykhs. In December of 1858, a muleteer named Tanyus Shahin took charge of the agitation, which quickly turned into a revolt against the feudal order. The peasants rallied to his leadership and Shahin established his control over most of the villages of the Kisrawan by the summer of 1859.

Although there was little physical violence directed against the persons of the leading feudal families, there were wide-scale destruction of olive and mulberry trees and the theft of the harvests from the lords' lands. The rebels did, however, succeed in driving most of the elite Maronite families

[39] al-Ustawani, *Mashahid wa ahdath*, 162.
[40] Ibid., 153–4.
[41] Bakhkhash, *Akhbar halab*, vol. II, 32.

out of the district to seek safety in Beirut. Sensing a growing tide of victory as Maronite peasants flocked to his standard, Shahin and his men moved into the religiously mixed district of the Matn. In the early spring of 1860, he announced he would defend the Maronite peasants against their Druze overlords. As the Maronite peasants began to agitate in the Druze country, however, some of the Druze peasants became alarmed at what they viewed as increasingly aggressive Christian actions. Individual killings of Druzes by Maronites and Maronites by Druzes became increasingly frequent. What had begun as potentially a social revolution was rapidly disintegrating into a sectarian civil war.[42]

In May open battles between the two communities erupted in the Matn region of central Lebanon. When armed Christians from the predominantly Melkite Catholic market town of Zahle came to the assistance of the Christian peasants in the mountains, a combined force of Druzes and Shia from the Biqʿa Valley attacked Zahle on 18 June 1860 and quickly took the town with a great loss of Christian lives. Soon after, Druze forces captured and sacked Dayr al-Qamar, the seat of the Shihabi emirate. Both towns were symbols of Christian wealth and influence in Lebanon and their destruction sent shock waves throughout the region, as well as thousands of Christian refugees to the coast.[43] The rumors emanating from the conflict zone created the conditions for the next major rupture in sectarian relations that would occur in Damascus.

The riot in Damascus began on 9 July 1860 and lasted eight days. Its duration and intensity were more severe than those of its predecessor in Aleppo. In its aftermath, most of the Christian Quarter of Damascus was turned to rubble and between several hundred and several thousand Christians lost their lives. The estimates of the dead varied widely and unlike the case of Aleppo ten years earlier, no attempt was ever made by the authorities to tally their number. In another difference between the two uprisings, Ottoman troops did not forcefully restore order and there were no reported Muslim casualties in the violence. Rather the city quieted down and those Ottoman troops that had originally failed to move to stop the riots patrolled the city's streets without incident. The shock of the severity of the outburst pushed the French to send an expeditionary

---

[42] Makdisi, *Culture of Sectarianism*, 96–134.

[43] Leila Fawaz, "Zahle and Dayr al-Qamar: Two Market Towns of Mount Lebanon during the Civil War of 1960" In *Lebanon: A History of Conflict and Consensus*, edited by Nadim Shehadi and Danna Haffar Mills (London: The Centre for Lebanese Studies and I. B. Tauris, 1988): 49–63.

force to Lebanon and the Ottoman government to dispatch the foreign minister, Fuad Pasha, to Damascus to investigate.[44]

In the aftermath of the riot, the Christian Quarter of Damascus was a smoldering ruin. Thousands of Christians fled the city for what was seen as the relative safety of the coast or north to Aleppo. The Ottoman authorities originally housed those who remained in the city's mosques, much to the ire of the Muslims. Eventually, the authorities requisitioned houses from Muslims in the Qanawat Quarter and transferred the Christians into them. This action angered Muslims, who felt that those who were not guilty were receiving collective punishment.[45] As was the case in Aleppo, a military tribunal was established and guilt was apportioned. Initially, those arrested (more than 800) and executed (167) were, as was the case in Aleppo ten years earlier, from the Muslim lower classes. As the investigations proceeded, however, some of those arrested were from the Muslim elite, including most of the members of the *meclis*, as Christians accused them of participation in the riots.[46] According to al-Ustuwani, these charges were largely baseless:

For about the last five days the Christians have been acting outrageously, as both men and women go around confronting people. They grab a man and say to him, "This is our robe (*qunbaz*)," for example, or "You killed so-and-so." "You looted this." "You burned that." And women grab women and say "That is our wrap (*izar*). I see what you have there, under your arm." And if the person has an article of clothing, they claim, "It's ours." They are thus accused. The government takes the thing from them and they are judged guilty. In this way, the misfortune and despair of all the Muslims has intensified.[47]

With civil order restored, a new *meclis* was established in October with several of those from the previous body, including al-Ustawni, serving once again. From that point on, however, the Ottoman authorities insisted that there be a Christian representative participating in its deliberations. Tensions between Muslims and Christians remained high throughout Syria in the aftermath of the riot in Damascus. Mistrust did not disappear overnight and rumors of impending doom continued to circulate in the religious communities. There were occasional murders

---

[44] Fawaz, *Occasion for War*, 78–100; Schilcher, *Families in Politics*, 87–106; Philip Khoury, *Urban Notables and Arab Nationalism: The Politics of Damascus 1860–1920* (Cambridge: Cambridge University Press, 1983), 8–25.

[45] al-Ustuwani, *Mashahid*, 183–4.

[46] Fawaz, *Occasion for War*, 140–2.

[47] al-Ustuwani, *Mashahid*, 199.

that were sectarian in nature and more commonly there were insults,[48] but Syria did not experience any further outbreaks of sectarian violence. This was all the more remarkable as in the Anatolian and Balkan provinces, sectarian/ethnic animosities would literally tear the empire apart beginning in the last decades of the nineteenth century and culminating in World War I.

Historians have advanced our understanding of why the middle decade of the nineteenth century was marked by sectarian strife in Syria and Lebanon, but perhaps the more pertinent question is why there were no further social upheavals in the region as the century progressed and the Ottoman Empire unraveled. Part of the answer lies in the way that the Muslim elite in Aleppo responded to the events in Damascus in 1860. In the summer of 1860, rumors of the fighting in Lebanon reached Aleppo and the poorer Muslim classes began to agitate against perceived Christian privilege once again. This was met by a firm show of force by the city's governor; a bribe was also paid by the Christians to the potential rioters, while the Muslim notables, in a demonstration of civic responsibility, organized patrols to quiet the city down. [49] When Damascus erupted in July, order was maintained in Aleppo through the combined efforts of the foreign consuls, the Ottoman officials, and the Muslim notables.[50] Elsewhere, anti-Christian incidents did not become deadly when sectarian tensions flared up again in Damascus during the economic depression in the 1870s, and we must assume that the city's Muslim notables had become more vigilant to prevent a repetition of the sectarian violence of 1860.[51]

The leading Muslim families of both Damascus and Aleppo witnessed the destruction wrought by a mob that they constructed in their imagination to be composed of outsiders or low-class elements from within their cities. That shift in blame made it easier for the Muslim elite to act as their predecessors had done at the start of the Greek War for Independence to intervene to restore civic order. In part, their willingness to do so was based in their understanding of political reality. The region's Christians, unlike the case of the various Christian populations of the Balkans or Anatolia, had no aspirations for a separate state of their own. Without nationalist emotions conflating with religious sentiment, Arabic-speaking Christians posed no existential threat to their Muslim

[48] Some of these are recorded by Bakhkhash, *Akhbar halab*, vol. III, 202, 204, 215, 279.
[49] Fawaz, *Occasion for War*, 77.
[50] Letter Consul Skene to Lord J. Russell, August 18, 1860, London, PRO FO 406/n. 8, 378.
[51] Khoury, *Urban Notables and Arab Nationalism*, 45.

neighbors. In addition, the changing economic situation in the Ottoman Arab provinces made it once again possible for the Muslim elite to envision their future as both secure and rosy as the sultan's subjects. It was in their best interests that sectarianism was removed from the public discourse, even if not all of its wounds were healed.

EMPOWERING THE *A*ᶜ*yan*

The intervention by Muslim notables to dampen the flames of sectarian antagonism in Aleppo after 1850 demonstrated their reemergence as brokers of political power in the city. They were not unique as across the Arab provinces individuals from the notable Muslim families began to reclaim a role in civil society in the latter part of the Tanzimat period. In some cases, those individuals were from the same families that had had been prominent for a century or more. But there were also new family names among the elite as individuals who served the state in the military or civilian bureaucracy established their own dynasties.

Two reforms, introduced by the government in Istanbul, were vital for the reemergence of the *a*ᶜ*yan* and their integration into the Tazimat project: the Tapu (Land-Deed) Code of 1858 and the Vilayet (Province) Law of 1864. The first was based on a seemingly very liberal idea: the lands the state, as representative of the Muslim community at large, had administered for centuries as *timar*s or tax farms should be distributed to the peasants who worked them. The second strengthened the political power of the elite Muslim families by providing them with a greater voice in the provincial administration. That would at times put them at odds with the Ottoman provincial governors and the imperial program of "reform," as was the case in 1873, when Shaykh al-Ustawani resigned from the Damascus council to protest the imperial order that allowed foreigners to purchase property in the province of Syria.[52]

The Hatt-ı Şerif of 1839 promised the end of tax farming. With that mandate, the bureaucrats in Istanbul were confident that the Tapu Law of 1858 would transform the agricultural sector of the empire by giving the peasants clear title (*tapu*) to their land. The bureaucrats imagined that the registration of individual rural proprietors on the land they farmed would lead to more effective tax collection. Individual responsibility for taxes had been the motivation behind the institution of the tax on adult males, the *ferde vergüsü*, in the cities, and it was now to be extended

---

[52] al-Ustawani, *Mashahid*, 51.

to the agricultural sector, which constituted the potentially largest single source of revenue for the state's coffers. The plan had a serious flaw, however, that underscored the gap between the theoretical construction of Ottoman society that the bureaucrats possessed and the reality of conditions on the ground in the provinces. In order to receive title to the lands they worked, the peasants had to register it with state agents.

The peasants had already experienced the conscription of their sons. For most, the new law, which was probably poorly explained to them in the first place, must have seemed yet another government intrusion into their lives. The collective strategy of resistance that was employed by many peasants across the Arab provinces was to allow the prominent families that had been involved in moneylending to the villagers for generations to register the lands in their names. With that result, scholars have argued that the new law did not result in anything new. It simply made a de facto practice that had come into being with the creation of the *malikane*s in the eighteenth century de jure.[53] Other peasants who registered land in their own names soon found that the taxes were too burdensome and sold it to those who had ready cash. In Beirut, Mosul, and Aleppo provinces a newly emerging commercial class took advantage of the peasants' dilemma to secure their wealth by acquiring rural holdings. In areas that were farther removed from the urban centers, the strategy the peasants employed was to allow tribal chieftains to register the land in their names.[54] That pattern of land registration was common in central and southern Iraq, where Bedouin chieftains were among the largest landowners by the end of the nineteenth century. In some cases, there was coercion to force the peasants to sign over their lands, but generally they acquiesced to the reduction of their status from peasant proprietors to sharecroppers. There was no armed resistance to the new laws in any of the Arab lands in the nineteenth century.

The pace of the implementation of the new land law was uneven. There is little evidence of its effects in Damascus province until the 1870s,

---

[53] Peter Sluglett and Marion Farouk-Sluglett, "The Application of the 1858 Land Code in Greater Syria: Some Preliminary Observations" In *Land Tenure and Social Transformation in the Middle East*, edited by Tarif Khalidi (Beirut: The American University of Beirut, 1984): 409–24; James Reilly, "Status Groups and Propertyholding in the Damascus Hinterland, 1828–1880" *IJMES* 21 (1989): 517–39.

[54] Khoury, *Urban Notables*, 26–44; Mannaᶜ, *Ta'rikh Filistin*, 192–4; Dina Rizk Khoury, "The Introduction of Commercial Agriculture in the Province of Mosul and its Effects on the Peasantry, 1750–1850" In *Landholding and Commercial Agriculture in the Middle East*, edited by Çağlar Keyder and Faruk Tabak (Albany: The State University of New York Press, 1991): 155–72; Batatu, *Old Social Classes*, 73–6.

for example.[55] With its implementation, individual peasant proprietors did not disappear, but they controlled a shrinking percentage of the cultivatable land. Data from 1909 from what would become the Palestine Mandate listed 16,970 families cultivating 785,000 *dunum*s (a *dunum* is approximately 1,000 square meters, or a quarter of an acre), at an average of 46 *dunum*s each, while 144 families held 3,130,000 *dunum*s, at an average of 22,000 *dunum*s each.[56] The pattern of landownership varied across the region and even within a particular region. In Palestine, large landowners were more common in the coastal plain than in the rugged terrain of Jabal Nablus, where smallholders prevailed. In the rich farmland to the south of Damascus, the Ghuta, smallholdings were the norm while in villages farther removed from the metropolis in the hinterlands of Homs and Hama, large landowners, often drawn from the military, predominated.[57] With the privatization of farmland and the possibility for the creation of large estates, however, many of the traditional Muslim *aᶜyan* families, as well as Christian entrepreneurs, became wealthy. The potential for creating wealth arose as the commercial relations between the Ottoman Empire and its Western trading partners underwent a major transformation.

The Anglo-Ottoman Commercial Treaty of 1838 was the key to that shift. Sultan Mahmud and his court were desperate in that year. They had failed to dislodge the Egyptian occupation of Syria and needed British support and British arms if they were to recover the lost provinces. The partial cost of that support was a commercial treaty that allowed British traders to settle anywhere in the empire and eliminated all internal tariffs charged on them. Those internal tariffs, however, remained in place for Ottoman merchants. Although the actual tariff on imports was raised from 3 percent to 5 percent for the British merchants and export duties from 3 percent to 12 percent, the elimination of the internal duties gave them a substantial advantage over their Ottoman competitors for whom those duties were still in place.[58] Similar treaties were soon granted to the other European powers. The impact was almost immediate. In customs receipts from Aleppo in 1841, 1851, and 1852, foreign passport

[55] Reilly, "Status Groups and Propertyholding."
[56] Alexander Schölch, *Palestine in Transformation 1856–1882: Studies in Social, Economic and Political Development*, translated by William Young and Michael Gerrity (Washington, DC: Institute for Palestine Studies, 1993).
[57] Reilly, "Status Groups and Propertyholding," 529–30.
[58] Şevket Pamuk, *The Ottoman Empire and European Capitalism, 1820–1913: Trade, Investment and Production* (Cambridge: Cambridge University Press, 1987), 18–21.

holders or locally based merchants who enjoyed protégé status from one
of the European states constituted the top ten taxpayers on imported
goods.[59] More than half of the city's import trade, in terms of its mone-
tary value, was in the hands of those who were legally foreigners.

The effects of these trade treaties on the local economy are debated.[60]
What is clear from the surviving customs receipts is that most imported
goods from Europe were manufactured and most exports to it were
raw agricultural products. Not surprisingly, the balance of trade was in
Europe's favor. A British consular report for Aleppo in 1890 reported
figures for Britain's trade with the province for the past five years. With
the exception of 1887, when imports were double the value of exports,
exports were typically valued at two-thirds the value of imports.[61] If
money was to be made from the export trade of the Arab provinces in
the second half of the nineteenth century, control of rural resources was
where the action was. The governor of Aleppo province received an order
in July 1872 announcing that subjects of the United Kingdom, France,
Italy, Austria, Belgium, Sweden, and Denmark could purchase land in the
province. That did not set off a land rush by the European trading houses,
however. Members of the Marcopoli and Poche families, both holders of
Austrian nationality, did take advantage of the new law and purchased
rural estates in the vicinity of Aleppo, but most of the fertile land that was
opened up along the Euphrates for purchase by the pacification of the
Bedouin was bought either by local Muslim notable families or by agents
of the House of Osman.[62]

If the land law enhanced the economic status of the sultan's Arab
Muslim elite families, the provincial law promulgated in 1864 helped
to secure their political position. The framers of the law envisioned that
the empire would be governed by a civilian bureaucracy that would
implement civic and economic reforms throughout the provinces, in
effect establishing the rational and just administration that the Reform
Edict of 1856 had promised. Each province would have its own salaried

---

[59] Bruce Masters, "The Political Economy of Aleppo in an Age of Ottoman Reform" *JESHO*
53 (2010), 305.
[60] Abdul-Karim Rafeq, "The Impact of Europe on a Traditional Economy: The Case of
Damascus 1840–1870." In *Économie et sociétiés dans l'empire ottoman: actes du colloque de Strasbourg*, edited by Jean Louis Bacqué-Grammont and Paul Dumont, 3
vols. (Paris: Centre National de la Recherche Scientifique, 1983), 3, 419–32; Quataert,
Ottoman Manufacturing, 49–79; Pamuk, *Ottoman Empire and European Capitalism*,
108–29.
[61] Masters, "Political Economy," 310.
[62] Ibid., 309–10.

bureaucracy and an advisory council to the governor. While in the Arab provinces, almost all of the governors were of Anatolian or Balkan origin, and thereby in local eyes Turks, the provincial bureaucracies and councils were staffed by locals, who were in most cases Arabs. Among the other functions that these new bureaucrats would perform was the publication of an official provincial gazette that would keep the public informed of new regulations as well as laud new improvement schemes put into place by the provincial government. These gazettes, published in the Arab provinces in bilingual editions with Arabic alongside Ottoman Turkish columns, were followed by privately published journals that were generally in Arabic only. The official gazette of Aleppo province, *Furat/Fırat,* at different periods of its existence, also published the news in Armenian.

The presence of Armenian in the gazette of Aleppo points to new boundaries that were created for the provinces that did not conform to their historical boundaries or reflect any attempt to draw the provinces' boundaries along ethnic lines. Under the new law, Aleppo province was extended northward to include the largely Turkish-speaking cities of Marash (Kahramanmaraş), Ayntab (Gaziantep), and Urfa (Şanlıurfa), thereby creating a province in which Arabic speakers and Turkish speakers were roughly equal in number, with a large Armenian-speaking minority. In 1870, a new province was created along the Euphrates River in what had been Aleppo province to be governed from the garrison town of Dayr al-Zawr. This reflected the hopes of the central government that with the pacification of the Bedouins, the new province would become a major wheat producer for the empire.[63] Iraq was reduced to two provinces, Baghdad and Mosul. The formerly autonomous Kurdish province of Şehrizor was absorbed under the governor of Mosul, creating a province where Kurds and Arabs were roughly equal in number. Basra, formerly a sometimes-separate province, was governed from Baghdad until 1884, when it again emerged as a separate province.

The new provincial law was implemented in Damascus in 1865 with the newly reconstituted province named *Suriyya/Suriye.* The new/old name reflected a growing historical consciousness among its inhabitants, or at least the intellectuals, that connected them with an ancient, pre-Islamic past. Because of Western concerns over the holy places in Palestine, Jerusalem and most of what would become the Palestine Mandate were designated as a separate district (*sancak*) under its own governor, who reported directly to Istanbul and not Damascus. Mount Lebanon was

[63] Ibid., 308–9.

made into a self-governing unit, *mütesarrifiye*, in 1864 with an advisory council that was composed under a formula that institutionalized confessional administration. The governor, or *mütesarrif*, was appointed by the sultan but from a list that was made up of Ottoman Catholics who were not Maronites.[64] The rest of Lebanon was folded into the Suriyya province, thereby depriving Beirut of its newly won status as a provincial capital. That act stirred resentment in that city's growing and increasingly self-confident bourgeoisie, who lobbied Istanbul incessantly until 1888, when Sultan Abdülhamid II (1876–1909) reestablished the province of Beirut. The province in its new incarnation included most of the Mediterranean coast of historic Syria from just north of Jaffa to the port city of Lattakia.[65]

In a break with the past, many of the governors of the newly formed provinces were career bureaucrats rather than military officers, an indication of the rise of a civil bureaucracy in the Tanzimat era.[66] Representative of that new class was Midhat Pasha, who governed Baghdad province from 1869 until 1872. Midhat had helped write the new provincial law and had administered the first "model" province in what is today Bulgaria. He arrived in Baghdad with the zeal of a committed reformer who viewed modernization as the means to reestablish Ottoman control in what had long been an imperial backwater. He embarked on a number of projects including the creation of a state-operated steamship company on the Euphrates to challenge the monopoly held by the company run by the British Lynch family. While he tore down Baghdad's ancient city walls, Midhat Pasha built a hospital, an orphanage, and a number of schools. His main ambition was, however, to implement more fully the *tapu* scheme in the province and to settle the Bedouins, turning them into taxpaying peasants.

Midhat largely failed in that ambition, but he did manage to break the power of the Muntafiq confederation by exploiting a rivalry within the ruling family. The brother he supported, later to be called Nasir Pasha, was made governor of a new *sancak* called Muntafiq with the newly built city al-Nasiriyya as its capital. Elsewhere, however, Midhat's plans to exploit a similar quarrel within the *ahl al-bayt* (the ruling family) to break the powerful Shammar tribe ended only in schism in the tribe with

[64] Engin Akarlı, *The Long Peace: Ottoman Lebanon, 1861–1920* (Berkeley: University of California Press, 1993).

[65] Hanssen, *Fin de Siècle Beirut*, 40–54.

[66] Carter Findley, *Bureaucratic Reform in the Ottoman Empire: The Sublime Porte 1789–1922* (Princeton, NJ: Princeton University Press, 1980), 151–220.

a small branch settling down while the majority chose to keep their camels and old ways of doing things.[67] Exploiting yet another familial rift, this time within in the ibn Saᶜud family, Midhat dispatched an Ottoman army to the oasis town of al-Hasa in the eastern Najd in 1870 which he reestablished as an imperial province after two centuries of official neglect. The newly reconstituted, al-Hasa province would serve as a base for Ottoman intrigues in the various shaykhdoms of the Persian Gulf until the onset of World War I.[68]

THE CONSTITUTION OF 1876 AND THE FIRST OTTOMAN PARLIAMENT

Although Midhat Pasha's reign as governor was a significant turning point in Iraq's modern history, he is best known by historians of the empire for his dogged pursuit of a constitution. The Ottoman bureaucrats and intellectuals who had come of age in the Tanzimat era had appropriated much from the West in terms of institutions. The reformers sought primarily to preserve the Ottoman state, but they also found much that was praiseworthy in the West that they felt should be adapted into an Ottoman context. For them, modernization did not necessarily mean wholesale Westernization, although they recognized that their vision of modernity did, in fact, entail the importation of some modified Western institutions.

The central ambition of their political modernization program was a constitution that would set out the responsibilities and the limits of the sultanate. In the past, the limits on the powers of the sultans were only those that the collective agreement of the ulama placed on them. Their sanction, of course, did not always work to curb imperial tendencies toward absolutism. In a constitution, the limits of the sultan's authority would be spelled out for all to read. The Tanzimat reformers had already produced a transformation of the centuries-old sharia traditions of personal law into a written code (*mecelle*) that was inspired by the Muslim legal tradition even as it looked like the civil code of a Western European nation. New commercial codes promulgated in the Tanzimat era, however, followed the Muslim traditions of commerce and finance less than they resembled similar codes in France. The drafters of the constitution sought a balance between the two political traditions: Islamic and

---

[67] Longrigg, *Four Centuries*, 298–311.
[68] Frederick Anscombe, *The Ottoman Gulf: The Creation of Kuwait, Saudi Arabia, and Qatar* (New York: Columbia University Press, 1997), 16–53.

Western. It would be a document that would not stray from the ideals of a just government in the Islamic tradition even if it embodied language imported from the European liberal lexicon, for which properly Ottoman Turkish neologisms were coined, usually from Arabic roots, as in *Kanun-ı Esasi*, "constitution." The crowning result of the reform movement was the Ottoman Constitution of 1876. Its text embodied some of the liberal economic and political ideas its framers had appropriated from Western European models, but it gave no guarantees for either political parties or the freedom of expression. Although the Constitution established that Islam was the religion of the state (article 11) and the Turkish of the Ottoman court was the official language of the empire (article 18), article 8 stated, "everyone who is within the Ottoman state, whatever his religion or sect, is without exception to be labeled as an Ottoman." The document was a physical manifestation of the hopes of the Tanzimat reformers that Ottomanism could provide the ideological foundations of a modern state. Ethnically and religiously diverse, the population of the empire would be united by the institution of a constitutionally defined sultanate. Loyalty to the House of Osman would guarantee these newly constituted Ottoman subjects the rule of law and responsible government. In addition, those subjects would have a voice in the regime through their representatives in an Ottoman Parliament that would meet on a regular basis in Istanbul.[69]

The promulgation of the Constitution, however inclusive its language and optimistic its framers were, came about under murky circumstances. In an increasingly volatile atmosphere of street agitation in the capital against Sultan Abdülaziz for his reluctance to sign the Constitution into law, several of the leading ministers and military commanders instigated a coup whereby his nephew, Murad V, was brought to the throne on 30 May 1876. Not long afterward, the former sultan committed suicide and the new sultan seemed to become unhinged both by his sudden rise to power and by the death of his uncle. He too dithered over promulgating the Constitution. Within three months of his ascending the throne, Murad was declared insane and his brother Abdülhamid, who affirmed that he would issue the Constitution immediately, took the throne on 31 August 1876.[70] The new Constitution had come into effect with rumors circulating in the capital of a power grab by elements within the military.

[69] Robert Devreux, *The First Ottoman Constitutional Period: A Study of the Midhat Constitution and Parliament* (Baltimore: The Johns Hopkins Press, 1963).
[70] Hanioğlu, *Brief History*, 108–23.

To make matters worse for the fledgling constitutional sultanate, the intrigues of the palace occurred at a time of trouble for the empire. In 1875, Serbian peasants in Herzegovina initiated an insurrection over taxes that quickly spread to Bosnia. Bulgarian peasants rose in rebellion in the spring of 1876 in what seemed to be a widespread nationalist uprising for independence. This was met by severe retribution by Muslim irregular forces in actions that gained notoriety in the West as the "Bulgarian Massacres" even though in the original rising it had been Muslims, not Bulgarian Christians, who had been massacred. Russia, who posed as the "Big Brother" of the sultan's Slavic subjects, used the violence in Bulgaria as pretext for war. Russian forces advanced across the Ottoman frontier in the Balkans and along the eastern flank of the empire in 1877.

Despite the crisis in the Balkans, the Ottoman Parliament met in March 1877. There were two sessions and although provisions were made for 130 members, only 119 showed up in Istanbul for the first session, of which 18 were from the Arab provinces, and 113 for the second, which included 16 parliamentarians from the Arab provinces. Yemen, which had been represented by 2 delegates in the first session, sent none to the second. The provinces of Syria and Aleppo were overrepresented with both sending 4 delegates when each had only been allotted 3 seats. Baghdad province, which had been allotted 14 delegates, sent only 3 men to both sessions, and Basra, given 3 delegates, sent none. The Lebanese of the *mütesarrifiye*, citing their autonomy, declined to fill the seat allotted to them, although Khalil Ghanim represented Beirut, which was still at that time a part of the province of Suriye in both sessions.

There were no elections for the delegates but rather the provincial consultative bodies named their representatives. Not surprisingly, the delegates were often members of those same councils. Among those who traveled to Istanbul were Yusuf Ziya al-Khalidi from Jerusalem, Nafiᶜ al-Jabiri from Aleppo, Shaykh Ahmad Darwish al-ᶜAjlani from Damascus, Khalid al-Atassi from Homs, and Husayn Bayhum from Beirut.[71] Not all the delegates were so prominent and there was a smattering of Christians and Jews, as well as a few self-made men. Most of the surnames of the Arab delegates, however, would have been recognized a century before by the ancestors of those they represented. As in the case of the provincial governments, the *aᶜyan* were well represented in the imperial parliament.[72]

---

[71] Devreux, *First Ottoman Constitutional Period*, 140–1, 259–75.
[72] Christoph Herzog, "Some Notes about the Members of Parliament from the Province of Baghdad." In *The First Ottoman Experiment in Democracy*, edited by Christoph Herzog

The records of the proceedings show that the Arab delegates took an active part in the proceedings, adding their regional perspective. They were also keenly aware of developments both throughout the empire and in the wider world.[73] Their experience on the imperial stage was short-lived, however. Sultan Abdül Hamid II, citing the exigencies of the war with Russia, dissolved parliament and suspended the constitution on 13 February 1878. But the experience of serving their constituencies in Istanbul had a normative effect on those who did so. Most of the Arab delegates were relatively young, and they continued to dominate the politics of their respective provinces through the end of the empire as committed Ottomanists. In that regard, at least, the framers of the Constitution of 1876 had at least partially realized their goals.

NORTH AFRICA IN THE ERA OF THE TANZIMAT

By 1876, the bureaucrats in Istanbul had established effective control over the Arab provinces of the Fertile Crescent, but they were less effective in reasserting the sultan's authority in his North African provinces. The exception was Libya. In 1831, France invaded Algeria, which was officially an Ottoman province but which, as was the case in Tunisia and Libya, had long enjoyed autonomy under the reign of a hereditary dynasty of governors. Sultan Mahmud II protested the action but could do little else. The Ottomans were fearful of both Mehmed Ali's ambitions and those of the French and took a preemptive strike, sending an expeditionary force to Tripoli in 1835 to secure what remained of their North African territories. It quickly ousted the last of the Karamanlı governors. The army took longer to secure the rest of the province. But by the 1840s, the Ottoman governors in Tripoli reached a modus vivendi with the Sanusi order in Cyrenaica (Barqa), the eastern half of the province, and that alliance of sorts kept the province quiet and at least nominally Ottoman.

The Sanusi Sufi order was founded by Muhammad al-Sanusi in the early nineteenth century. As a student in Mecca, he joined the Naqshbandi order and was influenced by the writings of Muhammad ibn ᶜAbd al-Wahhab. Al-Sanusi sought to reform Islam internally and to

and Malek Sharif (Würzburg: Ergon Verlag, 2010): 275–84; in the same volume, Malek Sharif, "A Portrait of Syrian Deputies in the First Ottoman Parliament," 285–311.
[73] Hasan Kayalı, *Arabs and Young Turks: Ottomanism, Arabis, and Islamism in the Ottoman Empire, 1908–1918* (Berkeley: University of California Press, 1997), 25–30.

resist the steady encroachment of the Western imperialists. He was born in Algeria, but was in Arabia when his homeland was occupied. Choosing not to return to a land where Christians were in control, he settled in Libya, where his order soon established contacts across the Sahara Desert through a combination of trade and active proselytism. His anti-Western ideology fit well with Ottoman ambitions for the region and the province of Libya (for the Ottomans, Trablus-ı Garb) was politically fully incorporated into the empire with a governor appointed from Istanbul, although it sent no delegates to the first Ottoman Parliament.[74]

The Ottoman reoccupation of Libya put the Husayni dynasty ruling in nearby Tunisia in a difficult position, stuck between the French, who clearly had designs on the country, and the Ottomans, who sought to draw Tunisia back into their fold as a loyal province. During the reign of Ahmad Bey in Tunis (1837–53), Ottoman pressure was intense. In return for a letter of his appointment as governor, Ahmad had to send an annual tribute to the sultan and to recognize him as sultan-caliph. In 1840, Istanbul informed him that he must impose all the new regulations of the Tanzimat in his province, but he equivocated and never complied. Tunisia did, however, dispatch troops to aide the Ottomans in the Crimean War in 1853.

Not fully accepting the Ottoman version of reform, Tunisia experienced its own reform under the guidance of the minister Khayr al-Din (d. 1889), who had been a protégé of Ahmad Bey. Tunisia's governor, Muhammad al-Sadiq Bey, agreed to Khayr al-Din's Constitution in 1860, although he suspended it four years later. Khayr al-Din was an Abkhaz from the Caucasus who had started his early career as a mamluk in Istanbul. Perhaps because of his origins, he had pro-Ottoman sentiments. In 1871, he negotiated an imperial order from Sultan Abdülaziz, affirming the Husayni line as the hereditary governors of the province. In return, the governors would send Istanbul a yearly tribute, contribute military forces if called upon to do so, require that the Ottoman sultan's name be mentioned first in the Friday prayers offered across the province, and promise that all coins minted in the province would bear his name. The old formula for legitimating political autonomy first suggested by al-Mawardi in the eleventh century had made a comeback.

Despite Khayr al-Din's efforts, Tunisia was slowly moving into the French sphere of political influence. Faced with mounting debts to fund its modernization schemes, the province declared bankruptcy and an

---

[74] Abun-Nasr, *History of the Maghrib*, 303–12.

international conglomeration of banks took over its finances in 1869. French commercial interests soon controlled much of the province's economy. The Congress of Berlin in 1878 placed Tunisia in the French political sphere of influence and in 1881, French forces occupied the country. The French occupiers allowed the Husayni dynasty to maintain the facade that it was still in control, but it was the French rather than the Ottomans who were the country's "protectors."

The situation in Egypt after the death of Mehmed Ali bore some superficial resemblance to that in Tunisia. In the deal brokered by the British to end the Egyptian occupation of Syria, Sultan Abdülmecid granted to Mehmed Ali's descendants the right to serve as the hereditary governors of Egypt in return for a yearly tribute and the understanding that any agreement between the Ottomans and a European power would be valid in Egypt as well. The latter requirement was clearly in Britain's interests as it imposed the terms of the Anglo-Ottoman Treaty of 1838 on the country. The sultan theoretically appointed which of Mehmed Ali's descendants would govern but that was purely a formality. In fact, Egypt acted as an independent state after 1841 although the ruler was technically simply a governor (*vali*) of one of the sultan's "protected domains." In 1867, Sultan Abdülaziz granted Saꜥid the newly minted title of khedive (*hıdıv*) to indicate that he was not just an ordinary Ottoman governor but had a special place in the empire's hierarchy. In reality, the title meant little and the status quo remained.

Ironically given the virtual independence of Egypt in the mid-nineteenth century, Ottoman cultural influences had probably never been stronger in the country. Ottoman Turkish was the language at the khedive's court and of administration. The leading bureaucrats and military officers were Turkish speakers who were recruited by the governors starting with Mehmed Ali from the empire. They were handsomely rewarded with gifts of land by the governors and constituted along with the ruling dynasty the largest landowners in the country. The Arabic-speaking natives of the country called the ruling elite collectively "Turks," although many actually were of Balkan or Circassian origin, and deeply resented their privileges.

The tension would give rise to Egypt's first populist leader, Colonel Ahmad ꜥUrabi, who effectively staged a coup d'etat in 1881 and was named prime minister by the parliament against the khedive's wishes. That set off a series of events that ultimately led to a British occupation of the country in 1882. Great Britain continued to maintain the fiction that the khedive in Cairo was merely an official in the Ottoman government who received a letter of appointment upon his accession from the sultan. Tellingly, however, Egypt was colored red as a part of the larger empire on the world map in every British child's classroom. The practice of a formal Ottoman investiture of each new khedive continued until the outbreak of World War I, when Khedive Fuad was elevated to the rank of king under British "protection."

CONCLUSION: THE TANZIMAT IN RETROSPECT

In October 1875, six months before the promulgation of the Constitution, the Ottoman government placed a discreet announcement in an Istanbul newspaper that it was not going to service all the interest it owed on outstanding loans to European banks. In effect, it was bankrupt. The juxtaposition of the two events, bankruptcy and the proclamation of the Constitution, illustrates a glaring weakness facing the Tanzimat reformers. While they could, and did, implement reforms that would lead to greater political control over the Arab provinces, they were in the process of losing economic control as the empire could not produce sufficient revenues to fund those reforms. The difference could only be made up through borrowing from Western banks, under extremely unfriendly terms. After it declared its bankruptcy, the European powers established the Public Debt Administration in 1881 to pay back the empire's creditors. From that point on, the Ottoman bureaucrats were no longer totally in control of significant portions of the empire's finances and resources.

On the political front, however, the Ottoman officials could look back over the decades of the Tanzimat with some satisfaction. The Asian Arab provinces had largely been secured, and indeed in 1872 under the Vilayet Law, an Ottoman province was constituted in remote Yemen for the first time since the seventeenth century. Yemen was nonetheless hardly a model province as many of its tribes remained resistant to rule from Istanbul. The same could be said for the easternmost province of al-Hasa established by Midhat Pasha. Ottoman control in both those provinces continued to be contingent upon control of the tribes as it had in the centuries past. Modernity occurred more slowly in some parts of the other Arab lands than it did in others.

The Tanzimat era had started in the Syrian provinces in the aftermath of the Egyptian occupation. It was not clear to the Muslim elites at that time whether it would mean a restoration of the status quo that existed before the occupation or a continuation of the radical reforms imposed by the Egyptian regime. The Christian minority of the provinces fervently hoped for the latter. In retrospect, the Tanzimat was a little bit of both. The centralizing regime of Ibrahim Pasha was continued under the Ottomans, replete with the two most hated innovations of that regime: conscription and direct individual taxation of the Muslims. Yet it was balanced by giving a greater voice in the local provincial administration to the ulama, as well as the *aʿyan*. A new civil commercial code replaced the sharia, but for the most part it was administered by the same people, or at least members of the same families. New *aʿyan* families emerged in the Syrian cities in the Tanzimat period, but that had happened in the eighteenth century as well. Some of the names of the notable families had changed, but urban Arab society was as stratified as it had been before the Tanzimat. Under the administration of governors appointed from Istanbul, the *aʿyan* secured both their political and economic position. As a class, they clearly benefited as the centralizing measures from the capital secured their status locally.

For poorer Muslims, the rage at social inequalities that might have been directed at the *aʿyan* was deflected instead toward their Christian neighbors. A similar conclusion was reached by Frederick Anscombe for the Muslim populations in the Balkans.[75] Not unlike the poor whites of the "Jim Crow" era southern states of the United States, potential class anger was directed at more easily assailable targets. In the case of Aleppo, economic grievances were not openly voiced in the rioters' demands in 1850, but the fact that they targeted the wealthy Christian neighborhoods and left alone the poorer ones provided a hint that it was perceived Christian economic privilege, as well as their new social freedom, that embittered the rioters and not necessarily their religion. In Damascus, the mob had been more indiscriminate in their targets, although Christians in poorer, religiously mixed quarters, such as Maydan, survived, protected by their Muslim neighbors. Whatever the initial causes of the unrest, the heavy hand of Ottoman retribution fell disproportionally on the poorer classes in both Aleppo and Damascus.

The integration of the empire into the capitalist world of trade and finance created definite winners and losers. Chief among the former were the *aʿyan* families and to a lesser extent the merchant families, both Muslim and Christian, who handled the distribution of Western manufactured goods from the main commercial ports to the inland cities and towns of the empire. European bankers and investors also profited, and

[75] Frederick Anscombe, "Islam and the Age of Ottoman Reform" *Past and Present* 208 (2010): 159–89.

they would oversee most of the economic development in the region in the last decades of the empire. The losers were the peasants, who increasingly found their position reduced to impoverished sharecroppers on someone else's lands, and the urban working class, faced with loss of jobs due to the increasing availability of manufactured European goods and rising prices as local agricultural commodities were exported to foreign markets and European imports took the place of locally produced goods.

7

The End of the Relationship

The consolidation of Ottoman rule over the Asian Arab provinces that began with the Ottoman reoccupation of Syria in 1840 was nearly complete at the start of the reign of Sultan Abdülhamid II (1876–1909). By the end of his reign, new technologies, such as the telegraph and railroad, linked many of the provincial capitals to Istanbul. No place was quite as distant as it once had been. There were nonetheless regions in the Arab lands that seemed alien and distinctly uncivilized to the Ottoman bureaucrats posted there. Underscoring that perception, Arabistan emerged as trope in the Ottoman discourse on civilization and progress. With their gaze fixed on the West, Ottoman would-be modernizers viewed the Arab lands as socially backward, undeveloped economically, and ignorant.[1] In securing his provinces in the east and south, Abdülhamid could rely on an increasingly professional bureaucracy and disciplined officer class. Both included Arabs although they were significantly underrepresented in either in terms of their percentage of the empire's population. Despite the changes that were occurring, most European observers were unimpressed by the empire's faltering steps toward modernity.[2] Perceptions of both reform and modernity, it seems, were relative.

---

[1] Christoph Herzog, "Nineteenth-Century Baghdad through Ottoman Eyes" In *The Empire in the City: Arab Provincial Capitals in the Late Ottoman Empire*, edited by Jens Hanssen, Thomas Philipp, and Stefan Weber (Beirut: Orient-Institut der deutschen morgenlädischen Gesellschaft, 2002), 311–28; Selim Deringil, "'They Live in a State of Nomadism and Savagery': The Late Ottoman Empire and the Post-Colonial Debate" *Comparative Studies of Society and History* 45 (2003), 311–42; Ussama Makdisi, "Ottoman Orientalism" *AHR* 107 (2002), 768–96.

[2] Mark Sykes, *Dar al-Islam: A Record of a Journey through Ten of the Asiatic Provinces of Turkey* (London: Bickers and Sons, 1904).

Better communication and an expanded bureaucracy facilitated greater surveillance by the state's security apparatus as independence movements, propelled by ethnically based nationalist ideologies, blossomed in the Balkans and took tentative first steps in Anatolia. The Arabic-speaking population of the empire was not immune from the siren song of cultural nationalism as pride in the glories of the Arabs' past was a hallmark of the intellectual discourse in the closing decades of Ottoman rule. In contrast to the troubled Tanzimat era for the region, however, Abdülhamid's reign was spared outbreaks of sectarian violence in the Arab lands. But storm clouds were emerging in the distant Balkans and closer still in southeastern Anatolia.

Despite concerns over what the future might hold, there were few in the Arab provinces who longed for the overthrow of the regime that had governed the region for four centuries. For most of the Muslim Arab population, and even for some among the region's Christian and Jewish minorities, the Ottoman Empire seemed to be all that stood in the way of a European land grab in the Fertile Crescent. The fate of the empire's former North African provinces and Egypt stood as clear warning to them of what might be in their future. Nonetheless, many intellectuals in the Arab provinces of the empire envied the relative freedom of the press available to their contemporaries in a British-"protected" Egypt, and some voted with their feet by settling in Cairo. Most Arab subjects of the sultan were, however, unwilling to trade a repressive Ottoman regime for a "liberal" British one. The compact between the sultan and his Arab subjects that had been forged in the sixteenth century still held. Their continued loyalty was partly due to fear, both of internal repression and of external aggression, but there were also optimistic voices that expressed hopes for a reinvigorated sultanate that would restore the Constitution and guide the empire's inhabitants to a better future as Ottoman citizens.

No period in Ottoman history has been the subject of such intense historical revisionism as that of its last absolutist sultan. In his lifetime, Abdülhamid II was excoriated by the *Times* of London as the "red Sultan" or "Abdul the Damned" for his alleged complicity in ethnic violence in the Balkans and eastern Anatolia.[3] Nationalist historians in the empire's successor states have characterized his reign as a period of unbridled despotism, marked by the brutal suppression of the national aspirations of their respective peoples. Although Abdülhamid II does not emerge out

---

[3] Andrew Wheatcroft, *The Ottomans: Dissolving Images* (London: Penguin Books, 1995), 231–47.

of recent historical revisionism as a sympathetic character, his policies are recognized as being predicated on a mission to save the empire, both by suppressing nationalism and by promoting an agenda that put Islam in the forefront of the Ottoman Empire's political identity.[4] The nature of Abdülhamid's rule was debated fiercely by his subjects in the various new print media increasingly available in Arabic during his reign, although more often from outside the empire's borders than within them. Absolutism versus constitutional monarchy, Ottomanism versus ethnic nationalism, a central role for Islam in the state versus tentative calls for secularism were all questions that roiled the intellectual circles in the empire in its final decades.

The ubiquitous censors in every provincial center limited the free expression of these debates but did not suppress them entirely. There was a growing diaspora of Arab intellectuals outside their control in Cairo, Europe, and the Americas, and newspapers and journals published in Arabic abroad took note of conditions in the "old country" and discussed options for its future.[5] These were often smuggled back to the empire through the various postal companies that had been granted to the European powers as concessions by the Ottoman government. All of the myriad political options known in the West as well as "home-grown" ideologies seemed to have been embraced by one segment or other of the intelligentsia in the Arab lands. The diversity displayed in the Arabic-language print media at the dawn of the twentieth century serve as testimony to a growing middle class that had its origins in a wide spectrum of the population.[6] Members of the *aʿyan* families still dominated the political life of the Arab cities, but the scions of the notable families in the Arab cities faced the sometimes-differing aspirations of an emerging middle class in the last decades of Ottoman rule.

THE NEW BOURGEOISIE

Modernity in the Arab lands had both physical and psychological dimensions. The first signs of its arrival were civic improvements that appeared

---

[4] Deringil, *Well-Protected Domains*, 16–43; Kemal Karpat, *The Politicization of Islam: Reconstructing Identity, State, Faith, and Community in the Late Ottoman Empire* (Oxford: Oxford University Press, 2001).

[5] Ilham Khuri-Makdisi, *The Eastern Mediterranean and the Making of Global Radicalism, 1860–1914* (Berkeley: University of California Press, 2010).

[6] Keith Watenpaugh, *Being Modern in the Middle East: Revolution, Nationalism, Colonialism and the Arab Middle Class* (Princeton, NJ: Princeton University Press, 2006).

in the coastal cities of the empire where the European investors had staked out their claims. Izmir, Iskenderun, Beirut, Haifa, and Jaffa received a Western façade in the form of Western-style architecture, tramway lines, street lights, and that ubiquitous sign of Ottoman modernity, a clock tower, first.[7] The inhabitants of the inland cities in Syria – Damascus, Homs, and Aleppo – in turn received those new symbols of the modern age after those who lived along the coast but before those living in Iraq or the Arabian Peninsula. To be truly appreciated, however, the physical manifestations of modernity required a new way of thinking, and that was to be found in the newly emerging bourgeoisie in those same cities.

The formation of a bourgeoisie in the cities of the Ottoman Arab provinces added a new dimension to the relationship between the sultan and his subjects, as its members were much more likely to question the political status quo than had their parents. The presence of a literate middle class signaled that the authority that had been exercised by the *aʿyan* for almost two centuries might find potential challengers. Real political power for the middle class was still a long way off, however. The new middle class was comparatively small, as it conservatively constituted no more than 10 percent of the total population. The vast majority of the sultan's Arab subjects continued to live in villages, in the crowded quarters that housed the urban poor, or in tribal encampments. But as more and more of their children and grandchildren were educated in the national schools to be created and staffed by members of the new middle class with the establishment of the European mandates, the impact of that first generation of "modern" Arabs on Arab cultural and political institutions for most of the twentieth century would be perhaps the strongest legacy of the Ottoman era in the Arab lands.

The members of the new bourgeoisie constituted the first generation in the Arab world to receive an education in schools with curricula shaped by Western models, methods, and subject matter. Missionaries from Europe and North America, both Protestant and Roman Catholic, had led the way in starting these schools. The Catholic project had begun tentatively in the seventeenth century, but Protestant missionary teachers from the United Kingdom and United States were rapidly catching up with them by the middle of the nineteenth century. The success of the Westerners in poaching some of the best and brightest of the youth of the Arabic-speaking Orthodox communities led the Orthodox patriarch

---

[7] Cem Emrence, *Remapping the Ottoman Middle east: Modernity, Imperial Bureaucracy, and the Islamic State* (London: I. B. Tauris, 2012), 34–53.

of Moscow to dispatch teachers to Syria and Palestine toward the end of the nineteenth century. With an openly missionary agenda behind the schools, those benefiting from this new window on the West were at first predominantly Christians. Jewish philanthropists in Europe seeking to "uplift" their coreligionists in the empire with benefits of a modern education started the Alliance Israélite Universelle in 1860, an early version of a philanthropic NGO that established schools for Jewish boys and girls in the empire.

Partly in response to the missionary schools, the Ottoman government in the Hamidian era embarked on an ambitious program to provide state-funded schools in the principal cities of the empire.[8] Government officials and local notables alike regarded these schools as symbols of progress, and each province's yearbook (*vilayet salnamesi*) proudly listed the number of schools and their pupils, as well as the names of those who were engaged to teach the sultan's youngest subjects in a wide variety of courses, from the Qur'an to French to chemistry. In addition, Muslim notables founded schools, funded by religious endowments, in Beirut, Jerusalem, Aleppo, Damascus, and Baghdad to provide a modern education for their sons that would equal that on offer in the missionary schools.[9] Schools for girls lagged behind those for boys, although the "gender gap" in education was greater in the Muslim community than among the religious minorities.

Literacy was still relatively rare in the Arab provinces outside the cities with estimates ranging between 10 and 20 percent of the total adult population being able to read in 1914. Within the cities, however, there was by that date an educated generation that sought to understand the advances in political institutions, science, and technology that were occurring in Europe and to apply them to Ottoman society. A new world was in the making, and the record left by the various journals and newspapers that were created to cater to this emerging social class shows that it was as a group optimistic and even enthusiastic about the future.[10] At the time, there was no talk about the inevitability of a "clash of civilizations" between Europe and the Middle East. That would come later for some, born of their disillusionment with the postwar settlement

[8] Benjamin Fortna, *Imperial Classroom: Islam, the State, and Education in the Late Ottoman Empire* (Oxford: Oxford University Press, 2002); Deringil, *Well-Protected Domains*, 93–111.
[9] Hanssen, *Fin de Siècle Beirut*, 162–89.
[10] Ibid., 213–35; Watenpaugh, *Being Modern in the Middle East: Revolution*, 68–94.

imposed on the former empire by the imperial powers in 1920.[11] In the waning decades of the empire, however, most of the discussions centered on how European-defined modernity might be introduced to Middle Eastern societies.

Modernity is a difficult concept to define whether in a European or Middle Eastern context.[12] Can being modern be measured with statistical data? If so, which data are significant? Or is modernity simply a state of mind? The two words Arabic writers at the turn of the twentieth century chose to convey the idea of "modern" were *hadith* and *ᶜasri.* Both terms convey the sense of what is present or in the "now" and so do not contribute substantially to our understanding of what the authors thought the terms meant. In the Middle East, its proponents understood modernity to be a break with the past. Which part of the past could be discarded and what might be upgraded to fit within a permeable continuum of modernity were, however, issues in the ongoing debate carried out in the print media. There were a few radicals who wanted to jettison all of the inherited traditions, but most did not. Rather, most intellectuals sought a compromise by which the morality of tradition could be cloaked in the scientific garb of the future. What most of those writing about the modern age sought was a transformation of Arab society rather than a major social or political revolution.

For those of the Arab middle class who would define themselves as "presentist" (*muᶜasir*) in the Hamidian era, modernity could be most easily expressed in the material culture they were adopting. It was, after all, a lot less jarring to import actual objects from the West than to embrace Western ways of thinking. European clocks, whether freestanding or the mantlepiece variety, had been popular among the Ottoman elite for centuries and faced no religious sanction as innovations. Clothing was a different matter for the Muslim religious establishment. The eminent Ottoman legal scholar Ebu's-su'ud had ruled in the sixteenth century that if a Muslim put on infidel clothing for any reason other than to save his life, he had become an infidel.[13] At the start of the Tanzimat era, the young Christian men of Aleppo had donned the fez as a symbol of their enthusiasm for the new regime. By the end of it, their sons had abandoned the *qunbaz* (caftan) and *sirwal* (baggy trousers) of their forefathers for the

---

[11] William Cleveland, *Islam against the West: Shakib Arslan and the Campaign for Islamic Nationalism* (Austin: University of Texas Press, 1985).

[12] See "AHR Roundtable: Historians and the Question of 'Modernity'" in *AHR* 116 (2011), 631–740.

[13] *Ebussuud Efendi Fetvarları,* 118.

frock coat, trousers, and cravat of the Europeans, while still retaining the fez. Their daughters also adapted to Western-style dress, and some tentatively began to appear in public unveiled at the start of the twentieth century.

The transformation of sartorial fashion lagged more slowly in Muslim households than in those of the religious minorities, but by the end of the nineteenth century many Muslim men in the upper and middle economic classes also sported the latest fashions, whose inspiration was imported from Europe even if local tailors produced them. Where once what one wore signaled the wearer's confessional identity, clothing had become semiotic of class differences. The poorer urban dwellers and peasants of all religious communities stuck to the same modes of dress that their fathers and grandfathers had worn while the male members of the bourgeoisie dressed like their counterparts in Paris or London, albeit while still sporting a fez. The conservative nature of society meant that bourgeoisie Muslim women were slower to dress in Western fashion, at least outside of their homes. Almost all remained veiled in public, although the debate raged over whether it should be a full opaque face veil (*niqab*) or something less restrictive (*hijab*). That debate has continued to the present.

Accompanying the shift to Western-style clothing, new city quarters sprang up outside the periphery of the old city walls in Jerusalem, Baghdad, Damascus, and Aleppo as members of the upper and middle classes sought to import Western-style family residences as well as dress. In addition to grand single-family homes, the new quarters included multifamily apartment blocks housing nuclear families, some of whom were not related by ties of blood or marriage. The new suburbs were laid out in an urban grid pattern with tramways and streetlights to serve their inhabitants. As was the case with dress, modernity for fashionable Arabs in the late Hamidian period was often a mixture of local tradition and European imports. Many of the windows in the upper story of the grandest houses were equipped with the traditional, carved wooden balconies (*mashrabiyya*) that allowed the women of the household to watch the traffic below unobserved. Many of these new houses, as well as those designed in the more traditional fashion employing central courtyards, were replete with wall paintings, which showed emblems of modernity such as steamships, railroads, and in at least one case an airplane.[14] In

[14] Stefan Weber, "Images of Imagined Worlds: Self-image and Worldview in Late Ottoman Wall Paintings of Damascus." In *The Empire in the City: Arab Provincial Capitals in the Late Ottoman Empire*, edited by Jens Hanssen, Thomas Philipp, and Stefan Weber (Beirut: Orient-Institut der deutschen morgenlädischen Gesellschaft, 2002), 145–71.

addition to the houses, the modernizing middle class increasingly appropriated European-style furniture, the ubiquitous Louis XIV style that still has currency throughout much of the Middle East, and dining conventions such as sitting on chairs at a dining table and using forks for meals as a mark of their having become modern.

The economic base of the emerging bourgeoisie was mixed. Some of those who can be subsumed into that class were engaged in trade or banking, others in small-scale manufacturing or in the employ of the state as bureaucrats or in the modern professions opened up by the Tanzimat reforms: medicine, education, and law. Some young men found their way to the middle class through service in the military as the empire's military academies, while still limited to Muslims, actively sought to recruit non-Turks, and especially those from Arab or Kurdish tribes, into the officer class.[15] In contrast to the diversity of the economic base of the new middle class, the truly wealthy *aʿyan* families were still largely vested in urban real estate and in agricultural lands in nearby villages.

Although non-Muslims predominated in both the commercial and banking spheres of the Arab cities, they did not monopolize them and many non-Muslim entrepreneurs had Muslims as silent partners. The continued presence of Muslims in the commercial sphere in the Arab lands contrasted sharply with conditions in the empire at large, where non-Muslims dominated the commercial and financial life of Izmir, Istanbul, and Thessaloniki. Such commercial partnerships may have also helped to dampen the passions of sectarianism in the Arab provinces in the closing decades of the empire as individuals cooperated in the pursuit of profits across religious lines.

COMPETING IDEOLOGIES

The Arab middle class provided an audience for the dissemination of a wide range of political and social ideologies at the start of the twentieth century. One of the defining features of modernity in the Middle East was the possibility for those who composed the new middle class to explore and reimagine their political identities. At the forefront of their options were the ideologies of Ottomanism and Islamic modernism as neither required a major reconfiguration of the primary political and social identity as Muslim held by the majority of the region's population. The two

[15] Eugene Rogan, "Aşiret Mektebi: Abdülhamid II's School for Tribes (1892–1907)" *IJMES* 28 (1996), 83–107.

were not mutually exclusive, and both could be embraced by a single individual without apparent contradiction. Both ideologies embraced modernity from the comfort of tradition. In addition, as neither was particularly threatening to the political establishment, writers exploring them were less likely to incur the wrath of the ubiquitous government censor than those promoting more radical alternatives.

Ottomanism had been advanced by the reformers of the Tanzimat and enshrined in the Constitution of 1876. Loyalty to the sultan was a relatively easy concept to understand, but it was rather more complicated for the proponents of Ottomanism to advance a coherent platform as to what their ideology embodied beyond that. As a result of that ambiguity, Arabic-speaking Christians and Jews could also feel comfortable under the Ottoman tent without having to question the communal identities that they had inherited from their forefathers as tradition. The Constitution of 1876 mandated that everyone who lived within the sultan's realm was an Ottoman, with the exception of resident foreigners and those formerly Ottoman subjects who enjoyed foreign "protection." Ottomanism as embodied by that constitution privileged the Ottoman Turkish spoken in Istanbul as the language of state and Islam as its religion, but it did not impose either on those who spoke another language or believed in a different faith. Without a clear articulation of the rights and privileges of the newly minted Ottomans in that constitution, however, Ottomanism was not a cause that might engender a popular groundswell of enthusiasm. It could shelter a vast array of identities for the sultan's Arab subjects, but it did not replace them. A robust patriotism required a cause more ennobling than simply preserving the status quo.

Not entirely sure they were Ottomans, for the majority of the sultan's Sunni Arab subjects Islam continued to provide the bedrock of political and social identity. Notions of what Islam meant were, however, more in flux at the dawn of the twentieth century than they had ever been before. There were, however, strong echoes of the various strands of Muslim intellectual thought that had been debated throughout the Ottoman centuries. Muslim intellectuals had digested both the Wahhabi and Naqshbandi critiques of Islam as practiced in the eighteenth century. They were also painfully familiar with the writings of those from among the European Orientalists who proposed that Islam was the root cause of the Muslim peoples' backward political and technological position in relation to the West. A growing number of Muslim intellectuals agreed with the critics, from both within and outside the faith, that many of the practices and ways of thinking that had come down to them under the rubric of tradition (*taqlid*) were ossified and a hindrance to both social and scientific progress. Rather than reject Islam wholesale and embrace the West, or alternatively to reject the West to find solace solely in a purified Islam as the Wahhabis proposed, these intellectuals believed in establishing a middle ground that would resuscitate the elements of their faith that they viewed as being authentically Muslim, while casting off those that might be construed as backward.

As Muslims had once led the world in scientific discoveries, Muslim modernists reasoned that Islam was not inherently inimical to knowledge and progress. Rejecting the agnosticism of the European Enlightenment, Muslim modernists might have agreed with the Enlightenment thinkers who held that Christianity as a system of religious beliefs was a detriment to scientific progress. Islam, however, was for them decidedly progressive. A return to the Islam as practiced in the first centuries of the community, they reasoned, would create the harmony between faith and science that had enabled Islamic society to flourish and would allow Muslims to take their rightful place *again* among the progressive civilizations as they had during Islam's "golden age."

The majority of these Muslim progressives were subsumed into the movement known as the Salafiyya, a neologism that was derived from *salaf*, meaning "ancestors." They believed a return to the simpler, and therefore purer, Islam of the first generations of Muslims who had been inspired by the living example of the Prophet Muhammad would free contemporary Muslims from the obscurantist baggage that the Muslim community had collectively acquired in its own "dark ages," after the destruction of Baghdad in 1258. Today, the term *Salafiyya* conjures up for many in the West images of Taliban-like Muslim fundamentalists. Muhammad ibn ᶜAbd al-Wahhab had called Muslims to return to the practices of the original Muslim community surrounding the Prophet Muhammad, and his strictly literalist and fundamentalist vision of Islam lies at the core of twenty-first-century Islamists' beliefs. But nothing could have been further from the meaning of *salafiyya* as it was understood in the first decade of the twentieth century in Cairo, where under the intellectual leadership of Muhammad ᶜAbduh (d. 1905), Muslim scholars sought to harmonize Muslim principles with Western innovations, whether scientific, technological, social, or political. Both evocations of the *salafiyya*, ibn ᶜAbd al-Wahhab's and Abduh's, could claim to be returning to the Islam of the ancestors. It was simply a very different understanding of what that meant when either man made that claim.

Although those who would have described themselves as belonging within the camp of the Salafiyya in Cairo at the start of the twentieth century would have ascribed to the notion that Islam and modernity as it was manifest in the West were not at odds, there were cultural lines that some were not prepared to cross. Qasim Amin (d. 1908), a student of ʿAbduh who was of Syrian-Kurdish origins, published a bombshell of a book entitled *Tahrir al-marʾa* (Women's Liberation) in 1899 in Cairo. Relying on a liberal reading of Muslim texts, Amin argued that the decline of Muslim society vis-à-vis the West was due in part to the social isolation of Muslim women. The key for progress lay in education for both Muslim men and women so that they could participate fully in building a modern Muslim society in which women would have the right both to appear in public unveiled and to earn their own income through gainful employment. Although Amin cited both the Qurʾan and the traditions of the Prophet to make his case, he was severely criticized by Muslim conservatives, who charged that he was seeking nothing less than the destruction of the Muslim family.

ʿAbduh failed to come to his pupil's defense and Amin published a second book in 1901, entitled *al-Marʾa al-jadida* (The New Woman). His arguments for women's rights in the revised work drew heavily on European social theorists, rather than on Islamic precedents. In his revision of his own work, Amin shifted much of the blame for the unequal status of women in Muslim society to Islam as a system of belief rather than just its social construction by Muslim men.[16] The debate over Qasim Amin's works demonstrated a growing rift among those Muslim intellectuals who sought to modernize their societies over the question of whether it was Islam that blocked progress toward some articulated vision of modernity or rather it was simply ill-informed Muslims who were the problem. In short, did they agree with Amin's analysis in his first book or in his second one? It is an ongoing debate that echoes down to the present.

Although Cairo was the focus of much of the Salafi debate over Islamic modernity, Damascus also produced scholars who contributed to the discourse of reform in the last Ottoman century.[17] Syrian scholars tended to be more conservative than their contemporaries in Cairo both in their

---

[16] Albert Hourani, *Arabic Thought in the Liberal Age 1798–1939* (Oxford: Oxford University Press, 1962), 164–70.
[17] Itzchak Weismann, *Taste of Modernity: Sufism, Salafiyya, and Arabism in Late Ottoman Damascus* (Leiden: Brill, 2001); David Commins, *Islamic Reform: Politics and Social Change in Late Ottoman Syria* (Oxford: Oxford University Press, 1990).

outlook and in the texts from which they drew their inspiration. The British occupation of Egypt in 1882 had forced intellectuals there to question how it had happened and more pressingly how it might be reversed. As such, the status quo was not an option for many Egyptian intellectuals and radical change had at least to be considered. Ripples set off by European developments were slower to reach inland Syria, and the question of what constituted modernity was less existential in Damascus or Aleppo than it was in Cairo. While Sufism and the works of ibn al-ᶜArabi were largely discarded in the intellectual discourse in Cairo as being in part the cause of Islam's descent into obscurantist traditionalism, some intellectuals in Damascus, including ᶜAbd al-Qadir al-Jaza'iri (d. 1883) who was buried in ibn al-ᶜArabi's mosque and Ahmad ᶜAbidin (d. 1889), kept the tradition of ibn al-ᶜArabi alive. Perhaps it was harder for them to let go of the man who had been so closely associated with their city during the Ottoman centuries. Another of Damascus's adopted sons, ibn al-Taymiyya, was the inspiration for other scholars in the city, providing continuity with the alternative intellectual tradition to Sufism that had sustained scholars in the city for generations. Those who based their scholarship in the latter camp, including Tahir al-Jaza'iri (d. 1920) and ᶜAbd al-Razzaq al-Bitar (d. 1917), took direct inspiration from the writings of Muhammad ibn ᶜAbd al-Wahhab and called for societal reform, based on a stricter interpretation of Islam and without the inspiration of European social theory.[18] As Damascus remained within the empire, its scholars had a different set of concerns than their counterparts in Cairo when it came to cultural nationalism as well.

Arab nationalism was potentially more disruptive of a continuing relationship between the Ottoman sultan and his Arab subjects than was the discourse on Islamic modernism as it could potentially lead to a breakup of the empire along ethnic lines. Scholars of Arab nationalism have debated when the ideology emerged as a truly widespread popular phenomenon, with some in the early twentieth century proposing that Arab nationalism was already a well-articulated ideology by the end of the Hamidian era. Historians writing later in the twentieth century pushed the rise of a political Arabism back at least to the Young Turk period, if not later.[19] The new consensus posits that an Arab movement for independence from the empire occurred relatively late and was supported

[18] Weismann, *Taste of Modernity*, 275–91.
[19] C. Ernest Dawn, *From Ottomanism to Arabism: Essays on the Origins of Arab Nationalism* (Urbana: University of Illinois Press, 1973); Kayalı, *Arabs and Young Turks*.

largely by those members of the new middle class who felt passed over for patronage from the state. In contrast, those individuals, largely drawn from the old a*ʿyan* families, who benefited from their connection to the state either by serving in the military or in acquiring land remained loyal Ottomans until it was no longer feasible for them to do so.[20]

While there were probably very few among the sultan's Arab subjects who sought independence, it is safe to say that most Arabic-speaking intellectuals, whether in the sultan's Arab provinces or under British "protection" in Cairo, were proudly aware of their cultural inheritance. The exception to that generalization was presented by some Maronite intellectuals who sought to promote a Lebanese national identity whose origins they argued predated the arrival of the Arab conquerors in the seventh century. But they were a distinct minority within a minority, and other Christian intellectuals in Beirut, such as Butrus al-Bustani (d. 1883), embraced the notion of an Arab cultural unity that transcended sectarian divisions.[21] For Muslim intellectuals, pride in the Arab past had been a dominant motif throughout the first three centuries of Ottoman rule. That pride only intensified in the empire's last century.

The new middle class sought out information on their ancestors' past, and popular writers such as Jurji Zaydan (d. 1914) capitalized on that interest by churning out a number of fictionalized histories of past heroes and their exploits. Presses, beginning with the Bulaq Press in Cairo, commissioned by Mehmed Ali, and later others in Beirut and Istanbul printed editions of some of the works produced in Islam's "golden age," making them available to a wider reading public for the first time. Some of the presses like the Bulaq Press were state enterprises, but others were privately financed by local investors or supported by missionary groups. Although perhaps only a few of the new middle class read these classics, as the language in which they were written remained difficult for most, they were frequently summarized in the popular newsprint media and taught in the curricula of the new schools. Soon almost every Arab city had a bookstore that sold affordable editions of both the classics of the Arab tradition and translations of Western works. New works of poetry and history and on scientific subjects were also produced as a new literary Arabic language was taking shape. As a sign of this growing historical cultural consciousness, streets in the new residential quarters bore names

---

[20] Michael Provence, "Ottoman Modernity, Colonialism and Insurgency in the Interwar Arab East" *IJMES* 43 (2011): 205–25.

[21] Ussama Makdisi, *Artillery of Heaven: American Missionaries and the Failed Conversion of the Middle East* (Ithaca, NY: Cornell University Press, 2008), 187–213.

of cultural heroes of the Arab past: ibn Sina, Abu Nuwas, ibn Khaldun, among others.

Pride, however, did not necessarily create a sense of an Arab ethnic identity for all those who spoke Arabic. Intellectuals in North Africa and Egypt did not necessarily imagine themselves to be Arabs. Across North Africa, the region's occupation by European powers made the national question a local one for the Arabic-speaking intellectuals, even while they recognized a cultural affinity with their putative cousins in the Ottoman Empire. The nationalist slogan that would emerge with the populist agitator Saᶜd Zaghlul (d. 1927) was "Egypt for the Egyptians." Perhaps because of the British occupation of the country, a regional rather than an ethnic identity took pride of place in the popular press in Egypt. Some intellectuals, such as Yaᶜqub Sannuᶜ (d. 1912), even promoted the use of colloquial Egyptian Arabic in mass-circulation newspapers and on the stage in Cairo.[22] That would be considered an anathema to the cultural nationalists who urged the use solely of the modern standard Arabic that was emerging in the print media as a new badge of a pan-Arab cultural identity.

In Baghdad, Damascus, and Aleppo, Arab identity remained closely intertwined with Islam, as most Muslims did not see any contradiction in conflating the two. Pride in an Arab past was necessarily for them a pride in a Muslim past. Christian intellectuals such as Shibli Shumayyil (d. 1917) and Farah Antun (d. 1922) who were based primarily in Beirut had begun to articulate their identity as Arabs in the second half of the nineteenth century.[23] This social construction filtered down to some Christians in the new middle class, who began to articulate themselves as Arabs in the last decades of the empire. It is not clear how extensive that identification was, however, as most of those who reached the United States before World War I identified themselves as Syrians to the immigration officials rather than as Arabs. Muslim authors were ready to extend membership in the Arab family to those who did not share their faith, but most writing in the first decade of the twentieth century would have rejected any attempt to cast Arab identity as purely a secular one. By 1914, important psychological steps had been taken by many Arabic-speaking intellectuals who envisioned the "nation" as being inclusive of religious differences and defined by mother tongue alone.

[22] M. M. Badawi, "The Father of Modern Egyptian Theatre: Yaᶜqub Sannuᶜ" *Journal of Arabic Literature* 16 (1985), 132–45.
[23] Hourani, *Arabic Thought*, 245–59.

Given the sectarian divisions that had divided the populations of what
would become Syria, Palestine, and Lebanon only a few decades before,
the tentative step toward an ethnic definition of the Arabs as a unitary
people was significant. It was even more remarkable in that in the rest of
the empire, religion trumped language even when the collective identity
bore a seemingly ethnic label: Greeks, Bulgarians, and so on. Despite a
common language, Greek-speaking Muslims on the island of Crete were
configured as Turks by their Christian neighbors, as were Slavic-speaking
Muslims in Bosnia and Bulgaria. In Anatolia, Turkish-speaking Christians
were either Greeks or Armenians depending on which rite they celebrated
on Sunday, and neither they nor their Muslim neighbors would have considered them to be Turks. Outside the Arab provinces, only in what would
become Albania did the intellectuals imagine their national community
to be based solely on language.[24] Arab nationalism was in the context of
the Ottoman Empire relatively unique in its inclusive and nonsectarian
definition of the "nation."

THE CALIPHATE QUESTION

The caliphate served as a prism through which various issues of religious
and national identities were refracted during the reign of Abdülhamid.
Articles 3 and 4 of the 1876 Constitution established that the Ottoman
sultan as caliph was the "protector of the religion of Islam." As discussed before, the sultanate and the caliphate were often conflated by
the Ottoman religious establishment in the earlier centuries, although
few Arab authors commented on the legitimacy of the sultan's claim to
that title. That indifference changed in the nineteenth century, as many
Muslim observers were faced with the stark reality of European imperial ambitions in the Middle East. Sultan Abdülhamid II further raised
the issue to one of international concern by reviving the claim advanced
in the sixteenth century that the House of Osman was alone entitled to
claim the office. In stark contrast, his grandfather, Sultan Mahmud II, had
been willing to share that title with Iran's Fath ʿAli Shah in the treaty of
Erzurum in 1823.[25] Despite Abdülhamid's claim, neither Sultan Mawlay
Hasan in Morocco nor Khedive Ismaʿil in Egypt, much less Nasir al-Din
Shah in Tehran, acknowledged him as caliph. Muslims living under

[24] Stavro Skendi, *The Albanian National Awakening* (Princeton, NJ: Princeton University
Press, 1967).
[25] Bruce Masters, "The Treaties of Erzurum (1823 and 1848) and the Changing Status of
Iranians in the Ottoman Empire" *JSIS* 24 (1991), 3–16.

European colonial rule in India, Southeast Asia, and Africa were, however, more willing to accede that title to him, if for no other reason than that the Ottoman Empire seemed to be the last Muslim state still standing and capable of aiding them against the European imperialists.

For Muslim Arab intellectuals, whether living under Abdülhamid's authority within the empire or in Cairo, the question of what constituted a legitimate claim to the caliphate was more complicated. Some, like their ancestors, would cite the saying attributed to the Prophet Muhammad that only one of those of the Quraysh could serve as imam of his community. Those within the empire might agree that the sultan deserved their loyalty in his capacity as protector of Islam, but they reasoned that he was not the caliph. The hesitancy to acknowledge Abdülhamid's claim diminished, however, as one Muslim territory after another was occupied by Christian armies. Even so, there was often a disclaimer to the effect that Abdülhamid's caliphate was not the same as that of the four "Rightly Guided Caliphs" of Muslim tradition. Over time, however, some scholars presented a more convoluted line of reasoning that would make the case that the Ottoman sultan alone had the right to the title, in line with the propaganda emanating from Istanbul. In doing so, they often invoked the necessity to preserve the community of Muslims from occupation by nonbelievers or heretics as providing legitimacy to the Ottoman sultan's claim to the prerogatives of the caliphate.

As we have seen in Chapter 5, one of the first Arab scholars to have recognized an Ottoman sultan as caliph was the Damascene scholar Muhammad Amin ibn ʿAbidin. Living under Ibrahim Pasha's occupation, he must have considered his political choices stark. He could acquiesce to the rule by a man he considered to be an apostate or justify why rebellion was necessary. Ibn ʿAbidin chose the latter course by acknowledging that Sultan Mahmud was the rightful caliph. Even while doing so, however, he made a distinction between the "greater" caliphate of the "Rightly-Guided Caliphs" and the "lesser" caliphate of the House of Osman. Nonetheless, he wrote, Muslims were obliged to render their fealty to the Ottoman sultan as caliph as long as he maintained the rule of law and fought the jihad against infidels and heretics.

A half-century later, ʿAbd al-Razzaq al-Bitar also in Damascus provided a different rationale for the legitimacy of the House of Osman as sole claimant to the title of caliph. In his entry for Sultan Abdülhamid II in his biographical dictionary, al-Bitar listed among the sultan's titles "Sultan of the Sultans of the Arabs and Foreigners (ʿAjam)" and, more significantly, "Shadow of God on Earth" and "Commander of the Faithful."

Historically, Arab authors had applied the last two titles to the caliphs alone.[26] Further on, al-Bitar discussed the rising of Muhammad Ahmad against the Egyptian administration in Khartoum in 1883 and, therefore, against Abdülhamid as lawful sovereign over Egypt. Al-Bitar embarked on a lengthy discussion of whether Muhammad Ahmad could rightly claim the title of *mahdi*, the person who Muslims believe will arrive at the end of time to usher in an age of justice before the final day of judgment. Al-Bitar noted various historical personages who had falsely made that claim, as well as an exposition of the Shi'i belief that the last imam, Muhammad Mahdi al-Muntadhar, would fulfill that function.

Al-Bitar then curiously cited the text *al-Shajara al-nuʿmaniyya* (discussed in Chapter 4), which foretold that the House of Osman would hold the sultanate until the coming of the *mahdi*, although he gave as the text's author al-Shaykh Salah al-Din al-Safadi, a thirteenth-century Sufi, rather than ibn al-ʿArabi.[27] Al-Bitar was a a student in the tradition of of ibn Taymiyya and the reason for his misidentification of the author of the text was most probably due to his having written essays equating ibn al-ʿArabi's writings to heresy. Nevertheless, al-Bitar seemingly accepted the prophecy as authentic and concluded his discussion of the revolt in the Sudan with a circular argument. As Sultan Abdülhamid was the universal, legitimate caliph of all Muslims, Muhammad Ahmad could not be the *mahdi*, as he claimed, because he was in revolt against his legitimate liege lord. The "true" *mahdi* would not break God's law by rising against his rightful sovereign. Muhammad Ahmad had, therefore, proven with his actions that he could not be that whom he claimed to be. But even in granting Sultan Abdülhamid the title of caliph, al-Bitar maintained the distinction established by ibn ʿAbidin between the "greater" caliphate of the "Rightly-Guided" Caliphs" and the "lesser" one of the Ottoman sultans.

Not surprisingly given his high praise of the rule of Sultan Abdülhamid, al-Bitar was associated with Abu al-Huda al-Sayyadi (d. 1909), perhaps the most prominent Arab promoter of the sultan's claim to the caliphate.[28] Abu al-Huda had risen quickly from the obscurity of his rural origins in a village in northern Syria by aligning himself with the royalist faction in Aleppo against another faction also made up of prominent families who

[26] ʿAbd al-Razzaq al-Bitar, *Hilyat al-bashar fi ta'rikh al-qarn al-thalith ʿashar*, 3 vols. (Damascus: Majmaʿ al-Lugha al-ʿArabiyya bi-Dimashq, 1961,1963), vol. I, 797.
[27] Ibid., vol. I, 804.
[28] Thomas Eich, "The Forgotten Salafi-Abu l-Huda As-Sayyadi" *WI* 43 (2003): 61–87.

were staunch constitutionalists. Although there were some in Aleppo who were dubious of Abu al-Huda's claim to *sharif* status, he was able to acquire the prestigious office of *naqib al-ashraf*, "head of the Prophet's descendants," at a young age in 1873. The office, although largely ceremonial, had great prestige in Aleppo and historically belonged to a scion of one of the city's *aᶜyan* families. Abu al-Huda had bigger ambitions, however, and by 1878 he had ingratiated himself with the sultan.

According to one story, he presented himself at Yıldız Palace in Istanbul, saying that the Prophet Muhammad had visited him in a dream and given him an important message for Sultan Abdülhamid that he must deliver in person and in privacy. But as he apparently could speak no Turkish and the sultan no Arabic, Abu al-Huda was dismissed by the sultan's aides. He returned two days later speaking fluent Turkish and was thus able to relay the Prophet's message to the sultan without an intermediary. The sultan was intrigued by the transformation and when his spies in Aleppo informed him that indeed Abu al-Huda had known no Turkish when he lived there, he was enchanted. It would seem that the Prophet had worked a linguistic miracle so as to demonstrate the legitimacy of Abu al-Huda's claim to esoteric knowledge.[29] After the incident, Abu al-Huda served as spiritual adviser to the sultan and initiated him into the Rifaᶜiyya Sufi order, which was popular in the Arab lands but practically unknown in Istanbul. The Young Turk faction in the capital viewed Abu al-Huda as a religious charlatan who exercised unnatural control over the sultan. They also made much of his Arab origins, invoking the trope of supposed Arab superstition and backwardness.[30] But with his position at court secured, Abu al-Huda promoted himself as one of the sultan's Arab experts while urging his fellow Arabs to acknowledge his sultan's claim to the universal caliphate.

Not everyone was prepared to do so, however. The most famous of the Arab dissenters was ᶜAbd al-Rahman al-Kawakibi (d. 1903). Al-Kawakibi was the son of an *aᶜyan* family that had been prominent in Aleppo from at least the sixteenth century if not before. With his business partner Hashim al-Kharrat, he attempted to publish Aleppo's first private newspaper in 1878 but was stopped by the Ottoman authorities. In 1880, a new governor, Cemal Pasha, was appointed to Aleppo

[29] Ibrahim al-Muwaylihi, *Spies, Scandals, and Sultans: Istanbul in the Twilight of the Ottoman Empire*, a translation of *Ma Hunalik*, translated by Roger Allen (Lanham, UK: Rowman & Littlefield, 2008), 134–6.

[30] Butrus Abu-Manneh, "Sultan Abdulhamid II and Shaikh Abulhuda Al-Sayyadi" *MES* 15 (1979), 131–53.

province, and he shut down the pair's second attempt, *al-Iᶜtidal*, which was a bilingual newspaper in Arabic and Ottoman Turkish. That was not the end of al-Kawakibi's run-ins with the authorities. In 1886, Zirun Chikmakiyan, a disgruntled lawyer, attempted to assassinate Cemal Pasha. Cemal Pasha was convinced that Chikmakiyan had not acted alone and arrested Husam al-Din al-Qudsi, Nafiᶜ al-Jabiri, and al-Kawakibi as coconspirators. All were very prominent members of the city's *aᶜyan*. Al-Jabiri had represented Aleppo in the Ottoman Parliament, and both al-Qudsi and al-Kawakibi were associated with the constitutionalist faction in the city and among those who had opposed Abu al-Huda's rise to power. All three were eventually released without charge.[31] Al-Kawakibi chafed under the regime of press censorship in Aleppo, however, and in 1898, he sought the relative freedom of Cairo, where he published two works: *Taba'iᶜ al-istibdad* (The Characteristics of Tyranny) and *Umm al-qura* (The Mother of Cities). The latter title invoked the sobriquet of Mecca and al-Kawakibi argued in it that the Turks had allowed Islam to decay under their watch. In his view only a revived Arab caliphate, with its capital in Mecca, could preserve the faith and keep the Muslim lands free of European domination.

Al-Kawakibi's analysis echoed the anti-Hamidian line taken by another Syrian exile in Cairo, Louis Sabunji, in his newspaper, entitled appropriately enough *al-Khilafa* (The Caliphate), starting in 1881. In a similar vein, Wilfred Blunt, a British scholar of Islam and a former Foreign Office employee, proposed a return to an Arab caliphate in his *The Future of Islam*, published in 1882.[32] Blunt's book, which may have inspired al-Kawakibi's, listed several possible Arab contenders for the title of caliph and seemingly settled on the Hashemites of Mecca as the most logical choice, given the fact that they were indisputably descendants of the Quraysh. The British shadow government in Cairo was worried about the potential of Abdülhamid's claim to the caliphate to foment political unrest in Egypt should war between the two empires break out. As a result, al-Kawakibi's critique of Ottoman despotism was elevated to the forefront of their strategic thinking. British agents smuggled copies of the work into the Ottoman Arab lands, where they hoped it would lay the foundation for rebellion.

[31] al-Tabbakh, *Aᶜlam al-nubala*, vol. III, 381–3, 393–4; al-Ghazzi, *Nahr al-dhahab*, vol. III, 410–11.

[32] Wilfrid Blunt, *The Future of Islam* (London: Keegan Paul, Trench, 1882), 90–118; Ş. Tufan Buzpınar, "Opposition to the Ottoman Caliphate in the Early Years of Abdülhamid II: 1887–1182" *WI*, new series, 36 (1996), 59–89.

There were few echoes of al-Kawakibi's call for an Arab caliphate, however, among other Arab intellectuals either in Cairo or in the Arabic-speaking diaspora. That would have been impossible, of course, in the Ottoman-controlled Arab lands, where censors carefully removed any item that might undermine the sultan's authority even tangentially.[33] The burning political issue for Arab exiles from the Ottoman Empire was not, however, whether Abdülhamid had the right to claim the caliphate, but rather the necessity to restore the Constitution of 1876 so that the Ottoman Empire could rouse itself to its own defense and thereby prevent the further occupation of Muslim territories by the European powers. The caliphate was, with historical hindsight, an exaggerated issue for European imperial planners, creating either paranoia of a mass Muslim uprising in their own empires or optimism that if an alternate Arab claimant to the office emerged, the Ottoman Empire would unravel. It engendered very little discussion among most Arab Muslim intellectuals, however, except among those who sought to play the role of sycophants to Abdülhamid's ego. The question of what role the sultanate/caliphate should play within the Ottoman regime itself was soon to be decided in the capital itself.

THE YOUNG TURK REVOLUTION

The Ottoman Third Army, headquartered in Thessaloniki (Selanik, Salonica), mutinied in April 1908 and demanded the reinstatement of the Constitution of 1876. The city lay in the contested region of Macedonia, which was among the last vestiges of the Ottoman Empire on the European continent. Greeks, Bulgarians, and Macedonians all claimed the city as their own, and the Ottoman officers felt that desperate times required desperate measures. They were members of a secret society that called itself the Young Turks (Jön Türkler) and sought the end of Abdülhamid's autocracy as the only way to save the empire. The agitation spread to the capital, where the First Army joined with the rebels and on 23 July 1908, a group of officers forced Sultan Abdülhamid to reinstate the Constitution of 1876. New elections were held and the Ottoman Parliament convened on 17 December 1908.

[33] Cesar Farah, "Censorship and Freedom of Expression in Ottoman Syria and Egypt" in *Nationalism in a Non-National State: The Dissolution of the Ottoman Empire*, edited by William Haddad and William Ochsenwald (Columbus: Ohio State University Press, 1977); 151–94.

On 31 March 1909, conservatives staged an uprising in Istanbul, supported by religious students and a shadowy organization known as the İttihad-i Muhammadi (Muhammadan Union). The aims of the counter-revolutionaries were to restore full power to Abdülhamid and to dissolve the parliament. Conservative groups in many parts of the empire used the uprising as opportunity to voice their grievances. In the province of Adana in southeastern Anatolia, those grievances turned sectarian. Muslim mobs attacked Armenian quarters in the region's towns and cities, killing hundreds if not thousands of their neighbors. In nearby Aleppo, sectarian violence was controlled through the prompt action of the Muslim *a'yan* to defuse tensions, although the Armenians of the city stayed home for days in anticipation of trouble.[34] Local notables in both Damascus and Baghdad used the attempted coup to rally support against the Constitution and for a return of absolutism as they felt rule by a strong sultan would serve their interests best.[35] Although the uprising demonstrated deep social cleavages within the empire, the Ottoman army was able to restore order. Sultan Abdülhamid was deposed in favor of his brother, Mehmed IV. The former sultan was ironically exiled to Thessaloniki, the city that had given rise to the revolution.

The reception of the Young Turk coup was mixed in the Arab lands. The new middle class welcomed it as a move toward progress, but many of the old *a'yan* families who had benefited from the sultan's regime were not as sanguine about a return to the principle of a sultanate governed by laws. Nonetheless, many stood for election and by and large, as was the case with the first parliament, the majority of the sixty delegates elected in 1908 from the Arab provinces were from *a'yan* families. Nafi' al-Jabiri, one of Aleppo's delegates, had the distinction of serving in both the parliaments of 1876 and 1908. Despite the participation of delegates from the Arab provinces, there were complaints in Arabic-language periodicals in Europe and within the empire itself, as press laws were suddenly much freer than before, that the Arabs were underrepresented. There were 275 delegates in all, giving the Arab provinces approximately 24 percent of the total, while some historians estimate that those provinces held approximately a third of the empire's population. In the Parliament elected in 1914, however, the percentage of delegates from the Arab provinces increased to 32 percent.[36]

---

[34] Masters, *Christians and Jews*, 182–3.
[35] Kayalı, *Arabs and Young Turks*, 72–4.
[36] Ibid., 175.

Rather than reflecting ethnic divisions, the major point of debate between Muslim members of the new parliament was ideological. Whether Turkish- or Arabic-speaking, members of the Muslim middle class tended to support the Committee of Union and Progress (Cemiyet-i İttihad ve Terakki) [CUP], which embodied the party agenda of the Young Turks. That faction promoted a strong centralized state with an ideology of rein-vigorated Ottomanism, but with an emphasis on Turkish as the national language and Islam as the religion of state. Non-Muslim minorities and the old, elite Muslim families in the Arab lands supported parties that favored greater decentralization and local autonomy. The interests of the latter coalesced into the Moderate Liberal Party (Mutedil Hürriyetperveran) established in 1909. The Moderate Liberals dissolved in 1911, but other parties with similar political aspirations took their place. Although many of the Arab members of Parliament gravitated toward the opposition par-ties, Hasan Kayalı's groundbreaking study of Arab politics in the Young Turk era has shown it is wrong to construct an Arab-Turkish split over the question of decentralization, as some of the Arab members of Parliament favored the Young Turks on all issues except their increasing insistence on making Turkish the sole language of imperial administration.[37]

There was, however, one issue that concerned delegates from the Syrian provinces as a regional concern: Jewish immigration to what would become the Mandate of Palestine. There had been limited immigration by eastern European Jews to the region in the late nineteenth century, but after the creation of the World Zionist Congress and Jewish Agency at the end of the century, there was a systematic attempt by the Zionists to acquire land in what they considered to be Eretz Yisrael (the Land of Israel). Taking advantage of the more liberal press laws following the Young Turk coup, Arabic-language newspapers in Haifa began to draw attention to the purchase of agricultural lands by the Jewish Agency and the subsequent dispossession of peasant farmers. In the 1911 Parliament, two delegates from Jerusalem, Ruhi al-Kalidi and Saʿid al-Husayni, tried to stop further sales of land to the newly arrived immigrants. They were joined by one of the representatives of Damascus, Shukri al-ʿAsali, who feared that the Zionists had designs on territory throughout the region. They were supported in their opposition by Aleppo's veteran del-egate Nafiʿ al-Jabiri.[38] They failed, however, to get a consensus as the

---

[37] Ibid., 81–102.
[38] Rashid Khalidi, *Palestinian Identity: The Construction of Modern National Consciousness* (New York: Columbia University Press, 1997), 80–4, 135–6.

Young Turk faction in the Parliament saw the Zionists as potential allies. Although Arabs generally may not have felt an existential threat from outsiders that elicited a counterstrategy of Arab nationalism, such sentiments were clearly in the making among the intelligentsia who published and read the newspapers. Their editors and columnists were increasingly drawing their readers' attention to developments throughout the empire, in addition to those occurring in Palestine, which might augur further disruption of the status quo.

The empire faced two major crises in 1912 that forced those elites to question their future. Italian forces occupied five ports in the Ottoman province of Libya in October 1911. Initially, the Ottomans attempted to aid local resistance, which was headed by the Sanusi Sufi order. In October 1912, however, Italy threatened to extend the war to the Aegean Sea. Sultan Mehmed IV capitulated and declared Libya autonomous on 17 October 1912. The declaration was simply a fig leaf for Italy's imperial schemes. The sultan as caliph was to remain as the spiritual head of the province's Muslims, but its administration would be Italian. A rebellion against the Italian occupation continued, however, and during the First World War, Ottoman and German officers arrived in Cyrenaica to help direct it. Even after their departure at the end of the war, the rebellion was not completely suppressed until 1931 with the execution of the charismatic rebel ʿUmar Mukhtar.[39]

The Ottoman Empire had little choice but to abandon the Libyans to their own fate as its neighbors in the Balkans were mobilizing their forces on its borders in the autumn of 1912. On the day following Sultan Mehmed's announcement on Libya, Bulgaria, Serbia, Montenegro, and Greece declared war on the empire. Despite a spirited Ottoman defense of western Thrace, elsewhere in the Balkans, the Ottoman armies crumbled under the combined assault. On 8 November 1912, the Ottoman garrison in the city of Thessaloniki surrendered to the Greek army. Armistice talks among the parties began in December in London but collapsed at the end of January 1913. With renewed vigor, the Bulgarian army captured the city of Edirne (Adrianople) on 26 March 1913. The more than five centuries of Ottoman rule in the Balkans had come to an end.

Many Arab intellectuals saw the war in Libya as a clear sign that the European imperial powers had ambitions that included them. They reacted to that reality in two ways. The most common reaction was to rally around the Ottoman throne as the last chance to save their

---

[39] Abun-Nasr, *History of the Maghrib*, 377–85.

provinces from European occupation. That was the line put forward most vigorously by Rashid Rida, the Lebanese intellectual and student of Muhammad ᶜAbduh, based in Cairo. The second was to imagine an alternative to Istanbul's rule. Among Muslims who would embrace that option, the only alternative seemed to have been an Arab caliphate, as put forward by al-Kawakibi and British propagandists operating out of Cairo. In addition to the Hashemite Sharifs in Mecca and Khedive ᶜAbbas Hilmi in Egypt, Sayyid Ahmad al-Sanusi, who had captured Arab popular imagination with his ongoing war of resistance in Libya, joined the list of potential monarchs for an independent Arab state. The possibility of an Arab republic had not yet entered into the public discourse on the Arabs' political future.

Although far away, the Ottoman defeat in the Balkans also had an impact on the Arab imagination.[40] The coup of 1908 had greatly reduced the role of the government censor in shaping how the press reported events in the empire and abroad. Muhammad Kurd ᶜAli (d. 1953), a budding intellectual from the new middle class, took the opportunity and moved his newspaper, *al-Muqtabas*, which he had founded in the more liberal atmosphere of Cairo, back to his hometown of Damascus in December 1908. It was in operation until 1914, when a new regime of extreme censorship was imposed by the CUP junta in Istanbul. Although Kurd ᶜAli was emerging in his editorials as an Arab cultural nationalist, he, like his colleagues elsewhere in Syria and Iraq, took a supportive stance to the Ottoman war effort in the Balkans. In part, those sympathies were due to the fact that Arab conscripts, both Muslims and non-Muslims, were fighting and dying for the empire for the first time in large numbers. But Arab intellectuals also used the defeat in the Balkans to press for greater liberalization in the provincial administration at home. A key demand echoed throughout the various newspapers was that Arabic should be official along with Turkish in the Arab provinces. The language question was becoming politicized, and with it, the stirrings of an Arab nationalist sentiment could be observed in the press.

The Ottoman grand vizier Kamil took the opportunity of the peace talks in London in December 1912 to advance his own agenda of decentralization. He consented to a request from notables in Beirut to establish

---

[40] Abdul-Rahim Abu-Husayn, "One Ottoman Periphery Views Another: Depictions of the Balkans in the Beirut Press, 1876–1908." In *Istanbul as Seen from a Distance: Centre and Provinces in the Ottoman Empire*, edited by Elisabeth Özdalga, M. Sait Özervarlı, and Feryal Tansuğ (Istanbul: Swedish Royal Institute in Istanbul, 2011), 155–70.

a reform committee. Another committee was set up in Damascus. Both committees produced a list of very similar requests to address grievances felt by the Arab subjects of the sultan. These included that Arabic be cofficial with Ottoman Turkish in provincial administration in the Arab lands, the reduction of time of military service for draftees, and the provision that Arab enlisted men serve only in the Arab provinces. The Beirut Reform Committee also sought greater autonomy for the provincial government, including its right to hire foreign experts as advisers. The Damascus Committee made no such appeal for local autonomy. The concerns of both committees demonstrated that there were the stirrings of a common political identity shared by those who spoke Arabic in the two provinces that led them to act in coordination to voice their concerns to the government.[41]

Unfortunately for the moderates, the hardliners in the CUP took the opportunity of the defeat of the Ottoman army in the Balkan War to stage a coup in January 1913 to remove Kamil Pasha. The recommendations of the Arab reform committees were shelved, although the Ottoman regime issued a new provincial law in March 1913 that granted greater autonomy to the provinces in the spending of their revenues. It did not, however, address the issue of cultural autonomy. To the contrary, the next few years would witness the increasing linguistic Turkification of the provincial administration and the state school system in the Arab lands. Furthermore, the reform committees that had given voice to local concerns were disbanded. Some of those who formed the committee in Beirut went to Paris, where a group of Syrian émigrés had called for an Arab Congress, which met 18–24 June 1913. The meeting produced a list of requests to the Ottoman government that echoed those for cultural autonomy issued by the reform committees. But again, events in Istanbul rendered the call for reform in the Arab provinces largely unheeded. On the eve of the Great War, most Arabs in the empire were still loyal to the sultan. The debates over which language was to be used by the state, however, had highlighted the distinction between Turks and Arabs as significant for the first time in four centuries of Ottoman rule in the Arab lands and had pushed to the forefront the issue of ethnic identity.[42]

[41] Kayalı, *Arabs and Young Turks*, 128–30; Hanssen, *Fin de Siècle of Beirut*, 78–81; Kurd ʿAli, *Khitat al-sham*, vol. III, 126–7.
[42] Dawn, *From Ottomanism to Arabism*, 148–58; Kayalı, *Arabs and Young Turks*, 135–41.

THE ARABS IN THE GREAT WAR

The four-hundred-year-old relationship between the Ottoman sultans and their Arab subjects ended abruptly with the First World War. There are several competing narratives of the part the Arabs played in that war. The one most familiar in the West is of the Arab Revolt, put forward by T. E. Lawrence in his *Seven Pillars of Wisdom* (1935) and promoted through numerous lectures and slide shows by Lowell Thomas in Europe and North America in the war's aftermath. In that version presented to a new generation with David Lean's epic film *Lawrence of Arabia* (1962), Lawrence almost singlehandedly won the war for Sharif Faysal al-Hashimi, only to be betrayed in the war's aftermath by Arab bickering and British duplicity. Faysal's revolt also plays a major role in Turks' historical memory of the war, the Arap hiyâneti (Arab Betrayal), albeit with a much reduced role for Lawrence. Then, there is the story favored by Arab nationalists of Turkish oppression (*zulm al-Turk*), Arab heroism, and British treachery advanced by Muhammad Kurd ʿAli in his monumental *Khitat al-Sham* (1925–8) and later by George Antonius in *The Arab Awakening*.[43] But perhaps the most compelling of the narratives to have come out of the Great War is that of the Safarbarlik, remembered by a generation of Arabs who had endured it.[44]

Safarbarlik is the Arab pronunciation of the Ottoman Turkish *seferbirlik*, meaning "mobilization for war." In the Arab lands, the word came to mean specifically conscription and more generally the whole war experience. Young Arab men had been conscripted for the war with Russia (1877–8), the Balkan Wars, and the campaigns to pacify the Yemeni tribes. Conscription was widely unpopular, as no one had made a case that the empire was a cause worth dying for. One of the key demands of the reform committees in both Beirut and Damascus in 1913 had been that Arab draftees be posted solely to their home provinces. That, like the other calls for reform, went nowhere. During the war, more than a hundred thousand men were conscripted from the Arab provinces with the heaviest burden falling on the territories that would be constituted after the war as the Mandates of Syria, Lebanon, and Palestine.

[43] George Antonius, *The Arab Awakening: The Story of the Arab National Movement* (New York: G. P. Putnam's Sons, 1946).
[44] Najwa al-Qattan. "*Safarbarlik*: Ottoman Syria in the Great War." In *From the Syrian Land to the States of Syria and Lebanon*, edited by Thomas Philipp and Christoph Schumann (Beirut: Orient-Institut der deutschen morgenlädischen Gesellschaft, 2004): 163–74.

There was more than conscription, however, to darken the Arabs' collective memory of the war years in the Levant. Although there were almost no military engagements in the region, it was hit by drought and locust infestation. Adding to the misery, the Allied blockade of the Levantine coast meant that the Ottoman Arab provinces were cut off from food imports from Egypt that had traditionally fed the population in hard times. Remittances in the form of cash from Syrian and Lebanese emigrants in the Americas were also cut off, creating hardship for the families whom they had left behind. The U.S. consular and missionary letters are replete with accounts of starvation and death during the war years, although it is impossible to know how many people actually died. Muhammad Kurd ʿAli claimed that 120,000 people had died of famine or disease in Lebanon and 300,000 in Syria during the war years.[45] A more recent estimate places the loss of life in Palestine at 6 percent of the total population with a guess that the percentage of the population that perished during the war was higher in Syria.[46]

The Ottoman Empire entered the war in late October 1914, but there had already been intense activity by the Ottomans, British, and French to line up allies among the Arabs for the anticipated struggle. The British were particularly worried about the potential effects that a call for jihad by the Ottoman sultan/caliph might have on the subject Muslim peoples of their empire. To forestall that possibility, they pursued contacts with various prominent men who might emerge as a rival caliph to the House of Osman. The most serious contender for that role was Sharif Husayn of Mecca, who was wooed by both British and Ottoman officials. Husayn had spent much of his life in Istanbul, but he had also spoken out against the Ottoman use of force in Yemen. As such, both Ottoman and British officials were uncertain as to which side he would support should it come to war.

At the start of the hostilities, a British expeditionary force, made up largely of Indian soldiers, landed in Basra on 6 November 1914; there the local power broker Sayyid Talib, who was a former member of the Ottoman Parliament, welcomed them. Sayyid Talib, like many of the Arab parliamentarians, had fallen out with the CUP faction and asked the British to make him the emir of Basra. Instead they sent him to India.[47] Not long afterward, the British force began to move up the Tigris River

[45] Kurd ʿAli, *Khitat al-sham*, vol. IV, 133.
[46] Justin McCarthy, *The Ottoman Peoples and the End of the Empire* (London: Arnold, 2001),165.
[47] Charles Tripp, *A History of Iraq*, 3rd ed. (Cambridge: Cambridge University Press, 2007), 24–9.

toward Baghdad. There had been Iraqi officers in the Ottoman forces who belonged to the secret Arab Nationalist society *al-ʿAhd* and were sympathetic to an Arab revolt. Most of those had been previously identified by the Ottoman authorities, however, and had fled to Egypt or Arabia at the start of the war. As a result, there was no popular rising across the province, although there was local resistance limited to Hilla in protest of conscription that simmered between 1914 and 1916.[48] Generally, however, the leading Shi'i clergy viewed the Ottomans as the lesser of two evils. Their representatives went to the tribes of southern Iraq in January 1915 and urged them to resist the British advance. It is reported that eighteen thousand volunteers were recruited to fight the jihad against the British, and these were placed under Ottoman command.[49] The tribesmen contributed to a vigorous Ottoman defense that stalled the British advance just south of Baghdad in late November 1915. The Anglo-Indian forces retreated to al-Kut, where they endured a siege, lasting until 29 April 1916, when they surrendered. British forces continued to hold Basra, however.

If the dominant personality in the Western narrative of the Arabs lands during the First World War was T. E. Lawrence, that role in the popular Arab memory of the war belonged to Ahmed Cemal Pasha, who was given by them the unsavory nickname al-Saffah (the Bloodthirsty). Cemal Pasha, along with Talat Pasha and Enver Pasha, seized control of the CUP government in the spring of 1914. Sultan Mehmed Reşad remained on the throne and the Parliament met in session throughout the war years, but the three officers controlled the conduct of the war with only minimal consultation with either. Cemal took control of the Fourth Army, which had responsibility for a wide swath of territory running from Adana in the north to Medina. He arrived in Damascus after the declaration of war to prepare an Ottoman offensive against Egypt. Before departing the city for the campaign, he reportedly delivered a stirring speech in which he invoked various Arab heroes of the past and urged his men, the ranks of whom were largely filled with Arab conscripts, to fight as bravely for their faith as had their forefathers under the leadership of Salah al-Din.[50]

---

[48] Christoph Herzog, "The Ottoman Politics of War in Mesopotamia, 1914–1918, and Popular Reactions: The Example of Hilla" In *Popular Protest and Political Participation in the Ottoman Empire*, edited by Eleni Gara, M. Erdem Kabadayı, and Christoph Neumann (Istanbul: İstanbul Bilgi Üniversitesi Yayınları, 2011), 303–18.

[49] Ibid, 305–6; Nakkash, *The Shi'is of Iraq*, 60–1; Eric Davis, *Memories of State: Politics, History, and Collective Identity in Modern Iraq* (Berkeley: University of California Press, 2005), 44.

[50] Kurd ʿAli, *Khitat al-sham*, vol. III, 133–4.

The operation to "liberate" Egypt began on 4 February 1915. Cemal Pasha was convinced that the Egyptian masses would rise up in rebellion against their British masters when news reached them that the caliph's army was at the Suez Canal. They did not, and the British army dealt Cemal an inglorious defeat. He returned to Damascus, where, according to the historian Kurd ʿAli, he began to see traitors everywhere. Of course, there were some real traitors around. French diplomats had neglected to destroy incriminating correspondence with various Arab officials, clergy, and intellectuals when they were ordered to leave Syria at the outbreak of the war. Cemal had apparently known about the letters before the Egyptian campaign, but only started to act on them in its aftermath. He also arrested many who were not implicated in treason, but who had supported political parties other than the CUP.

The first public execution of the reputed traitors occurred on 21 August 1915 in Beirut's clock-tower square, where eleven men who were largely from the new middle class were hanged. More executions followed in spring 1916 in both Damascus and Beirut. Among those executed were members of Syria's *aʿyan* families, including Shukri al-ʿAsali and ʿAbd al-Hamid al-Zuhrawi who had served in the Ottoman Parliament before the war.[51] Sharif Husayn's son, Emir Faisal, was staying with friends just outside Damascus when he heard the news of the executions. He was reportedly shocked by the execution of so many leading men. His father had been in secret correspondence with Sir Henry McMahon, His Majesty's high commissioner in Egypt, for more than a year about the possibility of an Arab revolt. In Antonius's reading of history, however, it was the severity of Cemal's treatment of the reputed traitors that encouraged Faisal to initiate his own treason against his sultan.[52]

Faysal was not alone in feeling outrage. The execution of the "martyrs" in Beirut provided a turning point in his view of Ottoman legitimacy for at least one Arab serving in the Ottoman army, Ihsan Turjman of Jerusalem. Although he seemed previously ambivalent in his diary entries concerning the Ottoman Empire, his entry for 1 September 1915, which gave an account of the executions in Beirut, ended with the lines "I do not know any of these patriots, but I was deeply shaken by this news. Farewell to you brave compatriots. May our souls meet when your noble objectives are realized."[53] The martyrs (Shuhada) of Cemal's purge

[51] Khoury, *Urban Notables*, 75–6.
[52] Antonius, *Arab Revolt*, 188–91.
[53] Salim Tamari, *The Year of the Locust: A Soldier's Diary and the Erasure of Palestine's Ottoman Past* (Berkeley: The University of California Press, 2011), 130–2.

entered into the Arab nationalist pantheon of heroes, and both Beirut and Damascus have a square named in their honor. In hindsight, Cemal Pasha had made a colossal misstep that soured many individual Arabs' views toward the continued legitimacy of the sultanate.

Faysal's Arab Revolt began on 5 June 1916, and although it would become the stuff of legend, it had very little impact on Arabs outside the Hejaz. Cemal had hoped for a general rising by the Egyptians in 1915 and the British were hoping for one from among the sultan's Arab subjects in 1916. Neither event occurred. There were some further defections from the Ottoman army by Arab nationalist officers to join Faysal's army, but there were few outward signs of how the rest of the population greeted the revolt that had been mounted in their name. Whatever their feelings, the populations of the cities remained quiet. In part, this may have been due to Cemal's policy to transfer most of the Arab officers and even enlisted men from the Fourth Army to serve at Gallipoli or on the Russian front. He then replaced them with presumably more loyal Turkish troops. He had also ordered the deportation of more than a thousand prominent Syrians to Anatolia.[54] Of course, the regime of censorship was extremely strong in Syria and there was little opportunity for public support of the rebels. Outside the cities, the tribes in Arabia loyal to the House of ibn Saʿud remained neutral while some of those in the trans-Jordan region joined the Ottoman cause. When added to those Bedouins already fighting the British in Iraq, more Arabs fought to maintain the sultan's rule over them than to overthrow it and that estimate does not include the thousands of conscripts who had no choice. Almost all of the Arabs who voluntarily took to the battlefield were, however, Bedouin tribesmen. Weary of war already and weakened by war-induced hunger, the urban populations and peasants alike chose to sit out the revolt.

Faysal's Arab army fought a brilliant guerrilla war, but the Bedouins had been waging classic hit-and-run tactics against Ottoman forces for almost four centuries. Still, it is questionable that his forces could have ended Ottoman rule in the Arab provinces outside Arabia on their own. A century before, Wahhabi warriors seized Arabia but had been unable to occupy Damascus. Faysal had, however, powerful allies. If 1917 witnessed a horrific stalemate on the Western Front in Europe, it saw major British breakthroughs in their campaign to knock the Ottoman Empire out of the war. Reinforcements were sent to Basra from India and Anglo-Indian troops entered Baghdad on 11 March 1917. To the west,

[54] Kurd ʿAli, *Khitat al-sham*, vol. III, 142,

the British and Commonwealth forces, under the command of General Edmund Allenby, were able to crush Ottoman resistance in the Sinai in the autumn of that year. British forces occupied Jaffa on 16 November 1917 and on 11 December, they entered Jerusalem.

The war in the Arab lands would go on for almost another year, but the outcome was certain after the British victories of 1917. More Bedouin tribes joined Faysal's army, which entered Damascus on 1 October 1918. The Ottoman forces had already withdrawn from the city, having been dealt a major defeat by the British forces in the Hawran. It is still debated by some scholars whether or not the troops under British command entered the city first. The question was not trivial, as the British had promised Faysal that whatever towns his army liberated would be included in the future Arab Kingdom. Whichever army reached Damascus first, as was the case with Selim's victory in 1516, it fell without a shot having been fired. On the first Friday after Faysal's entry into the city, he followed Selim's example, whether aware of the precedent or not, and attended prayers at the Ummayad Mosque. There the imam issued his sermon in the name of "the Commander of the Faithful, our Lord, the Sultan, the Sharif Husayn and his son the Emir Faysal."[55] It was four hundred and two years, almost to the day, after another imam had made his pledge of loyalty to Sultan Selim in that same mosque. The Arabs, at last, had found an alternate candidate for the sultanate. Ottoman rule had ideologically come to an end in the Arab lands.

Arab forces soon afterward occupied Aleppo, but the war did not officially end until 30 October 1918, when the Ottoman government signed an armistice with the Allies, but not with Emir Faysal, at Mudros. Although Faysal would establish a de facto Arab government in Damascus and Aleppo in the aftermath of the Great War, Ottoman sovereignty over the Arab territories was not ceded until the Treaty of Sèvres in 1920, and then it was not to the Arab Kingdom. Rather, the Treaty of San Remo in that same year divided the former Ottoman Arab provinces in the Fertile Crescent into League of Nations mandated territories to be administered either by the United Kingdom or France. The boundaries were remarkably similar to those proposed in the secret deal known as the Sykes-Picot Agreement of 1915, the existence of which the British had fervently denied to Faysal. In the view of the Arab nationalists, one colonial power had simply replaced another.

[55] A. L. Tibawi, *A Modern History of Syria, including Lebanon and Palestine* (London: Macmillan St. Martin's Press, 1969), 271.

POSTMORTEM

Multiethnic, dynastically based empires did not fare well in the Great War (1914–18). The realms of the Hapsburg kaiser and the Romanov czar dissolved into the newly minted nation-states of central and eastern Europe. The Bolsheviks were able to regain much of the latter's territories in Eurasia in a "union of the proletariat," but nobody was really fooled. It was still Russia and an empire, simply under another name. Ethnic nationalism, although brutally suppressed, did not disappear and would eventually help bring down the USSR. Even the United Kingdom of Great Britain and Ireland, arguably the strongest militarily and most socially cohesive of the multiethnic monarchies going into the war, could not retain sovereignty over the entirety of Ireland in the war's aftermath. Ideologies of nationalisms, based on a nation that was defined by imagined ties of blood and history, as well as faith and mother tongue, had triumphed. The stage was set for even more bitter conflicts to be waged on European soil throughout the twentieth century

At first glance, the Ottoman Empire was yet another victim of the rising tide of nationalism. That, at least, is how the historians of the various subject peoples of the Ottoman sultan, including the Turks, have represented their national histories in the aftermath of the empire's demise. But that is really only part of the story. For the Muslim peoples of the empire, there was no clear moment when they stood up, united as one, to say that they no longer wanted to be the sultan's subjects. The one Muslim people that did so, the Albanians, did so reluctantly in 1912 to assert their own national identity in the face of neighbors who coveted their land and denied their national identity. Albanian reformers had been in the forefront to push for greater autonomy of their provinces, but they had remained loyal to the sultan as long as it was a feasible political option for them to do so. In the end, they were fairly reluctant rebels.

In spite of the Arab Revolt, many Arab intellectuals had also remained loyal to the House of Osman until it was no longer a political option. Inertia and fear of change were undoubtedly at play in their making of that decision. There was, however, also still hope that the Constitution could be restored and with it, a decentralized sultanate that would provide for cultural autonomy in the Arab lands. We cannot be sure what the majority of Arab Muslims felt about the retreat of the Ottoman armies from what would become Syria and Iraq. Those in towns occupied by the Allied Forces definitely did not feel that they had been liberated by the British and French armies, even though there were some among the

Christian population in what would become Lebanon who welcomed the change in masters.

Nonetheless, the relationship between the sultan and his Arab subjects was in transition before the war. The dominance of the CUP ideology among those who ruled in the capital had created a rift over the question of cultural rights for Arabic speakers. The history of Turkish nationalism in the twentieth century and its troubled relations with the Kurds hints that had the empire not entered the Great War, a rupture between Arabs and Turks would have most probably occurred eventually. Without a clean break of their own making, however, the Arabs were ill prepared to stand united against the designs of the European imperialists. The majority of them, like their ancestors, had trusted in the Ottoman sultan's promise to preserve the integrity of the lands of Islam from all enemies and that trust was broken.

Conclusion

For the Faith and State

They (Europeans) began their new life in the fifteenth century, while we
were delayed by the Ottoman Turks until the nineteenth century. If God
had preserved us from the Ottoman Conquest, we should have remained
in unbroken touch with Europe and shared in her renaissance. This would
have fashioned a different kind of civilization from the one in which we
are now living.[1]

Taha Husayn

Taha Husayn (d. 1973), who was arguably among the most formidable intellectuals of twentieth-century Egypt, did not think much of the
Ottoman legacy in his country. He was not alone in his opinion, as most
Arabs of his generation judged the Ottoman centuries harshly. At the
end of the empire, the Arabs had become a trope for cultural backwardness and religious obscurantism for "progressive" Ottomans. Many Arab
intellectuals in the twentieth century would characterize the Ottoman
Empire as having those same negative qualities. Added to the consensus
that the Ottoman regime had retarded Arab intellectual, social, and political progress was the stereotype of brutish behavior by Ottoman soldiers
and officials, which is often featured in literary and cinematic representa-
tions of the Ottoman past in Arabic-language media. When asked about
the Ottoman centuries, many elderly Arabs will respond with a simple
phrase, *zulm al-turk*, the "oppression of the Turks." It is safe to say that
there is little nostalgia for the ancien régime in the Arab lands, although

---

[1] From Taha Husayn, *The Future of Culture in Egypt* Reproduced in John Donohue and
John Esposito, eds. *Islam in Transition: Muslim Perspectives* (Oxford: Oxford University
Press, 1982), 77.

the complete proverb from which the phrase is taken is more ambivalent: *Zulm al-turk wala ʿadil al-ʿArab*, "The oppression of the Turks is better than the Bedouins' justice."

It is not hard to understand why the Arab nationalists of the twentieth century sought to place some distance between themselves and the Ottoman Empire. The ideology of Turkish nationalism that prevailed in its dying days soured its memory for those who could not share in that narrowing vision of whom the empire should serve. Moreover, the "oppression of the Turks" as a shorthand summation of the past provides a convenient scapegoat to explain the causes of underdevelopment in the Arab nations, as is implied in Taha Husayn's quote. The simplicity of the assertion, however, takes away agency for the vast majority of the sultans' Arab subjects who over the course of those centuries did not revolt against Ottoman hegemony. If the "backward" state in which the Arabs found themselves in the twentieth century was simply the fault of the Ottoman occupation, then their ancestors had sat by and endured four hundred years of oppression in silence. That possibility leads us back to the question posed by the historian of Rome Clifford Ando: "What induced quietude rather than rebellion?"

I have argued in the preceding chapters that many individual Arabs in the ranks of the ulama and from the notable urban families did more than simply acquiesce to Ottoman rule: they collaborated with it. If the history of empires is to be about relationships of power between the rulers and the ruled, then it must be acknowledged that individual Arabs of the elite classes played a part within the Ottoman administration, somewhere along a continuum between the empire's true subalterns and the Ottoman elite ruling class dispatched from Istanbul. The inhabitants of Damascus, which produced no rebels against the sultan, chose to honor the ʿAzms as the city's heroes of the period. It is an appropriate choice. The ʿAzm family epitomizes the relationship that many urban Sunni Arabs had with the Ottoman regime.

The ʿAzm governors served the regime as it was in their own best interests to do so. At the same time, it was in the best interests of those at the imperial court in Istanbul to allow members of the family to administer an important imperial center in the sultan's name. The partnership between sultan and his "loyal servants" allowed the ʿAzm family to acquire wealth. They used a part of that wealth to build a palatial residence, a madrasa, and a caravansary in their adopted city, all of which are proudly shown to visitors by contemporary Damascenes as examples of their city's glorious history. In return, the ʿAzm governors provided some measure of security along the hajj route, although they proved ultimately ineffective against the Wahhabi threat. While it lasted, both sides profited from the relationship. The empire endured in Damascus throughout much of the eighteenth century, in no small part, as the ʿAzms had enabled it to do so. In return, the family would take its place among the notables of their adopted city.

Relationships in which individuals, families, and tribes linked their fortunes to that of the state were common throughout the Ottoman Empire in the early modern period. We have to go no further geographically than the Greek Orthodox Phanariot families who lived within the walls of the imperial capital. In their compromise with the Ottoman state, the Phanariots tendered their services as translators at court and represented the sultan's interests as ambassadors to the West. In return, they dominated the hierarchy of the Orthodox Church in the empire and served as tax farmers and governors in what was for them the very profitable province of Wallachia. It is doubtful that the members of those families felt any deep ideological commitment to the empire that they served other than perhaps gratitude for the sultan's support of the supremacy of the Orthodox faith in the face of Catholic encroachment and for the order that his army maintained that allowed their families to prosper. With the introduction of the new ideology of nationalism, however, their loyalty came into question. Their subsequent fall from power with the Greek War for Independence was calamitous for some of them. Nonetheless, Greeks continued to serve the Ottoman state until its demise in 1918.

Beyond self-interest, there was the ideology of the Islamic sultanate that supported the Ottoman Empire. It was the invocation of its role as the protector of a shared faith that provided the strongest bond between the House of Osman and its Sunni subjects. It proved to be an effective strategy for ruling the Arab lands as members of the Sunni scholarly class, the ulama, became the most enthusiastic supporters of the dynasty in the regions to the south of the Taurus Mountains and along the southern shores of the Mediterranean Sea as they identified the fortunes of the House of Osman with the welfare of Sunni Muslims. As such, they were willing to give the Ottoman state their loyalty. It was not quite unconditional, as the state had to demonstrate that its goals were "commanding right and forbidding wrong." The Ottoman elite grasped that reality and they constructed mosques, fountains, marketplaces, caravansaries, and bridges throughout the Arab lands funded by pious foundations, leaving a physical mark of their presence in the Arab provinces. They also funded other endowments to feed the poor and aid pilgrims to the holy cities of

Mecca and Medina, of which the sultans were the self-proclaimed protectors. Beyond concrete examples of piety, the state invoked its role as
the protector of the "people of the Sunna" against attacks from Christian
infidels and Shi'i, and later Wahhabi, "heretics." In short, the administrators of the Ottoman state sought to promote themselves as the righteous
upholders of Muslim traditions and institutions.

The authors whose works inform much of the discussion in this book
often linked Islam to the Ottoman regime with the phrase *din wa dawla*
"the faith (religion) and state," which they invoked when speaking of
an individual's willingness to sacrifice himself for the greater good. The
faith of Islam came first in importance, but it was followed by the state
in an acknowledgment that it was the state that upheld the faith. Islam,
in turn, legitimated the state's actions. It is, of course, impossible to know
whether the larger Sunni Arab population of the empire shared that perception. In their petition to Sultan Abdülmecid I, the rebels in Aleppo in
1850 stated: "if our lord sultan should command it, we would willingly
surrender our wealth, our lives, and our children as martyrs for our lord,
the sultan, and the faith of Islam."[2] The petition was signed, "the common people of Aleppo" (*ahali Halab ᶜamm*). It may have been simply a
formulaic expression, but the connection between their religion and the
sultan's state was clearly there.

The rebels had taken up arms, they said, because Islamic justice had
been overturned. They were appealing to their lord sultan to set the world
right for them again. We can assume that in their worldview the fact that
the sultan was a Turk and they were Arabs was of little relevance. That
does not mean that awareness of ethnic differences was not present in the
relationship between the rebel subjects and their sultan. Underscoring
that difference, their petition was written in a childish calligraphy and
in an Arabic that bordered on the colloquial. Attached to it, however,
was a translation in highly formulaic Ottoman Turkish so that the sultan might understand what his subjects were humbly beseeching him to
do. History, unfortunately, does not record the petitioners' reaction to
the sultan's response, which took the form of a shower of artillery shells
on the quarters in which they lived. But the two chroniclers of Aleppo,
Muhammad Raghib Tabbakh and Kamil al-Ghazi, representing *aᶜyan*
interests, wholeheartedly approved of the methods by which the "rabble"
was punished.[3]

---

[2] Istanbul, BOA, İrade Dahiliye 13185/14.
[3] al-Ghazzi, *Nahr al-dhahab*, III, 365–6; al-Tabbakh, III, 351–3.

The urban notables, the *a^cyan*, also played a role in maintaining the sultan's empire, although we might wonder whether they were motivated to do so for the faith or for more mundane reasons that were more closely aligned to those of the Phanariots than to those invoked by the ulama. Throughout history, self-interest has been a powerful incentive for those who would collaborate with empires. Nevertheless, resting on those twin pillars of Sunni Arab society, the ulama and the notables, the Ottoman Empire's control over most of the Arab lands was secure between 1516 and 1798. The only long-term successful challenges to it before Napoleon's foray into Egypt were mounted by armies that were sustained by alternative Islamic ideologies: Shi'i in the cases of Yemen and the Iranian borderlands, a contending dynasty with more distinguished ancestors in Morocco, or desert warriors motivated by an intolerant Muslim Puritanism. An ideology of state that did not stand on some version of Islam for its legitimacy was most probably inconceivable to most Muslims in the Middle East in the early-modern period.

After 1798 when it became painfully obvious to Muslim observers in the Arab lands that the House of Osman was no longer invincible, Mehmed Ali offered an alternative version of a modernizing Muslim state. It was a vision based solely on military might and no ideology other than that the dynasty knew what was best for its subjects. As a result, the majority of the population under Ibrahim Pasha's rule rejected his regime either passively or actively. The Ottomans' version of modernity introduced with the Tanzimat reforms (1839–76) was initially as disruptive in the Arab lands as that of Ibrahim Pasha as it seemed to replicate the tighter controls instituted in the Egyptian occupation, coupled with greater freedoms for the non-Muslim population. That set off a series of sectarian riots that further destabilized the Arab provinces. When order was restored, however, it became apparent to both the ulama and the *a^cyan* that collaboration with the reforms would ensure their continued status within the empire as the "natural" leaders in the Arab cities.

Collaboration rather than resistance was the dominant response to the Ottoman Empire in the Arab lands. Their collaboration did not mean that there was an absence of a strong cultural pride among educated Arabs in the Ottoman centuries. Their surviving literary works demonstrate that they were acutely aware that there were cultural differences between them and the sultans and most of the governors who ruled them. But Ottoman rule was not entirely a foreign occupation, as many Arab nationalist authors in the twentieth century would have us believe. Apart from the chief judges in the large cities and most of the governors,

Ottoman administration in the Arab provinces was carried out by local actors: judges, clerks, acting governors, tax collectors, and janissaries. All of these were willing participants in the running of the empire.

Nonetheless, there are scattered hints in some works that the author preferred Arab to Turkish rule. The best example of that sentiment is in the chronicle written by the Orthodox priest Mikha'il Burayk in Damascus who noted that the ʿAzms were the first from among the *awlad al-ʿarab*, Arabs, to serve as governors in Damascus.[4] That he frequently praised the ʿAzms for being good governors has been taken to indicate that Fr. Burayk equated their good government with their ethnicity. Elsewhere, however, in other chronicles and biographical dictionaries, good governors and judges were praised and bad ones excoriated without reference to their ethnicity. Indeed, ethnicity seemed to have been just one category of identity to be noted, with an individual's membership in a particular Sufi order often given more prominence in a biographical entry than his mother tongue. Outward shows of piety by a governor rather than his ethnicity seemed to have been the prerequisite for a favorable review either in biographical dictionaries or in chronicles that were written for the most part by members of the Arabic-speaking ulama.

Ethnicity as a political category was introduced relatively late to the Arab provinces. The reign of Abdülhamid II (1876–1909) vigorously reinserted Islam as one of the pillars of the Ottoman state and most Sunni Arabs responded favorably to his call for a more pronounced role for Islam in the ideology of the state. But an emergence of a middle class in the region's cities meant that not everyone in the sultan's Arab provinces was willing to buy uncritically into the old slogan of *din wa dawla*. Local issues such as the selling of land to Zionist settlers in what would become Palestine or what language would be used in provincial administration or taught in the government schools became Arab issues with the proliferation of print media. With provincial administration much more centralized at the start of the twentieth century, the presence of Ottoman officialdom in the Arab provinces proliferated. Ironically, at a time when more Arabs could actually understand Ottoman Turkish because of its incorporation in the curricula of both the state- and religiously run schools, there was a push for a greater use of Arabic in that administration. A pride in Arab cultural identity provided the basis for the creation of a potential national question within the empire in its last decade.

---

[4] Burayk, *Ta'rikh al-Sham*, I-II, 7–9, 13–14, 36.

By 1914, ethnicity was becoming increasingly politicized, but there was still no groundswell of Arab public opinion calling for an independent Arab state. The absence of nationalist sentiment was especially noticeable among the ranks of the ulama and the old established *a'yan*. Those two groups that had supplied the most willing collaborators to the Ottoman enterprise for four centuries, by and large, remained loyal to the end. The tie of religious solidarity between Arabs and Turks was weakening in the last decade of the Ottoman Empire but it still held firm for many Arabs. Given the dominance of Islam as a political ideology for fourteen centuries and the role that their ancestors had played in establishing and maintaining that dominance, it is easy to understand why it was difficult for some Arabs to let go and try to recast their identities as something else. The Ottoman sultans had convinced their ancestors that they were best prepared to protect and preserve the "people of the Sunna." Many Arabs even in 1918 were not ready to let relinquish that compact. Those resisting the French occupation in northern Syria appealed to Mustafa Kemal for support on the basis of Muslim, rather than national, solidarity. "Faith and state" still provided a formidable combination to elicit their loyalty.

Bibliography

Archives Consulted

Dar al-Watha'iq (Syrian National Archives): Damascus
    Aleppo sijillat
    Aleppo al-Awamir al-Sultaniyya (Aleppo AS)
    Damascus al-Awamir al-Sultaniyya (Damascus AS)
Başbakanlık Osmanlı Arşivi, BOA, (Prime Minister's Ottoman Archives): Istanbul
    Hatt-ı Hümayun
    İrade Dahiliye
    İrade Hariciye
    İrade Meclis-i Vâlâ
Public Records Office, PRO: London
    Foreign Office (FO)
    State Papers (SP)

Published Primary Sources

ᶜAbbud, Yusuf Dimitri al-Halabi, al-Murtad fi ta'rikh halab wa baghdad, edited by Fawwaz Mahmud al-Fawwaz, M.A. Thesis, University of Damascus, 1978.

al-ᶜAbid, Hasan Agha, Ta'rikh Hasan Agha al-ᶜAbid: hawadith sanah 1186 ila sanah 1241. Damascus: Wizarat al-Thaqafa wa al-Irshad al-Qawmi, 1979.

Abu Yusuf, Yaᶜqub. Kitab al-kharaj. Cairo: al-Matbaᶜa al-Salafiyya, 1962.

Aigen, Wolffgang. Sieben Jahre in Aleppo (1656–1663), edited by Andreas Tietze. Vienna: Wiener Zeitschrift für die Kunde des Morgenlandes, 1980.

al-Ansari, Sharaf al-Din Musa. Nuzhat al-khatir wa bahjat al-nathir, 2 vols. Damascus: Wizarat al-Thaqafa, 1991.

Bakhkhash, Naᶜum. Akhbar halab, edited by Fr. Yusuf Qushaqji, 4 vols. Aleppo: Matbaᶜat al-Ihsan, 1987–92.

Barker, Edward, editor, *Syria and Egypt under the Last Five Sultans of Turkey: Being Experiences, during Fifty Years, of Mr. Consul-General Barker*, 2 vols. 1876, reprint, New York: Arno Press, 1973.

al-Bitar, ᶜAbd al-Razzaq. *Hilyat al-bashar fi ta'rikh al-qarn al-thalith ᶜashar*, 3 vols. Damascus: Majmaᶜ al-Lugha al-ᶜArabiyya bi-Dimashq, 1961, 1963.

Bowring, John. *Report on the Commercial Statistics of Syria*. 1840, reprint New York: Arno Press, 1973.

Burayk, Mikha'il al-Dimashqi, *Ta'rikh al-sham, 1720–1782*. Harissa, Lebanon: Matbaᶜat Qadis Bulus, 1930.

Burckhardt, John. *Travels in Syria and the Holy Land*. London: John Murray, 1822.

al-Damanhuri, Ahmad ibn ᶜAbd al-Munᶜim, *al-Nafaᶜ al-ghazir fi salah al-sultan wa al-wazir*. Alexandria: Mu'assasat Shabab al-Jamᶜa, 1992.

al-Dimashqi, Mikha'il. *Ta'rikh hawadith jarrat bi-al-sham wa sawahil barr al-sham wa al-jabal, 1782–1841*. Amman: Dar Ward al-Urduniyya, 2004.

Düzdağ, M. Ertuğrul. *Şeyhülislam Ebussuud Efendi Fetvaları Işığında 16. Asır Türk Hayatı*. Istanbul: Enderun Kitabevi, 1983.

Elias al-Musuli, *An Arab's Journey to Colonial Spanish America: The Travels of Elias al-Musili in the Seventeenth Century*. Translated and edited by Caesar Farah. Syracuse, NY: Syracuse University Press, 2003.

Evliya Çelebi, *Evliya Çelebi Syahatnamesi*, vols. 9–10. Istanbul: Üçdal Neşriyat, 1984.

al-Ghazali, Muhammad. *Al-Ghazali's Path to Sufism; His Deliverance from Error (al-Munqidh min al-Dalal)*, translated by R. J. McCarthy, S.J. Louisville, KY: Fons Vitae, 2006.

ibn ᶜAbd al-Razzaq, ᶜAbd al-Rahman al-Dimashqi. *Hada'iq al-inᶜam fi fada'il al-sham*. Beirut: Dar al-Diya', 1989.

ibn ᶜAbd al-Wahhab, Muhammad. *Kitab al-tawhid alladhi huwwa haqq Allah ᶜala al-ᶜabid*. Cairo: Dar al-Maᶜarif, 1974.

ibn Abi al-Surur, Muhammad. *al-Minah al-rahmaniyya fi al-dawla al-ᶜuthmaniyya*. Damascus: Dar al-Basha'ir, 1995.

   al-Tuhfa al-bahiyya fi tamalluk al ᶜuthman al-diyar al-misriyya. Cairo: Dar al-Kutub wa al-Watha'iq al-Qawmiyya, 2005.

ibn al-ᶜArabi, Muhiyy al-Din. *Ibn al-'Arabi: The Bezels of Wisdom*, translated by R. W. J. Austin. Mahwah, NJ: Paulist Press, 1980.

ibn al-Hanbali, Radi al-Din Muhammad al-Halabi. *Durr al-habab fi ta'rikh aᶜyan halab*, 2 vols. Damascus: Wizarat al-Thaqafa, 1972–3.

ibn al-Himsi, Shihab al-Din Ahmad. *Hawadith al-zaman wa wafiyyat al-shuyukh wa al-aqran*, 3 vols. Sidon: al-Maktaba al-ᶜAsriyya, 1999.

ibn Kaldun, ᶜAbd al-Rahman. *The Muqaddimah: An Introduction to History*, translated by Franz Rosenthal, 3 vols. New York: Pantheon Books, 1958.

ibn Kannan, Muhammad al-Salihi. *Yawmiyyat shamiyya*. Damascus: Dar al-Tibaᶜ, 1994.

ibn Sanad, ᶜUthman al-Basri. *Mataliᶜ al-Suᶜud* (Mosul: Wizarat al-Thaqafa wa al-Iᶜlam, 1992).

ibn Taymiyya, Taqi al-Din. *Ibn Taymiyyah Expounds on Islam: Selected Writings of Shaykh al-Islam Taqi ad-Din Ibn Taymiyyah on Islamic Faith, Life, and*

Society, translated by Muhammad `Abdul-Haqq Ansari. Riyadh: General Administration of Culture and Publication, 1421/2000.

ibn Tulun, Shams al-Din Muhammad. *I^clam al-wara' bi-man wulliya na'iban min al-atrak bi-dimashq al-sham al-kubra.* Damascus: al-Matba^ca wa al-Jarida al-Rasmiyya, 1964.

Mufakahat al-khillani fi al-zaman ta'rikh misr wa sham, 2 vols. Cairo: al-Mu'assasa al-Misriyya al-^cAmma li-al-Ta'lif wa al-Anba wa al-Nashr, 1964.

al-Jabarti, ^cAbd al-Rahman. *^cAja'ib al-athar fi al-tarajim wa al-akhbar*, 7 vols. Cairo: Lajnat al-Bayan al-^cArabi, 1958–67.

Kayat, Assaad. *A Voice from Lebanon.* London: Madden, 1847.

al-Khiyari, Ibrahim al-Madani, *Tuhfat al-udaba' wa salwat al-ghuraba'*, 3 vols. Baghdad: Wizarat al-Thaqafa wa al-I^clam, 1979.

Kritovoulos. *History of Mehmed the Conqueror*, translated by Charles Riggs. Princeton, NJ: Princeton University Press, 1954.

al-Makki, Muhammad. *Ta'rikh hims.* Damascus: Institute Français de Damas, 1987.

al-Mawardi, ^cAli. *al-Ahkam al-sultaniyya wa al-wilaya al-diniyya.* Cairo: al-Matba^ca al-Tawfiqiyya, 1978.

Mishaqa, Mikhayil. *Murder, Mayhem, Pillage, and Plunder: The History of Lebanon in the 18th and 19th Centuries*, translated by Wheeler Thackston, Jr. Albany, NY: State University of New York Press, 1988.

Mustafa Nuri Paşa, *Netayic ül-Vukuat*, 2 vols. Ankara: Türk Tarih Kurumu, 1979.

al-Muwaylihi, Ibrahim. *Spies, Scandals, and Sultans: Istanbul in the Twilight of the Ottoman Empire*, a translation of *Ma Hunalik*, translated by Roger Allen. Lanham, UK: Rowman & Littlefield, 2008.

al-Nabulusi, ^cAbd al-Ghani. *al-Haqiqa wa al-majaz fi rihlat bilad al-sham wa misr wa al-hijaz.* Damascus: Dar al-Ma^carifa, 1989.

Wasa'il al-tahqiq wa rasa'il al-tawfiq, edited by Samer Akkach and published under the title *Letters of a Sufi Scholar: The Correspondence of ^cAbd al-Ghani al-Nabulusi (1641–1731).* Leiden: Brill, 2010.

Nagata, Yuzo, Toru Miura, and Yasuhisa Shimizu, editors. *Tax-Farm register of Damascus Province in the Seventeenth Century: Archival and Historical Studies*, Tokyo: Tokyo Bunko, 2006.

Naima, Mustafa. *Tarih-i Naima*, 6 vols. Istanbul: Matba'a-yı Amire, 1864–6.

Neophitos of Cyprus, *Extracts from the Annals of Palestine, 1821–1841*, translated by S. N. Spyridon in *The Journal of the Palestine Oriental Society* 18 (1938). Reprinted under the title, *Farqim be-Toldot Eretz Yisrael [1821–1841]*. Jerusalem: Ariel Publishing House, 1979.

Qara'li, Yusuf, editor. *Ahamm hawadith halab fi nifs al-awwal min al-qarn al tasi^c ^cashar.* Cairo: Imprimerie Syrienne, 1933.

Russell, Alexander. *The Natural History of Aleppo*, 2 vols. London: G. G. and J. Robinson, 1794.

Sykes. Mark. *Dar al-Islam: A Record of a Journey through Ten of the Asiatic Provinces of Turkey.* London: Bickers and Sons, 1904.

al-Suwaydi al-^cAbbasi, al-Sayyid ^cAbdallah ibn al-Husayn. *Mu'tammar najaf.* Cairo: al-Matba^ca al-Salafiyya, 1393/1973.

Tamari, Salim. *The Year of the Locust: A Soldier's Diary and the Erasure of Palestine's Ottoman Past.* Berkeley: University of California Press, 2011.

Tansel, Salahattin. "Şilahsor'un Feth-name-i Diyar-ı Arab Adlı Eseri" *Tarih Vesikaları* 4 (1955): 294–320.

al-Turk, Niqula. *Hamalat Bunabart ila al-sharq.* Tripoli, Lebanon: Jirus Burs, 1993.

Volney, Constantine. *Travels through Syria and Egypt in the Years 1783, 1784, and 1785.* English translation, 2 vols. London: G. G. and J. Robinson, 1787.

al-ʿUmari, Yasin ibn Khayr-Allah. *Zubdat al-athar al-jaliyya fi al-hawadith al-ardiyya.* Najaf: Matbaʿat al-Adab, 1974.

al-ʿUrdi, Abu al-Wafa'al-Halabi. *Maʿadan al-dhahab fi al-acyan al-musharrafa bihim halab.* Aleppo: Dar al-Mallah, 1987.

al-Ustuwani, Muhammad Saʿid, *Mashahid wa ahdath dimashqiyya fi muntasaf al-qarn al-tasiʿ al-ʿashar 1256 h.-1277 h. 1840 m.-1861 m.* Damascus: Wizarat al-Iʿlam, 1994.

Secondary Sources

ʿAbd al-Rahim, ʿAbd al-Rahim. *al-Rif al-misri fi qarn al-thamin ʿashar.* Cairo: Maktabat Madbuli, 1974.

Abdel-Nour, Antoine. *Introduction à l'histoire urbaine de la Syrie ottomane (XVIᵉ-XVIIIᵉ siècle).* Beirut: Lebanese University 1982.

Abdullah, Thabit. *Merchants, Mamluks, and Murder: The Political Economy of Trade in Eighteenth-Century Basra.* Albany: State University of New York Press, 2001.

Abu-Lughod, Janet. *Before European Hegemony: The World System A.D. 1250–1350.* Oxford: Oxford University Press, 1989.

Abu-Husayn, Abdul-Rahim. "One Ottoman Periphery Views Another: Depictions of the Balkans in the Beirut Press, 1876–1908." In *Istanbul as Seen from a Distance: Centre and Provinces in the Ottoman Empire*, edited by Elisabeth Özdalga, M. Sait Özervarlı, and Feryal Tansuğ. Istanbul: Swedish Royal Institute in Istanbul, 2011, 155–70.

Abu-Manneh, Butrus. "The Islamic Roots of the Gülhane Receipt" *WI* 34 (1994): 173–203.

"The Naqshbandiyya-Mujaddidiyya in the Ottoman Lands in the Early Nineteenth Century" *WI* 22 (1982): 131–53.

"Salafiyya and the rise of the Khalidiyya in Baghdad in the early nineteenth century" *Die WI* 43 (2003): 349–72.

"Sultan Abdulhamid II and Shaikh Abulhuda Al-Sayyadi" *MES* 15 (1979): 131–53.

Abun-Nasr, Jamil. *A History of the Maghrib.* Cambridge: Cambridge University Press, 1975.

Adanır, Fikret. "Semi-Autonomous Forces in the Balkans and Anatolia." In *The Cambridge History of Turkey.* Vol 3. *The Later Ottoman Empire, 1603–1839*, edited by Suraiya Faroqhi. Cambridge: Cambridge University Press, 2006, 157–85.

"AHR Roundtable: Historians and the Question of `Modernity'" *American Historical Review* 116 (2011): 631–740.

Akarlı, Engin. *The Long Peace: Ottoman Lebanon, 1861–1920.* Berkeley: University of California Press, 1993.

Akdağ, Mustafa. "Celali İsyanlarında Büyük Kaçgun" *Tarih Araştırmaları Dergisi* 2 (1964): 1–49.

Aksan, Virginia. *Ottoman Wars 1700–1870: An Empire Besieged.* Harlow, UK: Pearson Longman, 2007.

Allen, Roger and D. S. Richards, editors. *The Cambridge History of Arabic Literature: Arabic Literature in the Post-Classical Period.* Cambridge: Cambridge University Press, 2006.

Ando, Clifford. *Imperial Ideology and Provincial Loyalty in the Roman Empire.* Berkeley: University of California Press, 2000.

Amin, Samir. *The Arab Nation: Nationalism and Class Struggle*, translated by Michael Pallis. London: Zed Press, 1976.

Anscombe, Frederick. "Islam and the Age of Ottoman Reform" *Past and Present* 208 (2010): 159–89.

The Ottoman Gulf: The Creation of Kuwait, Saudi Arabia, and Qatar. New York: Columbia University, 1997.

Antonius, George. *The Arab Awakening: The Story of the Arab National Movement.* New York: G. P. Putnam's Sons, 1946.

Ashtor, Eliyahu. *Levant Trade in the Later Middle Ages* (Princeton, NJ: Princeton University Press, 1983).

al-ᶜAzzawi, ᶜAbbas. *Ta'rikh al- ᶜiraq bayn al-ihtilalayn*, 5 vols. Baghdad: Matbaᶜat Baghdad, 1935–56.

Badawi, M. M. "The Father of Modern Egyptian Theatre: Yaᶜqub Sannuᶜ" *Journal of Arabic Literature* 16 (1985): 132–45.

Baer, Gabriel. "The Administrative, Economic and Social Functions of the Turkish Guilds" *IJMES* 1 (1968): 28–50.

Baer, Marc David. *Honored by the Glory of Islam: Conversion and Conquest in Ottoman Europe.* Oxford: Oxford University Press, 2008.

Bakhit, Muhammad Adnan. *The Ottoman Province of Damascus in the Sixteenth Century.* Beirut: American University in Beirut, 1982.

Barbir, Karl. *Ottoman Rule in Damascus, 1708–1758.* Princeton, NJ: Princeton University Press, 1980.

Barnard, Toby. *A New Anatomy of Ireland: The Irish Protestants, 1649–1770.* New Haven, CT: Yale University Press, 2003.

Batatu, Hanna. *The Old Social Classes and the Revolutionary Movements of Iraq.* Princeton, NJ: Princeton University Press, 1978.

Syria's Peasantry, the Descendants of Its Lesser Rural Notables, and Their Politics. Princeton, NJ: Princeton University Press, 1999.

Blunt, Wilfrid. *The Future of Islam.* London: Keegan Paul, Trench, 1882.

Bodman, Herbert. *Political Factions in Aleppo, 1760–1826.* Chapel Hill: University of North Carolina Press, 1963.

Boyar, Ebru and Kate Fleet, *A Social History of Ottoman Istanbul.* Cambridge: Cambridge University Press, 2010.

Braudel, Fernand. *The Mediterranean and the Mediteranean World in the Age of Philip II*, translated by Siân Reynolds, 2 vols. New York: Harper & Row, 1972.

Brummett, Palmira. *Ottoman Seapower and Levantine Diplomacy in the Age of Discovery*. Albany: State University of New York Press, 1994.

Buzpınar, Ş. Tufan. "Opposition to the Ottoman Caliphate in the Early Years of Abdülhamid II: 1977–1882" *WI*, new series, 36 (1996): 59–89.

Casale, Giancarlo. "The Ottoman Administration of the Spice Trade in the Sixteenth-Century Red Sea and Persian Gulf" *JESHO* 49 (2006): 170–98.
  The Ottoman Age of Exploration. Oxford: Oxford University Press, 2010.

Ceccato, Rosella Dorigo. "Drama in the Post-Classical Period: A Survey." In *The Cambridge History of Arabic Literature: Arabic Literature in the Post-classical Age*, edited by Roger Allen and D. S. Richards. Cambridge: Cambridge University Press, 2006, 347–68.

Ceylan, Ebubekir. *The Ottoman Origins of Modern Iraq: Political Reform, Modernization and Development in the Nineteenth-Century Middle East*. London: I. B. Tauris, 2011.

Charles-Roux, François. *Les échelles de Syrie et de Palestine au XVIIIe siècle*. Paris: Paul Guenther, 1928.

Chaudhuri, K. N. *Asia before Europe: Economy and Civilisation of the Indian Ocean from the Rise of Islam to 1750*. Cambridge: Cambridge University Press, 1990.

Cleveland, William. *Islam against the West: Shakib Arslan and the Campaign for Islamic Nationalism*. Austin: University of Texas Press, 1985.

Cohen, Amnon. *The Guilds of Ottoman Jerusalem*. Leiden: Brill, 2001.
  Palestine in the 18th Century: Patterns of Government and Administration. Jerusalem: Hebrew University Press, 1973.

Cole, Juan. *Napoleon's Egypt: Invading the Middle East*. New York: Palgrave Macmillan, 2007.

Coller, Ian. *Arab France: Islam and the Making of Modern Europe, 1798–1831*. Berkeley: University of California Press, 2011.

Colley, Linda. *Britons: Forging the Nation 1707–1837*. New Haven, CT: Yale University Press, 1992.

Commins, David. *Islamic Reform: Politics and Social Change in Late Ottoman Syria*. Oxford: Oxford University Press, 1990.

Cook, Michael. *Commanding Right and Forbidding Wrong in Islamic Thought*. Cambridge: Cambridge University Press, 2000.

Copty, Atallah. "The Naqshbandiyya and Its Offshoot, the Naqshbandiyya-Mujaddiyya in the Haramayn in the 11th/17th Century" *WI* 43 (2003): 321–48.

Cory, Stephen. "Sharifian Rule in Morocco (Tenth-Twelfth/ Sixteenth-Eighteenth Centuries)." In *The New Cambridge History of Islam*. Vol. 2. *The Western Islamic World, Eleventh to Eighteenth Centuries*, edited by Maribel Fierro. Cambridge: Cambridge University Press, 2010, 453–79.

Crecelius, Daniel. "Egypt in the Eighteenth Century." In *The Mamluks in Egyptian Politics and Society*, edited by Thomas Philipp and Ulrich Haarmann. Cambridge: Cambridge University Press, 1998, 59–86.

Cuno, Kenneth. *The Pasha's Peasants: Land, Society, and Economy in Lower Egypt, 1740–1858*. Cambridge: Cambridge University Press, 1992.

Davis, Eric. *Memories of State: Politics, History, and Collective Identity in Modern Iraq*. Berkeley: University of California Press, 2005.

Dawn, C. Ernest. *From Ottomanism to Arabism: Essays on the Origins of Arab Nationalism*. Urbana: University of Illinois Press, 1973.

Deringil, Selim. "'They Live in a State of Nomadism and Savagery': The Late Ottoman Empire and the Post-Colonial Debate" *Comparative Studies of Society and History* 45 (2003): 311–42.

The Well-Protected Domains: Ideology and the Legitimation of Power in the Ottoman Empire 1876–1909. London: I. B. Tauris, 1998.

Devreux, Robert. *The First Ottoman Constitutional Period: A Study of the Midhat Constitution and Parliament*. Baltimore: The Johns Hopkins Press, 1963.

Dresch, Paul. *Tribes, Government and History in Yemen*. Oxford: Oxford University Press, 1989.

Dykstra, Darrell. "The French Occupation of Egypt, 1798–1801." In *The Cambridge History of Egypt*. Vol. 2. *Modern Egypt, from 1517 to the End of the Twentieth Century*, edited by M. W. Daly. Cambridge: Cambridge University Press, 1998, 113–38.

Eich, Thomas. "The Forgotten *Salafi* Abul-Huda as-Sayyadi" *WI* 43 (2003): 61–87.

El Moudden, Abderrahmane. "The Idea of the Caliphate between Moroccans and Ottomans: Political and Symbolic Stakes in the 16th and 17th Century-Maghrib" *Studia Islamica* 82 (1995): 103–12.

Eldem, Edhem, Daniel Goffman, and Bruce Masters. *The Ottoman City between East and West: Aleppo, Izmir, and Istanbul*. Cambridge: Cambridge University Press, 1999.

El-Rouayheb, Khaled. "The Myth of 'the Triumph of Fanaticism' in the Seventeenth-Century Ottoman Empire" *WI* 48 (2008): 196–221.

"Opening the Gate of Verification: The Forgotten Arab-Islamic Florescence of the 17th Century" *IJMES* 38 (2006): 263–81.

Emrence, Cem. *Remapping the Ottoman Middle East: Modernity, Imperial Bureaucracy, and the Islamic State*. London: I. B. Tauris, 2012.

Establet, Colette and Jean-Paul Pascual, *Families et fortunes à Damas: 450 foyers damascains en 1700*. Damascus: Institute Français de Damas, 1992.

Fahmy, Khaled. *All the Pasha's Men: Mehmed Ali, His Army and the Making of Modern Egypt*. Cambridge: Cambridge University Press, 1997.

Farah, Cesar. "Censorship and Freedom of Expression in Ottoman Syria and Egypt." In *Nationalism in a Non-National State: The Dissolution of the Ottoman Empire*, edited by William Haddad and William Ochsenwald. Columbus: Ohio State University Press, 1977, 151–94.

Faroqhi, Suraiya. *Pilgrims and Sultans: The Hajj under the Ottomans, 1517–1683*. London: I. B. Tauris, 1994.

Towns and Townsmen of Ottoman Anatolia: Trade, Crafts and Food Production in an Urban Setting, 1520–1650. Cambridge: Cambridge University Press, 1984.

Fawaz, Leila Tarazi. *Merchants and Migrants in Nineteenth-Century Beirut*. Cambridge, MA: Harvard University Press, 1983.

An Occasion for War: Civil Conflict in Lebanon and Damascus in 1860. Berkeley: University of California Press, 1994.

"Zahle and Dayr al-Qamar: Two Market Towns of Mount Lebanon during the Civil War of 1960." In *Lebanon: A History of Conflict and Consensus,* edited by Nadim Shehadi and Danna Haffar Mills. London: The Centre for Lebanese Studies and I. B. Tauris, 1988, 49–63.

Ferguson, Niall. *Empire: The Rise and Demise of the British World Order and the Lessons for Global Power.* London: Allen Lane, 2002.

Findley, Carter. *Bureaucratic Reform in the Ottoman Empire: The Sublime Porte 1789–1922.* Princeton NJ: Princeton University Press, 1980.

Finkel, Caroline. *Osman's Dream: The Story of the Ottoman Empire 1300–1923.* New York: Basic Books, 2005.

Fleischer, Cornell. *Bureaucrat and Intellectual in the Ottoman Empire: The Historian Mustafa Ali.* Princeton, NJ: Princeton University Press, 1986.

"Shadows of Shadows: Prophecy in Politics in 1530s Istanbul." In *Identity and Identity Formation in the Ottoman World: A Volume of Essays in Honor of Norman Itzkowitz,* edited by Baki Tezcan and Karl Barbir. Madison: University of Wisconsin Press, 2007, 51–62.

Fortna, Benjamin. *Imperial Classroom: Islam, the State, and Education in the Late Ottoman Empire.* Oxford: Oxford University Press, 2002.

Frank, Andre Gunder. *ReOrient: Global Economy in the Asian Age.* Berkeley: University of California Press, 1998.

Gerber, Haim. "Guilds in Seventeenth-Century Anatolia Bursa" *Asian and African Studies* 11 (1976): 59–86.

al-Ghazzi, Kamil. *Nahr al-dhahab fi ta'rikh halab al-shahba,* 3 vol. Aleppo: al-Matbaᶜa al-Marwaniyya, 1923–6.

Gibb, Sir Hamilton and Harold Bowen, *Islamic Society and the West: A Study of the Impact of Western Civilization on Moslem Culture in the Near East,* 2 vols. London: Oxford University Press, 1950, 1957.

Gillespie, Raymond. *Devoted People: Belief and Religion in Early Modern Ireland.* Manchester, UK: Manchester University Press, 1997.

Grehan, James. *Everyday Life and Consumer Culture in 18th-Century Damascus.* Seattle: University of Washington Press, 2007.

"Street Violence and Social Imagination in Late-Mamluk and Ottoman Damascus (ca. 1500–1800)" *IJMES* 35(2003): 215–36.

Gülsoy, Ufuk. *Osmanlı Gayrimüslimlerinin Askerlik Serüveni.* Istanbul: Simurg, 2000.

Haarmann, Ulrich. "Ideology and History, Identity and Alterity: The Arab Image of the Turks from the 'Abbasids to Modern Egypt" *IJMES* 20 (1988): 175–96.

Haddawy, Husain, translator, *The Arabian Nights.* New York: W. W. Norton, 1990.

Halaçoğlu, Yusuf. *XVIII. Yüzyılda Osmanlı İmparatorluğu'nun İskân Siyaseti ve Aşiretlerin Yerleştirilmesi.* Istanbul: Türk Tarih Kurumu, 1988.

Hämäläinen, Pekka. *The Comanche Empire.* New Haven, CT: Yale University Press, 2008.

Hanioğlu, M. Şükrü. *A Brief History of the Late Ottoman History.* Princeton, NJ: Princeton University Press, 2008.

Hanna, ⁽Abdullah. *Harakat al-ᶜamma al-dimishqiyya fi al-qarnayn al-thamin ᶜashar wa-al-tasiᶜ ᶜashar.* Beirut: Dar ibn Khaldun, 1985.

Hanna, Nelly. "Culture in Ottoman Egypt." In *The Cambridge History of Egypt.* Vol. 2. *Modern Egypt from 1517 to the end of the Twentieth Century,* edited by M. W. Daly. Cambridge: Cambridge University Press, 1998, 87–112.

In Praise of Books: A Cultural History of Cairo's Middle Class, Sixteenth to the Eighteenth Century. Albany: State University of New York, 2003.

Making Big Money in 1600: The Life and Times of Ismaᶜil Abu Taqiyya, Egyptian Merchant. Albany: State University of New York, 1998.

Hanssen, Jens. *Fin de Siècle Beirut: The Making of an Ottoman Provincial Capital.* Oxford: Oxford University Press, 2005.

Hathaway, Jane. *The Arab Lands under Ottoman Rule, 1516–1800.* Harlow, UK: Pearson Longman, 2008.

"The *Evlâd-i ᶜ Arab* (Sons of the Arabs) in Ottoman Egypt: A Rereading." In *Frontiers of Ottoman Studies: State, Province, and the West,* Vol. 1, edited by Colin Imber and Keiko Kiyotaki. London: I. B. Tauris, 2005, 203–16.

The Politics of Households in Ottoman Egypt: The Rise of the Qazdağlıs. Cambridge: Cambridge University Press, 1997.

A Tale of Two Factions: Myth, Memory, and Identity in Ottoman Egypt and Yemen. Albany: State University of New York, 2003.

Hattox, Ralph. *Coffee and Coffeehouses: The Origins of a Social Beverage in the Medieval Near East.* Seattle: University of Washington Press, 1985.

Herzog, Christoph. "Nineteenth-Century Baghdad through Ottoman Eyes." In *The Empire in the City: Arab Provincial Capitals in the Late Ottoman Empire,* edited by Jens Hanssen, Thomas Philipp, and Stefan Weber. Beirut: Orient-Institut der deutschen morgenländischen Gesellschaft, 2002, 311–28.

"The Ottoman Politics of War in Mesopotamia, 1914–1918, and Popular Reactions: The Example of Hilla." In *Popular Protest and Political Participation in the Ottoman Empire,* edited by Eleni Gara, M. Erdem Kabadayı, Christoph Neumann. Istanbul: İstanbul Bilgi Üniversitesi Yayınları, 2011: 303–18.

"Some Notes about the Members of Parliament from the Province of Baghdad." In *The First Ottoman Experiment in Democracy,* edited by Christoph Herzog and Malek Sharif. Würzburg: Ergon Verlag, 2010, 275–84.

Hess, Andrew. *The Forgotten Frontier: a History of the Sixteenth-century Ibero-African Frontier.* Chicago: University of Chicago Press, 1978.

Heyd, Uriel. *Ottoman Documents on Palestine, 1552–1615.* London: Oxford University Press, 1960.

Holt, P. M. *The Age of the Crusades: The Near East from the Eleventh Century to 1517.* London: Longman, 1986.

Egypt and the Fertile Crescent, 1516–1922. London: Longmans Green, 1966.

"Some Observations on the `Abbasid Caliphate of Cairo" *BSOAS* 47(1984): 501–7.

Hourani, Albert. *Arabic Thought in the Liberal Age 1798–1939.* Oxford: Oxford University Press, 1962.

"Ottoman Reform and the Politics of the Notables." In *Beginnings of Modernization in the Middle East*, edited by William Polk and Richard Chambers. Chicago: University of Chicago Press, 1968.

al-Husri, Sati^c. *al-Bilad al-ᶜarabiyya wa al-dawla al-ᶜuthmaniyya*. Beirut: Dar al-ᶜIlm lil-Milayin, 1960.

Hütteroth, Wolf-Dieter. "Ecology of the Ottoman lands." In *The Cambridge History of Turkey*. Vol. 3. *The Later Ottoman Empire, 1603–1839*, edited by Suraiya Faroqhi. Cambridge: Cambridge University Press, 2006, 18–43.

İnalcık, Halil. "Osmanlı Pamuklu Pazarı, Hindistan ve İngiltere: Pazar Rekabitinde Emek Maliyetinin Rolü" republished in Halil İnalcık, *Osmanlı İmparatorluğu: Toplum ve Ekonomi* (Istanbul: Eren, 1993), 259–319.

The Ottoman Empire: The Classical Age 1300–1600, translated by Norman Itzkowitz and Colin Imber. London: Weidenfeld and Nicholson, 1973.

"Sened-i İttifak ve Gülhane Hatt-ı Hümayûn" *Beletin* 28 (1964): 603–22.

İnalcık, Halil and Donald Quataert, editors, *The Economic and Social History of the Ottoman Empire, 1300–1914*. (Cambridge: Cambridge University Press, 1994).

Inber, Colin. *Ebu's-su'ud: The Islamic Legal Tradition*. Stanford, CA: Stanford University Press, 1997.

Irwin, Robert. "Mamluk History and Historians." In *Arabic Literature in the Post-Classical Period*, edited by Roger Allen and D. S. Richards. Cambridge: Cambridge University Press, 2006, 159–70.

Jasanoff, Maya. *Edge of Empire: Lives, Culture, and Conquest in the East 1750–1850*. New York: Alfred Knopf, 2005.

Johansen, Baber. *The Islamic Law on Land Tax and Rent: The Peasants' Loss of Property Rights as Interpreted in the Hanafite Legal Literature of the Mamluk and Ottoman Periods*. London: Croom Helm, 1988.

Just, Roger. "Triumph of the Ethnos." In *History and Ethnicity*, edited by Elizabeth Tonkin, Maryon McDonald, and Malcolm Chapman. London: Routledge, 1988, 71–88.

Kafescioğlu, Çiğdem. "'In the Image of Rum': Ottoman Architectural Patronage in Sixteenth-Century Aleppo and Damascus" *Maqarnas* 16 (1999): 70–96.

Karamustafa, Ahmed. *God's Unruly Friends: Dervish Groups in the Islamic Middle Period 1200–1550*. Oxford: Oneworld, 2006.

Karpat, Kemal. *The Politicization of Islam: Reconstructing Identity, State, Faith, and Community in the Late Ottoman Empire*. Oxford: Oxford University Press, 2001.

Kayalı, Hasan. *Arabs and Young Turks: Ottomanism, Arabism, and Islamism in the Ottoman Empire, 1908–1918*. Berkeley: University of California Press, 1997.

Kemp, Percy. *Territoires d'Islam: Le monde vu de Mossoul aux XVIIIe siècle*. Paris: Sindbad, 1982.

Khalidi, Rashid. *Palestinian Identity: The Construction of Modern National Consciousness*, New York: Columbia University Press, 1997.

Khater, Akram. *Sources in the History of the Modern Middle East*. Boston: Houghton Miflin Company, 2004.

Khoury, Dina Rizq. "The Introduction of Commercial Agriculture in the Province of Mosul and its Effects on the Peasantry, 1750–1850." In *Landholding and Commercial Agriculture in the Middle East*, edited by Çağlar Keyder and Faruk Tabak. Albany: State University of New York Press, 1991, 155–71.

State and Provincial Society in the Ottoman Empire: Mosul, 1540–1834. Cambridge: Cambridge University Press, 1997.

Khoury, Philip. "Continuity and Change in Syrian Political Life: The Nineteenth and Twentieth Centuries" *AHR* 96 (1991): 1374–407.

Urban Notables and Arab Nationalism: The Politics of Damascus 1860–1920. Cambridge: Cambridge University Press, 1983.

Khuri-Makdisi, Ilham. *The Eastern Mediterranean and the Making of Global Radicalism, 1860–1914.* Berkeley: University of California Press, 2010.

Hilary Kilpatrick, "Journeying towards Modernity: The 'Safrat al-Batrik Makariyus' of Bulus al-Zaʿim al-Halabi" WI 37 (1997): 156–77.

Kunt, I. Metin *Sancaktan Eyalete: 1550–1650 arasında Osmanlı Ümerası ve İl İdaresi.* Istanbul: Boğaziçi Üniversitesi Yayınları, 1978.

Kurd ʿAli, Muhammad. *Khitat al-sham*, 6 vols. Beirut: Dar al-qalam, 1969–72.

Kuroki, Hidemitsu. "Mobility of Non-Muslims in Mid-Nineteenth-Century Aleppo." In *The Influence of Human Mobility in Muslim Societies*, edited by Hidemitsu Kuroki (London: Kegan Paul, 2003): 117–50.

Lewis, Norman. *Nomads and Settlers in Syria and Jordan, 1800–1900.* Cambridge: Cambridge University Press, 1987.

Lier, Thomas. *Haushalte und Haushaltepolitik in Baghdad 1704–1831.* Wurzburg: Ergon Verlag, 2004.

Longrigg, Stephen. *Four Centuries of Modern Iraq.* Oxford: Clarendon Press, 1925.

Makdisi, Ussama. *The Artillery of Heaven: American Missionaries and the Failed Conversion of the Middle East.* Ithaca, NY: Cornell University Press, 2008.

The Culture of Sectarianism: Community, History, and Violence in Nineteenth-Century Lebanon. Berkeley: University of California Press, 2000.

"Ottoman Orientalism" *AHR* 107 (2002): 768–96.

Mannaʿ, ʿAdel. "Continuity and Change in the Socio-Political Elite in Palestine during the late Ottoman Period." In *The Syrian Land in the 18th and 19th Century*, edited by Thomas Philipp. Stuttgart: Franz Steiner Verlag, 1992, 69–90.

"Eighteenth- and Nineteenth-Century Rebellions in Palestine" *Journal of Palestine Studies* 24 (1994): 51–66.

Ta'rikh filastin fi awakhir al-ʿahd al-ʿuthmani: qira'a jadida. Beirut: Mu'assasat al-Dirasat al-Filastiniyya, 1999.

Ma'oz, Moshe. "Changes in the Position and Role of the Syrian 'Ulama in the 18th and 19th Centuries." In *The Syrian Land in the 18th and 19th Century*, edited by Thomas Philipp. Stuttgart: Franz Steiner Verlag, 1992, 109–19.

Ottoman Reform in Syria and Palestine: The Impact of the Tanzimat on Politics and Society. Oxford: Clarendon Press, 1968.

Marsot, Afaf Lutfi al-Sayyid. *Egypt in the Reign of Muhammad Ali.* Cambridge: Cambridge University Press, 1985.

Masters, Bruce. "The 1850 Events in Aleppo: An Aftershock of Syria's Incorporation into the Capitalist World System" *IJMES* **22** (1990): 3–20.

"Aleppo's Janissaries: Crime Syndicate or *Vox Populi?*" In *Popular Protest and Political Participation in the Ottoman Empire: Studies in Honor of Suraiya Faroqhi,* edited by Eleni Gara, M. Erdem Kabadayı, and Christoph Neumann. Istanbul: İstanbul Bilgi Üniversitesi Yayınları, 2011, 159–75.

Christians and Jews in the Ottoman Arab World: The Birth of Sectarianism. Cambridge: Cambridge University Press, 2001.

"The Establishment of the Melkite Catholic Millet in 1848 and the Politics of Identity in Tanzimat Syria." In *Syria and Bilad al-Sham under Ottoman Rule: Essays in Honour of Abdul-Karim Rafeq,* edited by Peter Sluglett with Stefan Weber. Leiden: Brill, 2010, 455–74.

"Patterns of Migration to Ottoman Aleppo in the 17th and 18th Centuries" *International Journal of Turkish Studies* **4** (1987): 75–89.

The Origins of Western Economic Dominance in the Middle East: Mercantilism and the Islamic Economy in Aleppo, 1600–1750 (New York: New York University Press, 1988).

"The Political Economy of Aleppo in an Age of Ottoman 'Reform'" *JESHO* **52** (2010): 290–316.

"The Treaties of Erzurum (1823 and 1848) and the Changing Status of Iranians in the Ottoman Empire" *The Journal of the Society for Iranian Studies* **24** (1991): 3–16.

"The View from the Province: Syrian Chroniclers of the Eighteenth Century" *JAOS* **114** (1992): 353–62.

McCarthy, Justin. *The Ottoman Peoples and the End of the Empire.* London: Arnold, 2001.

Meriwether, Margaret. *The Kin Who Count: Family and Society in Ottoman Aleppo, 1770–1840.* Austin: University of Texas Press, 1999.

Mikhail, Alan. *Nature and Empire in Ottoman Egypt: An Environmental History.* Cambridge: Cambridge University Press, 2011.

Mundy, Martha. "Islamic Law and the Order of State: The Legal Status of the Cultivator." In *Syria and Bilad al-Sham under Ottoman Rule: Essays in Honour of Abdul-Karim Rafeq,* edited by Peter Sluglett with Stefan Weber. Leiden: Brill, 2010, 399–419.

Murphey, Rhoads. *Ottoman Warfare 1500–1700.* New Brunswick, NJ: Rutgers University Press, 1999.

"Syria's 'Underdevelopment' under Ottoman Rule: Revisiting an Old Theme in the Light of New Evidence from the Court Records of Aleppo in the Eighteenth Century." In *The Arab Lands in the Ottoman Era: Essays in Honor of Professor Caesar Farah,* edited by Jane Hathaway. Minneapolis: University of Minnesota Press, 2009, 209–30.

el-Nahal, Galal. *The Judicial Administration of Ottoman Egypt in the Seventeenth Century* Minneapolis, MN: Bibliotheca Islamica, 1979.

Nakash, Yitzhak. *The Shi'is of Iraq.* Princeton, NJ: Princeton University Press, 1994.

Necipoğlu, Gülru. *The Age of Sinan: Architectural Culture in the Ottoman Empire.* Princeton, NJ: Princeton University Press, 2005.

Neumann, Christoph. "Ottoman Provincial Towns from the Eighteenth to the Nineteenth Century: A Re-Assessment of their Place in the Transformation of the Empire." In *The Empire in the City: Arab Provincial Capitals in the Late Ottoman Empire*, edited by Jens Hanssen, Thomas Philipp, and Stefan Weber. Beirut: Orient-Institut der deutschen morgenländischen Gesellschaft, 2002, 133–44.

Nieuwenhuis, Tom. *Politics and Society in Early Modern Iraq: Mamlūk Pashas, Tribal Shayks and Local Rule between 1802 and 1831*. The Hague: Martinus Nijhoff, 1982.

Ochsenwald, William. *Religion, Society and the State in Arabia: The Hijaz under Ottoman Control, 1840–1908*. Columbus: Ohio State University Press, 1984.

O'Fahey, R. S. and Bernard Radtke, "Neo-Sufism Reconsidered" *Islam* 70 (1993): 52–87.

Özbaran, Salih, "Osmanlı İmperatorluğun Hindistan Yolu" *Tarih Dergisi* 31 (1977): 65–146.

Özoğlu, Hakan. *Kurdish Notables and the Ottoman State: Evolving Identities, Competing Loyalties, and Shifting Boundaries*. Albany: State University of New York Press, 2004.

Pamuk, Şevket. "Money in the Ottoman Empire, 1362–1914." In *An Economic and Social History of the Ottoman Empire 1300–1914*, edited by Halil İnalcık and Donald Quataert. Cambridge: Cambridge University Press, 1994, 953–70.

The Ottoman Empire and European Capitalism, 1820–1913: Trade, Investment and Production. Cambridge; Cambridge University Press, 1987.

Panzac, Daniel. "Mourir à Alep au XVIIIᵉ siècle." *RMMM* 62 (1991–4): 111–22.

Parsons, Timothy. *The Rules of Empires: Those Who Built Them, Those Who Endured Them, and Why They Always Fall*. Oxford: Oxford University Press, 2010.

Pascual, Jean-Paul. "The Janissaries and the Damascus Countryside at the Beginning of the Seventeenth Century According to the Archives of the City's Military Tribunal." In *Land Tenure and Social Transformation in the Middle East*, edited by Tarif Khalidi. Beirut: The American University in Beirut, 1984, 357–65.

Petry, Carl. "The Military Institution and Innovation in the Late Mamluk Period." In *The Cambridge History of Modern Egypt*. Vol. 1. *Islamic Egypt, 640–1517*, edited by Carl Petry. Cambridge: Cambridge University Press, 1998, 462–89.

Philipp, Thomas. *Acre: The Rise and Fall of a Palestinian City, 1730–1831*. New York: Columbia University Press, 2001.

Philipp, Thomas, and Ulrich Haarmann, editors. *The Mamluks in Egyptian Politics and Society*. Cambridge: Cambridge University Press, 1998.

Philliou, Christine. *Biography of an Empire: Governing Ottomans in an Age of Revolution*. Berkeley: University of California Press, 2010.

Polk, William. *The Opening of Southern Lebanon, 1788–1840: A Study of the Impact of the West on the Middle East*. Cambridge, MA: Harvard University Press, 1963.

Provence, Michael. "Ottoman Modernity, Colonialism and Insurgency in the Interwar Arab East" *IJMES* 43 (2011): 205–25.

Quataert, Donald. *Ottoman Manufacturing in the Age of the Industrial Revolution*. Cambridge: Cambridge University Press, 1993.

al-Qattan, Najwa. "*Safarbarlik*: Ottoman Syria in the Great War." In *From the Syrian Land to the States of Syria and Lebanon*, edited by Thomas Philipp and Christoph Schumann. Beirut: Orient-Institut der deutschen morgenländischen Gesellschaft, 2004, 163–74.

Rafeq, Abdul-Karim. *al-ᶜArab wa al-ᶜUthmaniyyun*. Damascus: Matbaᶜ Alif Ba', 1974.

Dirasat iqtisadiyya wa-al-ijtimaᶜiyya fi ta'rikh bilad al-sham al-hadith. Damascus: Maktabat Nubil, 2002.

"Economic Relations between Damascus and the Dependent Countryside, 1743–71." In *The Islamic Middle East, 700–1900*, edited by A. L. Udovitch. Princeton, NJ: Darwin Press, 1981, 653–86.

"The Impact of Europe on a Traditional Economy: The Case of Damascus 1840–1870." In *Économie et sociétiés dans l'empire ottoman: actes du colloque de Strasbourg*, edited by Jean Louis Bacqué-Grammont and Paul Dumont, 3 vols., Vol. III. Paris: Centre National de la Recherche Scientifique, 1983, 419–32.

The Province of Damascus, 1723–1783. Beirut: American University in Beirut, 1966.

"Relations between the Syrian Ulama and the Ottoman State in the Eighteenth Century" *Oriente Moderno* 18/79 (1999): 67–95.

Raymond, André. *Artisans et commerçants au Caire au XVIIIᵉ siècle*, 2 vols. Damascus: Institute Français de Damas, 1973, 1974.

Grandes villes arabes á l'époque ottomane. Paris: Sindbad, 1985.

The Great Arab Cities in the 16th–18th Centuries: An Introduction. New York: New York University Press, 1984.

Reilly, James. "Rural Waqfs of Ottoman Damascus: Rights of Ownership, Possession and Tenancy" *Acta Orientalia* 51 (1990): 27–46.

"Status Groups and Propertyholding in the Damascus Hinterland, 1828–1880" *IJMES* 21 (1989): 517–39.

Roded, Ruth. "Ottoman Service as a Vehicle for the Rise of New Upstarts among the Urban Elite of Syria in the Last Decades of Ottoman Rule." In *Studies in Islamic Society: Contributions in Memory of Gabriel Baer*, edited by Gabriel Warburg and Gad Gilbar. Haifa: Haifa University Press, 1984, 63–94.

Rogan, Eugene. "Aşiret Mektebi: Abdülhamid II's School for Tribes (1892–1907)" *IJMES* 28 (1996): 83–107.

Rood, Judith Mendelsohn. *Sacred Law in the Holy City: The Khedival Challenge to the Ottomans as Seen from Jerusalem, 1829–1841*. Leiden: Brill, 2004.

Sadgrove, Philip. "Pre-Modern Drama." In *The Cambridge History of Arabic Literature: Arabic Literature in the Post-Classical Age*, edited by Roger Allen and D. S. Richards Cambridge: Cambridge University Press, 2006, 369–83.

Salzman, Ariel. *Tocqueville in the Ottoman Empire: Rival Paths to the Modern State*. Leiden: Brill, 2004.

Schilcher, Linda. *Families in Politics: Damascene Factions and Estates of the 18th and 19th Centuries.* Stuttgart: Franz Steiner Verlag, 1985.

Schölch. Alexander. *Palestine in Transformation 1856–1882: Studies in Social, Economic and Political Development,* translated by William Young and Michael Gerrity. Washington, DC: Institute for Palestine Studies, 1993.

Seikaly, Samir. "Land Tenure in 17th Century Palestine: The Evidence from the *al-Fatawa al-Khairiyya.*" In *Land and Social Transformation in the Middle East,* edited by Tarif Khalidi. Beirut: The American University in Beirut, 1984, 397–408.

Sharif, Malek., "A Portrait of Syrian Deputies in the First Ottoman Parliament." In *The First Ottoman Experiment in Democracy,* edited by Christoph Herzog and Malek Sharif. Würzburg: Ergon Verlag, 2010, 285–311.

Shimizu, Yasuhisa. "Practices of Tax Farming under the Ottoman Empire in Damascus Province." In *Tax-Farm Register of Damascus Province in the Seventeenth Century: Archival and Historical Studies.,* edited by Yuzo Nagata, Toru Miura, and Yasuhisa Shimizu. Tokyo: The Tokyo Bunko, 2006, 23–52.

Shuval, Tal. "The Ottoman Algerian Elite and Its Ideology" *IJMES* 32 (2000): 323–44.

Singer, Amy. *Palestinian Peasants and Ottoman Officials: Rural Administration around Sixteenth-Century Jerusalem.* Cambridge: Cambridge University Press, 1994.

Sirriyeh, Elizabeth. *Sufi Visionary of Ottoman Damascus: ʿAbd al-Ghani al-Nabulusi, 1641–1731.* London: Routledge Curzon, 2005.

Skendi, Stavro. *The Albanian National Awakening.* Princeton, NJ: Princeton University Press, 1967.

Sluglett, Peter and Marion Farouk-Sluglett. "The Application of the 1858 Land Code in Greater Syria: Some Preliminary Observations." In *Land Tenure and Social Transformation in the Middle East,* edited by Tarif Khalidi. Beirut: The American University of Beirut, 1984, 409–24.

Steensgaard, Niels. *The Asian Trade Revolution of the Seventeenth Century: The East India Companies and the Decline of the Caravan Trade.* Chicago: The University of Chicago Press, 1974.

Steppat, Fritz. "Kalifat, *Dār al-Islām* und die Loyalität der Araber zum osmanischen Reich bei Hanafitschen Juristen des 19. Jahrhunderts." In *Correspondance d'Orient No 11: Ve Congrès International d'Arabisants et d"Islamisants,* Brussels: Centre pour l'Étude des Problèmes du Monde Musulman Contemporain, 1970, 443–62.

Johann Strauss, "Ottoman Rule Experienced and Remembered: Remarks on Some Local Greek Chronicles of the *Tourkokratia.*" In *The Ottomans and the Balkans: A Discussion of Historiography,* edited by Fikret Adanır and Suraiya Faroqhi. Leiden: Brill, 2002, 193–221.

Tabbakh, Muhammad Raghib. *Iʿlam al-nubala bi-taʾrikh halab al-shaba,* 3 vols. Aleppo: Dar al-Qalam al-ʿArabi, 1977.

Tamari, Steve. "Arab National Consciousness in Seventeenth- and Eighteenth-Century Syria." In *Syria and Bilad al-Sham under Ottoman Rule: Essays in Honour of Abdul-Karim Rafeq,* edited by Peter Sluglett with Stefan Weber, Leiden: Brill, 2010, 309–22.

"Ottoman *Madrasa*s: The Multiple Lives of Educational Institutions in Eighteenth-Century Syria" *Journal of Early Modern History* 5 (2001): 99–127.

Tezcan, Baki. *The Second Ottoman Empire: Political and Social Transformation in the Early Modern World.* Cambridge: Cambridge University Press, 2010.

Thomas, Lewis. *A Study of Naima*, edited by Norman Itzkowitz, New York: New York University Press, 1972.

Thompson, Elizabeth. "Ottoman Political Reform in the Provinces: The Damascus Advisory Council in 1844–45" *IJMES* 25 (1993): 457–75.

Tibawi, A. L. *A Modern History of Syria, Including Lebanon and Palestine.* London: Macmillan St. Martin's Press, 1969.

Touati, Houari. "Ottoman Maghrib." In *The New Cambridge History of Islam.* Vol. 2. *The Western Islamic World Eleventh to Eighteenth Centuries*, edited by Maribel Fierro Cambridge: Cambridge University Press, 2010, 503–45.

Todorova, Maria. "The Ottoman Legacy in the Balkans." In *Imperial Legacy: The Ottoman Imprint on the Balkans and the Middle East*, edited by L. Carl Brown. New York: Columbia University Press, 1996, 45–77.

Tripp, Charles. *A History of Iraq*, 3rd ed. Cambridge: Cambridge University Press, 2007.

Uzunçarşılı, İsmail Hakkı. *Mekke-i Mükerreme Emirleri.* Ankara: Türk Tarih Kurumu, 1972.

van Bruinessen, Martin. *Agha, Shaykh and State: The Social and Political Structures of Kurdistan.* London: Zed Books, 1992.

Wallerstein, Immanuel. *The Modern World System*, 3 vols. New York: Academic Press, 1974, 1980, 1989.

Watenpaugh, Heghnar Zeitlian. "Deviant Dervishes: Space, Gender and the Construction of Antinomian Piety in Ottoman Aleppo" *IJMES* 37 (2005): 535–65.

The Image of an Ottoman City: Imperial Architecture and Urban Experience in Aleppo in the 16th and 17th Centuries. Leiden: Brill, 2004.

Watenpaugh, Keith. *Being Modern in the Middle East: Revolution, Nationalism, Colonialism and the Arab Middle Class.* Princeton, NJ: Princeton University Press, 2006.

Weber, Stefan. "Images of Imagined Worlds: Self-Image and Worldview in Late Ottoman Wall Paintings of Damascus." In *The Empire in the City: Arab Provincial Capitals in the Late Ottoman Empire*, edited by Jens Hanssen, Thomas Philipp, and Stefan Weber. Beirut: Orient-Institut der deutschen morgenländischen Gesellschaft, 2002, 145–71.

Weintritt, Gotfried. "Concepts of History as Reflected in Arabic Historiographical Writing in Ottoman Syria and Egypt (1517–1700)." In *The Mamluks in Egyptian Society*, edited by T. Philipp and U. Haarmann. Cambridge: Cambridge University Press, 1998, 188–95.

Weismann, Itzchak. *Taste of Modernity: Sufism, Salafiyya, and Arabism in Late Ottoman Damascus.* Leiden: Brill, 2001.

Wheatcroft, Andrew. *The Ottomans: Dissolving Images*, London: Penguin Books, 1995.

White, Sam. *The Climate of Rebellion in the Early Modern Ottoman Empire.* Cambridge: Cambridge University Press, 2011.

Wilkins, Charles. *Forging Urban Solidarities: Ottoman Aleppo 1640–1700.* Leiden: Brill, 2010.

Winter, Michael. "Attitudes towards the Ottomans in Egyptian Historiography during Ottoman Rule." In *The Historiography of Islamic Egypt (C. 950–1800),* edited by Hugh Kennedy. Leiden: Brill, 2001, 195–210.

Egyptian Society under Ottoman Rule 1517–1798. London: Routledge, 1992.

"Historiography in Arabic during the Ottoman period" In *Arabic Literature in the Post-Classical Period,* edited by Roger Allen and D. S. Richards. Cambridge: Cambridge University Press, 2006, 194–210.

"Ottoman Egypt, 1525–1609." In *The Cambridge History of Egypt.* Vol. 2. *Modern Egypt from 1517 to the End of the Twentieth Century,* edited by M. W. Daly. Cambridge: Cambridge University Press, 1998, 1–33.

"A Polemical Treatise by ʿAbd al-Ġani al-Nabulusi against a Turkish Scholar on the Religious Status of the *Dhimmi*s" *Arabica* 35 (1988): 92–103.

"The Re-Emergence of the Mamluks following the Ottoman Conquest" In *The Mamluks in Egyptian Politics and Society,* edited by Thomas Philipp and Ulrich Haarmann, Cambridge: Cambridge University Press, 1998, 87–106.

"A Seventeenth-Century Arabic Panegyric of the Ottoman Dynasty" *Asian and African Studies* 13 (1979): 130–56.

Winter, Stefan. *The Shiites of Lebanon under Ottoman Rule, 1516–1788.* Cambridge: Cambridge University, 2010.

Winter, Tim. "Ibn Kemal (d.940/1534) on Ibn ʿArabi's Hagiography" In *Sufism and Theology,* edited by Ayman Shihadeh. Edinburgh: Edinburgh University Press, 2007, 137–57.

Wood, Alfred. *A History of the Levant Company.* London: Oxford University Press, 1935.

Yi, Eunjeong. *Guild Dynamics in Seventeenth-Century Istanbul: Fluidity and Leverage.* Leiden: Brill, 2004.

Ze'evi, Dror, "Back to Napoleon? Thoughts on the beginning of the Modern Era in the Middle East" *MHR* 19 (2004): 73–94.

"The Use of Ottoman Sharica Court Records as a Source for Middle Eastern Social History: A Reappraisal" *Islamic Law and Society* 5 (1998): 35–56.

Zilfi, Madeline. "The Kadizadelils: Discordant Revivalism in Seventeenth-Century Istanbul" *JNES* 45 (1986): 251–69.

Index

Abaza Hasan Pasha (grand vizier), 46, 68
ᶜAbbas Hilmi (khedive), 215
Abbas I, Shah, 31, 32, 56
Abbasid Caliphate, 28, 41, 48, 52,
    107, 128
ᶜAbbud, Yusuf Dimitri, 84, 104, 131, 136
ᶜAbduh, Muhammad, 201, 215
Abdülaziz, Sultan, 35, 184, 187, 188
Abdülhamid I, Sultan, 184, 206, 212
Abdülhamid II, Sultan, 19, 182, 186, 192,
    193, 206, 207, 230
Abdülmecid I, Sultan, 157, 163, 165, 173,
    188, 228
ᶜAbid, Hasan Agha, 131, 132–4, 136, 144
ᶜAbidin, Ahmad, 203
Abkhaz, 24
absolutism
    caliphate precedence and, 4
    constitutionalism and, 183, 194, 212
    Mughal, 125
Abu Bakr (caliph), 50, 124
Abu Hanifa, 31
Abu Risha, 97
Abu Yusuf, Yaᶜqub, 88
Aceh, 35
Acre, 87, 148
Adige, 24
Adile (daughter of Hasan Pasha,
    Baghdad, 40
agriculture, 74, 100
ahl al-bayt (ruling family in a Bedouin
    tribe), 182
ahl al-sunna (people of the Sunna), 21

Ahmad Bey (Tunisia), 187
Ahmed I, Sultan, 38
Ahmed II, Sultan, 98
Aigen, Wolffgang, 46
ᶜA'isha (wife of Prophet Muhammad), 50
ᶜAjlani, Shaykh Ahmad Darwish al-, 185
Akbar, Emperor, 125
ᶜAlawis (Moroccan dynasty), 36
Albania, 5, 206, 223
Albanians, 5, 68
Aleppo, 6, 24, 25, 28, 42, 60, 67, 76, 77,
    78, 79, 86, 131, 139–45, 146,
    159, 163, 178, 185, 190, 195,
    198, 228
Alexandria, 133
Algeria, 36, 186
ᶜAli, Caliph/Imam, 50
Ali Rıza Pasha (grand vizier), 149
al-insan al-kamil (perfect man in Sufi
    Tradition), 116
Alioğlu, Hüseyin, 39
Alliance Israélite Universelle, 196
al-Muqtabas (newspaper), 215
alterity, cultural, 12
American Board of Commissioners for
    Foreign Missions (ABCFM), 160
American University (Beirut), 161
Amin, Qasim, 202
Amin, Samir, 75
amir al-ᶜArab (commander of the
    Bedouins), 96
amir al-jabal (Commander, or Prince, of
    Lebanon), 165

amir al-mu'minin (Commander of the Faithful), 51
Anatolia, 25, 63, 193, 206
Ando, Clifford, 3, 5, 226
Anglo-Ottoman Commercial Treaty (1838), 179, 188
Ankara (battle), 25
Ansari, Sharaf al-Din Musa al-, 65
Anscombe, Frederick, 190
ᶜAntar, 127
ᶜAntun, Farah, 205
Arab Congress, 216
Arab sciences, 107
Arab Spring (2011), 2
ᶜArab wa al-ᶜuthmaniyyun al-, 1516–1916 (The Arabs and the Ottomans, Rafeq), 10
ᶜArabi (plural *ᶜArab,* or *ᶜUrban,* those who speak Arabic as their native tongue, or a Bedouin, or an inhabitant of Arabia), 14
Arabian Nights, The, 127
Arabistan (country of the Bedouin/Arabs), 15, 96, 150
Arutin, Bishop Bulus, 140, 170
ᶜAsali, Shukri al-, 213
Ashraf al-Ghawri al-, Sultan, 28
ᶜAshura (Shi'i holy day), 31
askeri (soldier class), 37
Atassi, Khalid al-, 185
Atatürk, Mustafa Kemal, 17
autonomy, 187
    Albanian, 223
    Beirut Reform Committee and, 216
    governors and, 39
    guild, 81
    Lebanese, 185
    Libyan, 186
    local, 164, 166, 213
    North African, 40
    sultanate, 102
avariz hane (taxable units), 93
awlad al-ᶜArab (Arabic-speakers), 14, 65, 230
Awrangzeb, Sultan, 125
aᶜyan (elite local families), 8, 18, 42, 83–8, 140, 177–83, 190, 194, 229, 231
ayan (plural *ayanlar,* local strong man), 87, 139
Aydınlı Abdullah Pasha, 86
ᶜAyn Jalut (battle), 22
Ayntab (Gaziantep), 146, 181

Ayşe (daughter of Hasan Pasha, Baghdad), 41
Azeban (infantry corps), 68
ᶜAzm, Sulayman al-; (brother of ᶜAzm Isma'il al-Pasha), 86
ᶜAzm, ᶜAbdallah al-, 136, 147, 169
ᶜAzm, Asᶜad al- Pasha, 86
ᶜAzm, Isma'il al- Pasha, 86

Bab al-Nayrab quarter in Aleppo), 169
Bab Musalla (quarter in Damascus), 69
Babnisi, ᶜAbdallah al-, 169
Badawi, Ahmad al-, 112
Baghdad, 20, 22, 30, 31, 32, 62, 76, 104, 149, 181, 198
    Province, 185
Bakhkhash, Naᶜum, 152, 159, 170, 172, 173
Balkans, 193
Banqusa (quarter in Aleppo), 69, 169
Banu Hilal, 127
Barker, Edward, 153
Bashir II, Emir, 165
Bashir III, Emir (Bashir Qasim), 165
Basra, 32, 62, 77, 149, 181, 185
batin (inner truth), 105, 115
Baybars, 23
bayᶜa (profession of loyalty), 28
Bayezid II, Sultan, 25
Bayhum, Husayn, 185
bedel-i askeri (tax instead of conscription), 172
Bedir Xan, Emir, 167
Bedouins, 14, 27, 32, 62, 68, 74, 77, 95–8, 135, 139, 155, 163, 178, 181, 182
Beirut, 77, 160, 178, 182, 195
Beirut Reform Committee, 216
bidᶜa (heresy), 123
Bira (Birecik), 77
Birgili Mehmed (Mehmed of Birgi), 119, 122
Bitar, ᶜAbd al-Razzaq al-, 203, 207
Blunt, Wilfred, 210
Bodman, Herbert, 67
Bonaparte, Napoleon, 130–4
Bosniaks, 5
Botan, 166
bourgeoisie, 159, 182, 194–9
Bowen, Harold, 12
Bowring, Sir John, 79
Braudel, Fernand, 164

Bulaq Press, 204
Bulgaria, 5, 214
Bulgarian Massacres, 185
Bulut Kapan Ali Bey, 44, 130
Burayk, Mikha'il, 230
Bustani, Butrus al-, 204
Büyük Süleyman Pasha (Iraq), 136

Çağalzade Sinan Pasha, 38
Cairo, 6, 20, 24, 25, 27, 43, 76, 78, 133
Çaldıran (battle), 26
caliphate, 206–11
  evolution of office of, 50, 51
  greater and lesser, 207
  model, 5
  sultanate and, 206
  universal, 52
Caliphs, Rightly Guided, 53
Canpulatoğlu ʿAli, 47
Canpulatoğlu, Hüseyin, 38
Çapanoğlu Celalettin Mehmed Pasha,
    138, 141
Cebel-i Dürüz (Mountain of the Druzes,
    Lebanon), 164
Cem, Prince, 25
Cemal Pasha, 209
Cemiyet-i İttihad ve Terakki (Committee of
    Union and Progress, CUP), 213
centralization, 154, 164
Çerkes Osman Pasha (Abu Tawq), 86
Cezire (northern Iraq and eastern Syria), 146
Cezzar Ahmed Pasha, 87, 132, 137, 146
Chechen, 24
Chikmakiyan, Zirun, 210
Chingiz Khan, 4
Christians
  Balkan, 5
  Catholic, 152
  Greek Orthodox, 142, 227
  Maronite, 152, 165–6, 173, 182, 204
  Melkite, 142, 152
  Nestorian (Assyrians), 167
  Uniate, 152
Circassians, 24
Cizre, 167
clothing, 197
coffee, 77, 119, 120, 137
  houses, 121, 126–8
commerce, 73, 75–9, 160, 183
conscription, 7, 13, 19, 37, 67, 144, 149,
    150, 153, 157, 163, 168, 172,
    178, 190, 215, 217

Constantinople, 25
Constitution of 1876, 183–6, 211
courts
  Arabic language and, 59, 109
  authority of, 151, 162
  commercial, 161
  Muslim law, 71
  qadis and, 63
  religious, 12, 16
  sharia, 161
Cyrenaica (Barqa), 186

Damanhuri, Ahmad ibn ʿAbd al-Munʿim
    al-, 28, 44
Damascus, 6, 20, 24, 25, 26, 28, 42, 45, 60,
    64, 76, 77, 86, 87, 110, 131, 149,
    160, 163, 190, 195, 198, 226
Dar al-Islam (House of Islam, the lands
    under Muslim rule), 20
Darʿiyya, 139
Davud Pasha (Iraq), 144, 149
Dayr al-Qamar, 174
Dayr al-Zawr, 181
decentralization, 215
derebey (lord of the valley), 87, 161
Derviş Pasha (Damascus), 147
devşirme (boy-tax), 13, 37, 67
dhikr (Sufi practice), 113, 123
Dimashqi, Mikha'il al-, 132
diwan (informal council), 130, 161
Diyarbakır, 90, 167
diyar-ı mahrusa (well-protected domains), 4

Ebu's-suʿud Efendi, 54, 197
economy
  Ottoman, 74–75, 101–02, 179–80,
      189–91
  commanding right and forbidding
      wrong, 101
  decline of, 74
  revenues and, 101
  trade treaties and, 180
  world, 74
Edirne (Adrianople), 214
Egypt, 23, 42–5, 62, 91, 130–9, 188
  occupation of, 146–54
*Egypt and the Fertile Crescent 1616–1922
    A Political History* (Holt), 10
Elias al-Musili, 104
elite, 180, 214, 227
  Sunni, 7
  Turks, 188

emirs (commanders), 23, 52
  Egyptian, 43
empire
  Ottoman
    Islam and the, 8
    periods of, 4, 16
      decline (1566–1808 or 1839), 16
      height (1453–1566), 16
      origins (1300?–1453), 16
      revived (1839–1908), 16
      revolution and collapse
        (1908–1918), 17
    ruler power in, 8
  paradigm, 3
  Roman, 3
Erdoğan, Recep Tayyip, 2
Eretz Yisrael (the Land of Israel), 213
Esad Muhlis Pasha, 159
ethnicity, 206, 230
Evliya Çelebi, 15, 103, 116
exceptionalism, Arab, 11, 12
expansion
  Ottoman
    eastward, 30–3
    North African, 35–7
    southward, 33–5
exports, 77, 180
  crop, 92

families, clans, and tribes, 176
  Abbasid (Banu Abbas), 51
  ʿAnaza, 97, 146, 170
  Ayyubid, 23
  ʿAzm, 42, 85, 91, 98, 226
  Bani Lam, 98
  Banu Tamim, 98
  Bekirli, 98
  Druze, 147, 164, 165, 174
  Fatimid, 110
  Fatlah, 98
  Harfush, 89
  Hashemite, 210
  Hayar, 96
  Husayni, 187
  ibn Saʿud, 134, 139, 183
  İlbeklü, 98
  Jalili, 42, 85, 91, 149
  Karamanlı, 186
  Khazaʾil, 98
  Khazin, 173
  Kurdish, 164
  Lynch, 182

Maʿn al-, 89, 147
Marcopoli, 180
Mawali, 97
Muntafiq, 98
Poche, 180
Quraysh, 51, 207
Shammar, 98, 134, 182
Shihab al-, 147, 165
Faqariyya (faction), 43
Farhad Pasha (Damascus), 117
Farhi, Haim, 147
Fath ʿAli Shah (Iran), 206
fatwa (legal ruling), 126
fellahin (peasants), 15
ferde vergüsü (tax on adult males),
    169, 177
Feyzullah Efendi, 120, 121
fez, 160, 197
finance, 79, 150, 183, 190
frontier, tribal, 95–100
Fuad (Khedive), 189
Fuad Pasha (grand vizier), 175
Furat/Fırat (newspaper), 181
Future of Islam, The (Blunt), 210

Gaylani (al-Kaylani), ʿAbd al-Qadir al-, 31
gedik (guild membership certificate), 80
Genç Yusuf Pasha, 137
gender
  gap, 196
  God's, 115
  roles, 106, 202
Georgians, 24
Ghanim, Khalil, 185
Ghazali, Janbardi al-, 28, 117
Ghazali, Muhammad al-, 55, 125
Ghazzi, Kamil al-, 90, 228
Ghuta, 162, 179
Gibb, Sir Hamilton, 11
governors
  hereditary, 40, 188
  meclis and, 162
  military, 39–40
  Ottoman, 38–9
  professional, 37, 42
  provincial, 58–63, 177, 181
  self-made, 37–42
Granada, 36
Greece, 5, 214
Greek War for Independence, 142, 144,
    145, 176, 227
Grigorios V, Patriarch, 142

guilds, 79–82, 101, 137, 161
  membership, 81

hadith (traditions of the Prophet
  Muhammad), 197
Hafız Ahmed Pasha (grand vizier), 56
Haifa, 195
hajj, 21, 40, 51, 78, 97, 103, 134, 136,
  163, 227
Hakkari, 167
Halakha (religious law), 106
Hama, 86, 146, 179
Hanafi (legal tradition), 31, 53, 58, 63
Hanbali (legal tradition), 63
hanedan (hereditary dynasties), 87
Hanioğlu, Şükrü, 157
Hanna, Nelly, 104
Harim, 146
Hasa, al-, 183, 189
Hasan (grandson of Muhammad), 51
Hasan Pasha (Baghdad), 32
Hashemite clan (Banu Hashim), 61
Hathaway, Jane, 29
Hatt-ı Şerif (Gülhane Decree), 157, 159,
  162, 172, 177
Hawran, 137, 222
Hawza (council of the leading Shi'i
  clergy), 135
hijab (veil), 198
Holt, P. M., 10
Homs, 95, 146, 179, 195
Hourani, Albert, 83, 84, 86
House of Osman, 156, 184, 206, 207,
  227, 229
Hülegü, 23
Hungary, 5
Hürrem (wife of Süleyman, 111
Hürşid Pasha (governor, Aleppo), 140
Husayn, Imam, 30, 51, 52
Husayn, Taha, 225
Husayni, Sa'id al-, 213
Hüsrev Pasha (grand vizier), 111

ibn Abi al-Surur, Muhammad, 22, 49,
  54, 119
ibn Abi al-Wafa, Shaykh Abu Bakr, 114
ibn 'Abidin, Muhammad Amin, 154, 207
ibn al-'Arabi, Muhiy al-Din, 110, 112–26,
  131, 208
ibn al-Himsi, Shihab al-Din Ahmad, 56
ibn Ayas, Muhammad, 27, 49
ibn Ayyub, Salah al-Din (Saladin), 23

ibn 'Abd al-Wahhab, Muhammad, 71,
  122–4, 134, 155, 186, 201
ibn Hamid al-Din, Yahya Muhammad, 35
ibn Hanbali, Radi al-Din Muhammad, 56
ibn Hanbali, Radi al-Din Muhammad, 64
ibn Kannan, Muhammad, 57, 86, 103,
  118, 119
ibn Khaldun, 'Abd al-Rahman Abu-Zayd,
  53, 76, 108, 205
ibn Sa'ud, 'Abd al-'Aziz, 134, 155
ibn Sa'ud, Sa'ud, 135
ibn Sina, 205
ibn Taymiyya, Taqi al-Din, 53, 110, 122, 123
ibn Tulun, Muhammad, 27, 55, 64, 83, 115
Ibrahim Pasha (governor of Syria), 139,
  144, 146–54, 161, 169, 190,
  207, 229
identity, 12–16
  Arab, 205
  ethnic, 8, 15
  religious, 163
  shared religious, 8
  topographical, 15
ijtihad (individual reasoning), 124
iltizam (tax farms), 88
Ingush, 24
*International Journal of Middle Eastern
  Studies*, xiii
İrak-ı Arap (Iraq of the Arabs), 15
Iran, 32, 229
Iraq, 33, 74
Iskanderun, 149, 195
Islahat fermanı (Reform Decree), 172
Islam
  Constitution of 1876 and, 184
  Ottoman Empire and, 5, 6, 8, 21, 48
  state and, 10
Islamic Society and the West (Gibb and
  Bowen), 11
Isma'il, 206
Istanbul, 4, 104, 109, 164, 199
İttihad-i Muhammadi (Muhammadan
  Union), 212
Izmir, 195, 199

Jabarti, 'Abd al-Rahman al-, 44, 54
Jabiri, Nafi' al-, 185, 210, 212, 213
Ja'fari (Islamic legal tradition), 31, 33
Jaffa, 182, 195
Jalili, Yahya al-, 150
janissaries (Ottoman infantry), 8, 48, 66–9,
  132, 138, 141, 144, 150

Jaza'iri, ᶜAbd al-Qadir al-, 203
Jaza'iri, Tahir al-, 203
Jeddah, 42, 44
Jerusalem, 42, 104, 198
Jewish Agency, 213
Jisr al-Shughur, 146
jizya (poll-tax on non-Muslims, 153
Jön Türkler (Young Turks), 211
Judayda (quarter of Aleppo), 170
judges
  chief, 13, 59
  provincial, 59, 63–6
    decentralization of, 59

Kadızade Mehmed, 120
Kadızadeli (follower of Kadizade
    Mehmed), 120
Kaimmakam (governor), 166
Kamil Pasha, grand vizier, 215
kanun (sultanic decrees), 63, 71, 125
Kanun-ı Esasi (constitution), 184
Karagöz (shadow puppet theater), 127
Karamanlı Ahmed, 39
Karbala, 104, 134, 155
Karim Khan Zand, 32
Karmi, Marᶜi al-, 49
Katib Çelebi, 121
Katırağası Ibrahim Pasha (Aleppo), 136
Kawakibi, ᶜAbd al-Rahman al-, 209–11
Kayalı, Hasan, 213
Kemalpaşazade Ahmed, 116
Kha'ir Bek, 22, 28
Khalidi, Ruhi al-, 213
Khalidi, Yusuf Ziya al-, 185
khalifat Rasul Allah (Successor of God's
    Messenger), 50
khaluw (guild membership certificate), 80
khans (caravansaries), 159
Kharrat, Hashim al-, 209
Khayr al-Din (Tunisia), 187
khedive (*hıdıv*, governor of Egypt), 188
Khilafa, al- (newspaper), 210
Khiyari, Ibrahim al-, 55, 57, 98, 103, 109,
    111, 118, 119, 121, 123, 126
Khoury, Philip, 87
Kisrawan, 173
Kızıl Baş, 116
Konya, 149
Kritovoulos, 4
Kurd ᶜAli, Muhammad, 215
Kurdistan (Country of the Kurds), 15, 59,
    164, 167
Kurds, 5, 68, 95

Lala Mustafa Pasha, 57
land
  ownership, 178
  registration, 178
landowners, 8
language, 6, 12, 16, 59, 206, 215
  Arabic, use of, 103, 107, 108, 109
  Ottoman Turkish, 184, 188, 200, 213,
    216
  Persian, 107
Lattakia, 182
Lebanon, 46, 60, 89, 92, 146, 147, 148,
    164, 176
legitimacy, 6, 7, 10, 18, 21, 54, 55, 61, 155
  non-Muslim, 30
Levant Company, 77
Libya, 186, 214
literacy, 104, 196
literature, 93, 107, 108, 128
Little Ice Age, 74, 94, 97

Maᶜarrat al-Nuᶜman, 86, 146
Macedonia, 211
Maᶜn, Fakhr al-Din, 89
madhhab (mezhep, Muslim legal tradition),
    64–5
madrasa (religious school), 13, 106
  Khusrawiyya (madrasa complex), 111
  Süleymaniye, 111
maghariba (irregular soldiers), 67
Maghrib (Arabic for North Africa, 36
Mahmud I, Sultan, 40, 57, 179, 207
Mahmud II, Sultan, 137, 138, 139, 142,
    147, 148, 154, 186, 206
majlis (diwan) al-shura (consultative
    assembly), 151
Makdisi, Ussama, 164
Makki, Muhammad al-, 95, 99
malikane (life-time tax farm), 90–1
malikaneci (possessor of a malikane), 82
Maliki (legal school), 63
mamluk (male slave), 22
Mamluk Sultanate, 21–30
Mannaᶜ, ᶜAdel, 85, 155
Mar Shimᶜun, 167
Mar'a al-jadida, al- (*The New Woman*,
    Amin), 202
Marash (Kahramanmaraş), 181
Marj Dabiq, 21, 26
Matn, 174
Mawardi, ᶜAli al-, 52, 187
Mawlay Hasan, Sultan, 206
Maydan (quarter in Damascus), 69, 190

Maydanjik (quarter in Aleppo), 69
Mazlum, Maksimus, 152
Mecca, 20, 61, 135, 210
mecelle (written legal code), 183
meclis (provincial governing body), 161
Medina, 20, 61
Mehmed (Vani) Efendi, 120, 121
Mehmed Ali, 137, 139, 144, 147, 154, 155,
  186, 204, 229
Mehmed I, Sultan, 53
Mehmed II, Sultan, 4, 21, 25
Mehmed IV, Sultan, 46, 57, 103, 120,
  212, 214
merchants, 8
  ethnicity of, 78–9
Meriwether, Margaret, 85
Midhat Pasha, 182, 189
military, 5, 150, 184
  Arabistan Ordusu (Army of the Land of
    the Arabs), 163
  Fifth Army (*Arabistan Ordusu*, Army of
    the Land of the Arabs), 163
  İrak Ordusu (Army of Iraq), 163
  Maronite Christian, 152
  provincial, 66–9
millets (non-Muslim religious
  communities), 172
miri (state lands), 88
mirs (Kurdish chieftains), 166
missionaries, 195
Mocha, 34
modernity, 197
  political identity and, 199
monarchy, constitutional, 194
Montenegro, 214
Morocco, 49, 229
Mosul, 28, 30, 32, 42, 60, 62, 76, 149,
  166, 178, 181
mufti (chief legal theorists), 65
Muhammad Ahmed (Mahdi), 208
Muhammad al-Makki, 118
Muhammad al-Muntadhar (Mahdi), 208
Muhammad al-Mutahhar (Mahdi), 34
Muhammad al-Sadiq Bey (Tunisia), 187
Muhammad Bey (Abu Dhahab), 44
Muhammad, Prophet, 50
Muhammad Taqi (Imam), 30
mujtahids (Shi'i legal authorities), 31, 124
mulk (private property), 88
Muntafiq, 182
Muqaddima (ibn Khaldun), 53
Murad IV, Sultan, 120
Murad V, Sultan, 184

Musa al-Kadhim, Imam, 30
music, 120
Muslims
  Albanian, 7
  Arab, 6
  Balkan, 7
  Bosniak, 7
  Imami Shia, 51
  Naqshbandi, 200
  Shia, 26, 30, 31, 51, 56, 83, 104, 123,
    124, 134, 135, 155, 174, 229
  Imami, 34, 51, 116
  Ismaili, 34, 110
  Zaydi, 34
  Sunni, 5, 48, 51, 71, 110, 135,
    155, 227
  legal traditions of, 63
  Wahhabi, 200
  Yemeni, 34
Mustafa Zarif Pasha, 169, 170, 171
Muta'sim (caliph), 28
Mutawakkil 'ala Allah al-, Caliph, 27,
  28, 112
mütesarrifiye (Lebanon), 182
Muwahhidun (Wahhabis), 122

Nabulusi, 'Abd al-Ghani al-, 103, 113,
  118–19, 120, 126
Nadir Shah, 32, 58
Naima, 96
Najaf, 104, 135
Najaf, Council of, 32
Najd, 139, 146, 183
Napoleon, 130–9
naqib al-ashraf (head of the Prophet's
  descendants), 209
Nasir al-Din Shah, 206
Nasir Pasha (Iraq), 182
Nasiriyya, al-, 182
Nasser, Gamal Abdul-, 2
nationalism, 19, 176, 193, 206, 227
  ethnic, 194
Necib Pasha (Aleppo), 160
Nelson, Lord, 131
neo-Mamluks, 29, 70
Neophytos, 143, 148
Nezip, 153, 167
niqab (full opaque face veil), 198
Niqula al-Turk, 14
Nizam al-Mulk, 110
Nizam-ı Cedid (, 132
Nizamiyya (madrasa), 110
North Africa, 45, 186–9

Ömer, Governor (Baghdad), 41
Osman Gazi, 12, 49
Osman, House of, 5, 7, 18, 27, 31, 44, 46, 54, 55, 117, 155
Osmanlı (Ottoman), 12
Ottomanism, 194, 200, 213

Palestine, 179, 213, 217, 230
Palestine Mandate, 181
Parliament, First Ottoman, 183–6
Parliament, Second Ottoman, 211–14
Passarowitz, Treaty of, 40
pastoralists, 9, 14, 95
Patras, 142
patronage, 109
peasants, 60, 75, 76, 88, 91, 92–5, 98, 102, 177, 191
 Christian, 15, 174
 Druze, 174
 Serbian, 185
Peloponnesus, 139–45
periodization, 16–19
Philliou, Christine, 6
pilgrimages, 104
piracy, 39, 40, 57
Piri Reis map, 73
plural, 51
poetry, 106, 107, 109
 folk, 128
 mawal (multi-versed), 128
poll-tax, 150, 153
population, 76
 Muslim Arab, 193
 non-Muslim, 172
 rural depopulation, 93–5
Portugal, 33, 35
presidios (Spanish garrisons), 36
provinces
 Arab, 11–12, 17–19
 Balkan and Anatolian, 11, 62, 71
 Iraqi, 32, 62, 150
 North African, 39
 peripheral, 163–8
 Roman power and, 3
 Syrian, 65, 86, 92, 139, 161
Public Debt Administration, 189

qadis (Muslim judges), 63, 101
Qajar, Shah Mohammad, 150
Qalawun (Kalavun), 23
Qansuh al-Ghawri, Sultan, 21, 112

qanun (sultan's law), 63
Qarliq (quarter in Aleppo), 69, 169
qasaba (Ottoman fortified city), 36
Qasim (al-Kabir), (Yemen), 35
Qasimiyya (faction), 43
Qazdughliyya (faction), 44, 45
Qom, 104
Qudsi, Husam al-Din al-, 210
qunbaz (caftan), 197
Qur'an, 107, 124
Qutuz, 22

Rafeq, Abdul-Karim, 10, 11
Ragib Pasha, 138
Rashid ibn Mughamis, 32
Raydaniyya (battle), 27
Raymond, André, 10, 11
Razzaq, ᶜAbd al-al-Rahman ibn ᶜAbd al-, 118
reaya (Ottoman subjects, literally, the flock), 5, 37
rebellions and revolutions
 Aleppo, 139–45, 168, 169
 Anatolia, 142
 Arab Revolt, 72, 217, 219, 220, 221
 Bosnia, 185
 Bulgaria, 185
 Celali, 95
 Damascus, 168, 174
 Diyarbakır, 140
 Egyptian, 29
 Herzegovina, 185
 Istanbul, 212
 Kızıl Baş, 26
 northern Syria, 38
 Wallachia, 142, 145
 Young Turk, 211–16
reform, 2, 18, 61, 129, 139, 157–9, 177, 184, 186, 187, 203
 committee, 216, 217
Reform Decree, 172, 173
Reform Edict (1856), 180
regime, Mamluk and Ottoman continuities, 70
religion, 105, 206
 political ideology and, 10, 34
religious sciences, 107
renewal, religious, 119–26
Rida, Rashid, 215
riots, urban, 25
Rum (Anatolia and the Ottoman Balkan provinces), 13, 142

Rumi (plural *Arwam*, Ottoman, or
    Orthodox Christian), 13
Rumi, Jalal al-Din, 129
rural conditions, 88–95
Russell, Alexander, 127, 131
Russia, 172, 185

Sabunji, Louis, 210
Saʿdis (Moroccan dynasty), 36
Saʿid Baraka al- (Berke), 23
Safadi, al-Shaykh Salah al-Din al-, 208
Safavi, Shah Ismail, 26, 30, 31, 56
Safed, 104
Said Pasha (Damascus), 173
salaf (ancestors), 122
salafiyya (Muslim reform movement),
    122, 201
Saliba (quarter of Aleppo), 170
Salimiyya (Damascus), 117
Salzman, Ariel, 90
Sanʿa, 34, 35
sancak (district), 181
Sannuʿ, Yaʿqub, 205
Sanusi, Muhammad al-, 186
Sanusi, Sayyid Ahmad al-, 215
sarays (provincial palaces), 16, 142
Sayda (Sidon), 160
Sayyadi, Abu al-Huda al-, 208
scholarship, 106–12
schools, 110, 111, 195–6
    al-Azhar, 111
    awqaf and, 106
    Hanbali, 111
    Maliki, 111
    state-sponsored, 59
secularism, 194
Şehrizor, 181
Selim I, Sultan Yavuz, 20, 21–30, 55, 64
Selim II, Sultan, 6, 108, 117
Selim III, Sultan, 131, 133, 137
sema (Sufi performance), 113
Serbia, 5, 214
Şeyhülislam (chief legal scholar
    of the Empire), 40
Shafiʿi School, 109
Shahin, Tanyus, 173
Shahnamah (Persian epic), 107
Shahrizor, 59
*Shajara al-nuʿmaniyya fi al-dawla
    al-ʿuthmaniyya al-* (The
    Genealogical Tree in the
    Ottoman State), 117, 208

Sharaf al-Din, Imam (Yemen), 34
sharia (Islamic religious laws and
    moral code), 3, 53, 58, 63,
    71, 102, 115, 119, 125,
    172, 183, 190
sharif (plural *ashraf*, descendant
    of the Prophet Muhammad),
    37, 38, 42, 132, 138, 140,
    209, 215
shaykh (head of a guild or Bedouin
    tribe), 80
Shaykh al-balad (Cairo, "head of the
    town"), 44
Shaykh al-Islam (chief Muslim legal
    authority), 64
Shia, 20
Shiʿat Ali (party or faction of
    ʿAli), 51
Shihab, Bashir II, 146
Shihab, Emir Haydar al-, 147
Shumayyil, Shibli, 205
Sidon, 59, 87
silk, 165
silver, 74
Sinan (architect), 111
sipahis (cavalrymen), 60–1
Sirhindi, Shaykh Ahmad, 124
sirwal (baggy trousers), 197
slaves, 13, 29
    African, 15
    Egyptian, 24
    European, 36
    Qipchak Steppe, 24
    royal, 41
    Sultan's, 37
Sökeli Ali, 40
Spain, 36
Sufi
    Bektaşi, 112
    Mevlevi, 112, 113
    Naqshbandi, 113, 124–6
    orders (singular, *tariqa*), 112,
        230
    Qadiriyya, 112
    qalandars (mendicant Sufis), 113
    Rifaʿiyya, 112, 209
    Sanusi, 186, 214
Sufi doctrine, 112–26
Süleyman (Baghdad), 40
Süleyman Pasha, 137, 147
Süleyman, Sultan (Kanuni), 20, 28, 30–1,
    34, 56, 111

Sultanate
  al-Damanhuri and, 44
  as an institution, 19, 44, 52–8, 123
    constitutionally-defined, 184
    obligations of, 52, 183
  decentralized, 223
  House of Osman and, 208
  Mamluk, 21–30, 44
  North African, 40
  Ottoman, 70
Sumatra, 35
Suq Saruja (quarter in Damascus), 69
Suriyya/Suriye, 181
Syria, 23, 48, 74, 92, 171, 176, 185, 192
Syrian Protestant College, 160

Taba'i' al-istibdad (*The Characteristics of Tyranny*, al-Kawakibi), 210
Tabbakh, Muhammad Raghib al-, 153, 228
Tahrir al-mar'a (*Women's Liberation*, Amin), 202
ta'ifa (*tawa'if*, guilds), 80
taife (sect), 143
Ta'izz, 34
takfir (to name someone an infidel), 123
Takiyya (Damascus), 136
Talay, İstemihan, 1
Tanzimat (reordering), 157–59, 163, 177, 183, 189–91
Tanzimat Reforms, 160–63, 168–69, 178–80, 187, 229
Tapu (Land-Deed) Code (1858), 177–80
taqlid (tradition), 201
Tatarlar (quarter in Aleppo), 69
taxation, 63, 100
  collective, 178
  individual, 178, 190
  modernization and, 156
tax-farming, 60, 89–93, 157
Thessaloniki, 199, 211, 214
Thrace, 214
timar (fief granted to a cavalryman), 60–2, 88, 89
Timur-i lenk Han (Tamerlane), 25, 146
tobacco, 93, 119, 127
Topkapı Palace, 37
Tosun, son of Mehmed Ali, 138
Trablus-ı Garb (province of Libya), 187
trade, 46, 74, 136, 190
  Asian and European, 73

caravan, 75, 77, 78, 95, 146
  direct, 87
  Egyptian, 24
  export, 180
  import, 180
  patterns of, 76
  regional, 75
  routes, 33, 97
  silk, 92
  transit, 77, 79
transliteration, xiii
treaties, 159, 179
Tripoli (Lebanon), 59, 86
Tripoli (Libya), 36, 39, 186
Tuman Bay, Sultan, 27
Tunis, 36, 76
Tunisia, 186, 187–8
türbe (tomb), 111
Turkey, Republic of, 17
Turkmens, 68, 95, 98
Turks, 5, 13
  Anatolian, 5

ulama (Muslim religious scholars), 4, 16, 51, 64, 83, 103, 105, 106, 110, 121, 151, 162, 183, 226, 227, 231
ʿUmari, Yasin al-, 117, 119, 131
Umayyads (Banu Umayya), 50
Umm al-qura (*The Mother of Cities*, al-Kawakibi), 210
umma (Muslim polity), 50
ʿUrabi, Colonel Ahmad, 188
ʿUrdi, Abu al-Wafa, 38, 56
Urfa (Şanlıurfa), 181
Urumia, 38
Ustuwani, Muhammad Saʿid al-, 121, 160, 172, 175
ʿUthman, Caliph, 50

vali (governor), 188
Vasco da Gama, 24
vekil (deputy governor), 166
Vilayet (Province) Law (1864), 180–3, 189
vilayet salnamesi (provincial yearbook), 196
violence, sectarian, 168–77, 193, 212

wahdat al-wujud (unity of existence or being), 114

Wahhabis (followers of ibn ʿAbd
    al-Wahhab), 122, 134–9
wali (*awliya* (saints), 105
Wallachia, 5, 62
Wallerstein, Immanuel, 74
waqf (plural *awqaf*, pious endowment), 33,
    89, 106, 151, 161
Werry, Augustus William, 170, 171
World Zionist Congress, 213

Yahya Efendi, 121
Yemen, 34, 49, 62, 185, 189, 229
yerliyya (regiment in Damascus), 68

Yunan (Greece, ethnic Greeks), 142
Yusuf Ziya Pasha, 133

Zabid, 34
Zaghlul, Saʿd, 205
zahir (outer truth), 105, 115
Zahir al-ʿUmar, 44
Zahir Barkuk, al-, 24
Zahle, 174
zawiyya (*tekke*, Sufi hostels), 112
Zaydan, Jurji, 204
Zeytun, 153
Zohar (mysticism), 106

CPSIA information can be obtained
at www.ICGtesting.com
Printed in the USA
LVOW07s2045301117

558173LV00002B/208/P

9 781107 619036